The Mott's
Miniature Furniture
Workshop Manual

by Barbara and Elizabeth Mott

FOX BOOKS
Fox Chapel Publishing Co Inc.

Box 7948
Lancaster, PA 17604

The Mott's Miniature Furniture Workshop Manual is a re-issue of Mott Miniature
Workshop Manual with updated sources and information.

To order a copy of this book,
please send check or money order
for $19.95 plus $2.50 to:
Fox Chapel Book Orders
Box 7948
Lancaster, PA 17604

Try your favorite book supplier first!

DEDICATION

"It is only through sharing, that we can truly enjoy our treasures."

Allegra Irene Mitchell Mott

This book is dedicated, first, to our mother, Allegra Irene Mitchell Mott, whose overwhelming love of anything miniature soon instilled that love in our father, Dewitt Mott. Their dedication to their common interest was our inspiration, their patient training and insistence to surpass our ideas of our own limitations passed on to us this common love of collection and crafting miniatures.

Further, this book is dedicated to the Walter Knott Family of Knott's Berry Farm, who recognized the charm and educational appeal of our Mott Miniature Collection and put it on permanent public view at Knott's Berry Farm which, in turn, inspired thousands of men and women to take up the hobby of collecting and building miniatures.

We cannot omit Madge and Henry Wall or Bea and Jay De Armond, dear friends of our family, without whose confidence in our ability and their patient support, this book would never have been written.

Last, and most important, this book is lovingly dedicated to our three children, Polly, Christopher and Melissa, who have been initiated into the elite fraternity of the long-suffering children of authors. Yes, you have missed doing some of the fun things while this book was being written; but we truly hope that you, when you are grown, will find use for the information and techniques, herein, for they are passed on to you — through us — from your wonderfully wise and talented grandparents.

Barbara and Elizabeth Mott

ABOUT THE AUTHORS

It is no exaggeration to refer to the Motts as the First Family of Miniatures. Barbara and Elizabeth Mott, together with Elizabeth's son Chris, his wife, Kimberly, carry on a family tradition started over 80 years ago by their mother Allegra. Starting in their home in Iowa, the Motts now pursue their devotion to miniatures of every description in their adopted state of California.

In addition to the world famous Mott's Miniatures Museum, formerly located inside Knotts' Berry Farm from 1958 to 1992, the Mott family also holds the distinction of starting the miniatures organization called N.A.M.E. The National Association of Miniature Enthusiasts was the first nation wide organization ever established for the purpose of uniting all those who love miniatures. It is now an international organization with chapters in several countries around the globe. Barbara Mott, the first president of N.A.M.E., can still be found working in the Motts' dollhouse shop adjacent to their museum.

All of the Mott's are miniaturists who build from scratch, as well as collect the work of others. They have been instrumental over the years in assisting other persons involved in

miniatures and have been a driving force in the establishment of miniature construction and collecting as a truly recognized are form. The work of the Mott family is appreciated more one you realize that when the family put together most of the exhibits that now comprise their collection, there were not yet stores where you could walk in and furnish a miniature setting or dollhouse, what they could not find in antique shops or at rummage sales had to be made by hand. In fact, the Mott Miniatures _was_ the first miniature store and became a full-time business when they moved to Knott's in 1958.

In the 34 years that most of their work was displayed at Knott's Berry Farm, millions of people have viewed the collection. The Mott's left Knott's Berry Farm after several unsolicited attempts were made by the park to purchase the collection. Some of the collection is currently on display in the Mott's dollhouse shop, just on block north of the amusement park. But miniature lovers don't despair, the Mott family is working on plans to secure a new permanent home for their work in a brand new building where the entire collection could be viewed.

PREFACE

The return of the Workshop Manual.

This book is a reprint of the original Mott Miniature Workshop Manual Volume 1, released for the first time in 1978. With the exception of some changes in the introduction and a different cover and binding, this book is unchanged from the original.

We have had so many requests for this book over the years that we nearly ran out of copies, and we haven't even advertised it since 1980. We have been trying for four years to reprint the manual but every publisher we talked with either wanted us to sell them the rights, or wanted to chop the book into little tiny booklets. It seemed hopeless until we were recently contacted by Fox Chapel Publishing, who have agreed to re-release the book in its complete form.

We realized that there have been many changes to the world of miniatures since work on this book first began back in 1976, none the lease of which is the existence of *Full Line Miniature Shops*. Something that was quite rare back then. Because of a lack of miniature shops at the time, you will see references made as to the sources for tools, woods, glues, stains and other materials that you will need for these projects. These references will tell you to write to specialty tool companies, wood companies, glue companies, and other outlets such as hobby and craft stores as sources for your supplies. But today, all of these items (and a whole lot more) can be found at your local miniature shop.

In your local miniature shop you will find a large assortment of tools, many not listed in this book, from the X-Acto and Pro-Edge companies. If you don't have any tools yet, we recommend picking up one of their mini tool sets. There are sev-eral to choose from, each comes with an assortment of saw, knives, clamps, sanders, files and other items. Lumber for miniature projects is available in a variety of dimensions as well as wood types. The most common you will find is Basswood. It is a soft wood but is much more durable than Balsa. You will also find an entire assortment of stains, glues and varnished from several companies including the House of Miniatures company and the Shenandoah company. You will find that some of the glues have changed names over the years, and new and better products have replaced older ones. For example, Aliphatic Resin is not found widely in the yellow wood glues. Sobo & Yes glues are still around, but Permabond & Wilhold Flash Glues have been replaced by a product called ZAP. Ask your local miniature shop for their recommendations.

If you don't have a local shop, you can find one, or a mail order company, by looking in Magazines such as Nutshell News, and Miniature Collector. Nutshell News is produced by Kalmbach Publishing, 21027 Crossroads Circle, Waukesha, WI, 53186. Miniature Collector is put out by Scott Publications, 30595 Eight Mile Road, Livonia, MI, 48152-1798. In addition to these periodicals, there is an annual publication called *The Miniatures Catalog*, the industries largest source-book, also produced by Kalmbach. All of these publications are available through miniature shops as well.

In the introduction, we mention the National Association of Miniature Enthusiasts which was started by Allegra Mott in 1972. This organization has a quarterly publication called the N.A.M.E. Gazette and is available only to its members. N.A.M.E. sponsors conventions as well as local clubs. For more information about N.A.M.E., you can write to P.O. Box 69, Carmel, Indiana, 46032, or go in to your local miniature shop and pick up an application.

INTRODUCTION

Through the many years of displaying our miniature collection at Knott's Berry Farm, we became aware of the collector's need for information on techniques of building, products information, and plans for the construction of miniature furniture, accessories and toys.

For the five years prior to the original publishing of this book in 1978, we published the *Mott Miniature Workshop News* to share our knowledge, techniques we have found to be useful, and building plans to a small segment of ever-increasing number of miniaturists. It was through the dedication efforts of Louise Carter, Patricia and Abe Baron and their daughter, Cynthia, that this book was conceived and brought to the attention of a publisher. We shall be ever grateful to Louise, Pat, Abe & Cynthia for their reassuring encouragement during the long months while this book was being developed.

Through the counsel of many of our friends in the world of miniatures, we have chosen to present our book as a teaching manual, which will aid the novice as well as the accomplished builder.

Our father carved and constructed all of his miniature furniture without benefit of power tools. In those days, he had nothing but a pen knife and saw with which to work. With the use of these simple tools, he produced many of our treasured pieces of miniature furniture.

As you will see in our tool section, we do not call for any power tools; however, we recognize the benefit to those of you who may own them. All of the furniture, accessories and toys which are offered as projects in this book can be constructed with the tools which are listed. With these tools, your work will be relatively quiet and readily accessible while you are waiting for potatoes to boil for supper, the endless waiting in a doctor's office, watching over a napping child, or the long rides to work in a car pool. We have built our miniatures while doing all of the above.

The "How To" section will especially aid the beginning miniaturist and offers technical information to even the advanced builder. We have chosen to set aside a section for assembly directions, which saved repetition of many instructions and allowed us to include additional projects. These first two sections, 1 and 2, will be expanded as needed, in future volumes.

The furniture is separated into categories of chairs, tables, and so forth instead of furniture periods, so that you can easily find the "chair that was in grandmother's parlor" when building a replica of her home.

We have tried to be flexible with our instructions, so that the various pieces will appeal to all who desire to build them. There is a wealth of turnings, mouldings, woods, and so on, from which to choose, in most miniature supply stores. Of course, these can be substituted for those called for in the instructions, as long as the length, depth, diameter, and so forth are kept accurate. We have seen many beautiful pieces of furniture by makers who chose to use cardboard in place of some wood pieces. Remember many of our full-size pieces of antique furniture were constructed of paper maché.

Our addition of full-color prints to apply to some of the furniture, accessories and toys is a unique innovation which has never been offered through a book before this one. The color will add interest and charm to your miniature creations, and the designs are faithful reproductions of the antique counterpart.

We look forward to receiving your comments on these projects, and ones which you might like to be included in a future book. We would also like your comments on the binding we have chosen. We have selected a more traditional "glued" binding in contrast to the "spiral binding" we used on the first three printings of this book. Comments can be mailed to: The Mott Miniature Collection Booklet. To purchase your copy of any of the Mott books, see your local dealer or write to us at the above address.

We hope that through our book you will have as many happy days in your miniature endeavors as we have through the shared knowledge of our dear friends.

TABLE OF CONTENTS

Tools and Sources
2nd Edition Update

Since the first edition of this Workshop Manual, there are many more mailorder sources for the tools listed on the following pages.

You may contact the following for catalogs:

Leichtung Workshops
4044 Commerce Parkway
Cleveland, OH 44128

Wood Carvers Supply
Box 7500
Englewood, FL 34295

Woodcraft Supply
Box 1686
Parkersburg, WV 26102

Woodworkers Supply
5604 Alameda Place NE
Albuquerque, NM 87113

In addition, the Zona Company has come out with a number of new tools ideal for miniaturists. I've had an opportunity to try their Bernma Assemblers clamps and have found them to be exceptional tools.

Contact: ZONA Tool Company
                Box 502F
                Bethel CT 06801   1-800-696-3480

TOOLS 1-A

X-ACTO SAW 1-A-1: This tool has fine tooth hobby saw blades which are designed to cut two collective thicknesses of wood or metal. These blades fit into a tool handle which X-Acto also has available. These can be purchased from a hobby or miniature supplier.

1-A-1

SNAP SAW 1-A-2: This is a fine tooth hobby saw which is made of plastic with a stationary metal blade. This saw will also cut any of the thin woods or metals which the X-Acto saw will cut. The blades cannot be replaced in this saw. It can be purchased from a hobby or miniature supplier.

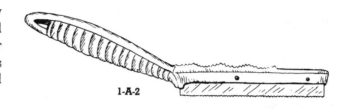

1-A-2

HAND SABRE SAW 1-A-3: This saw gets in where other saws cannot, and cuts either straight or curved lines. It can be purchased at some hardware stores or through the Brookstone "Hard-to-Find Tools" catalog.

1-A-3

X-ACTO KNIFE 1-A-4: This hobby knife has replaceable blades in a variety of shapes for your specialized needs in carving. It can be purchased at your hobby or miniature dealer.

1-A-4

STANLEY KNIFE 1-A-5: This hobby knife has replaceable blades that can be stored in the handle of the knife. This knife has blades with a variety of shapes for your specialized needs in carving. It can be purchased at a hardware store.

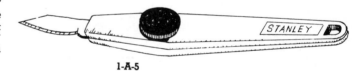

1-A-5

TWEEZERS 1-A-6: We use tweezers in most of our miniature work. I have shown tweezers with the long needle points. There is a great variety of tweezers on the market, and I am sure you will find quite a selection at your neighborhood drug store.

1-A-6

PLIERS 1-A-7 AND 1-A-8: I have shown two of the many types of pliers which are on the market and can be utilized in your miniature work. Check hardware stores, hobby and miniature shops.

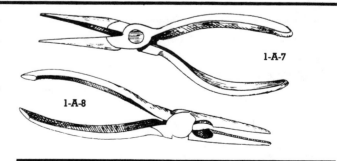

1-A-7

1-A-8

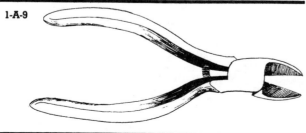

1-A-9

CUTTERS 1-A-9: You will find that you will need wire or metal cutters. They also can be purchased at your local hardware store.

1

AWL OR PUNCH 1-A-10: You will find many uses for this tool. It can be purchased at a hardware store.

1-A-10

HAND DRILL — PIN DRILL — PIN DRILL VISE 1-A-11: This tool is identified by these various names. You can get a large selection of sizes of bits, which you will find that you use constantly when making furniture, and so on. You can obtain the drill and bits at your local hardware store.

1-A-11

NAIL SET 1-A-12: This tool drives or sets brads and finishing nails up to 1 1/4" in length. You drop the brad head first into the tube, place the tube at the desired location, and push the knob down. The brad is forced into the wood. It is wonderful for hard to get to areas where you just cannot swing a hammer. This tool can be purchased at a hardware store.

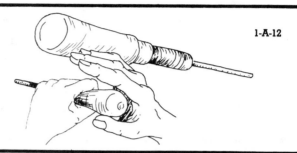

1-A-12

MITRE BOX 1-A-13: This tool is a most important part of your inventory of tools. You will need it constantly to cut mitre corners and straight cuts. The mitre box can be obtained from a hardware store, and many hobby and miniature shops carry the metal X-Acto mitre box.

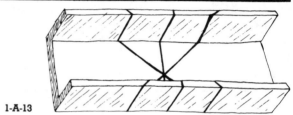

1-A-13

HAND VISE 1-A-14: This tool is excellent when you are doing hand turning of miniature spindles and posts. I am sure that you will find as many uses for it as I have. You may be able to find it at a hardware store; if not, it can be ordered from the Brookstone "Hard-to-Find Tools" catalog.

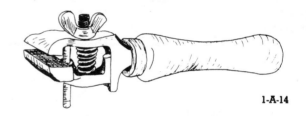

1-A-14

PAPER FASTENERS — WOOD CLOTHES PINS WITH SNAP 1-A-15: I have shown a metal paper fastener which you can find in many sizes. These fasteners and the wooden snap clothes pins are an excellent means of holding pieces while the glue is drying. I am sure you will find some around the house.

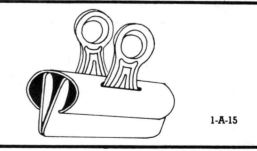

1-A-15

C CLAMP 1-A-16: These clamps can be found in many sizes and a variety of designs. They are also excellent for clamping joints of wood while the glue is drying. They can be purchased at a hardware store.

1-A-16

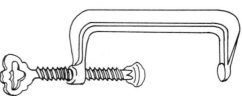

NYLON CLAMP 1-A-17: These nylon clamps hold small objects gently, without scratching delicate surfaces. A rubber band maintains the degree of tension that you want. I purchased mine from Brookstone's "Hard-to-Find Tools" catalog.

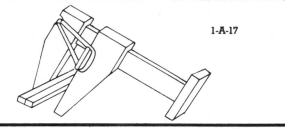

1-A-17

TABLE VISE 1-A-18: A table vise is a must for your workbench. You will find it so convenient to have that "third hand" when sawing or glueing a hard to handle item. Before hurrying out to the hardware store, first check the tool box, as you may just find one there. I have shown the vise I recently purchased from Brookstone; it is called the "PanaVise." The head rotates a full 360 degrees, and tilts 180 degrees from vertical to horizontal. You can imagine the variety of uses for this tool.

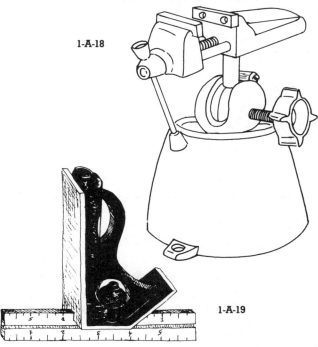

1-A-18

SQUARE AND LEVEL COMBINATION 1-A-19: This tool is indispensable when building, to make sure everything is perfectly squared and level. It can be purchased from a hardware store.

1-A-19

FILES 1-A-20: You will find files an important addition to your tool selection. They can be purchased from a hardware store. The files I have pictured are part of a set of individually shaped files I purchased from Brookstone's "Hard-to-Find Tools" catalog.

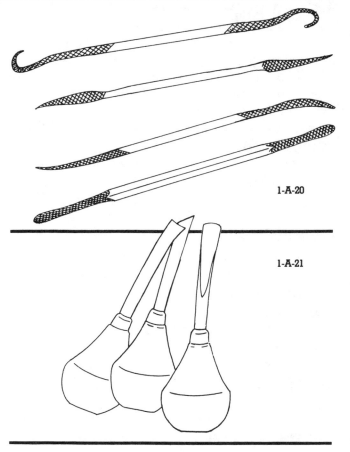

1-A-20

WOOD CHISEL 1-A-21: The variety of shapes of the wood chisels aids in carving chair seats and the fine carving on much Victorian furniture. These can be purchased at some hobby shops and hardware stores.

1-A-21

Before you run out to buy your supply of tools, look in your tool boxes and see what you already have on hand. When you do go to buy tools, you may find it useful to take this book along to aid you in identifying the tools you need.

The mailing address for the Brookstone "Hard-to-Find Tools" catalog is:

Brookstone Company
127 Vose Farm Road
Peterborough, New Hampshire 03458

*Note: Unless otherwise specified, the measurements for wood and other materials are given in the order of **thickness × width × length** (with the wood grain running the length of the board).*

You personal choice of woods will vary with the degree of importance each piece of furniture represents to you. The beginning miniaturist has heard the pros and cons of balsa wood. It is widely used in the construction of model airplanes, as it is lightweight and buoyant. We do not believe that a beginner must start with balsa wood; we prefer to recommend more durable woods in the construction of the various projects offered in this book. However, we do recommend balsa wood for specific structural detail in a few projects. Bass wood is readily available and is generally used by a great number of miniaturists. As you become a more proficient craftsman and your attention to detail becomes greater, you probably will desire to construct the miniature piece of furniture from the same variety of wood as its full-scale antique counterpart.

The following is a list of some woods, their colors, textures, and availability:

BALSA WOOD: An exceedingly lightweight and porous wood. It is easily sawed and carved. It can be purchased at most hobby and craft shops and some miniature supply shops. It is quite difficult to obtain a fine finish, as most finish materials *(including paint)* continue to raise the grain of the wood. Various colors of shoe wax can be used as stains and finishes. These shoe waxes will provide an acceptable finish.

BASS WOOD: This is a fine grained, creamy white wood which is readily found in hobby shops, miniature supply shops, and many mail-order lists. It can be stained to represent most of the major varieties of wood.

CHERRY: The color is light reddish-brown; it is straight grained and satiny. It is used in fine furniture and can be obtained from wood specialty houses.

EBONY: The color is dark brown to black; it is dense with a close grain. It is commonly used for inlays and ornamental work. It can be obtained from wood specialty houses.

HICKORY: The color is white to cream. It is very resilient. It is used for the bow-backs of the Windsor chairs. It can be obtained from wood specialty houses in veneer. You would have to request pieces in greater thickness.

MAHOGANY: The color is reddish-brown and tannish-brown. The grain is a plain stripe, mottled, with fine crotches. It is available from wood specialty houses.

MAPLE: The color is creamy to light reddish-brown. It is usually straight grained. The curly maple and bird's-eye maple woods are used in fine furniture. It can be obtained from wood specialty houses.

OAK: There are white and red colors in oak. There usually is a stripe figure in the pattern of the wood, and the wood is very durable. Many miniature suppliers and mail-order lists carry oak, as well as wood specialty houses.

PINE: The color is light brown to red. The wood is light, soft, with a close, straight grain. It will be found in most miniature supply shops, on some mail-order lists, as well as the wood specialty houses.

ROSEWOOD: The color is a variety of shades of dark brown. The wood texture ranges from porous to close, firm and hard. This wood was used in fine furniture. The wood can be obtained from wood specialty houses.

WALNUT: The color ranges from a light grey-brown to a dark purple-brown. There is a great variety of grain figures in this wood. The wood can be obtained from wood specialty houses.

The following is a list of the finer woods with the major periods in which they were most commonly used in furniture:

CHERRY: 1750-1820.

EBONY: Essentially ornamental work. The black keys of pianos were ebony, while the white keys were ivory.

HICKORY: 1750-1820. Windsor chair top rails.

MAHOGANY: Universally used throughout all of the various periods.

MAPLE: 1600-1825.

OAK: Very early English furniture, the "Golden Oak" period of 1890-1910.

PINE: 1600-1825.

ROSEWOOD: 1800-1875. Was used in fine pianos.

WALNUT: Early American through the Victorian era.

In addition to your local miniature dealer who stocks

a variety of woods, you can check the advertisements in *Miniature Collector* and other miniature-related publications, as well as the following wood specialty houses:

A. Constantine & Son, Inc.
2050 Eastchester Road,
Bronx, New York 10461
Catalogue available ($.50, 1978).

Craftsman Wood Service, Inc.
2727 South Mary Street
Chicago, Illinois 60608
Catalogue available.

GLUE 1-B-2

WOOD BONDING GLUES

TITEBOND GLUE: It is stronger than white glue, is excellent for bonding wood. Sets fast. Dries with a yellowish tint. Manufactured by The Franklin Glue Company, Columbus, Ohio 43207.

WILHOLD ALIPHATIC RESIN GLUE: It is stronger than white glue and is excellent for bonding wood. Manufactured by Wilhold Glues, Inc., Santa Fe Springs, California 90670 and Chicago, Illinois 60612.

WILHOLD WHITE GLUE: It dries clear and sets fast. Manufactured by Wilhold Glues, Inc., Santa Fe Springs, California 90670.

ELMER'S GLUE-ALL: Bonds wood, paper and cloth. Especially good for wood. Dries clear. Product of Borden, Inc., Department C.P., Columbus, Ohio 43215.

CLOTH GLUES

PACTRA SUPER THICK — SUPER STICK: It dries clear and sets fast. A product of Pactra Industries, Inc., Los Angeles, California 90028.

SOLOMON'S SOBO GLUE: Excellent for fabrics; dries clear. Manufactured by Solomon's Laboratories, New York, New York.

PAPER GLUES

YES: An all-purpose stick flat glue which we have found will not curl, wrinkle, or discolor any paper print, cloth, or leather. We use this glue for all of our paper prints and wallpaper glueing. Manufactured by Gane Brothers and Lane, Inc., Chicago, Illinois.

FAST BOND GLUES

PERMABOND GLUE: A "super" glue. Bonds in seconds. Read the directions carefully before using. It is excellent for a quick and permanent bond. Manufactured by Permabond International Corporation, Englewood, New Jersey 07631.

WILHOLD FLASH GLUE: An instant sticking "super" glue. Read the directions thoroughly before using. It is excellent for a quick and permanent bond. Manufactured by Wilhold Glues, Inc., Santa Fe Springs, California 90670 and Chicago, Illinois 60612.

GLUES FOR CEMENTING OBJECTS

WALTHER'S GOO: Tough and flexible glue. Excellent for attaching pictures to the wall and furniture to the floor, and so on. Read the directions thoroughly. A product of Walther's Specialties, Inc., Milwaukee, Wisconsin 53211.

GLUES FOR OUTDOOR SCENES

TOUCH-N-GLUE: Excellent adhesive which is especially effective for outdoor scenes. An extremely good bond. Dries a light brownish-grey. Manufactured by Champion International Corporation, Chemware Group, Weldwood Packaged Products, Kalamazoo, Michigan 49003.

SILICONE RUBBER HOBBY AND CRAFT ADHESIVE: It stays flexible, will not crack or shrink, dries a cloudy white. Excellent for use in cementing some objects in outdoor scenes. A product of Dow Corning Corporation, Midland, Michigan 48640.

S F CLEAR GLUE: Dries clear and makes an excellent facsimile of water in a sink or outdoors. Manufactured by Snow Foam Products, Inc., El Monte, California 91731.

TIPS: Read the directions by the manufacturer on the product, and allow all the time specified, or longer, for thorough drying. The more time you spend rubbing and polishing, the more beautiful and more durable the finish will be.

Gather all the tools and supplies required to apply the final finish before you start to work.

Never apply shellac after you have applied varnish.

Stain all wood before glueing.

PREPARATION: The old adage, "An ounce of prevention is worth a pound of cure," is well heeded when you are finishing a piece of furniture that has taken hours of your time and patience to create. Study the piece of furniture and the wood. Experiment with various stains and finishes on scraps of the wood you used to create your masterpiece; or try sample finishes on the bottom or back of the piece, where this experimentation will not show.

When you are satisfied with the final result, clean your work area so it will be free of dust. Shake dust out of your clothes before you start to work. Be sure the ventilation is good and the temperature is at least 70 degrees. If the weather is damp, do not use varnish or shellac.

Surfaces must be smooth and free of dust to take a good finish. Unless you want a distressed finished effect, any dents or gouges in the wood should be filled and sanded.

Open-grained woods such as walnut, oak and mahogany usually need filling in order to take a good finish; close-grained woods such as maple, pine, fir and birch can be finished without filling. Balsa wood is open-grained, while bass wood is close-grained.

Use stick shellac to fill dents and gouges for natural finishes. Stick shellac is available at most hardware and lumber supply stores in many colors, or you may choose to use plastic wood filler. Sand all fillers smooth.

When filling open-grained woods, a paste wood filler in a color to match the wood is used. Follow the manufacturer's directions, thin to the consistency of heavy cream, and apply the filler across the grain. When it dulls, wipe the surface across the grain and then with the grain, removing all traces of the filler. Let this dry for at least 24 hours.

FINISHES

STAINS: Add color to wood while allowing the grain to show. Stains can also be used to even the color of a wood or simulate another wood, such as bass wood stained like oak, walnut, or mahogany to simulate one of those woods which might not have been available when you were constructing your miniature piece of furniture. Remember to always stain the pieces of wood before glueing together. The glue fills the pores in the wood and will not allow the penetration of stain.

CLEAR PASTE WAX: Can be applied to any wood without much alteration of color, and is a very easy finish for beginners to use.

Rub on an even coat of the wax with a soft cloth, working with the grain of the wood. Let it stand 10 to 15 minutes, then polish and buff with a clean soft cloth. Let dry for 24 hours and then buff to a gloss. Paste wax can be applied over other finishes to protect them.

WHITE SHELLAC or an ACRYLIC (DECOUPAGE) SEALER: A clear finish which adds practically no tone at all, and either finish is excellent on light woods.

Use a good grade of shellac. Be sure that it is fresh and less than six months old. Thin the shellac 50-50 with alcohol and apply one coat. Let dry for four hours, rub the surface smooth with 3/0 steel wool or a very fine sandpaper. Apply a total of three or four thin coats, rubbing between each. Rub the last coat lightly with the steel wool.

We recommend that the acrylic *(decoupage)* sealer be used as a finish on all of the pieces of "stencilled" or decorated furniture and accessories which are first painted and then the color print is applied. Apply or spray three to six coats, allowing 24 hours drying time between applications.

VARNISH: Adds a slightly amber tone to the wood. Use a good quality of varnish, as it must be clear.

If you have previously filled the wood, apply an initial coat of thinned shellac before applying the varnish. *Note: Never* apply shellac *after* you have applied varnish, or your finish will not dry and will always remain tacky.

Apply the varnish full-strength with a clean brush,

using as few strokes as possible and letting the varnish flow. Let this dry at least 24 hours and up to a whole week. When dry, rub with 6/0 waterproof garnet paper used wet, doing the edges lightly, and using full-length strokes on flat surfaces. Wash off with clean rags and dry thoroughly. Apply a second coat, but do not sand. A paste wax can be applied for added beauty and protection.

LINSEED OIL: A clear finish and is quite beautiful when several coats are applied and rubbed thoroughly. This finish will grow slightly darker with time.

Mix two parts boiled linseed oil to one part turpentine. Place the container with the mixture in boiling water for 10-15 minutes to thin the oil properly. Using a soft cloth, spread generously on the wood and rub small areas for 10 to 20 minutes at a time. Wipe off the excess with a lint-free cloth. Using a polishing cloth, rub again for 10 to 20 minutes to bring out the luster. Let dry for 48 hours and apply a second coat. Let a week to a month pass before applying additional coats. Another coat should be applied each year.

OPAQUE FINISHES: These are accomplished with paints, from which you have an unlimited choice of colors.

We use acrylic paints which have a water base. These paints are virtually odor-free and are excellent to use when a room does not have open ventilation or when there are a number of people painting at one time.

These paints can be purchased at most miniature supply or craft stores in small jars or tubes. They are easily mixed to achieve any color match that may be required, and the clean-up is accomplished with water. When we have completed a painted project, especially where a color print has been applied, we spray with several coats of a good acrylic decoupage spray sealer.

The completed piece will have a matte finish that brings out the depth of the color.

We use enamel paints in the gilt, silver, or aluminum colors. These can be applied over any of the acrylic paints. You can purchase tiny bottles of the enamel paints in most hobby or craft stores.

HINGES 1-B-4

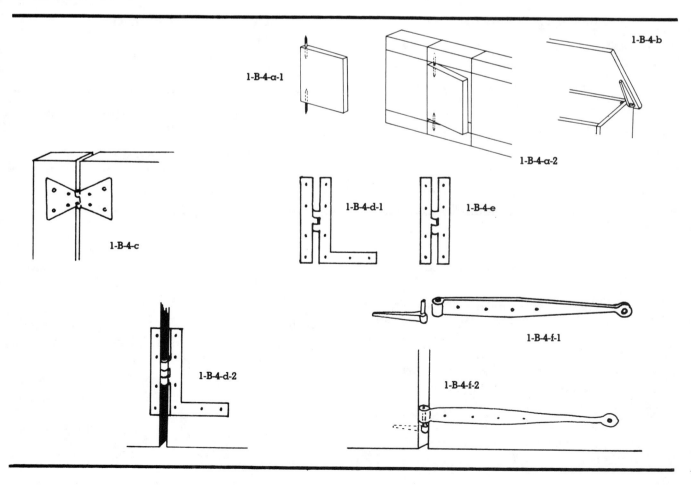

There is a great variety of hinges and drawer and door pulls available to you in the miniature marketplace through your miniature dealer and from many mail-order lists. We are illustrating only a few of the many which you can find.

1. Figure **1-B-4-a** is a pin hinge that you can make yourself. Figure **1-B-4-a-1** shows the insertion of a pin at the top and bottom of a door. Figure **1-B-4-a-2** shows the upper pin penetrating the upper frame of the opening, while the lower pin is pushed up through the lower frame and into the door.

2. Figure **1-B-4-b** shows the installation of a cleat hinge. This hinge can be made of wood or metal.

One cleat hinge is installed on either side of a box and is then attached to the lid. This type of hinge would be used for a blanket or dower chest.

3. Figure **1-B-4-c** shows the installation of a butterfly hinge or others of the same type.

4. Figures **1-B-4-d-1** and **1-B-4-d-2** show the installation of an H-L hinge.

5. Figure **1-B-4-e** shows the H hinge.

6. Figures **1-B-4-f-1** and **1-B-4-f-2** show the strap hinge and its installation. There are many designs of the strap hinge.

NAILS AND BRADS 1-B-5

When working with miniature furniture, you will find that ordinary nails and brads will be much too heavy and far too long. We have found that you must improvise, if you find that you have to use brads. Sequin pins are very fine in diameter and can be used

in place of a nail, especially if the length is cut to the depth of the wood, plus a minimal penetration. The tiny brads that usually accompany tiny hinges may still be too long and will penetrate the thickness of the wood. Measure them and snip off the excess length before installation.

DRAWER AND DOOR PULLS 1-B-6

1-B-6-c   1-B-6-d

1-B-6-a   1-B-6-b

You will find illustrations of four types of pulls. There is quite a variety now on the market from which to choose.

1. Figure **1-B-6-a** illustrates the tear drop drawer pull.

2. Figure **1-B-6-b** illustrates the bail drawer pull. This illustration is of the Chippendale variety.

3. Figure **1-B-6-c** illustrates a wooden drawer or door pull which you could carve yourself.

4. Figure **1-B-6-d** illustrates a metal drawer or door pull. You can paint the knob portion white and simulate old porcelain pulls.

SANDING 1-C-1

When you have completed cuts or carving, the wood must be sanded. We use emery boards for much of our sanding because of the rigid backing and the choice of two grades of sandpaper. When your piece has been rough sanded with the emery board, it must be finish-sanded with a very fine grade of sandpaper to smooth the surface. Be careful not to gouge the piece with the sandpaper.

After staining and sealing the wood, it must be steel-wooled. If a filler is going to be used, a light sanding

with 3/0 steel wool should be sufficient.

After the finish has been applied, the surface should again be sanded with either 4/0 steel wool or extra fine *(240 or 280 grit)* abrasive paper.

The surface should be sanded thoroughly, but do not go at it with a vengeance. Your touch should be light, but firm and steady. Be careful to get into the corners and edges. Too firm a touch will cut through the sealer coat and into the stain. After sanding, wipe all surfaces clean.

PREPARATION AND APPLICATION OF COLOR
PRINT 1-C-2

The insertion sheet contains numerous color prints to complete various projects offered in this book. Some are for furniture to simulate the antique stencilled pieces or painted decoration; some are for individual application, such as a clock face; and still others are applied to toys.

We have used this concept of the full-color print application on many of our previous projects and kits, to the delight of the craftsman. I have done all of the art work, attempting to copy as faithfully as possible the antique design and color. We hope you will be as pleased as others have been with our designs.

The various prints are identified on the color insert sheet with the project number, such as **8-H**. When you begin a project that requires a color print, study the insert sheet and find the print. Do not cut it out until you are ready to use it. This will save a misplaced print. When it is required, cut out the print or prints along the outside black line. When there might be interior cutting or curved cutting required, we recommend a pair of curved-end scissors, such as decoupage scissors or fingernail scissors.

We recommend that a good grade of paper paste be used to glue the print to the surface of the wood. We use "YES" bookbinder's paste which can be obtained from most good art stores, some stationery stores, and some miniature suppliers. This glue will not buckle or wrinkle your print as white glue will do. If this glue is not available to you, mix a batch of wheat or flour paste and use it.

Prior to the application of the color print, the furniture should be painted. You may want to match the background of the print, and this can be accomplished by mixing acrylic paints to the hue of the color being matched.

After the print has been applied and has thoroughly dried, I recommend the use of a decoupage sealer. I spray or coat my piece of furniture and so forth with at least six coats of the sealer. This prevents staining and fading.

HOW TO CARVE A STRAIGHT SPINDLE OR
POST 1-C-3-a

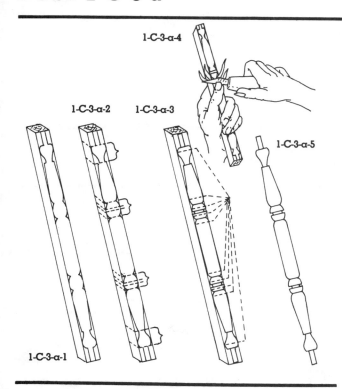

1-C-3-a-4
1-C-3-a-2
1-C-3-a-3
1-C-3-a-5
1-C-3-a-1

The preliminary step before making chairs, tables, beds, and so on, with delicately turned legs and spindles is to learn how to "turn" and carve. There are many finished products on the market at this time which were unavailable only a few years ago, and can be adapted to fill most of the needs of any plans in this book — but you cannot proclaim that the piece was made by you alone.

Carving and turning is really quite easy and can be done while you are on those endless phone calls or watching television. If you own or have access to a small wood-turning lathe and know how to use it, you may find that you do not need to study this section; but, if you are among the many who are approaching this aspect of miniature craftsmanship for the first time, read on.

I am going to show you how to make the blanket rail which is included in the basic assembly of the bed (**2-D-1**). This piece is rather bulky and perfect for a first-time carving. When you become proficient, you will be able to design your own shapes and do the most delicate spindle, leg, or finial.

Figure 1-C-3-a-1 shows a square stick of wood with the pattern drawn on the wood. Draw this design on all four sides of the piece of wood.

Figure 1-C-3-a-2 shows the placement of saw cuts (*use a fine hobby hand saw such as "X-Acto" or "Snap" saw*); the silhouette of one side of Figure 1-C-3-a-1 shows the depth of the saw cuts. These cuts aid in carving and help prevent chipping. Remember, you can always make a deeper saw cut later, but you cannot erase a cut that is too deep.

Figure 1-C-3-a-3 shows the placement of pencil lines to be drawn at the high point of each segment to be shaped. Mark these on the wood. Figure 1-C-3-a-4 shows how I hold wood to carve it. You will want to use a hobby knife such as "X-Acto" or "Stanley" for the carving. Both of these knives are very good and have a variety of blades from which to choose.

I "shave" the area away, turning the wood as I carve. You may use a variety of small files to achieve part of

the shaping, remembering to keep turning the wood around as you work. This assures a continuous balance in the cylindrical shaping.

Draw the knife or file down in a rounding motion from the pencil high-point to the saw cut. Continue in this manner until the segment is shaped as it is in Figure 1-C-3-a-5, to the depth of the saw cut. When the entire piece has been shaped in this manner sand carefully. I use emery boards for part of this sanding for they are firmer than just a piece of sandpaper. Be careful, for the original strength of the wood has been weakened by the carving.

If the spindle or post should break, you can repair it. Carefully and gently drill into each broken end of the post (*a tiny pin drill that is operated by hand is best for this purpose*) and place and glue a wooden dowel or peg or small brad *(with the head removed)* into the hole; then push and glue the second portion of the broken post over the other end of the peg. The two pieces are joined together. Let them dry. *Note:* Stain these pieces of wood before glueing, as the glue does not allow the stain to penetrate the wood.

HOW TO SHAPE A SPINDLE WITH A SPLAY
1-C-3-b

1. Refer to the diagram in your project which shows the side view of the spindle. Trace this shape onto the upright side edge of the board which you have cut to measure. Turn the tracing over, and trace this shape onto the opposite side edge of the board. Carve the board into this shape, using the drawn lines as your guide.

2. When the board has its initial shape, trace the diagram which shows the front view of the spindle onto the previously shaped board. Using these lines as your guide, cut the board to this shape. When this carving has been completed, sand the spindle rounded.

3. Drill any indicated holes at this time.

HOW TO CARVE A CURVED BOARD 1-C-3-c

Note: These instructions are for carving a curved board such as the top board of a chair back.

Cut a board the height × the width × the full depth of the curve. Draw a curve with pencil on the top surface of the board, and carve away the excess wood as you round the back, and carve the front into a concave curve. Sand the piece smooth after carving. See Figure 1-C-3-c-1 for the block of wood showing the areas to be carved away. See Figure 1-C-3-c-2 for the finished carving.

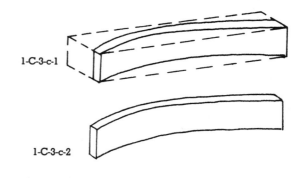

1-C-3-c-1

1-C-3-c-2

HOW TO CARVE A CABRIOLE LEG 1-C-3-d

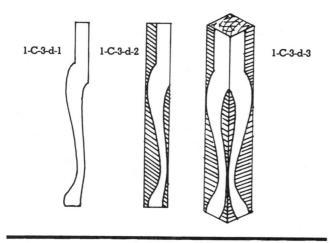

1-C-3-d-1   1-C-3-d-2   1-C-3-d-3

You can now find pre-carved cabriole legs on the market for your furniture projects, however you may not find just the size or shape that you may require.

These directions will be of help to you in your efforts to further your skill in miniature craftsmanship.

The leg that is offered here is for your practice in developing a skill. When you are designing your own piece of furniture, measure the length of the leg from the foot to the extreme height; the depth of the piece of wood is determined by the extreme dimension of the splay of the leg.

Trace the outline of the leg, as shown in Figure **1-C-3-d-1** and re-trace onto a piece of wood measuring 1/4" square. See Figure **1-C-3-d-2**. Mark the pattern on two adjoining sides; it is marked back to back, as shown in Figure **1-C-3-d-3**.

Carve the leg to shape with your knife. Cut the front and back of the leg first. Complete the shaping, and sand smooth.

HOW TO CARVE A WINDSOR TYPE CHAIR SEAT WITH SADDLE SHAPING 1-C-3-e

The grain in the wood runs sideways in the oval seat of a bow-back chair, and the grain runs from front to back in the shield-shaped seat of a continuous-arm Windsor. These "rules of thumb" are closely followed in the construction of the antique Windsors, and should be just as closely followed when you are attempting to make a copy of a Windsor in miniature.

Figure **1-C-3-e-1** shows the outline of the seat of the chair on a block of wood. The broken line which is shown in this drawing should be traced onto the bottom of your piece of wood, as it indicates the line from which the bottom should be rounded upward. The long diagram to the right of this drawing shows the side view of the shaping; and the long diagram below the drawing shows the front view of the shaping, which includes a view of the saddle shaping.

Cut the seat blank out and shape it as shown in Figure **1-C-3-e-1**. You will note that the sides are rounded down toward the bottom of the chair seat (*indicated by the broken line in the top view diagram*). The top area is dished out (*scooped*), and the front saddle area is shaped while the top back edge is left level (*this is the area that will be drilled for the placement of the back spindles*).

Sand the top and side areas smooth. The chair bot-

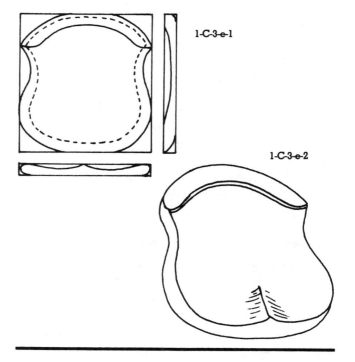

1-C-3-e-1

1-C-3-e-2

tom can be left with some roughness, as the antique Windsor chairs were all handmade and you will find that the chair bottoms still have the tool marks in evidence. Figure **1-C-3-e-2** shows the finished shaping of this chair seat.

11

HOW TO CARVE A SHAPED ARM WITH KNUCKLE CARVING 1-C-3-f

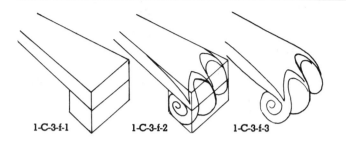

1-C-3-f-1   1-C-3-f-2   1-C-3-f-3

Fine bow-back Windsors can have an arm with knuckle carving at the front or hand rest.

When making a continuous arm bow-back Windsor,

shape the top of the piece of wood in a round or half-round and gradually blend into the arms which are flat. The next step is to bend the back as described in 1-C-6.

Stain the wood in the bow-back piece and two small blocks of wood which will be glued beneath the front of the arm. Glue this small block of wood beneath the hand rest as shown in Figure 1-C-3-f-1. When the glue is thoroughly dry, draw the knuckle shaping on the hand rest as shown in Figure 1-C-3-f-2. Carve the joined pieces, sand the finished carving, and re-stain where necessary. See Figure 1-C-3-f-3 for the finished carving.

SIMPLE UPHOLSTERY 1-C-4

1. Choose a fabric of the period you are attempting to reproduce. Use old materials, if possible, as new rayons, nylons and synthetics simply do not look old and tend to ruin the illusion which you have created with a reproduction of an antique piece of furniture.

Old fabrics can be found in many places. First, look in trunks in your own attic or basement. Second-hand stores, antique shops, rummage sales, and so forth, are all good sources of old materials. Look at old dresses, linings of coats and dresses, old linens, handkerchiefs (*some old lace trims are exquisite*) and curtains. Evening bags and compacts some-times have beautiful petit-point inserts. Old wallets make wonderful upholstery for leather chairs and foot stools. The worn edges, placed strategically on the arms of a chair, make the chair look old, worn

and comfortable.

2. When upholstering a slip seat of a chair or foot stool, follow these easy steps:
   a. Cut a piece of stiff cardboard slightly smaller than the shape of the opening. You must allow for the material to fold over the edges.
   b. Cut a piece of upholstery material at least 1/4" larger (*all edges*) than the piece of cardboard.
   c. Glue a tiny bit of cotton atop the cardboard, to form a cushion.
   d. Lay the upholstery over the cotton surfaces of the cardboard, bring all edges down and under the cardboard. Clip 1/8" cuts around the edges to allow the edges to fall into place. Glue down to the reverse side of the cardboard.

SIMULATING CARVING AND RELIEF DESIGN 1-C-5

Many pieces of furniture can be beautifully decorated with a substitute "carving."

1. Jewelry findings, tiny formed plastic pieces, moulded plastic wood, metal decorations, or paper laces are only a few of the types of decorations which can be glued on furniture to simulate carving. Beads or bead assemblies which are painted the color of

wood can be used in place of carved finials or even some legs or posts (*such as spool turnings*).

2. Spray the substitute materials with a coat of acrylic finish to seal the material before painting to match the wood. Choose a paint that is a close match to the finish on your piece of furniture. Acrylic paints can be easily mixed to match your chosen color. Try

a dab of paint on a piece of wood the color you are using; when you are satisfied with the match, it is time to paint. Paint the decoration *before* it is glued on your piece of furniture. These decorations can be touched up after they have been glued on, but you *must be careful* not to smear the paint on the finished wood.

3. Spray an acrylic finish on the completed piece to assure that the paint will not chip.

BENDING WOOD 1-C-6

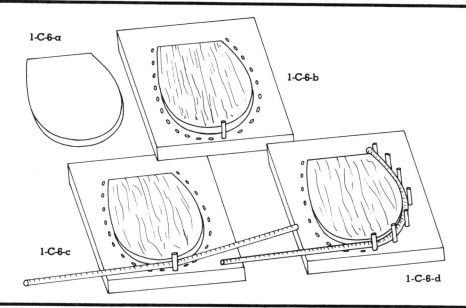

Once a piece of wood has been shaped, it is ready for bending. Several things must be considered before a piece of wood is chosen to be shaped and eventually bent.

Old chair makers chose green or unseasoned wood for bending purposes, because the wood held sufficient moisture to achieve the proper bending conditions. As a rule, the miniature builder does not have access to unseasoned wood in the proper thicknesses for his furniture project and must depend on a supplier.

When choosing wood for bending, always note the grain. It must run straight and smooth. Wavy grains or knots will make your piece split as it bends. The old Windsor chair makers chose hickory most often when making a bow-back chair, for this wood is the easiest to bend; they either boiled the wood or steamed it. The steaming process for a full-sized back lasts for several hours. Your small piece of wood should be placed on a rack in the top of a double boiler and steamed until it will not crack when bent. Be patient and wait the time, and keep sufficient water in the double boiler to produce the steam.

While the piece is being steamed, secure the bending block to your workbench, so you do not waste

time when the wood is removed from the steam. It is a very critical time, because, as the wood cools, it will break during the bending process. Draw the exact size and shape that you want your finished bow to be on a piece of 1/4" to 1/2" thickness wood and cut out. Secure this piece atop another block of wood with glue and nails. See Figure 1-C-6-a and Figure 1-C-6-b. Measure the thickness of the piece to be bent, and drill holes into the bottom block of wood along the outside line of this measurement. See Figure 1-C-6-b. Cut as many wooden pegs to fit into this series of holes as you have drilled holes.

When the wood has steamed sufficiently, remove it from the double boiler and immediately place it on the bending block. Find the center of the wood and place it at the center top of the bending block, placing a peg into the hole and wedging it firmly against the block. See Figure 1-C-6-c. One side of the wood piece is pulled into shape with a firm and steady motion. This side is now pegged against the bending block. The second side is now pulled into place with the same firm and steady motion. A quick motion can split the wood. Peg this side against the bending block. This wood should dry for several days before removing from the bending block. Remember this piece is fragile when you begin drilling for placement of back spindles.

RUSHING A CHAIR SEAT 1-C-7

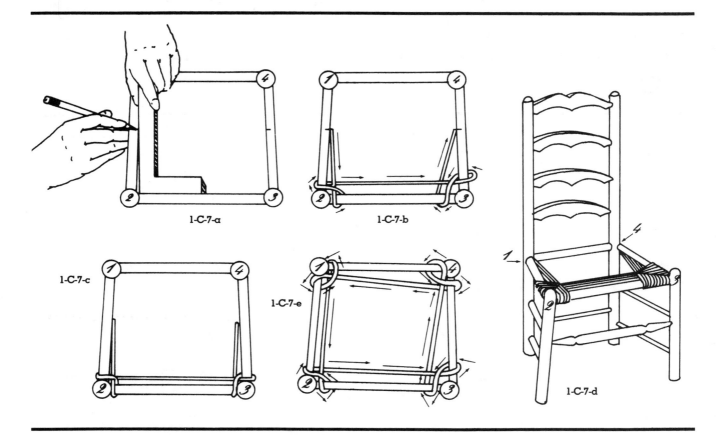

1-C-7-a

1-C-7-b

1-C-7-c

1-C-7-e

1-C-7-d

Rushing is a very old method of making seats of chairs or stools. During the seventeenth century, rushing was extensively used in England on spindle-backed and ladder-backed chairs.

The following directions and diagrams will aid in rushing the seats of chairs. Tan-colored carpet thread will be the material that we will use instead of the real rushes.

HOW TO WEAVE THE RUSH SEAT

The upper rungs of the chair, between the legs, form the seat frame. You will note in the chair (*or chairs*) that you have just made that the front and rear rungs are parallel, and the side rungs are at an angle.

This trapezoid shape opening must be reduced to a rectangle by weaving only along the sides and front.

1. To begin, hold a small square against the front rung, and mark each side rung where the square crosses it — as shown in Figure 1-C-7-a.

2. Cut a piece of carpet thread about 10" to a foot in length and glue (*using white glue or "Tacky"*) one end to the left side rail at the mark (*clamp the glued end with a small clamp or use a "spring" clothes pin*) and weave, bringing the thread over and under the front rung at the right of 2; left over and under the rung behind 2; across, over and under behind 3;

over and under at the left of 3; bring back to the right rung and glue at the mark. Clip off the excess thread. Figure 1-C-7-b illustrates this entire process, with arrows indicating the direction of the thread. Keep the thread taut and clamp the second end, as you did the first. Let the glue dry.

3. Figure 1-C-7-c shows how this process should look at the completion of this initial step of weaving.

4. Make equidistant pencil marks on the side rungs from the end of the glued thread to the rear of each side rung, keeping the last mark approximately 1/8" from the joint. The marks are spaced so that additional lengths of thread will be applied (*as the first one was*) and will fit snugly together. These threads, when glued in place and woven around the rungs will form a rectangular opening, as shown in Figure 1-C-7-d.

5. The diagonal lines which are formed when the threads cross will be kept straight by applying uniform tension. Remember, this is a miniature chair, and you must not pull too strongly or you will pull it apart or distort the shape of the chair.

6. When the opening is the rectangular shape, glue a long length of thread behind the last one attached on the left rung and continue weaving as before. *Do*

not glue to the right rung, but run the thread over and under the rear rung to the left of 4; over and under the right rung, in front of 4; over and under the left rung in front of 1; over and under the rear rung, to the right of 1. Continue to 2 and repeat the process, until the seat is filled. The final thread is then pulled through to the underside of the seat and tied. See Figure **1-C-7-e.**

AN ALTERNATE METHOD FOR ACHIEVING THE EFFECT OF A RUSHED SEAT IN A MINIATURE CHAIR 1-C-7-a

This method is especially good for the beginning craftsman and results in seats much like those found on antique doll house chairs. The antique seats were embossed paper to simulate rushing; we have provided color prints to simulate rushed seats. They are marked **1-C-7** on the color insert sheet.

1. While you are cutting the wood for your chair, trace the top view assembly diagram of the seat. Notch the corners of the seat to fit around the legs; retrace onto 1/8" thick wood and cut out. Use this seat blank instead of the seat framework when building the chair.

2. Apply the finish to the chair before applying the color print to the top surface of the seat blank. Refer to **1-C-2.**

CANING A MINIATURE CHAIR 1-C-8

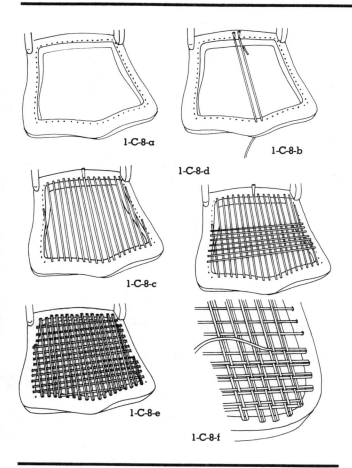

1-C-8-a

1-C-8-b

1-C-8-d

1-C-8-c

1-C-8-e

1-C-8-f

strands to simulate the strand of cane. Tan will most closely resemble the color of cane. You also need a tiny drill bit which is used in a pin drill, several shaped wooden pegs that will fit into the holes, a curved needle or small crochet hook, and dull-finish varnish to coat the "cane" when the seat is finished.

PREPARATION

First, be sure that the chair seat is thoroughly dry before beginning. The glue should set for at least 24 hours, or the tension of the cane or drilling holes may cause the pieces to separate. Drill holes 1/8" apart around the inside opening of the chair seat. See Figure **1-C-8-a.**

CANING

1. **BEGINNING VERTICAL WEAVE:** Push an end of the three strands of embroidery floss (*henceforth referred to as cane*) down through the center hole at the back of the chair seat. Secure this by looping it through the hole again and pushing a peg down into the hole. Pull the cane tight from the back rail and push the end down through the same hole in the front rail. Bring the end up through the hole to the left of the front hole (*secure with a peg*) and pull tight from the front rail to the same hole in the back rail. Continue in this manner, until one side of the chair is completed. See Figures **1-C-8-b** and **1-C-8-c.** An irregular side is filled in, as shown in the latter Figure. Attach another piece of cane to the right of the center

MATERIALS AND TOOLS REQUIRED

You will need cotton embroidery floss. Use three

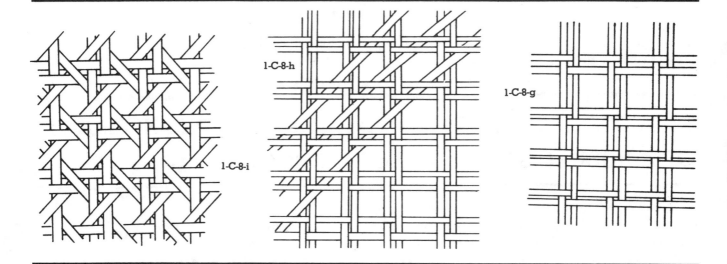

1-C-8-h

1-C-8-g

1-C-8-i

hole, insert a peg after it has been looped to secure the strand. Fill in the right side of the chair.

2. BEGINNING HORIZONTAL WEAVE: Attach a piece of cane at the center hole on one side rail, pull the cane across the chair frame on top of the first strands, from side rail to side rail. Work toward the front of the chair. See Figure **1-C-8-d**. Attach another piece of cane directly behind the first horizontal cane, and proceed to the back rail.

3. SECOND VERTICAL WEAVE: Repeat Step 1, pulling the cane parallel to the vertical strands and over both layers of cane which are now on the chair. See Figure **1-C-8-e**.

4. SECOND HORIZONTAL WEAVE: You will now actually begin to weave the chair seat. The cane runs from side rail to side rail. Weave the cane under the lowest vertical strand and over the top vertical strands to form a pattern of open squares. Pull these strands as tight as possible, and keep the strands together to form rows of pairs. See Figures **1-C-8-f** and **1-C-8-g**.

5. FIRST DIAGONAL WEAVE: Start at a corner and work toward the opposite corner hole. Draw each cane strand over all of the vertical weaves and under all of the horizontal weaves. Work all the way

to the opposite corner and then weave back to the first corner. The center is now clearly marked by two parallel strands of cane. See Figure **1-C-8-h**. Weave the cane on one side of the parallel strands through all of the opposite diagonal holes, keeping the lines parallel. If the seat is an irregular shape, you will skip some holes to keep to the parallel line. Repeat this weaving process on the opposite side of the parallel lines, until the first diagonal weave is completed.

6. SECOND DIAGONAL WEAVE: Start in one of the two remaining empty corner holes and weave the cane as you did in Step 5, with the following change: draw the cane over all horizontal strands and under all vertical strands. Each corner hole will have two strands running through it. See Figure **1-C-8-i** for a view of the completed caning.

7. FINISHING: A large chair would have a binding edge, which we are not including in these directions. A miniature chair can undergo so much stress and no more; by the time the caning is completed, the holes will be filled and would not be able to accept another two strands of cane.

You may wish to coat the cane with varnish to preserve the embroidery floss.

AN ALTERNATE METHOD FOR ACHIEVING THE EFFECT OF A CANE SEAT IN A MINIATURE CHAIR 1-C-8-a

This method is especially good for the beginning craftsman and results in seats much like those found on antique doll house chairs. The antique seats were embossed paper to simulate caning; we have provided color prints to simulate caning. They are marked

1-C-8 on the color insert sheet.

1. While you are cutting the wood for your chair, trace the top view assembly diagram of the seat. Notch the corners of the seat to fit around the four legs; re-trace onto 1/8" thick wood and cut out. Use

this seat blank instead of the seat framework when building the chair.

2. Apply the finish to the chair before applying the color print to the top surface of the seat blank. Cut the "cane" color print the same shape as the shape of the seat, but slightly smaller, as there is always wood around the edge of a cane seat. Refer to 1-C-2.

HOW TO ACHIEVE A MARBLE EFFECT FROM PAINT 1-C-9

You possibly have found, by now, that most marble that is available is far too thick even if it happens to be the correct dimension for your piece of furniture. By using the following method, you can simulate the effect of a marble-top table, and so forth, without sacrificing scale in your miniature project.

Practice this method on a scrap of wood until you have it perfected. Use two or more fast-drying enamel paints, such as the enamels produced for model airplanes and model trains. They can be purchased at most hobby and craft stores.

Apply the background enamel color, such as black or white. Then, while the background is still wet, apply the contrasting color or colors in wavy lines with a fine-tipped artist's brush. A wad of crumpled tissue paper may also be used to blend and soften the edges of the lines. Tipping the surface to cause slight running of the streaks adds to the realism of the veining.

Do not try this process with paints which are not compatible (such as paints from a variety of manufacturers or water and lacquer based paints) as they may lump or jell where they blend, probably remaining sticky.

Remember to "marble" the edges of the wood where they will be exposed, as on Victorian period table tops, dresser tops, fireplace mantles, and so on.

It really works. I used this process when we were constructing our miniature church which is on view at the Mott Miniature Museum at Knott's Berry Farm. We had marble pillar bases for all of the outside pillars — but one. These marble bases were several hundred years old and came from a castle in Europe. There was no chance to obtain another. Dad copied the shape in wood, and I painted it. You have to feel the marble bases (they are cold to the touch) to find the one that is a copy.

INSTALLING ROPE SPRINGS 1-C-10

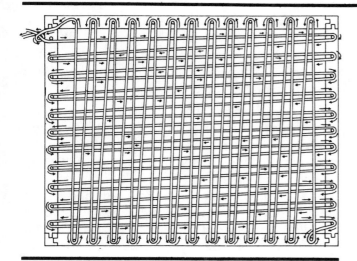

Rope was used on antique beds to perform the same function as metal springs today. I am sure many of you have seen antique beds (large of course) with pegs on the top surface of the side, foot and head rails. These pegs were used to lace the rope and hold it fast.

Because rope is out of scale for miniature beds, we use a twine in place of the rope.

1. The diagram shows a bed frame with pegs (circles) evenly spaced atop all of the rails. The arrows in the diagram indicate the direction of the rope lacing.

2. Leaving an end for tying, begin at the left peg on the foot rail, carry the rope (twine) up to the left peg on the head rail, bring the rope around the peg and down to and around the next peg on the foot rail. Continue in this manner until all pegs on the head and foot rails have been used.

3. Bring the rope around to the last peg on the right side rail, across to and around the last peg on the left side rail. Continue down the side rails, until you end at the end of the beginning end of rope. Tie the two ends together. Apply glue to the knot so that it will not become loose. Cut off excess end lengths.

ASSEMBLY OF BOW-BACK WINDSOR CHAIR 2-A-1

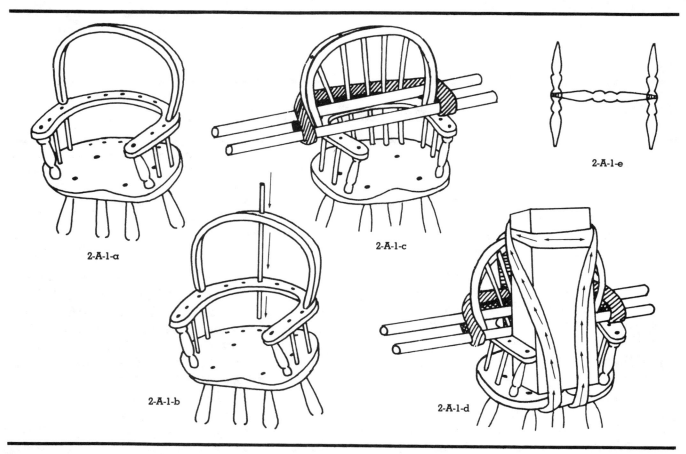

2-A-1-a

2-A-1-b

2-A-1-c

2-A-1-d

2-A-1-e

These directions are for the assembly of the bow-back Windsor baby chair, however, they can be adapted to any bow-back Windsor side chair or settee.

1. Glue the ends of the center leg stretcher into the two holes drilled in the side leg stretchers, as shown in Figure **2-A-1-e**.

2. Glue the ends of the side leg stretchers into the holes drilled into the legs.

3. Glue the legs into the holes drilled into the seat, being sure that they are inserted flush with the top surface of the seat. If any edges of the leg protrude through the seat, these can be sanded flush, when the glue has dried. Before the glue has set, be sure that the legs are even and hold the seat level. Allow the glue to dry overnight.

4. There are five spindles in the bow-back portion of the chair. These are inserted through the holes in the bow-back, the arm section, and on through the seat. See Figure **2-A-1-b**.

5. There are four spindles in the arm section, which are inserted through the holes in the arm and on through the seat.

Note: Insert the spindles very gently; do not force. If they do not insert easily, re-sand the diameter. The

bow-back or the arm section can be broken, if the spindles are forced.

6. Glue the front arm spindles in the first side front hole on each side of the seat. See Figure **2-A-1-a**.

When all of the arm and back spindles are in place and the back is sitting straight, carefully turn the chair upside down and place a dot of glue over the ends protruding through the seat. All of these spindles can be sanded flush with the bottom of the seat, the top of the arm and the top of the bow-back when the glue has dried overnight.

7. Carefully remove the bow-back from the jig. Place the bow-back in position (*do not glue at this time*). Beginning at the center drilled hole, insert the spindles from the top of the bow-back down through the hole, through the matching hole in the arm section, and through the hole in the seat. See Figure **2-A-1-b**. Repeat this process with the hole at the left of center, then right of center, then far left, then far right, until all spindles are in place. Using a pin, touch a dot of glue at each end of each spindle and under both ends of the bow. Allow the glue to dry overnight.

8. The bow ends can be held in place by laying one wood dowel piece behind both bows and another in

18

front of the bows. Attach a rubber band around both ends of the dowel. Place a piece of wood (*the width of the inside of the arm section*) inside the arm section to keep the arms from collapsing inward. Attach a rubber band around the top of this wood, bringing the rubber band down under the chair — up over the back — and again over this piece of wood. See Figures **2-A-1-c** and **2-A-1-d**. Keep the chair clamped in this manner until the glue is thoroughly dry. Carefully remove clamps.

9. Carefully sand all protruding spindle edges flush with the bow-back and underneath the bottom of the seat. Be extremely gentle as you sand; the chair is delicate and you have put too much time and patience into it to see it crumble.

10. Glue the foot rest in place, as shown in Figure **3-A**.

11. Apply the finish coat.

ASSEMBLY OF WINDSOR SIDE CHAIR 2-A-2

2-A-2-a

2-A-2-b

1. Figure **2-A-2-a** shows the assembly of the back and seat. The top back board mortises into the side posts and is glued in place. The spindles are glued into the holes in the back board. This assembly is then glued into the holes in the seat. The ends of the side posts and spindles will be flush with the bottom surface of the seat. Be sure that this assembly sits correctly before the glue has dried.

2. Figure **2-A-2-b** shows the assembly of the upper chair with the legs and their stretchers. Glue the front, back and side stretchers into the holes in the legs. They should go through the leg; the rough end can be sanded later. Glue the top of the legs up into the seat, with the top edges flush with the top of the seat (*the rough ends will be sanded after the assembled chair has been glued and it is dry*). Be sure that the chair is straight and level before the glue has dried.

3. Sand the ends of the posts, spindles and legs. Apply a finish coat.

ASSEMBLY OF SLAT BACK CHAIR 2-A-3-a

1. Be sure all wood has been stained before glueing.

2. Figure **2-A-3-a-1** shows the assembly of the chair back. Glue the pieces together, as shown. Lay the assembled back down on a piece of waxed paper; be sure that it is squared, and let the glue dry.

3. Figure **2-A-3-a-2** shows the assembly of the front section of the chair. Glue the pieces together, as shown. Lay this assembly down on a piece of waxed paper; be sure that it is squared, and let the glue dry.

4. Figure **2-A-3-a-3** shows the assembly of the side view of the chair. When the back and front assembled sections are dry, assemble the two sides, as shown. When the chair is completed, be sure it is squared and let the glue dry.

5. Finish the chair according to your choice. When the chair and the finish are thoroughly dry, you can begin to rush the seat.

ASSEMBLY OF SLAT BACK CHAIR WITH ARMS 2-A-3-b

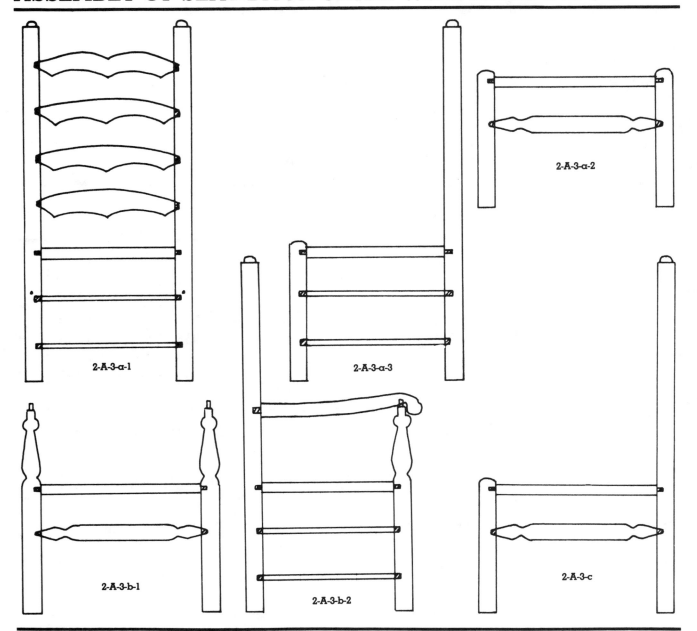

2-A-3-a-2

2-A-3-a-1

2-A-3-a-3

2-A-3-b-1

2-A-3-b-2

2-A-3-c

1. Follow Steps 1 and 2 in **2-A-3-a.**

2. Figure **2-A-3-b-1** shows the assembly of the front section of this chair. Glue the pieces together, as shown. Lay this assembly down on a piece of waxed paper; be sure that it is squared, and let the glue dry.

3. Figure **2-A-3-b-2** shows the assembly of the side

view of the chair. When the back and front assembled sections are dry, assemble the two sides, as shown. When the chair is completed, be sure that it is squared and let the glue dry.

4. Follow the directions in Step 5 in **2-A-3-a.**

ASSEMBLY OF SLAT BACK CORNER CHAIR 2-A-3-c

1. Be sure all wood has been stained before glueing.

2. Figure **2-A-3-a-1** shows the assembly of the back, with this exception: substitute the post shown in Figure **3-M-2** in place of the right-hand post in this diagram. Continue to assemble the chair back as shown.

3. Figure **2-A-3-c** shows the assembly of the front

section of the chair. You will see that the right-hand post in Figure **2-A-3-a-1** is now used as the right-hand post in the front assembly.

4. Lay these two assembled sections down on waxed paper and let the glue dry. Be sure that each section is squared.

5. The assembly of the left side of the chair remains

the same as it was in the previous two chairs, however the right side assembly is different. The extra set of slats is inserted into the upper portion of this side assembly, and the lower assembly remains the same.

6. When the chair is completed, be sure that it is squared and let it dry. Finish the chair according to your choice, and when this finish is thoroughly dry, you are ready to begin to rush the seat.

ASSEMBLY OF BANNISTER BACK CHAIR 2-A-4

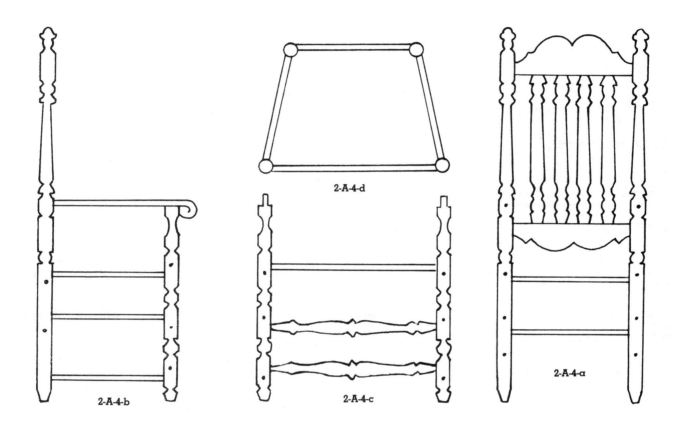

2-A-4-b

2-A-4-d

2-A-4-c

2-A-4-a

1. Stain all wood before glueing. Refer to Figures 2-A-4-a (*front view of back assembly*), 2-A-4-b (*left side view*), 2-A-4-c (*front view of front leg assembly*) and 2-A-4-d (*top view of seat frame assembly*).

2. Glue the four bannisters into the holes in the bottom edge of the top slat and into the holes in the top edge of the bottom slat. See Figure 2-A-4-a.

3. Glue the above assembly into the upper and lower mortise holes in each post. See Figure 2-A-4-a.

4. Glue the back seat rail and the back leg stretcher into the two holes on the interior surface of each back post. See Figure 2-A-4-a.

5. See Figure 2-A-4-b (*side view*). Glue the arm rests, the side seat rails and the side leg stretchers into the holes on the front surface of the back posts.

6. See Figure 2-A-4-c. Glue the front seat rail and the two front leg stretchers between the two front legs.

7. Glue the side seat rail and the side leg stretchers into the holes on the back surface of the front legs. Glue the arm rests onto the pegs at the top of the front legs.

8. See Figure 2-A-4-d, which is a top view diagram of the assembly of the seat frame. Be sure the frame is squared, as it is in the diagram, and be sure that the chair sits straight.

9. Let the glue dry for at least one week before rushing the seat. Refer to 1-C-7 for the rushing.

10. After the seat has been rushed, apply a finish coat to the chair and the seat.

ASSEMBLY OF CANE SEAT CHAIR 2-A-5

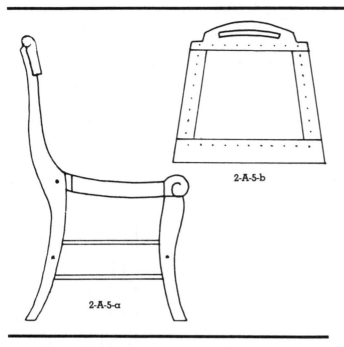

2-A-5-b

2-A-5-a

1. Figure **2-A-5-b** shows the assembly of the chair seat. Be sure that it is squared when the assembly is complete, and let the glue thoroughly dry.

2. Glue the back splat into the hole in the rear seat rail.

3. Glue a back leg on either side of the chair seat. The leg will fit into the notch in the rear seat rail. Insert a piece of 1/16" diameter wood dowel through the hole in the leg and into the rear seat rail. Clip off the excess length and sand smooth.

4. Glue the back rail into the lower hole of each back leg.

5. Glue the chair back into the notch at the top of each back leg and atop the top edges of the chair splat. See the picture of the chair in your work project.

6. Glue the front legs in place, and glue the side and front rails in place between the front legs and between the front and back legs. See Figure **2-A-5-a** and the picture of the chair on the project page.

7. When the assembly is completed, be sure that the chair is squared and sits level. When this has been done, let the glue dry thoroughly.

8. Apply the finish coat to the chair.

9. Refer to **1-C-8** to cane the chair seat. Do not attempt to cane the seat for at least one week after completion of the chair. This assures you that the glued joints will be thoroughly dry and tight.

ASSEMBLY OF CANE SEAT CHAIR WITH SPINDLES 2-A-6

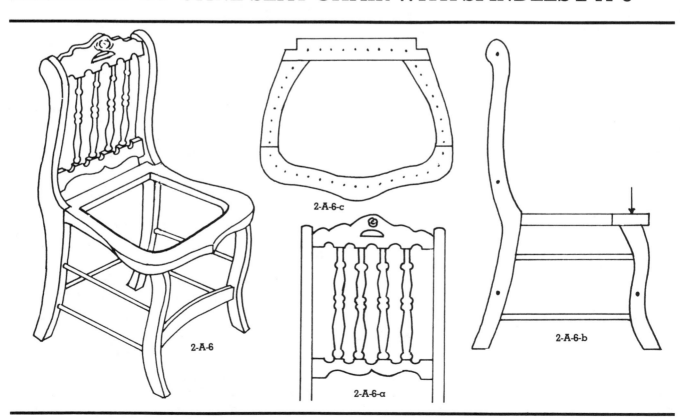

2-A-6

2-A-6-c

2-A-6-a

2-A-6-b

These assembly directions are for the chair which appears in 3-Q. The directions will also apply to other chairs of similar construction.

1. Stain all wood before glueing.

2. Refer to **2-A-6-d**, which is a top view diagram of the seat assembly. Glue the front, back and sides together as shown.

3. Glue the back spindles into the holes in the upper and lower back slats. See Figure **2-A-6-c**.

4. Glue the above assembly between the two back posts. See Figures **2-A-6-c** and **2-A-6-a**.

5. Glue the front leg stretcher between the two front legs. See Figure **2-A-6-a**.

6. Glue the back posts into the rear side notches of the chair seat, and the front legs pegged into the front of the chair seat. See Figures **2-A-6-a** and **2-A-6-b**.

7. Glue the side and back leg stretchers between the legs. Be sure the chair sits straight and level.

8. Apply a finish coat. Allow one week for the glue to dry.

9. Refer to **1-C-8** to cane the chair seat.

ASSEMBLY OF SLIP SEAT SIDE CHAIR 2-A-7

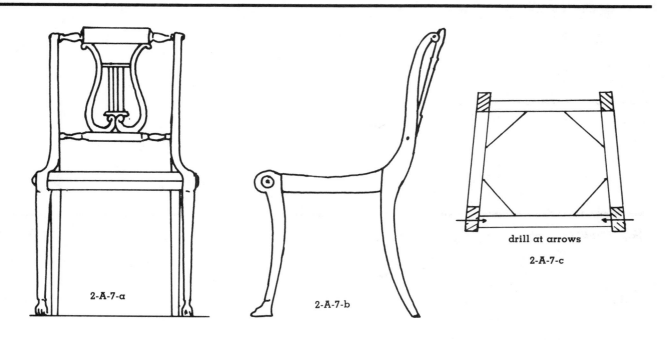

2-A-7-a

2-A-7-b

drill at arrows

2-A-7-c

This assembly is for the chair in 3-R, however it can be applied, with specific changes, to other slip seat chairs.

1. Construct the lyre back portion of the chair first. Refer to **3-R-13** for this assembly. The arrows in Figures **3-R-9** and **3-R-10** show the area in which the wire or pins must pass through the top board and down into the same area in the bottom board. The brass pins or wire must be 9/16″ in length. Glue this assembly between the lyre sides, as shown in the diagram. Glue the board and wire assembly in place. Place this completed assembly over the diagram to be sure it is straight. Let it dry.

2. Glue the above assembly between the back legs of the chair. The ends of the rungs will go through the holes drilled into the upper portion of the back legs.

3. Glue the side boards of the seat against the front edge of the back legs, continuing the curved line of the upper back portion of these legs. Glue the front legs against the front edge of the seat side board.

4. Glue the front board between the two front legs. Push a sequin pin through the hole in the leg and into the hole in the end of the front board. Be sure that the chair sits straight and level. Let the glue dry.

5. Glue the front and back seat braces (**K**) against the inside surfaces of the front and side boards. Be sure to place the front braces at the front and the back braces at the back, as they are different shapes and fit the assembled seat frame.

6. Apply a finish coat to the chair.

7. Refer to **1-C-4** and make the slip seat and upholster it. Slip the seat in place in the chair frame.

ASSEMBLY OF TABLE WITH CABRIOLE LEGS 2-B-1

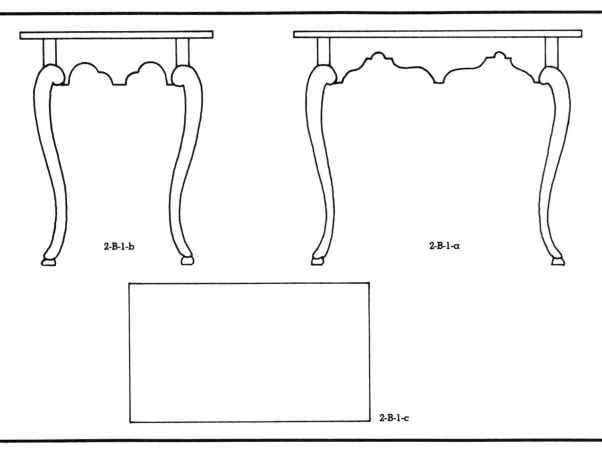

2-B-1-b

2-B-1-a

2-B-1-c

Note: The table shown in the diagrams is from project 5-D.

1. Stain all wood before glueing together.

2. Refer to Figure **2-B-1-a** which shows the front elevation of the table which you will be assembling. Lay a long piece of the apron down on a piece of waxed paper. Glue a leg against each edge of this piece of wood. Repeat this procedure for the second assembly, and let both dry thoroughly.

3. Trace Figure **2-B-1-c** onto a piece of paper. Place this piece of paper beneath a sheet of waxed paper. This shape will serve as the guide for the next step in the assembly of the table. Place the boards (*top edge downward*) against the inside surfaces of the lines (*the legs will be in the air*). Glue the end pieces of the apron (*top edge downward*) between the legs and against the back edge of the upper squared surface of the leg. Be sure this assembly is squared, and let it dry thoroughly.

4. Place the legs of the table downward, and set them on the work surface. Glue the table top (*centered*) on the top edges of the legs and apron pieces.

5. Finish the table to your choice.

ASSEMBLY OF DRESSING TABLE WITH MIRROR
STAND AND DRAWER 2-B-2

1. Stain all wood before glueing.

2. Figure **2-B-2-c** shows a top elevation of the assembly of the dressing table with the drawer. Glue the table back board against the edge of the bottom board, with all edges flush.

3. Glue the side boards against the end edges of the bottom board and against the upright end edges of the back board. See Figure **2-B-2-c**.

4. The front inner frame is glued atop the front edge of the bottom board and against the inside front edge of the side boards. The front facing boards glue against the pieces of the front inner frame and

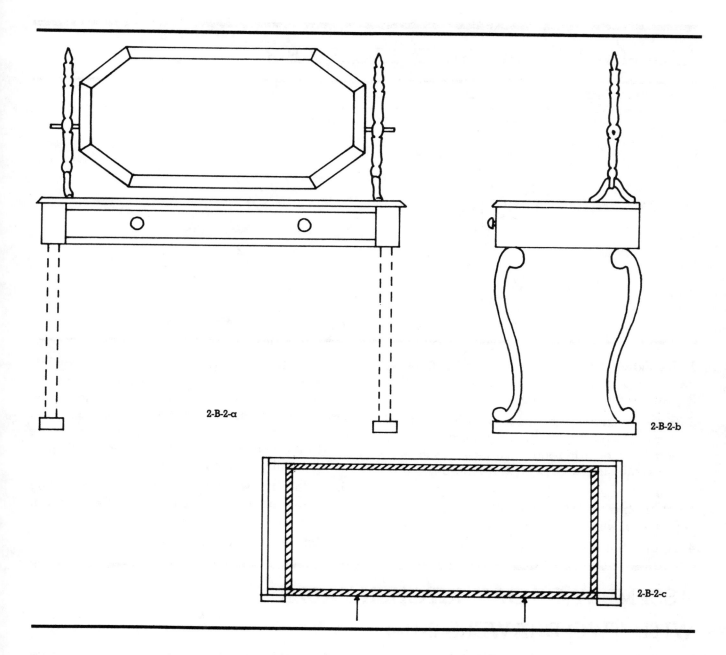

2-B-2-a

2-B-2-b

2-B-2-c

against the front upright edge of each side board. See Figure **2-B-2-c**.

5. The table top is glued atop the top edges of the framework with the beveled edges upward. See Figures **2-B-2-a** and **2-B-2-b**.

6. Glue the upper front frame beneath the top board and between the two front frame pieces. See Figure **2-B-2-a**.

7. See Figure **2-B-2-b** (*side elevation*). Glue two legs atop the leg support. Repeat, for the other pair of legs. Glue a leg assembly beneath each side of the dressing table, being sure that they are straight.

8. Glue the two mirror post legs against the lower turning of the mirror post, being sure the assembly is as shown in Figure **2-B-2-b**.

9. Glue the mirror frame moulding atop the mirror back, with the outside edges flush.

10. Insert the mirror pegs through the holes in the mirror posts and push into the upright side edges of the mirror back. See Figure **2-B-2-a** for the sites of insertion into the mirror back. Glue the mirror post legs atop the dressing table top at the back. See Figure **2-B-2-b**.

11. Refer to **2-E-1** for drawer assembly.

12. Apply a finish coat to this piece of furniture.

13. Glue the mirror inside the mirror frame moulding and against the mirror back board.

14. Attach two drawer pulls to the drawer front and slip the drawer in place.

25

ASSEMBLY OF SAWBUCK TABLE 2-B-3

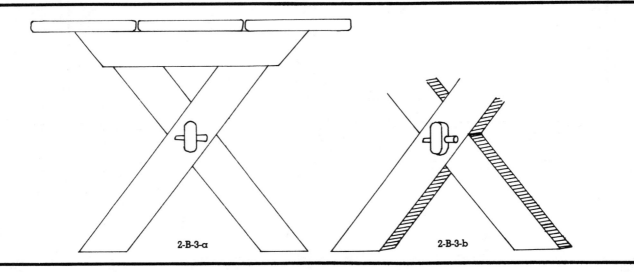

2-B-3-a   2-B-3-b

1. See Figure **2-B-3-a** (*end view of table*). Assemble the two legs together at the sites of the notches. Repeat, for the other pair of legs.

2. Glue the stretcher board into the hole cut into each pair of legs. Insert a wedge through the hole in the leg stretcher on the outside surface of each pair of legs and glue in place. See Figure **2-B-3-b**.

3. See Figure **2-B-3-a**. Glue a top leg brace (*drilled edge upward*) against the outside surface of each pair of legs, with the top edges flush.

4. Apply a thin line of glue to the top edge of the top leg brace board and put a table top board atop this piece, with the drilled holes matching. Apply the second and third boards, matching the drilled holes. Insert a peg down through the table top board and into the leg brace board; continue, until all holes are filled with pegs. Let the glue dry. Repeat this procedure for the other end of the table.

5. Using a flat wood rasp, smooth the protruding pegs at the table top, until they are level with the top. Finish sanding the pegs with an emery board.

6. Apply a finish coat to the completed table.

ASSEMBLY OF OAK KITCHEN TABLE WITH TWO DRAWERS 2-B-4

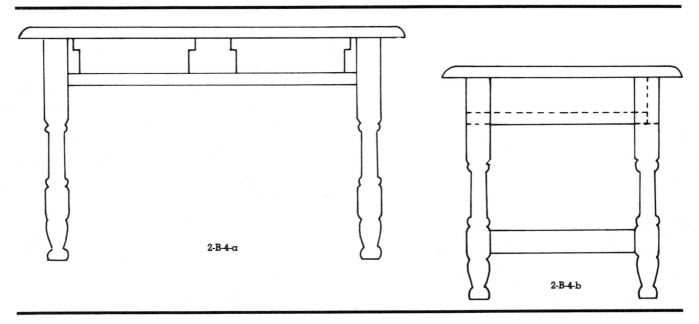

2-B-4-a   2-B-4-b

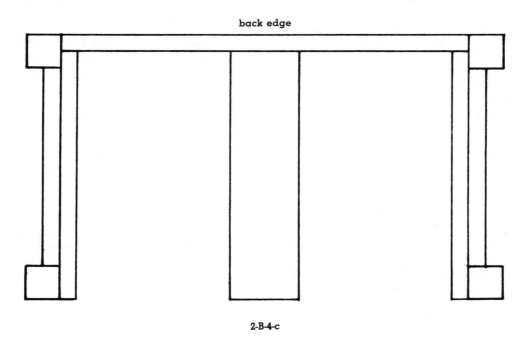

back edge

2-B-4-c

1. Stain all wood before glueing.

2. Figures **2-B-4-a** and **2-B-4-b** show the front and side elevations of the table.

3. Figure **2-B-4-c** shows the elevation of the underneath surface of the table top, showing the assembly of the legs, back, side boards, and drawer runners and divider.

4. Lay the table top board upside down on your work surface and glue the legs in place. Glue the two side boards between the legs and against the table top, with the inside surfaces of this board and the legs flush. Glue the back board between the legs and against the surface of the table top, with the back sur-

faces flush. Let dry.

5. Turn the table right side up, and glue the two shaped side drawer runners (*see Figures* **2-B-4-a** and **2-B-4-c**) against the inside surfaces of the table side boards and against the table top.

6. Glue the center shaped drawer divider down the center of the table, against the undersurface of the table top. See Figures **2-B-4-a** and **2-B-4-c**.

7. Glue the drawer base board against the inside surfaces of the table sides and back (*with bottom edges flush*) and against the bottom edges of the three drawer runners. See Figure **2-B-4-a**.

CHEST ASSEMBLY 2-C-1

These assembly directions are for the chest in **7**-C, *however, they can be adapted for the assembly of any chest of the type. Stain all wood before glueing.*

1. Refer to Figures **2-C-1-a** and **2-C-1-b**.

2. The sides are glued against the upright side edges of the back board, with the edges flush.

3. The top is glued atop the top edges of the side and back boards, with the back edges flush and an

equal side overhang.

4. The bottom (*rounded side up*) is glued against the bottom edges of the back and sides, with the back edges flush and with equal side overhang. *Be sure the chest frame is squared.*

5. Construct all of the drawers.

6. Insert one of the three lower drawers into the chest frame. Glue a drawer spacer directly above it; carefully remove the drawer without disturbing the spacer. Repeat this process twice more.

7. Insert the two deep drawers above the last spacer. Glue a spacer above them. Remove the right drawer, glue the drawer divider between the two spacers and along the right side of the remaining drawer. Carefully remove the drawer.

8. Glue a spacer between the chest sides and against the underneath surface of the top board.

9. The front legs splay to the front and toward the outside surface of the chest. The two front legs are glued in place. See Figures **2-C-1-a** and **2-C-1-b**.

10. The back legs splay only to the outside surface of the chest, with the back surface being straight. Glue these legs in place. Refer to Figure **2-C-1-b**.

11. Glue the front apron between the two front legs and against the underneath surface of the chest bottom. The side apron is glued between the front and back legs and against the underneath surface of the chest bottom.

12. Insert the drawers to assure a good fit. If they seem tight, they may need additional sanding. When assured of the fit, remove all of the drawers.

13. Apply the finish coat.

14. Attach drop pulls to all of the drawers. Refer to **1-B-6** for aid in identification.

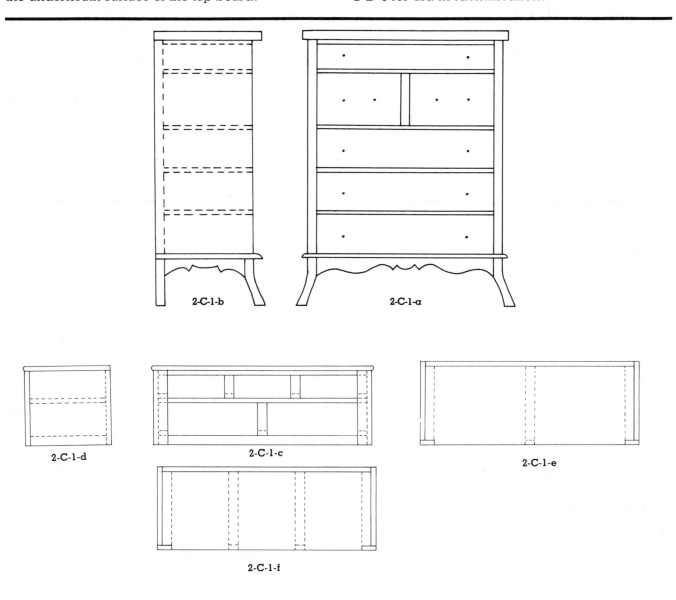

2-C-1-b   2-C-1-a

2-C-1-d   2-C-1-c   2-C-1-e

2-C-1-f

ASSEMBLY OF CABINET WITH DOORS 2-C-2

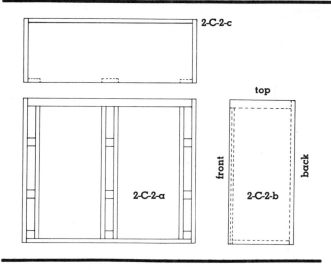

*This assembly is for the schrank, **8-K**, upper cabinet. These directions can, however, be adapted for other similar cabinets.*

1. Glue the side boards butted against the upright ends of the back board, with the back edges flush.

2. Glue the base board between the sides and against the back, with the bottom surfaces flush.

3. Glue the top board between the sides and against the back, with the top surfaces flush. See Figures **2-C-2-c** and **2-C-2-b**.

4. Glue the left and right facing boards atop the base and against the side walls, with the forward surfaces of these boards flush. See Figure **2-C-2-a**.

5. Glue the door divider board centered between the top and base boards, with the forward surfaces flush. See Figure **2-C-2-a**.

6. When the cabinet has had its finish coat, the doors are hinged to the front and the door knobs are attached. Refer to **1-B-4** and **1-B-6**.

ASSEMBLY OF CHEST ON FRAME 2-C-3

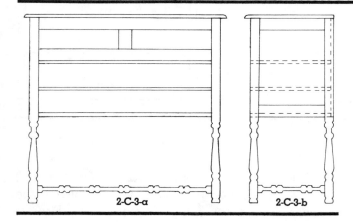

1. Glue the back leg stretcher between two legs (*a drilled hole will be on the front surface of each of these legs*). Glue the back board between these two legs, with the back and top edges flush. Refer to Figure **2-C-3-b**.

2. Glue the front leg stretcher between the remaining two legs (*the drilled hole will be on the back surface of each of these legs*). Glue the front board (*moulding surface forward*) between these two legs, with the top and front surfaces flush. Refer to Figure **2-C-3-a**.

3. Glue a separator board beneath the edge of the front board and against the inside surface of the back board. Be sure it is straight. Refer to Figure **2-C-3-b**.

4. Insert a drawer (*for measurement only*). Glue a second separator against the back wall beneath the drawer. Insert the second drawer and glue the chest bottom against the back wall beneath the drawer.

5. Glue the sides (*paneled surface toward the outside*) between the front and back legs and against the end edges of the two separators and the bottom board. Remove the drawers. See Figure **2-C-3-b**.

6. Glue the side leg stretchers in place. Refer to Figure **2-C-3-b**. Be sure the assembled chest is squared and level before the glue is dry.

7. Position the top board atop the top edges of the chest, with equal side overhang and the back edges flush. *Do not glue in place.* Glue a cleat hinge against the undersurface of the side overhang, resting but *not glued* against the side surface of the chest. Push a sequin pin through the rear side surface of the cleat hinge and through the side of the chest. Repeat for the other cleat hinge. Raise the lid and clip off the excess length of the pin.

8. Finish the chest to your choice. Attach the four drawer pulls.

ASSEMBLY OF DOWER CHEST 2-C-4

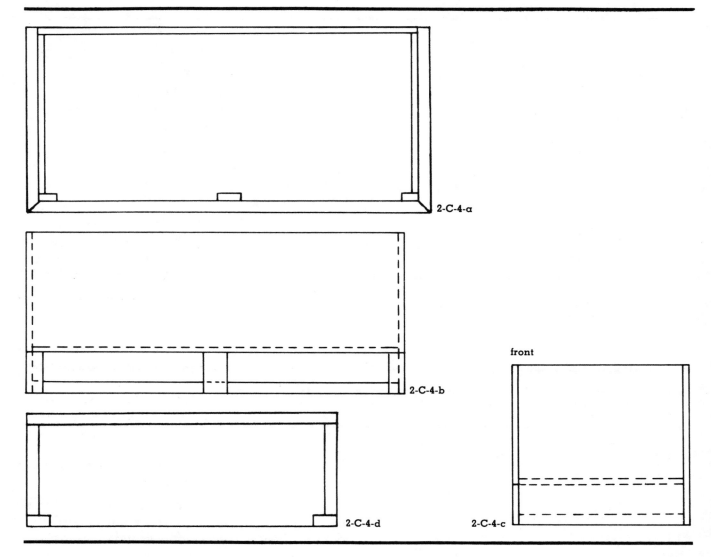

2-C-4-a

front

2-C-4-b

2-C-4-d

2-C-4-c

The directions which follow are for both dower chests **8-H** *(with drawers) and* **8-I**. *The directions dealing only with the chest with drawers will be marked with an asterisk.*

1. Glue the bottom against the two side boards, with all edges flush. See Figure **2-C-4-d** (*top view*).

2. Glue the back board against the rear edges of this assembly, with all edges flush. See Figure **2-C-4-d** (*top view*).

3.* Glue the lower front side facing boards against the front edges of the sides and bottom board, with the side and bottom edges flush. See Figure **2-C-4-d**.

4.* Insert a drawer against the interior left side. Glue the lower center facing board along the right side of the drawer, against the front edge of the bottom board, with the bottom edges flush. Insert the second drawer. See Figure **2-C-4-b**.

5.* Glue the drawer spacer between the side boards, against the back board and at the top edge of

the drawers. See Figures **2-C-4-b** (*front view*) and **2-C-4-c** (*side view*).

6. Glue the upper front board (*or front board*) against the front edges of the side boards and the drawer spacer (*or bottom board*). See Figures **2-C-4-b** (*front view*) and **2-C-4-c** (*side view*).

7. Glue the three base frame pieces together and glue centered beneath the chest, with back edges flush. See Figure **2-C-4-a**.

8. Refer to **1-B-4-b** (*cleat hinge*). Fashion two wood cleats. Glue these to the underside of the top board, following directions in **1-B-4-b**.

9. Paint the chest a color that will harmonize with the color prints marked either **8-H** or **8-I**.

10. Refer to **1-C-2**. Apply the color prints and finish as instructed.

11. Attach the cleat hinge as instructed in **1-B-4-b**. Attach the drawer pulls.

ASSEMBLY OF CABINET TOP WITH SHELVES AND PANELED DOORS 2-C-5

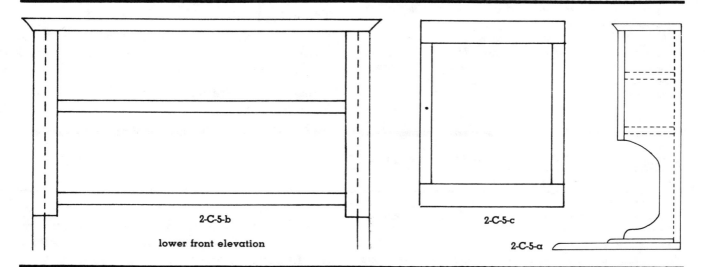

2-C-5-b

lower front elevation

2-C-5-c

2-C-5-a

1. Glue the sides against the edges of the back board, with the back and top edges flush. See Figure **2-C-5-a**.

2. Glue the top board atop the top edges of the previous assembly, with the back edges flush. See Figures **2-C-5-a** and **2-C-5-b**.

3. Glue a shelf or shelves in place, noting the placement of these shelves in the diagrams in the furniture project. See Figure **2-C-5-b**.

4. Glue the front side facing boards against the front upright edges of the side boards, and against the front edges of the shelves. See Figure **2-C-5-b**.

5. DOORS

   a. Glue the side frame boards against the center panel, with the top and bottom edges flush. See Figure **2-C-5-c**.

   b. Glue the top and bottom frame boards against the top and bottom edges of the side frame boards and the center panel. See Figure **2-C-5-c**. Let dry.

   c. Drill a hole or holes at the site of the black dot in the diagram to accept door pulls.

   d. Attach hinges to the door and the front side facing boards. Refer to **1-C-4-b** for instructions.

ASSEMBLY OF BED 2-D

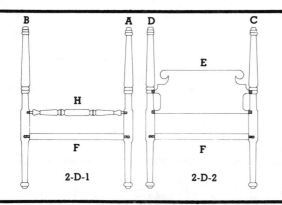

2-D-1

2-D-2

1. Figure **2-D-1** shows the inside view of the foot assembly. You will note the shaded squared areas show the insertion of the end brace and the blanket roll; the shaded circles show the holes which have been drilled to accept the side braces. Glue this sec-

tion of the bed together, as shown.

2. Figure **2-D-2** shows the inside view of the head assembly. Glue this section together, as shown. You will note that all of the beds will have the same letter identification of the major pieces of the bed, such as posts (**B**) and (**A**) will always be the foot posts, and posts (**C**) and (**D**) will always be the head posts.

3. When the head and foot sections have been glued together and are dry, you will glue the side braces into the head and foot posts, joining the two sections.

4. Glue a long brace against the inside surface of each of the side braces, with the bottom edges flush. This brace will support the mattress.

5. When the bed has been assembled and the glue is thoroughly dry, finish it to your choice.

ASSEMBLY OF DRAWERS 2-E

The measurements for the drawers which are given in this manual exactly fit the drawer opening. There is need for space tolerance for each drawer, and it is so minimal that the measurements would result in many various fractions of an inch. If you follow these easy steps, the drawers will not only fit the openings but will pull satisfactorily. The width and height of each drawer must be reduced the thickness of a piece of waxed paper. When you have cut the wood for each drawer, follow these directions.

1. Sand *both edges* of the width of the bottom board, back board and front board the thickness of a piece of waxed paper.

2. Sand *one edge* of the height of the back board, the two side boards and the front board the thickness of a piece of waxed paper.

3. Assemble the drawer as instructed. It should slide in and out with ease.

SIMPLE DRAWER ASSEMBLY 2-E-1

These instructions are for the simple way to put a drawer together. If you examine most drawers, you will find that the back board is set in between the two side boards. This necessitates cutting two different size boards for the front and back, and the assembly is more difficult. Our instructions call for the front and back boards to be of equal measurements to save cutting and assembly time.

1. The sides are glued against the side edges of the drawer bottom, with the bottom edges flush.

2. The back board is glued against the upright end edges of the sides and against the drawer bottom, with the bottom edges flush.

3. The front board, after the hole has been drilled for attachment of the drawer pull, is glued against the upright front end edges of the sides and against the drawer bottom, with the bottom edges flush. See Figure **2-E-1**.

DRAWER ASSEMBLY WITH FRONT OVERHANG 2-E-2

1. Assemble this drawer with the sides glued against the side edges of the drawer bottom, with the bottom edges flush.

2. Glue the drawer back board against the edge of the bottom board and against the upright end edges of the side boards, with all edges flush.

3. The front board, after the hole has been drilled for attachment of the drawer pull, is glued against the edge of the bottom board and against the upright end edges of the side boards, with equal overhang at each side and with the top edges flush. See Figures **2-E-2-a** and **2-E-2-b**.

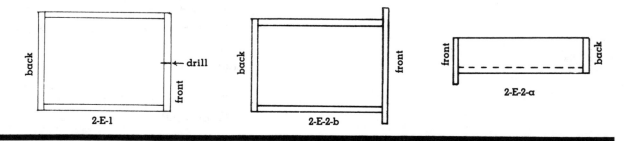

ASSEMBLY OF DRAWER WITH SIDE RUNNERS 2-E-3

1. Glue the sides butted against the side edges of the drawer bottom, with the bottom edges flush. See Figure **2-E-3-a**.

2. Glue the back board against the upright edges of the drawer sides and against the edge of the drawer bottom, with the bottom edges flush. See Figure **2-E-3-c**.

3. Glue the drawer runners along the drawer sides, with the top edges flush. See Figure **2-E-3-a.**

4. Glue the front board against the front edge of the drawer bottom, the upright front edges of the side boards, and the front edges of the drawer runners. See Figure **2-E-3-b.** The arrows in the diagrams indicate where the hole would have previously been drilled to accept a drawer pull.

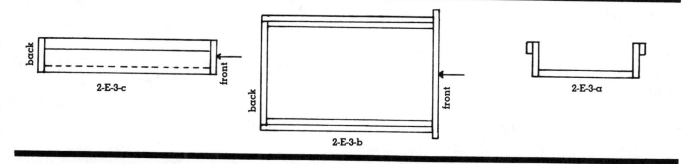

ASSEMBLY OF A BIN DRAWER 2-E-4

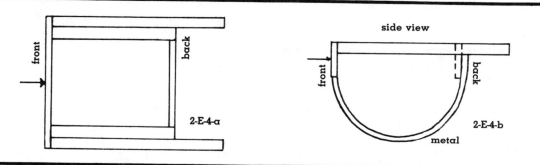

1. The arrows in the diagrams indicate where a hole would be drilled in the drawer front board to accept a drawer pull. Drill the hole before assembly.

2. Glue the drawer front board against the top front edges of the two shaped sides. See Figure **2-E-4-a** (*top view*).

3. Glue the drawer back between the two shaped sides, with the top and back edges flush. See Figure **2-E-4-a** (*top view*).

4. See the side view of this assembly (*Figure 2-E-4-b*). Using tiny brads, attach the thin metal piece, beginning beneath the bottom edge of the drawer front, and continue all around the edge of the curved side board. The metal will fasten against the back edge of the curved side and against the back surface of the drawer back board.

5. Glue the runners butted against the back surface of the drawer front board and along the outside surfaces of the side boards, with the top edges flush. These runners will extend behind the bin drawer assembly. See Figure **2-E-4-b** (*right side view*).

ASSEMBLY OF CLOCK 2-F

These directions are for the assembly of the grandfather clock 9-P, however, they can be adapted for other clocks. Stain all wood before glueing.

TOP SECTION

See Figures **9-P, 2-F-1** and **2-F-2.**

1. Glue the sides against the upright edges of the back board, with the edges flush. Glue the top and bottom boards against the back and between the side boards, with the edges flush.

2. Glue the color print of the clock face against the clock face backing board.

3. Finish the front board and glue the clock face board against the reverse side, allowing an equal distance on both sides. This assembled board will now fit into and against the top section assembly.

4. Glue the arched clock face moulding above the clock face. Glue the side moulding pieces against the sides of this unit, with the mitred ends joining the

mitred ends of the arched moulding.

5. Glue the top front moulding (*Figures* **9-P-4** *and* **9-P-5**) against the top front surface of the clock. Glue the two top side moulding pieces (*Figure* **9-P-6**) against the top side surfaces of the clock, with the mitred ends joining the front moulding pieces.

6. Glue the finial atop the finial base. Glue this assembled unit atop the center top surface of the clock.

CENTER SECTION

7. Glue the sides against the upright edges of the back board, with edges flush. Glue the top and bottom boards against the back and between the side boards, with edges flush. Glue the front board against the front edges of this assembly, with all edges flush.

8. Glue the door panel against the front board. See Figure **2-F-1**.

LOWER SECTION

9. Assemble the back, sides, top and bottom as you did for the center section. Glue the front board against this assembly, with the top edges flush, and the scallop toward the bottom.

10. Glue the front and back legs in position against the bottom board. See Figures **2-F-1** and **2-F-2**.

FINAL ASSEMBLY

11. Refer to Figures **2-F-1** and **2-F-2**. Glue the three sections together, with the back edges flush.

12. Glue the moulding joining the top and center sections atop the top surface of the center section and against the top section, with mitred ends joining.

13. Glue the moulding joining the center and lower sections atop the top surface of the lower section and against the center section, with mitred ends joining.

14. Apply a finish coat to the clock.

15. Attach a pull to the door panel.

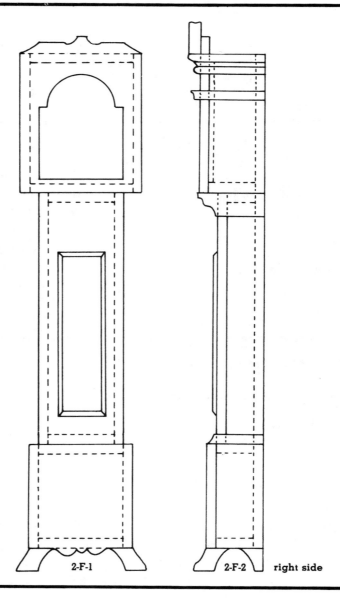

2-F-1   2-F-2   **right side**

GENERAL DIRECTIONS FOR LITHOGRAPHED DOLL HOUSES AND STABLE 2-G

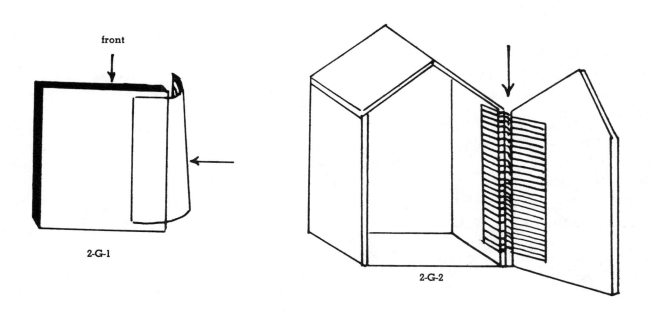

front

2-G-1

2-G-2

1. HO scale (*model railroad*) turned posts — Campbell Scale Models #HO-926-75 and fencing — Campbell Scale Models #HO-922-75 or Grandt Line #5035 — can be used in place of the round wood posts and fencing that are included in the directions for the houses. The length of these plastic pieces may have to be adjusted to the length called for in the directions. Many of the old lithographed doll houses had a brass porch rail that was a lattice weave. The tiny plastic lattice weave fencing can be painted with a gilt paint and substituted in place of the color print. These can be purchased from most hobby shops that carry model railroad supplies.

2. For a cloth hinge, cut two pieces of cloth 1 ″ wide × the height of the right edge of the front board of the house. Apply one piece against the front of the house, around the upright right edge of this board, and against the right side of the house. *Let dry.* See Figure **2-G-1**. Apply the second piece against the inside right wall of the house, against the upright front edge of this board, against the inner surface of the outside hinge, and against the inside surface of the front board of the house. *Let dry.* See Figure **2-G-2**. *Note:* Apply both hinge pieces before installing the second floor of the house.

3. Sand all edges of the wood.

4. You will find that the wooden ends of swab sticks and some toothpicks can be used for the 1/16″ diameter wood dowel.

5. If you prefer to cut part of the house structure from cardboard, it must be 1/16″ thick to correspond to the directions. The edge angles will have to be sanded to measurements that correspond to the diagrams. The edges of the cut cardboard will have to be sealed with a glue such as airplane cement to prevent separation when painted.

6. Balsa wood is easy to work with to cut dormer windows, porch roofs, and the center roof core of the stable.

7. Identify the individual pieces that make up the house by marking a divided box or egg carton spaces with the piece number (*such as* **10-A-1**) and keep the piece in its space until it is required.

8. Refer to **1-C-2** for application of the color print. Refer to **1-B-2** for glue.

9. We recommend acrylic paints, for they clean up with water. Paint all exposed surfaces that will not be covered by the color print *before* you glue on the print. Paint the interior walls, ceilings and floors — or use tiny print wallpaper. Cloth or paper prints can be used for floor coverings.

WINDSOR BABY CHAIR 3-A

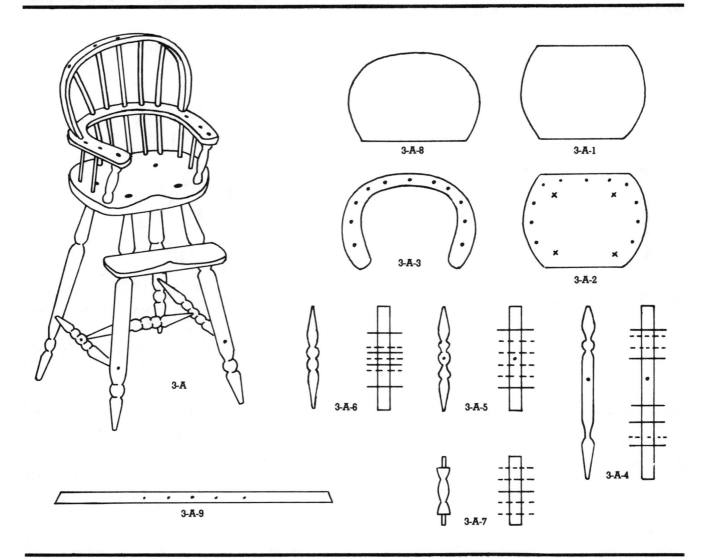

The miniature chair presented here is a copy of an antique Windsor baby chair my family owned and which was used by our Polly when she was a baby; it is also like a baby chair which was in Mount Vernon when we visited it years ago.

My father splintered a very old cobbler's hammer handle to provide the hickory for the bow-back of the miniature Windsor baby chair which I made. Search out second-hand stores for old tools, and so forth, for the hickory. If you are not sure about it, take the piece of wood to a lumberyard and ask if they can identify it. The bow must be made of hickory to assure proper bending. I made five bow-backs before I found my hickory; all of them failed and split in the bending, until I realized that those men of old really did know their business.

MATERIALS NEEDED FOR THIS PROJECT

You will need the various woods listed below. You will also need white glue, emery boards and sandpaper, stain, shellac and varnish, or a good decoupage spray for the finish. A saw, knife, a hand drill with a bit to drill 1/16″ diameter holes, rubber bands, clamps and small brads are also required. The woods you will be using are as follows.

HICKORY: For the bow-back.

OAK: For the arm section. 1/4″ × 1″ × 1 1/2″.

PINE or MAPLE: For the seat. 1/4″ × 1″ × 1 1/2″.

WOOD DOWEL: 1/8″ diameter × at least 13 1/2″ (longer, if there is breakage when turning the spindles).

PINE or MAPLE: For the foot rest. 1/8″ x 1/4″ x 1 1/8″.

WOOD DOWEL: Sanded to approximately 1/16″ in diameter × at least 12 3/4″ (longer, if there is breakage).

WOOD: For jig to shape the bow-back. 1/4″ × 1″ × 1 1/2″.

(A) HICKORY FOR BOW-BACK (Two): 3/32″ × 1/8″ × 2 7/8″. Find the hickory wood. Split the wood so you will have two pieces measuring 1/8" in width × 2 7/8" in length, and sand to a thickness of 3/32". Sand the edges rounded and drill holes at the sites of the black dots in Figure **3-A-9**.

(B) BACK JIG (One): Shape a piece of wood 1/4" × 1" × 1 1/4" for the back jig, as shown in Figure **3-A-8**. Trace this shape onto the wood and cut out.

BENDING THE BOW-BACKS: Refer to **1-C-6** (*bending wood*). Prepare the two bow-backs and steam both of them. If one should break while attaching it to the bending block, re-steam the second piece for a longer period of time and attach it to the bending block.

(C) SEAT (One): 1/4" × 1" × 1 1/2". Use the pine or maple piece. Trace the outline in Figure **3-A-1** onto the wood and cut out. Refer to **1-C-3-e** for aid in shaping the seat.

When the piece is carved to shape and has been thoroughly sanded, drill holes, as indicated in Figure **3-A-2**. Use tracing paper to copy the drill sites and transfer onto the seat, as it is extremely important that these holes be just as they are shown. If not, the back spindles will not be straight and the chair will not sit properly.

(D) ARM SECTION (One): Using the piece of oak which measures 1/4" × 1" × 1 1/2", trace the shape of the arm section onto the wood from Figure **3-A-3**. The black dots in the diagram indicate drill holes.

Drill the holes *before* any shaping is done. Carve this shape gently, as the piece will split if handled roughly. Sand gently.

(E) LEGS (Cut 4): 1/8" diameter wood dowel × 1 7/8". Figure **3-A-4** shows the shape. Refer to **1-C-3-a** for aid in shaping. Drill a hole through each leg at the site of the black dot.

(F) SIDE LEG STRETCHERS (Cut 2): 1/8" diameter wood dowel × 1 1/8". Figure **3-A-5** shows the shape. Refer to **1-C-3-a** for aid in shaping. Drill a hole through each piece at the site of the black dot.

(G) CENTER LEG STRETCHER (Cut 1): 1/8" diameter wood dowel × 1 1/8". Figure **3-A-6** shows the shape. Refer to **1-C-3-a** for aid in shaping.

(H) FOOT REST (One): 1/8" × 1/4" × 1 1/8". Use the pine or maple piece. Shape this piece as shown in Figure **3-A**. Refer to **1-C-3-e** for shaping.

(I) FRONT ARM SPINDLES (Cut 2): 1/8" diameter wood dowel × 3/4". Figure **3-A-7** shows the shape. Refer to **1-C-3-a** for aid in shaping.

(J) BACK SPINDLES (Five): Using the wood dowel sanded to approximately 1/16" in diameter, cut five pieces which measure at least 1 3/4" long.

(K) ARM SPINDLES (Four): Using the wood dowel sanded to approximately 1/16" in diameter, cut four pieces which measure at least 1" in length.

ASSEMBLY: Refer to **2-A-1**.

WINDSOR TYPE SIDE CHAIR 3-B

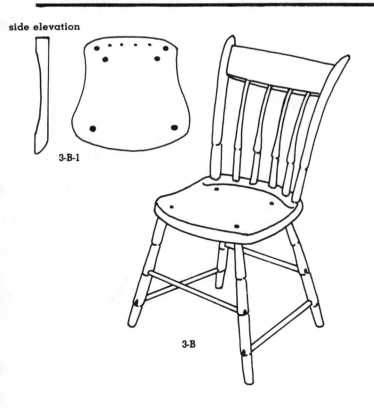

side elevation

3-B-1

3-B

(A) SEAT (Cut 1): 1/8" × 1 1/4" × 1 1/4". See Figure **3-B-1** for the shape. The side elevation shows the "dished" shaping of the seat. The black dots in the diagram indicate holes to be drilled through the seat.

(B) UPPER SIDE POSTS (Cut 2): 1/4" × 3/8" × 1 5/8". See Figure **3-B-4**. The left diagram shows the initial shaping. Refer to **1-C-3-b**. The right diagram shows the final shaping. The black mark in the left diagram indicates a mortise hole to be cut into the right side of the left post, and the left side of the right post to accept the upper back board.

(C) SPINDLES (Cut 4): 1/8" × 3/8" × 1 3/8". Refer to **3-B-5** for the shape. The left diagram shows the initial shaping and the right diagram shows the final shaping. Refer to **1-C-3-b**.

(D) TOP BACK BOARD (Cut 1): 1/4" × 1/4" × 1 3/8". Figure **3-B-3** shows the shaping. The top diagram shows the initial shaping. Refer to **1-C-3-c**. The middle diagram shows the final shaping. The lower

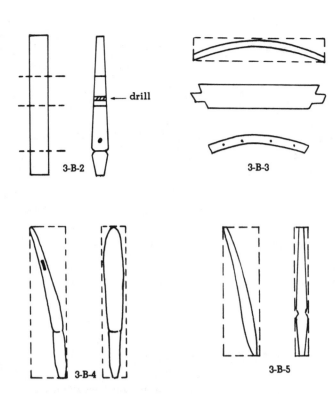

3-B-2

drill →

3-B-3

3-B-4

3-B-5

diagram shows four holes that are to be drilled into the bottom edge of the board (*indicated by black dots in the diagram*).

(E) LEGS (Cut 4): 3/16" diameter wood dowel × 1 1/2". Drill a hole through each leg at the site of the black dot. Drill a second hole through the other side of the leg at the site of the arrow in the diagram.

(F) FRONT AND BACK LEG STRETCHERS (Cut 2): 1/16" diameter wood dowel × 1 1/8".

(G) SIDE LEG STRETCHERS (Cut 2): 1/16" diameter wood dowel × 1 1/8".

ASSEMBLY: Stain all wood before glueing. Refer to **2-A-2**.

ARROW-BACK WINDSOR TYPE SIDE CHAIR 3-C

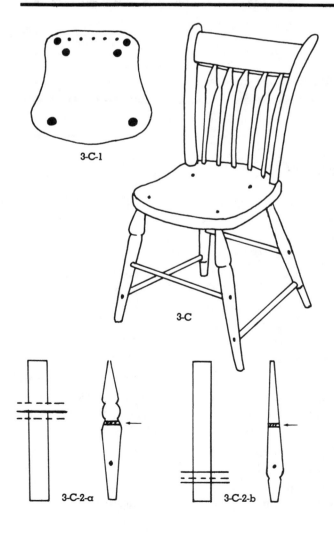

3-C-1

3-C

3-C-2-a

3-C-2-b

(A) SEAT (Cut 1): 1/8" × 1 1/4" × 1 1/4". See Figure **3-C-1** for the shape. Drill holes at the sites of the black dots in the diagram. Refer to **1-C-3-e** for the seat shaping.

(B) TOP BACK BOARD (Cut 1): 1/4" × 1/4" × 1 1/2". See Figure **3-C-3**. The top diagram shows the first step in shaping the board. Refer to **1-C-3-c**. The middle diagram shows the final shaping of this board. The lower diagram shows the placement of holes to be drilled into the bottom edge of the board, located by black dots in the diagram.

(C) UPPER SIDE POSTS (Cut 2): 3/16" × 3/8" × 1 5/8". Figure **3-C-4** shows the shaping. The left diagram shows the initial shaping of this board. Refer to **1-C-3-b**. The right diagram shows the final shaping. The black mark in the left diagram shows a mortise hole to be cut into the right surface of the left post and the left surface of the right post.

(D) BACK SPINDLES (Cut 5): 3/16" × 3/8" × 1 3/8". Figure **3-C-5** shows the shaping. The left diagram shows the initial shaping of the board. Refer to **1-C-3-b**. The right diagram shows the final shaping.

(E) FRONT LEGS (Cut 2): 3/16" diameter wood dowel × 1 1/2". Figure **3-C-2-a** shows the shaping. Refer to **1-C-3-a**. Drill a hole through each leg at the site of the black dot, and drill another hole through the leg in the opposite side at the site of the arrow.

3

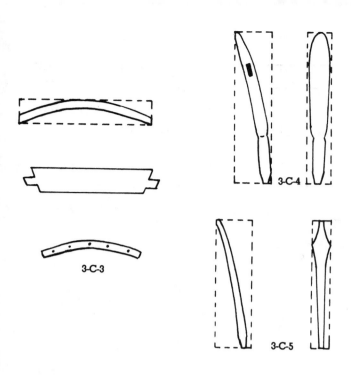

3-C-3

3-C-4

3-C-5

(F) BACK LEGS (Cut 2): 3/16" diameter wood dowel × 1 1/2". Figure **3-C-2-b** shows the shaping. Refer to **1-C-3-a**. Drill a hole through each leg at the site of the black dot in the diagram, and drill another hole through the leg in the opposite side at the site of the arrow.

(G) FRONT AND BACK LEG STRETCHERS (Cut 2): 1/16" diameter wood dowel × 1 1/8".

(H) SIDE LEG STRETCHERS (Cut 2): 1/16" diameter wood dowel × 1 1/8".

ASSEMBLY: Stain all wood before glueing. Refer to **2-A-2**.

WINDSOR TYPE BENCH
WITH FAN BACK AND EAR CARVING 3-D

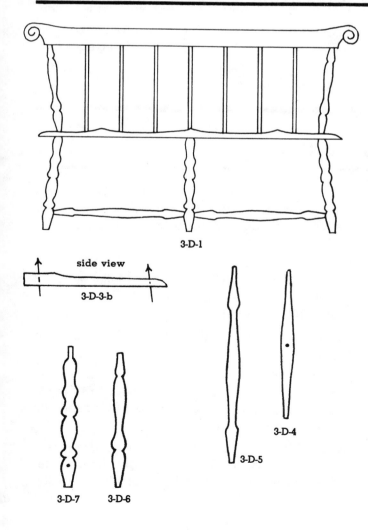

3-D-1

side view

3-D-3-b

3-D-4

3-D-5

3-D-7   3-D-6

(A) SEAT (Cut 1): 1/8" × 1 1/2" × 4 3/8". See Figures **3-D-3-a** (*top view diagram*) and **3-D-3-b** (*left side view diagram*). Drill 1/16" diameter holes through the seat at the sites of the black dots in the diagram. Refer to **1-C-3-e** for aid in shaping the saddle seat. The broken lines in the diagram indicate the areas of shaping.

(B) LEGS (Cut 6): 3/16" diameter wood dowel × 1 1/2". See Figure **3-D-7** for the shape. Drill a 1/16" diameter hole through the leg at the site of the black dot in the diagram. Refer to **1-C-3-a**.

(C) CENTER LEG STRETCHER (Cut 2): 1/8" diameter wood dowel × 2 1/8". See Figure **3-D-5** for the shape. Refer to **1-C-3-a**.

(D) SIDE LEG STRETCHER (Cut 3): 1/8" diameter wood dowel × 1 5/8". Drill a 1/16" diameter hole through each stretcher at the site of the black dot in the diagram in Figure **3-D-4**.

(E) BACK POSTS (Cut 2): 3/16" diameter wood dowel × 1 7/16". See Figure **3-D-6** for the shape. Refer to **1-C-3-a**.

(F) BACK (Cut 1): 1/8" × 5/16" × 4 13/16". See Figure **3-D-8** for the shape. Carve the "spiral" into the end "ears." Drill 1/16" diameter holes 1/16" deep into the bottom edge of this piece. See the arrows in the diagram.

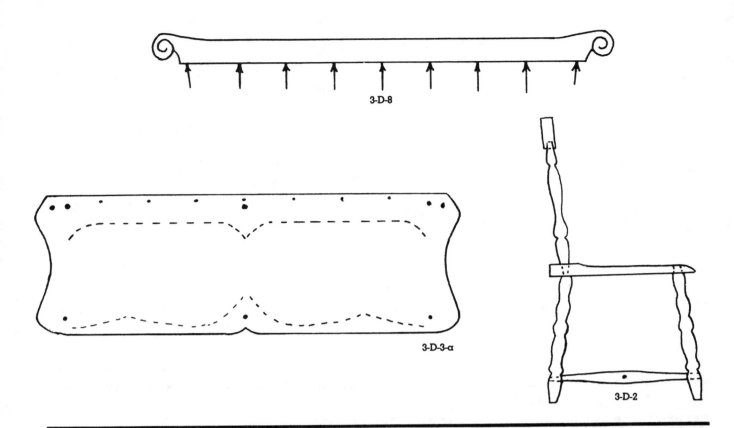

3-D-8

3-D-3-α

3-D-2

(G) BACK SPINDLES (Cut 7): 1/16" diameter wood dowel × 1 1/2".

ASSEMBLY: Stain all wood before glueing. See Figures **3-D-1** (*front view*) and **3-D-2** (*side view*).

1. Refer to **2-A-2** for general assembly of the bench.

2. Glue the center leg stretchers between the three side leg stretchers. Glue the three side leg stretchers between the three pairs of legs.

3. Apply a finish coat.

WINDSOR TYPE SIDE CHAIR WITH FAN BACK AND EAR CARVING 3-E

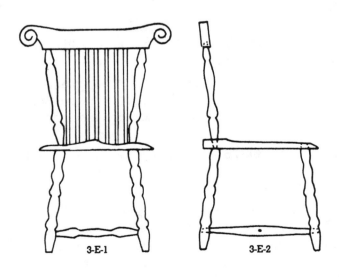

3-E-1   3-E-2

(A) SEAT (Cut 1): 1/8" × 1 1/2" × 1 5/8". See Figures **3-E-3-a** (*top view*) and **3-E-3-b** (*left side view*) for views of the shape. Drill 1/16" diameter holes through the seat at the sites of the black dots in the diagram. Refer to **1-C-3-e** for shaping of the saddle seat.

(B) BACK POSTS (Cut 2): 3/16" diameter wood dowel × 1 1/2". See **1-C-3-a** for aid in shaping and Figure **3-E-4** for the shape.

(C) BACK SPINDLES (Cut 7): 1/16" diameter wood dowel × 1 1/2".

(D) TOP BACK (Cut 1): 1/8" × 5/16" × 2". See Figure **3-E-8** for the shape. Carve the "spiral" in the end "ears." Drill 1/16" diameter holes 1/16" deep into the bottom edge of the back.

(E) LEGS (Cut 4): 3/16" diameter wood dowel × 1 1/2". See Figure **3-E-7** for the shape. Drill a 1/16" diameter hole through each leg at the site of the black dot.

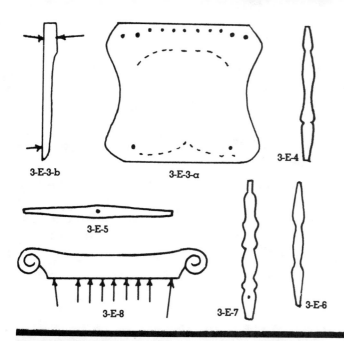

3-E-3-b   3-E-3-a   3-E-4

3-E-5

3-E-8   3-E-7   3-E-6

(F) CENTER LEG STRETCHER (Cut 1): 1/8" diameter wood dowel × 1 3/8". See Figure 3-E-6 for the shape. Refer to 1-C-3-a.

(G) SIDE LEG STRETCHER (Cut 2): 1/8" diameter wood dowel × 1 9/16". See Figure 3-E-5 for the shape. Drill a 1/16" diameter hole through the stretcher at the site of the black dot in the diagram.

ASSEMBLY: Stain all wood before glueing. Refer to Figures 3-E-1 (*front view*) and 3-E-2 (*side view*).

1. Refer to 2-A-2 for the general assembly.

2. Glue the center leg stretcher into the side leg stretchers. Glue the side leg stretchers into the front and back legs.

3. Apply a finish coat.

WINDSOR TYPE ARM CHAIR WITH COMB BACK AND ROCKERS 3-F

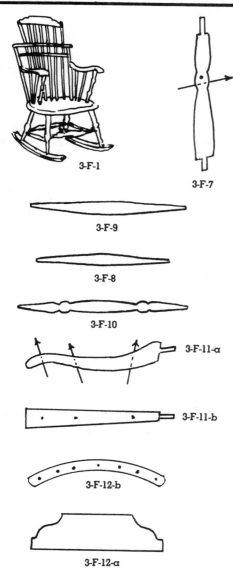

3-F-1   3-F-7

3-F-9

3-F-8

3-F-10

3-F-11-a

3-F-11-b

3-F-12-b

3-F-12-a

(A) SEAT (Cut 1): 1/8" × 1 1/2" × 1 11/16". See Figure 3-F-6 for the shape. Drill 1/16" diameter holes through the seat at the sites of the black dots in the diagram. The broken lines border the back edge of the "dish seat" shaping. Refer to 1-C-3-e.

(B) LEGS (Cut 4): 1/4" diameter wood dowel × 1 9/16". See Figure 3-F-7 for the shape. Refer to 1-C-3-a.

(C) FRONT LEG STRETCHER (Cut 1): 1/8" diameter wood dowel × 1 13/16". See Figure 3-F-10. Refer to 1-C-3-a.

(D) SIDE LEG STRETCHERS (Cut 2): 1/8" diameter wood dowel × 1 5/8". See Figure 3-F-9 for the shape.

(E) BACK LEG STRETCHER (Cut 1): 1/8" diameter wood dowel × 1 3/8". See Figure 3-F-8 for the shape.

(F) COMB TOP (Cut 1): 5/16" × 3/8" × 1 7/16". See Figures 3-F-12-a for the front view diagram of the shape and 3-F-12-b for a bottom view diagram showing the shape of the curve and the black dots which indicate placement of 1/16" diameter holes which will be drilled 1/16" into the bottom edge. Refer to 1-C-3-c for shaping the curve of the board.

(G) TOP BACK RAIL (Cut 1): 1/16" × 7/16" × 1 3/4". See Figure 3-F-13 (*top view*) for the shape. Drill 1/16" diameter holes through the board at the sites of the black dots in the diagram. Refer to 1-C-3-c for aid in shaping the curve of this board.

(H) LOWER BACK RAIL (Cut 1): 1/16" × 3/8" × 1 5/16". See Figure 3-F-14 (*top view*) for the shape. The black dots in the diagram represent 1/16" diameter holes to be drilled through the board. Refer to 1-C-3-c for aid in shaping this curved board.

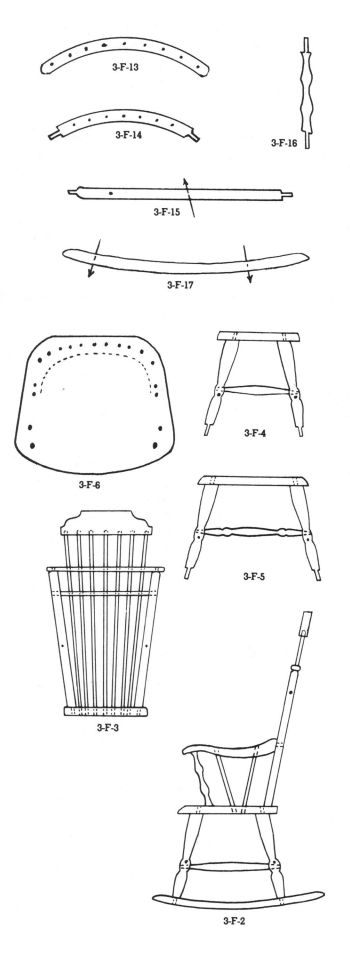

3-F-13

3-F-14

3-F-16

3-F-15

3-F-17

3-F-6

3-F-4

3-F-3

3-F-5

3-F-2

(I) BACK POSTS (Cut 2): 1/8″ diameter wood dowel × 2 3/8″. See Figure **3-F-15** for the shape. Drill a 1/16″ diameter hole through each post at the sites of the black dot and the arrow in the diagram.

(J) BACK SPINDLES (Cut 7): 1/16″ diameter wood dowel × 2 7/8″.

(K) ARM REST (Cut 2): 3/16″ × 1/4″ × 1 9/16″. See Figures **3-F-11-a** (*side view*) and **3-F-11-b** (*top view*) for the shape. Drill 1/16″ diameter holes through each arm rest at the sites of the arrows in the diagram.

(L) ARM POST (Cut 2): 1/8″ diameter wood dowel × 1 1/8″. See Figure **3-F-16** for the shape. Refer to **1-C-3-a**.

(M) ARM SPINDLES (Cut 4): 1/16″ diameter wood dowel × 1 1/8″.

(N) ROCKERS (Cut 2): 1/8″ × 1/4″ × 2 5/8″. See Figure **3-F-17** for a side view diagram of the shape. Drill 1/16″ diameter holes through each rocker at the sites of the arrows.

ASSEMBLY: Stain all wood before glueing. Refer to Figures **3-F-1**, **3-F-3** (*front view of upper back assembly*), **3-F-2** (*side view*), **3-F-4** (*front view of back leg assembly*) and **3-F-5** (*front view of front leg assembly*).

1. Insert the pegs of the lower back rail (**H**) into the upper holes in the back posts (**I**). Glue the top back rail (**G**) down upon the top pegs of the back posts. See Figure **3-F-3**.

2. Glue the back posts into the front left and right holes (*of the series of holes*) at the back of the chair seat. Insert the seven back spindles through the holes in the top back rail, the holes in the lower back rail, and glued into each of the seven holes at the back of the chair seat.

3. Glue the top ends of the seven back spindles into the holes in the comb top. See Figure **3-F-3**.

4. Glue the arm rests (**K**) into the lower front holes in the back posts. Glue the top peg of the arm post into the arm rest, and the lower peg into the hole in the chair seat. See Figure **3-F-2**.

5. Insert and glue the arm spindles (**M**) through the holes in the arm rest and down into the seat. See Figure **3-F-2**.

6. Glue the four legs into the seat. Glue the front, side and back leg stretchers between the legs.

7. Glue the leg pegs down into the holes in the rockers.

8. Sand off any excess lengths of pegs and spindles. Apply a finish coat.

BABY TENDER CRADLE 3-G

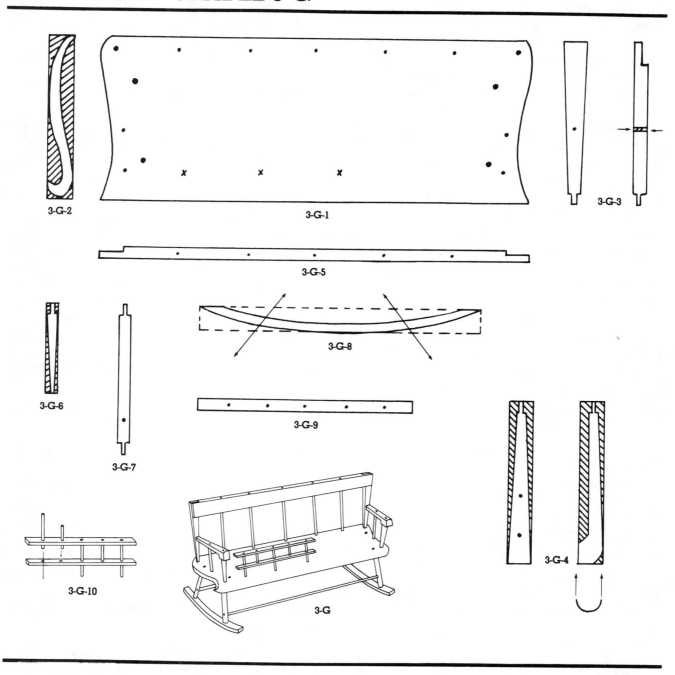

3-G-2

3-G-1

3-G-3

3-G-5

3-G-8

3-G-6

3-G-7

3-G-9

3-G-10

3-G

3-G-4

This rocking bench was used during the colonial period as a means of entertaining the baby while accomplishing work at the same time. Figures **3-G-1** through **3-G-9** show the various pieces required to complete this piece of furniture, with diagrams drawn to scale. Figure **3-G** shows the completed piece of furniture.

(A) BENCH SEAT (Cut 1): 1/4″ × 1 3/4″ × 4 1/2″. Refer to Figure **3-G-1**. Figure **3-G-2** shows the left end view of the seat shaping. Refer to **1-C-3-c** for aid in this carving. Drill 1/16″ diameter holes at the sites of the black dots and ×'s in this diagram. The holes indicated by ×'s are *not drilled through the seat.*

(B) BACK BOARD (Cut 1): 1/8″ × 3/8″ × 4 1/2″. See Figure **3-G-5** for a top view. The black dots in this diagram indicate 1/16″ diameter holes to be drilled through the board. Be careful when drilling these holes. Notch the back of each end, as shown in this diagram.

(C) BACK SPINDLES (Cut 5): 1/16″ diameter wood dowel × 1 3/4″. (*Wooden ends of cotton swab sticks do nicely.*) Carefully sand the diameter of one end along the length of 3/8″ and the other end along the length of 1/8″. Do this to each of the five pieces. The 3/8″ ends should easily insert (*carefully*) into the

43

holes in the back board and will protrude to the top. The ¼" ends will insert into the five holes in the rear of the seat, and will protrude through the bottom of the seat.

(D) BACK UPRIGHTS (Cut 2): 1/8" × 1/4" × 1 3/4". Shape and notch these pieces as shown in Figure **3-G-3**. Drill a 1/16" diameter hole at the black dot in the diagram. The notched end fits behind the notch in the back board. The peg end fits into the extreme left and right holes at the back of the seat, and protrudes through the bottom of the seat.

(E) ARM RESTS (Cut 2): 1/4" × 1/2" × 1 3/4". Cut from pine. Figure **3-G-4** shows the front, top and side shaping of these two pieces of wood. Drill 1/16" diameter holes at the sites of the two black dots in the diagram. The pegged end of each arm rest fits into the hole in each back upright piece.

(F) ARM SPINDLES — BACK (Cut 2): 1/16" diameter wood dowel × 1". These spindles will be inserted through the rear holes which were drilled into the arm rests, and down through the hole in the seat. The excess length which protrudes through the bottom of the chair seat should be sanded off.

(G) ARM SPINDLES — FRONT (Cut 2): 1/4" diameter wood dowel × 1". See Figure **3-G-6** for shaping these two spindles. These spindles will be inserted through the front hole which was drilled into the arm rests and on down through the holes in the seat. The excess length will be sanded smooth at the bottom of the seat.

(H) LEGS (Cut 4): 1/4" diameter wood dowel × 1 5/8". See Figure **3-G-7** for the shaping. Drill a 1/16" diameter hole at the site of the black dot in the diagram.

(I) LEG STRETCHERS (Cut 2): 1/16" diameter wood dowel × 4 3/4". These stretchers will be inserted

through the holes drilled through each pair of legs. They run the length of the cradle at the front and the back legs. Allow the legs to splay (*spread apart*) and sand the excess length away after this assembly has been glued.

(J) ROCKERS (Cut 2): 1/4" × 1/4" × 3". Figure **3-G-8** shows the shaping. Refer to **1-C-3-c** for aid in carving. Drill a 1/16" diameter hole at the site of each arrow in this diagram.

ASSEMBLY OF CRADLE: All pieces of the wood must be stained before they are glued into place. When the staining has been completed, the cradle may be assembled, following steps (**A**) through (**J**). Be sure the cradle is squared and let the glue dry thoroughly.

(K) BABY RAIL

(1) **RAILS** (Cut 2): 1/16" × 1/8" × 2 1/4". See Figure **3-G-9** (*top view*) for the black dots indicating the sites where 1/16" diameter holes are to be drilled through the 1/16" thickness of the wood.

(2) **SPINDLES — LONG** (Cut 3): 1/16" diameter wood dowel × 3/4". These will be inserted through the end holes and center holes of both pieces of the rail. They will protrude down into the seat, as shown in Figures **3-G-10** and **3-G**. This piece will *not* be glued into the seat of the cradle, but will peg in place and is removable.

(3) **SPINDLES — SHORT** (Cut 2): 1/16" diameter wood dowel × 1/2". See Figure **3-G-10** for assembly.

ASSEMBLY OF RAIL SECTION: After the rail section pieces of wood have been stained, they are ready for assembly. Follow steps (**K-1**) through (**K-3**) for assembly. Remember, the rail section is removable and is not glued into the seat of the cradle. The baby tender cradle is now ready for finishing.

WRITING-ARM CORNER CHAIR 3-H

3-H

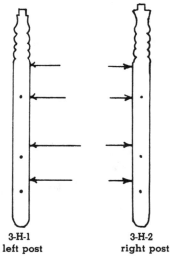

3-H-1
left post

3-H-2
right post

(A) LEFT POST (Cut 1): 3/16" diameter wood dowel × 2 5/16". See Figure **3-H-1** for the shape. The black dots in the diagram indicate 1/16" diameter holes to be drilled 1/16" deep. The arrows in the diagram indicate 1/16" diameter holes to be drilled into the post at these sites 1/16" deep.

(B) RIGHT POST (Cut 1): 3/16" diameter wood dowel × 2 3/8". See Figure **3-H-2** for the shape. Drill 1/16" diameter holes 1/16" deep at the sites of the black dots and arrows in the diagram.

(C) BACK POST (Cut 1): 3/16" diameter wood dowel × 2 3/8". See Figure **3-H-3** for the shape. Drill

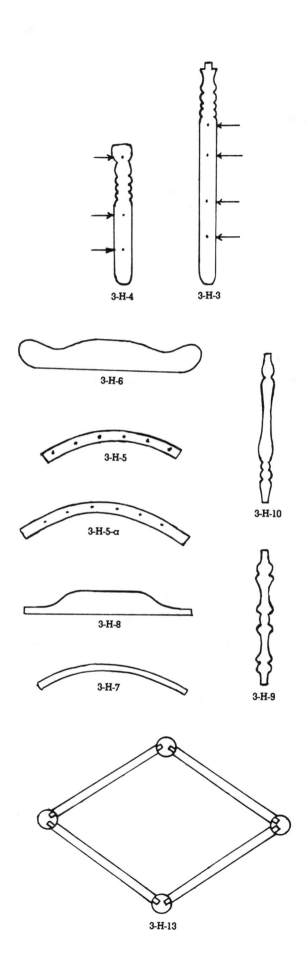

3-H-4

3-H-3

3-H-6

3-H-5

3-H-5-a

3-H-8

3-H-7

3-H-10

3-H-9

3-H-13

1/16" diameter holes 1/16" deep at the sites of the black dots and arrows in the diagram.

(D) FRONT POST (Cut 1): 3/16" diameter wood dowel × 1 1/2". See Figure **3-H-4** for the shape. Drill 1/16" diameter holes 1/16" deep at the sites of the black dots and arrows in the diagram.

(E) BASE OF COMB BACK (Cut 1): 1/8" × 3/8" × 1 1/2". See Figure **3-H-5** for the shape. Drill 1/16" diameter holes through the board at the sites of the black dots in the diagram. Refer to **1-C-3-c**.

(F) COMB BACK TOP (Cut 1): 1/8" × 3/8" × 1 1/2". See Figure **3-H-5-a** for a bottom view showing the initial shaping of the board. Refer to **1-C-3-c**. Drill 1/16" diameter holes 1/16" deep up into the bottom of this board at the sites of the black dots in this diagram. See Figure **3-H-6** for the final shaping.

(G) BACK SLATS (Cut 2): 1/4" × 3/8" × 1 5/8". See Figure **3-H-7** for the initial shaping. Refer to **1-C-3-c**. See Figure **3-H-8** for the final shaping.

(H) BACK LEG STRETCHERS (Cut 4): 3/32" diameter wood dowel × 1 3/8". Shape a 1/16" long peg at each end of each stretcher.

(I) FRONT LEG STRETCHERS (Cut 4): 3/16" diameter wood dowel × 1 7/16". See Figure **3-H-9** for the shape. Refer to **1-C-3-a**.

(J) BACK SEAT FRAME (Cut 2): 3/32" diameter wood dowel × 1 3/8". Shape 1/16" long pegs at each end of each piece.

(K) FRONT SEAT FRAME (Cut 2): 3/32" diameter wood dowel × 1 7/16". Shape 1/16" long pegs 1/16" in diameter at each end of each piece.

(L) WRITING-ARM SUPPORT (Cut 1): 1/16" × 3/4" × 1". See Figure **3-H-11** for the shape. Drill a 1/16" diameter hole through the wood at the site of the black dot.

(M) CURVED BACK (Cut 1): 1/16" × 1 5/8" × 3 9/16". See Figure **3-H-12** for the shape. Drill 1/16" diameter holes at the sites of the black dots in the diagram.

(N) COMB SIDE POSTS (Cut 2): 3/16" diameter wood dowel × 1 5/8". See Figure **3-H-10** for the shape. Refer to **1-C-3-a**.

(O) COMB POSTS (Cut 4): 1/16" diameter wood dowel × 1 5/8".

ASSEMBLY: Stain all wood before glueing. Refer to Figures **3-H** and **3-H-13** which show the assembly of the posts and seat frame. *Note:* If you are going to use a color print instead of rushing the seat, trace Figure **3-H-13** onto a piece of 1/8" thick wood. Drill a hole at the site of the leg peg at the front. Round off

45

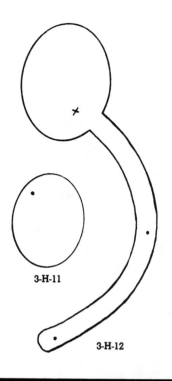

3-H-11

3-H-12

the top and bottom edges of the board. In the assembly use this board in place of the seat frame pieces.

1. Glue the comb side posts and four center posts into the base of the comb back (**E**). Glue the tops of these posts into the holes in the board which is the top of the comb back (**F**).

2. Refer to **3-M** and **2-A-3** for general assembly. Before glueing the curved back in place, glue the writing-arm support board atop the top pegged surface of the left post (**A**), being sure that this piece will be turned properly to fit under the writing-arm extension of the curved back (*the "×" in Figure* **3-H-12** *should fit directly over the peg*). Glue the writing-arm atop this support during assembly.

3. Glue the comb back centered atop the curved back and the back post.

4. Apply a finish coat.

5. Refer to **1-C-7** or **1-C-7-a**.

SETTLE CHAIR WITH HIGH BACK AND SIDE WINGS — SEAT FORMS A CHEST 3-I

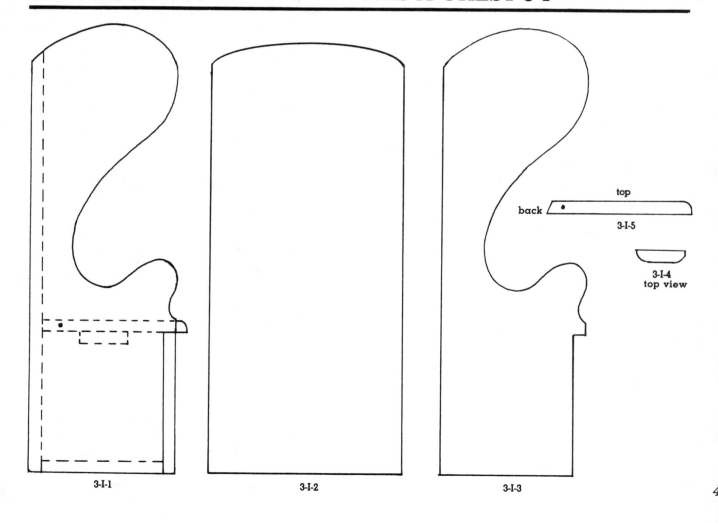

3-I-1

3-I-2

3-I-3

back | top

3-I-5

3-I-4 top view

(A) BACK (Cut 1): 1/8" × 2" × 4 5/8". See Figure **3-I-2** for the shape.

(B) FRONT (Cut 1): 1/8" × 1 1/2" × 2 1/4".

(C) SIDES (Cut 2): 1/8" × 1 1/2" × 4 13/16". See Figure **3-I-3** for the shape. Drill a 1/16" diameter hole through each side board at the site of the black dot in the diagram.

(D) SEAT (Cut 1): 1/8" × 1 1/2" × 1 15/16". See Figure **3-I-5** for a right side view of this board. Note the back edge angle and the rounding off of the front top edge. The black dot in this diagram represents a 1/16" diameter hole to be drilled 1/8" deep on each side surface of this board.

(E) BOTTOM (Cut 1): 1/8" × 1 1/4" × 2".

(F) SEAT BRACES (Cut 2): 1/8" × 1/8" × 1/2". See Figure **3-I-4** for a top view diagram of the shape.

(G) PEGS (Cut 2): 1/16" diameter wood dowel × 1/4".

ASSEMBLY: Stain all wood before glueing. See Figure **3-I-1** for a guide to the assembly.

1. Glue the sides against the upright side edges of the back board, with back and bottom edges flush.

2. Glue the bottom board between the side boards and against the back board, with bottom edges flush.

3. Glue the two seat braces against the inside surfaces of the side boards, with the top edge 1 1/4" above the top surface of the bottom board. See Figure **3-I-1** for the position of these braces.

4. Glue the front board against the front edges of the side boards and the bottom board, with all edges flush.

5. Apply a finish coat to the chair, seat and pegs. Let dry.

6. Place the seat between the sides and resting atop the top edge of the front board and the braces. Be sure that the back angle and front edge are in the correct position. See Figure **3-I-5**. Push a peg through the hole in the side board and into the hole in the seat. Do not glue. Repeat for the second peg. Do not glue. The seat will now raise.

BANNISTER-BACK ARM CHAIR 3-J

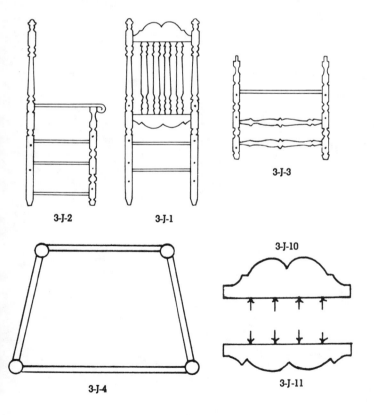

3-J-2   3-J-1   3-J-3

3-J-4   3-J-10   3-J-11

(A) BACK POSTS (Cut 2): 3/16" diameter wood dowel × 4 1/16". See Figure **3-J-5** for the shape. Drill 1/16" diameter holes through each post at the sites of the black dots and arrows in the diagram. Cut two 1/16" deep × 1/16" wide × 1/8" long mortise holes into each post at the site of the two notches in the diagram. Refer to **1-C-3-a** for aid in shaping.

(B) FRONT LEGS (Cut 2): 1/8" diameter wood dowel × 2 1/4". See Figure **3-J-6** for the shape. Drill 1/16" diameter holes through each leg at the sites of the black dots and arrows in the diagram. Refer to **1-C-3-a**.

(C) TOP BACK SLAT (Cut 1): 1/8" × 7/16" × 1 5/16". See Figure **3-J-10** for the shape. Drill 1/16" diameter holes 1/16" deep into the bottom edge at the sites of the arrows in the diagram.

(D) LOWER BACK SLAT (Cut 1): 1/8" × 5/16" × 1 5/16". See Figure **3-J-11** for the shape. Drill 1/16" diameter holes 1/16" deep into the top edge at the sites of the arrows in the diagram.

(E) ARM REST (Cut 2): 3/16" × 3/8" × 1 11/16". See Figures **3-J-9-a** (top view) and **3-J-9-b** (side view) showing the shape of the right arm rest. Reverse the diagrams for the left arm rest. Drill a 1/16" diameter hole through each arm rest at the site of the black dot in the diagram. Refer to **1-C-3-f** for aid in shaping the knuckle carving.

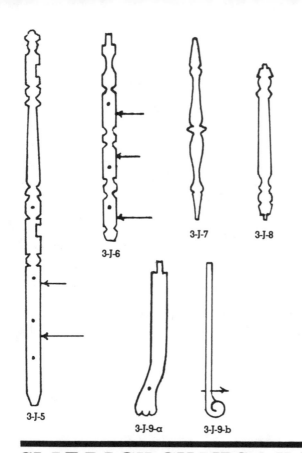

3-J-6

3-J-7

3-J-8

3-J-5

3-J-9-a

3-J-9-b

(F) BANNISTER (Cut 4): 1/16″ × 3/16″ × 1 11/16″. See Figure **3-J-8** for the shape.

(G) BACK SEAT RAIL (Cut 1): 1/16″ diameter wood dowel × 1 1/2″.

(H) SIDE SEAT RAIL (Cut 2): 1/16″ diameter wood dowel × 1 7/16″.

(I) FRONT SEAT RAIL (Cut 1): 1/16″ diameter wood dowel × 2″.

(J) BACK LEG STRETCHER (Cut 1): 1/16″ diameter wood dowel × 1 1/2″.

(K) SIDE LEG STRETCHER (Cut 4): 1/16″ diameter wood dowel × 1 7/16″.

(L) FRONT LEG STRETCHER (Cut 2): 3/16″ diameter wood dowel × 2″. See Figure **3-J-7** for the shape. Refer to **1-C-3-a**.

ASSEMBLY

1. Refer to **2-A-4** for the general assembly.

2. Refer to **1-C-7** for the seat rushing or **1-C-7-a**.

3. Apply a finish coat.

SLAT BACK CHAIRS 3-K-L-M-N

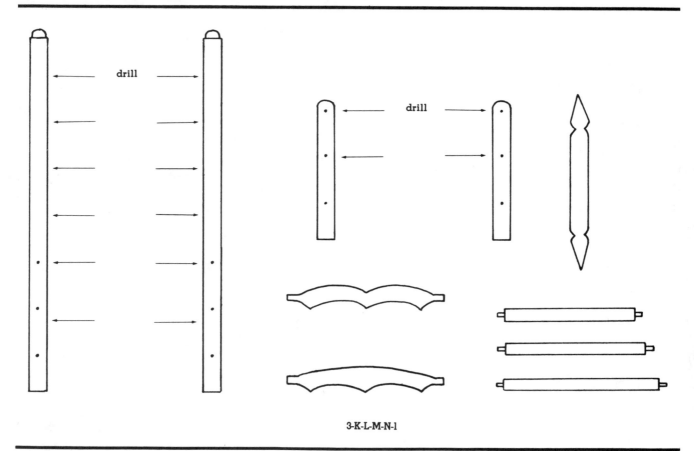

3-K-L-M-N-1

MEASUREMENTS

Width of back from outside measurement: 1 3/4″.

Width of front of seat from outside measurement: 1 15/16″.

Height of seat from floor: 1 1/2".

Height of arms from floor: 2 1/8".

MATERIALS NEEDED TO COMPLETE AN ENTIRE CHAIR

WOOD: For slats. 1/16" thick.

WOOD DOWEL: For upright posts and front stretchers. 3/16" in diameter.

WOOD DOWEL: For fine stretchers. 1/16" in diameter.

WOOD DOWEL: For seat rungs (*to form the frame for the rush seat*). 1/8" in diameter.

WOOD: For arms and rockers (*these will be carved to shape*). 1/4" × 1/4" square.

This wood is optional, if you choose to make the arm chair or the rocker.

Tan colored carpet thread, glue, stain and a finish are also needed.

Note: All working diagrams are drawn 1" = 1'.

SLAT BACK CHAIR 3-K

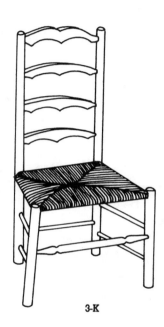

3-K

(A) POSTS (Cut 2): 3/16" diameter wood dowel × 3 7/8". See Figure **3-K-L-M-N-1** for the shape. Refer to **1-C-3-a** for aid in carving these pieces. Drill 1/16" diameter holes at the sites of the black dots, and at the sites of the arrows (*these holes will be at right angles to the first drilled holes*).

(B) POSTS (Cut 2): 3/16" diameter wood dowel × 1 1/2". See Figure **3-K-L-M-N-1** for the shape. Drill 1/16" diameter holes at the sites of the black dots, and at the sites of the arrows (*these holes will also be at right angles to the first drilled holes*).

(C) SEAT RUNGS

(1) **RUNG** (Cut 1): 1/8" diameter wood dowel × 1 9/16".

(2) **RUNG** (Cut 2): 1/8" diameter wood dowel × 1 5/8".

(3) **RUNG** (Cut 1): 1/8" diameter wood dowel × 1 13/16".

Shape the two ends of each piece as shown in the diagram. These pieces will form the rungs of the seat to hold the rushing.

(D) LEG STRETCHERS

(1) **STRETCHER** (Cut 1): 1/16" diameter wood dowel × 1 9/16".

(2) **STRETCHER** (Cut 4): 1/16" diameter wood dowel × 1 5/8".

(E) FRONT STRETCHER (Cut 1): 3/16" diameter wood dowel × 1 13/16". Shape this piece as shown in Figure **3-K-L-M-N-1**.

(F) SLATS (Cut 4): 1/16" × 1/4" × 1 1/2". Cut from the 1/16" thick wood. See Figure **3-K-L-M-N-1** and shape one piece as shown with the double arch; shape the remaining three as shown with the single arch.

ASSEMBLY: Stain all wood before glueing together. Follow assembly directions **2-A-3-a**.

49

SLAT BACK ARM CHAIR 3-L

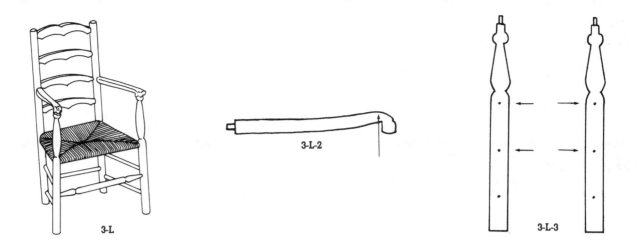

3-L

3-L-2

3-L-3

(A) POSTS: Follow directions in **(A)** for chair **3-K.** Drill an additional 1/16" diameter hole at the front of each post (*black dot area*) 2 1/4" above the base of the post.

(B) POSTS (Cut 2): 3/16" diameter wood dowel × 2 5/16". Figure **3-L-3** shows the shape to turn each post. Drill a 1/16" diameter hole at the site of each dot and each arrow. The second set of holes will be at right angles with the first set of drilled holes.

(C) through (F): Follow steps **(C)** through **(F)** in **3-K** exactly.

(G) ARMS (Cut 2): 1/4" × 1/4" × 1 3/4". Use the 1/4" × 1/4" square wood, and carve as shown in Figure **3-L-2.** Drill a 1/16" diameter hole at the site of the arrow in the diagram.

ASSEMBLY: Stain all wood before glueing. Follow the assembly directions in **2-A-3-b.**

SLAT BACK CORNER CHAIR 3-M

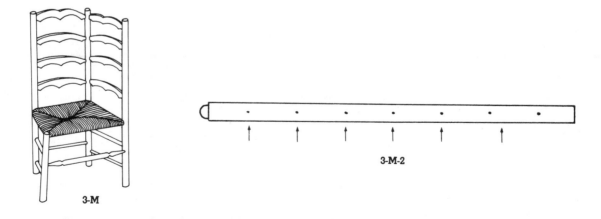

3-M

3-M-2

(A) POSTS: Follow the directions in **(A)** for chair **3-K.** Cut an additional piece of the 3/16" diameter wood dowel × 3 7/8" in length. Drill 1/16" diameter holes at the sites of the black dots and the arrows in Figure **3-M-2.**

(B) POST (Cut 1): 3/16" diameter wood dowel × 1 1/2". See Figure **3-K-L-M-N-1** for the shape. Drill 1/16" diameter holes at the sites of the black dots, and at the sites of the arrows (*these holes will also be at right angles to the first drilled holes*).

(C) through (F): Follow steps **(C)** through **(F)** in **3-K** exactly. Cut an additional slat and shape with the double arch. Cut three additional single arch slats.

ASSEMBLY: Stain all wood before glueing together. Follow assembly directions **2-A-3-c.**

SLAT BACK ROCKING CHAIR 3-N

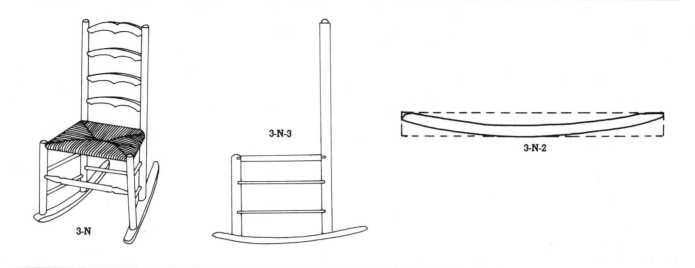

(A) ROCKERS (Cut 2): 1/8″ × 1/4″ × 2 3/4″. Shape the rockers as shown in Figure **3-N-2**. Refer to **1-C-3-c** for aid in carving a curved board.

(B) Figure **3-N-3** shows a side view of the rocker and the angled ends of the chair legs to fit the rockers. These rockers can be used for chairs **3-K** and **3-L**. Follow the directions for either chair and add the rockers, as shown in Figure **3-N-3**.

VICTORIAN PERIOD SIDE CHAIR WITH CANE SEAT AND BANJO BACK 3-O

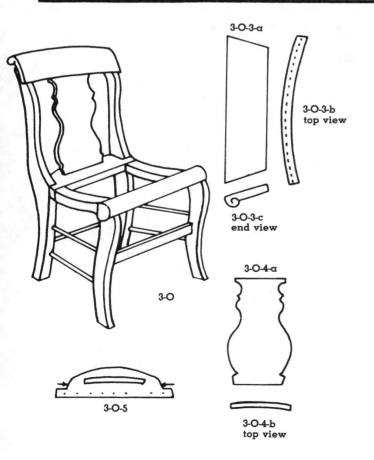

(A) BACK LEG (Cut 2): 1/8″ × 1/2″ × 3″. See Figure **3-O-1** for the shape. Drill 1/16″ diameter holes at the sites of the black dots and arrows in the diagram.

(B) FRONT LEG (Cut 2): 1/8″ × 3/8″ × 1 11/32″. See Figure **3-O-2** for the shape. Drill 1/16″ diameter holes at the sites of the black dots and arrows in the diagram.

(C) CHAIR BACK (Cut 1): 1/4″ × 7/16″ × 1 5/8″. See Figure **3-O-3-a** for the front view shape, Figure **3-O-3-b** for the top view curved shape, and Figure **3-O-3-c** for the shape to be carved into each end. *Note:* The dotted line in Figure **3-O-3-b** shows the depth that must be held for the major portion of the back, and the excess remains at the top for the scroll carving. Refer to **1-C-3-c** for aid in shaping a curved board.

(D) CHAIR SPLAT (Cut 1): 1/8″ × 3/4″ × 1 1/8″. See Figure **3-O-4-a** for a front view of the shape, and Figure **3-O-4-b** for the curve of the board. Refer to **1-C-3-c** for aid in shaping a curved board.

(E) CHAIR SEAT

　　(1) **BACK** (Cut 1): 1/8″ × 3/8″ × 1 1/4″. See Figure **3-O-5** for the shape and area to be cut away.

　　(2) **SIDES** (Cut 2): 3/16″ × 1/4″ × 15/16″. See

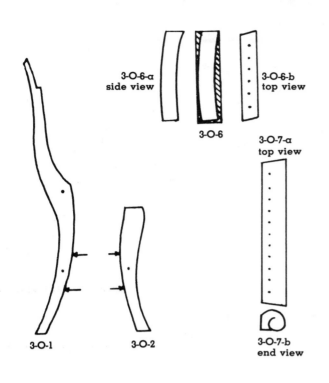

3-O-6-α side view

3-O-6-b top view

3-O-6

3-O-7-α top view

3-O-1

3-O-2

3-O-7-b end view

Figure **3-O-6-a** for the side view of the shape, and Figure **3-O-6-b** for the top view of the shape.

    (3) **FRONT** (Cut 1): 1/4″ × 1/4″ × 1 5/8″. See Figure **3-O-7-b** for the end view of the shape to be carved.

Note: Drill 1/16″ diameter holes at the sites of the black dots in all of the diagrams.

(F) BACK RAIL (Cut 1): 1/16″ diameter wood dowel × 1 1/4″.

(G) SIDE RAIL (Cut 4): 1/16″ diameter wood dowel × 1 3/8″.

(H) FRONT RAIL (Cut 1): 1/16″ × 1/8″ × 1 5/8″.

ASSEMBLY

1. Refer to **2-A-5** for the general assembly of this chair.

2. Apply the finish coat to the chair after the assembly has been completed and the glue is thoroughly dry.

3. Do not attempt to cane the chair seat for at least one week after the assembly has been completed. Refer to **1-C-8** for this procedure or **1-C-8-a**.

VICTORIAN CHAIR WITH CANE SEAT AND SHAPED SPLAT BACK 3-P

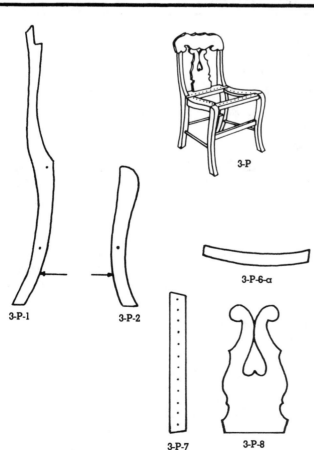

3-P

3-P-6-α

3-P-1

3-P-2

3-P-7

3-P-8

(A) BACK LEG (Cut 2): 1/8″ × 1/2″ × 3 1/16″. See Figure 3-P-1 for the shape. Drill 1/16″ diameter holes at the sites of the black dots and arrows in the diagram.

(B) FRONT LEG (Cut 2): 1/8″ × 3/8″ × 1 1/2″. See Figure 3-P-2 for the shape. Drill 1/16″ diameter holes at the sites of the black dots and arrows in the diagram.

(C) CHAIR BACK (Cut 1): 1/16″ × 1/2″ × 1 5/8″. See Figure 3-P-3 for the shape.

(D) BACK SPLAT (Cut 1): 1/16″ × 3/4″ × 1 3/8″. See Figure 3-P-4 for the shape.

(E) CHAIR SEAT

    (1) **BACK** (Cut 1): 1/8″ × 1/4″ × 1 5/16″. See Figure 3-P-5 for the shape and slot to be cut into this board.

    (2) **SIDES** (Cut 2): 3/16″ × 3/16″ × 1 1/8″. See Figure 3-P-6 for the shape (*top view*) and 3-P-6-a for the shape (*side view*).

    (3) **FRONT** (Cut 1): 1/8″ × 3/16″ × 1 1/2″. See Figure 3-P-7 for the shape. *Note:* Drill 1/16″ diameter holes at the sites of the black dots and arrows in all diagrams.

(F) BACK RAIL (Cut 1): 1/16″ diameter wood dowel × 1 1/4″.

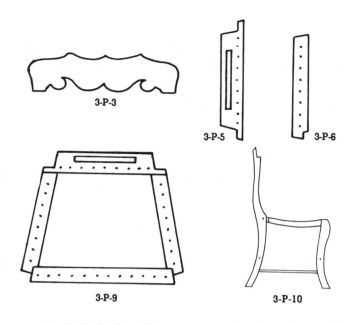

3-P-3

3-P-5   3-P-6

3-P-9   3-P-10

(G) SIDE RAIL (Cut 2): 1/16" diameter wood dowel × 1 1/2".

(H) FRONT RAIL (Cut 1): 1/16" × 1/8" × 1 13/16".

ASSEMBLY

1. Refer to **2-A-5** for general assembly of this chair. Figures **3-P-8** (*assembly of this chair seat*) and **3-P-9** (*side view of this chair showing the side rail*) will aid in the assembly.

2. When the chair has been assembled, it will be ready for a finish coat. Be sure to wait at least one week before you begin to cane the chair seat. Refer to **1-C-8** for instructions for cane. If you prefer to put in a slip seat, refer to **2-A-7** for information on how to cut support braces for the seat and how to measure for the slip seat, or refer to **1-C-8-a**.

VICTORIAN SIDE CHAIR
WITH SPINDLE BACK AND CANE SEAT 3-Q

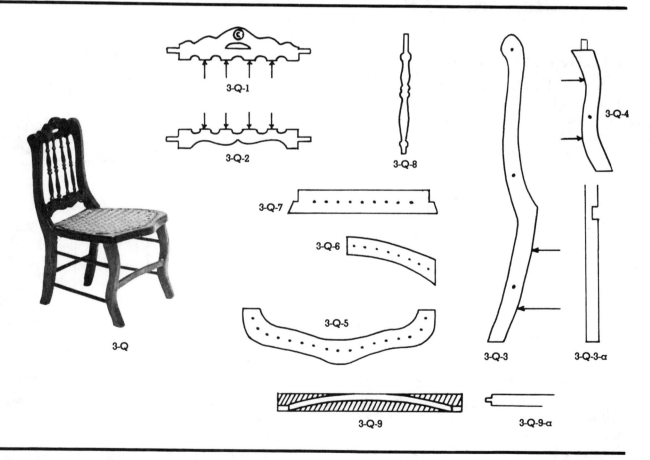

3-Q

3-Q-1

3-Q-2

3-Q-8

3-Q-7

3-Q-6

3-Q-5

3-Q-4

3-Q-3   3-Q-3-a

3-Q-9   3-Q-9-a

(A) UPPER BACK SLAT (Cut 1): 1/8" × 3/8" × 1 1/2". See Figure **3-Q-1** for the shape and carving. Drill 1/16" diameter holes at the sites of the arrows in the diagram.

(B) LOWER BACK SLAT (Cut 1): 1/8" × 3/16" × 1 1/2". See Figure **3-Q-2** for the shape. Drill 1/16"

diameter holes at the sites of the arrows in the diagram.

(C) BACK LEGS (Cut 2): 1/8" × 1/2" × 3 3/8". See Figure **3-Q-3** for the shape. Refer to **1-C-3-c** for aid in carving. Drill 1/16" diameter holes at the sites of the black dots and arrows in the diagram. See Figure

53

3-Q-3-a for the site of a mortise joint that must be cut into the inside of each leg.

(D) FRONT LEGS (Cut 2): 1/8″ × 7/16″ × 1 7/16″. See Figure 3-Q-4 for the shape. Drill 1/16″ diameter holes at the sites of the black dots and arrows in the diagram.

(E) CHAIR SEAT FRONT (Cut 1): 1/8″ × 5/8″ × 2″. See Figure 3-Q-5 for the shape. Drill 1/16″ diameter holes at the sites of the black dots in the diagram.

(F) CHAIR SEAT SIDES (Cut 2): 1/8″ × 1/4″ × 1 1/8″. See Figure 3-Q-6 for the shape. Drill 1/16″ diameter holes at the sites of the black dots in the diagram.

(G) CHAIR SEAT BACK (Cut 1): 1/8″ × 1/4″ × 1 9/16″. See Figure 3-Q-7 for the shape. Drill 1/16″ diameter holes at the sites of the black dots in the diagram.

(H) SPINDLES (Cut 4): 1/8″ × 1/8″ × 1 5/16″. See Figure 3-Q-8 for the shape. Refer to 1-C-3-a for aid in carving.

(I) FRONT STRETCHER (Cut 1): 1/8″ × 3/16″ × 1 15/16″. See Figure 3-Q-9 for the curved shape and Figure 3-Q-9-a for the shape of the ends. Refer to 1-C-3-c for aid in carving.

(J) SIDE LEG STRETCHERS
    (1) **SIDE LEG STRETCHERS** (Cut 2): 1/16″ diameter wood dowel × 1 3/4″.
    (2) **SIDE LEG STRETCHERS** (Cut 2): 1/16″ diameter wood dowel × 1 5/8″.

(K) BACK STRETCHER (Cut 1): 1/16″ diameter wood dowel × 1 1/2″.

ASSEMBLY: Refer to 2-A-6. Refer to 1-C-8 or 1-C-8-a.

DUNCAN PHYFE STYLE SIDE CHAIR WITH SLIP SEAT 3-R

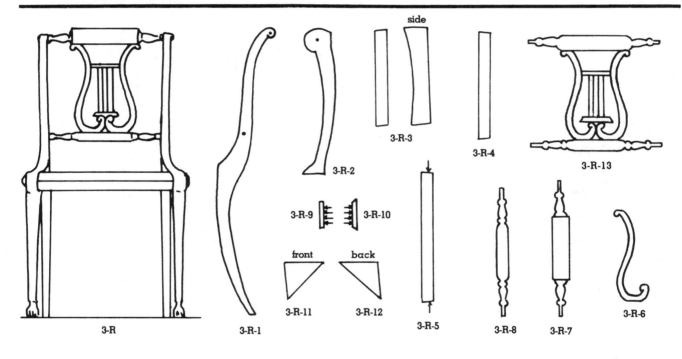

3-R   3-R-1   3-R-2   side   3-R-3   3-R-4   3-R-13   3-R-9   3-R-10   front   back   3-R-11   3-R-12   3-R-5   3-R-8   3-R-7   3-R-6

(A) BACK LEGS (Cut 2): 1/8″ × 5/8″ × 3 1/8″ (*cut with the grain of wood going the length*). See Figure 3-R-1 for the shape. Drill 1/16″ diameter holes at the sites of the black dots in the diagram.

(B) FRONT LEGS (Cut 2): 1/8″ × 3/8″ × 1 5/8″ (*cut with the grain of wood going the length*). See Figure 3-R-2 for the shape.

(C) SEAT FRONT (Cut 1): 1/8″ × 1/8″ × 1 3/8″. See Figure 3-R-5. Drill tiny holes at the sites of the arrows in the diagram.

(D) SEAT BACK (Cut 1): 1/8″ × 1/8″ × 1 3/16″. See Figure 3-R-4. Note the angle at the top and bottom of this board.

(E) SEAT SIDE (Cut 2): 1/8″ × 1/4″ × 1 1/16″. See Figure 3-R-3 for the shape.

(F) TOP-BACK RUNG (Cut 1): 3/16″ diameter wood dowel × 1 1/2″. See Figure 3-R-7 for the shape. Refer to 1-C-3-a.

(G) LOWER BACK RUNG (Cut 1): 1/8″ diameter

wood dowel × 1 3/8″. See Figure **3-R-8** for the shape. Refer to **1-C-3-a**.

(H) LYRE SIDES (Cut 2): 1/16″ × 1/2″ × 1″. Cut from 1/16″ thickness cardboard. See Figure **3-R-6** for the shape. Apply a coat of airplane cement to all surfaces of the two cut-out pieces. Let the glue dry. Match paint to the color of the wood you are using. Paint these two pieces and let the paint dry. Spray several coats of an acrylic sealer to all surfaces.

(I) TOP BOARD (Cut 1): 1/16″ × 1/16″ × 5/16″. See Figure **3-R-10** for end angles.

(J) BOTTOM BOARD (Cut 1): 1/16″ × 1/16″ × 1/4″.

(K) SEAT BRACES

(1) **FRONT** (Cut 2): Cut from 1/16″ thick wood. See Figure **3-R-11** for the shape.

(2) **BACK** (Cut 2): Cut from 1/16″ thick wood. See Figure **3-R-12** for the shape.

(L) SLIP SEAT (Cut 1): Cut from stiff cardboard after the chair has been assembled. Cut a piece slightly smaller than the shape of the seat opening. Refer to **1-C-4** for full directions and upholstery.

(M) FINE BRASS WIRE OR FINE PINS (Four lengths of wire or four pins): 9/16″ in length.

ASSEMBLY: Stain all wood before glueing. Refer to **2-A-7** for assembly of chair and **1-C-4** for assembly of slip seat.

OAK HALL CHAIR c. 1897 3-S

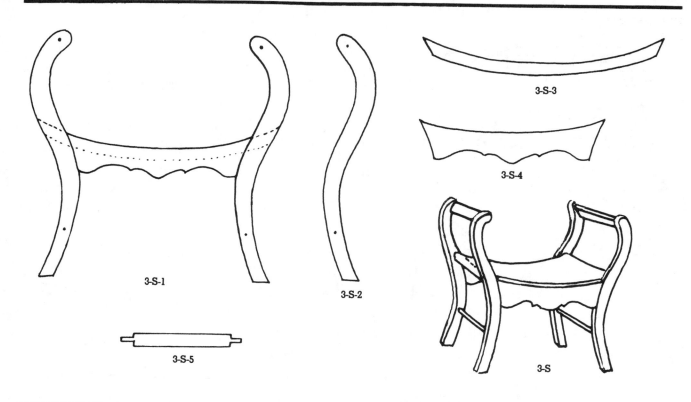

(A) LEGS (Cut 4): 1/8″ × 5/8″ × 2 5/8″. See Figure **3-S-2** for the shape. Drill a 1/16″ diameter hole through each leg at the site of the black dots in the diagram.

(B) APRON (Cut 2): 1/8″ × 1/2″ × 2″. See Figure **3-S-4** for the shape.

(C) SEAT (Cut 1): 7/16″ × 1″ × 2 1/2″. See Figure **3-S-3** for a side view of the shape. Refer to **1-C-3-c**.

(D) SPINDLE (Cut 2): 1/16″ diameter wood dowel × 1 1/4″.

(E) UPHOLSTERY (Cut 1): 1″ × 3 1/2″. Use silk

damask, tapestry, or other choice of material. *Note:* The 1″ width is the exact width which is a finished measurement; if you choose a fabric which will fray, you will need to add a measurement for turning under on each edge.

(F) ARM REST (Cut 2): 1/8″ × 1/8″ (*square*) × 1 1/4″. See Figure **3-S-5** for the shape. The arm remains square and the 1/16″ diameter pegs are rounded at each end.

ASSEMBLY: Stain all wood before glueing. Refer to Figures **3-S** and **3-S-1** for the assembly.

1. Glue the spindles into the lower holes in the legs with outside surfaces flush. See Figure **3-S-1** for the position of the legs.

2. Glue the arm rest boards into the holes in the upper portion of the legs, with the top surface of each board angled down toward the center of the seat.

3. Cover the top surface of the seat, leaving an equal amount of excess material at either end.

4. Refer to Figure **3-S-1** for the position of the two pieces of apron. Be sure that each piece is at this same level. The diagram can be used as a guide for placement. Glue the pieces in place.

5. Apply a finish coat to the chair.

6. Glue the upholstered seat between the legs and flush with the top surface of the apron.

OAK PARLOR ROCKER 3-T

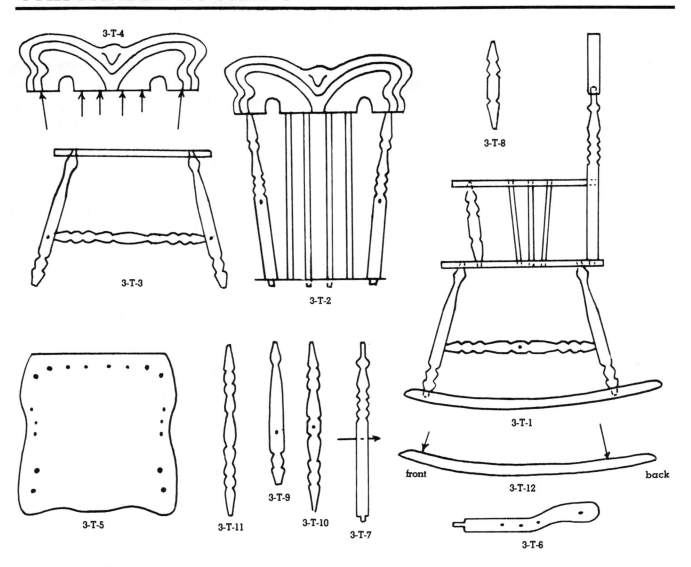

(A) SEAT (Cut 1): 1/16″ × 1 5/8″ × 1 11/16″. See Figure **3-T-5** for the shape. Drill 1/16″ diameter holes through the seat at the sites of the black dots in the diagram.

(B) LEGS (Cut 4): 3/16″ diameter wood dowel × 1 9/16″. See Figure **3-T-9** for the shape. Refer to **1-C-3-a.** Drill a 1/16″ diameter hole through the leg at the site of the black dot in the diagram.

(C) BACK POSTS (Cut 2): 1/8″ diameter wood dowel × 1 15/16″. See Figure **3-T-7** for the shape. Refer to **1-C-3-a.** Drill a 1/16″ diameter hole through the post at the site of the black dot in the diagram.

(D) BACK SPINDLES (Cut 4): 1/16″ diameter wood dowel × 1 15/16″.

(E) TOP BACK (Cut 1): 1/8″ × 5/8″ × 1 15/16″. See

Figure **3-T-4** for the shape. The lines in the diagram should be finely carved into the back. Drill 1/16″ diameter holes 1/16″ deep up into the bottom edge of the back, at the sites of the arrows in the diagram.

(F) ARM REST (Cut 2): 1/16″ × 5/16″ × 1 1/2″. See Figure **3-T-6** for the shape. Drill 1/16″ diameter holes through each arm at the sites of the black dots in the diagram.

(G) ARM POST (Cut 2): 1/8″ diameter wood dowel × 1″. See Figure **3-T-8** for the shape. Refer to **1-C-3-a**.

(H) ARM SPINDLES (Cut 6): 1/16″ diameter wood dowel × 15/16″.

(I) SIDE LEG STRETCHER (Cut 2): 1/8″ diameter wood dowel × 1 13/16″. See Figure **3-T-10** for the shape. Refer to **1-C-3-a**. Drill a 1/16″ diameter hole through the stretcher at the site of the black dot in the diagram.

(J) CENTER LEG STRETCHER (Cut 1): 1/8″ diameter wood dowel × 1 7/8″. See Figure **3-T-11** for the shape. Refer to **1-C-3-a**.

(K) ROCKER (Cut 2): 1/8″ × 1/4″ × 2 3/4″. See Figure **3-T-12** for the shape. Drill 1/16″ diameter holes 1/16″ deep down into the top edge of the rocker at the site of the black dot in the diagram.

ASSEMBLY: Stain all wood before glueing. See Figures **3-T-1** (*right side view*), **3-T-2** (*back assembly — front view*) and **3-T-3** (*front view of leg assembly*).

1. Refer to **2-A-2** for general assembly of the chair.

2. Glue the arm spindles into the three holes on each side of the seat and into the holes in the arm rest; glue the end peg of the arm rest into the back post. Glue the arm post into the holes in the chair seat and the arm rest.

3. Glue the center leg stretcher into the hole in each side leg stretcher. Glue the side leg stretchers into the holes in the front and back legs.

4. Glue the legs into the rockers.

5. Apply a finish coat.

PARLOR ARM CHAIR 3-U

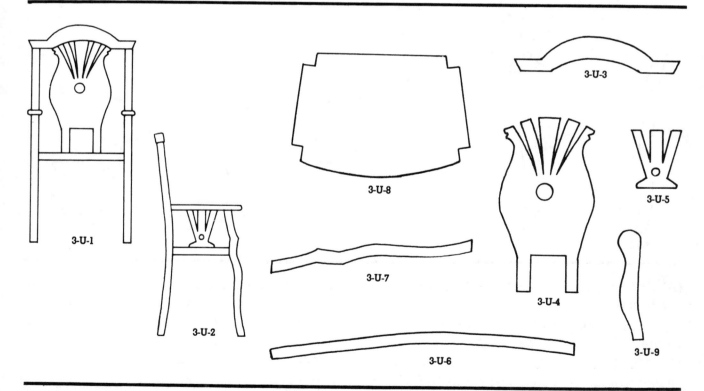

3-U-3
3-U-8
3-U-5
3-U-1
3-U-2
3-U-7
3-U-4
3-U-9
3-U-6

The parlor arm chair and parlor divan (3-V) were "Golden Oak" and were upholstered in high colored velours, crushed plush, mercerized tapestry, silk brocatelle and silk damask.

(A) SEAT (Cut 1): 1/8″ × 1 1/8″ × 1 5/8″. See Figure **3-U-8** for the shape.

(B) FRONT LEGS (Cut 2): 1/8″ × 1/4″ × 2 1/8″. See Figure **3-U-7** for the shape.

(C) ARM REST (Cut 2): 1/8″ × 1/4″ × 1 1/4″. Round off the top and front edges. See Figure **3-U-8** for the shape.

(D) ARM SUPPORT (Cut 2): 1/16″ × 1/2″ × 5/8″. See Figure **3-U-5** for the shape.

(E) BACK LEGS (Cut 2): 1/8″ × 3/8″ × 31/4″. See Figure **3-U-6** for the shape.

(F) UPPER BACK (Cut 1): 1/8″ × 3/8″ × 1 3/4″. See Figure **3-U-3** for the shape.

(G) LOWER BACK (Cut 1): 1/16″ × 1″ × 1 7/8″. See Figure **3-U-4** for the shape.

ASSEMBLY: Refer to **2-A-4**.

1. Upholster the seat with one of the above materials, or one of your choice, after assembly and after the finish coat has been applied to the chair.

2. Refer to **1-C-11** for aid in upholstering the seat of the chair.

PARLOR DIVAN 3-V

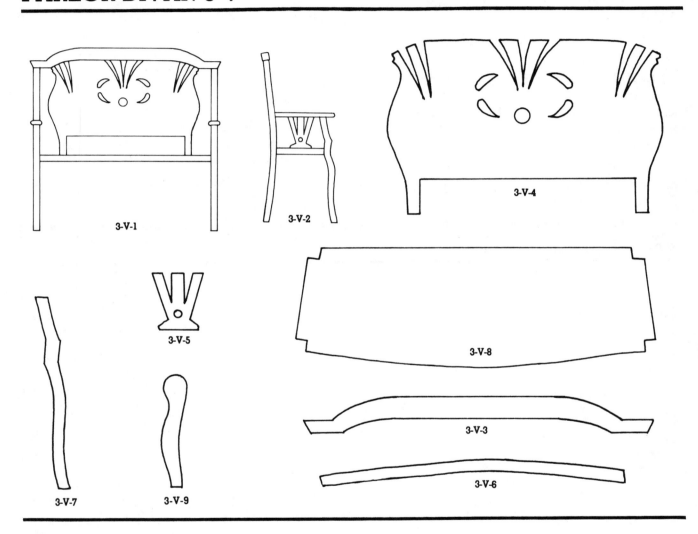

3-V-1   3-V-2   3-V-4

3-V-5   3-V-8   3-V-3

3-V-6

3-V-7   3-V-9

(A) SEAT (Cut 1): 1/8″ × 1 1/8″ × 3 1/2″. See Figure **3-V-8** for the shape.

(B) FRONT LEG (Cut 2): 1/8″ × 1/4″ × 2 1/8″. See Figure **3-V-7** for the shape.

(C) ARM REST (Cut 2): 1/8″ × 1/4″ × 1 1/4″. Round off the top and front edges. See Figure **3-V-8** for the shape.

(D) ARM SUPPORT (Cut 2): 1/16″ × 1/2″ × 5/8″. See Figure **3-V-5** for the shape.

(E) BACK LEGS (Cut 2): 1/8″ × 3/8″ × 3 1/4″. See Figure **3-V-6** for the shape.

(F) UPPER BACK (Cut 1): 1/8″ × 3/8″ × 3 5/8″. See Figure **3-V-3** for the shape.

(G) LOWER BACK (Cut 1): 1/16″ × 1 7/8″ × 2 7/8″. See Figure **3-V-4** for the shape.

ASSEMBLY: Refer to **2-A-4**.

1. Upholster the seat with one of the materials listed in **3-U**, or use one of your choice, after assembly and after the finish coat has been applied to the chair.

2. Refer to **1-C-11** for aid in upholstering the seat of the divan.

VICTORIAN PERIOD
BALLOON-BACK SIDE CHAIR 3-W

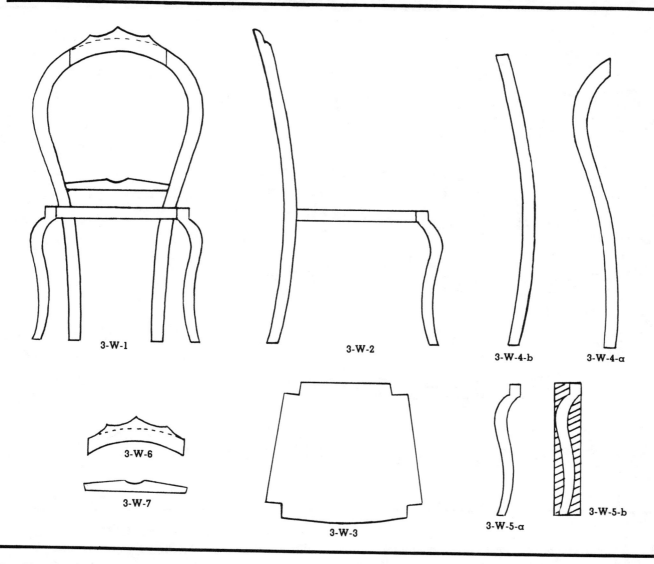

3-W-1

3-W-2

3-W-4-b

3-W-4-a

3-W-6

3-W-7

3-W-3

3-W-5-a

3-W-5-b

(A) SEAT (Cut 1): 1/8" × 1 1/2" × 1 5/8". See Figure 3-W-3 for the shape.

(B) BACK LEGS (Cut 2): 7/16" × 1 1/8" × 3 1/8". See Figure 3-W-4-b for the shaping of this board (*this is a side view diagram*). When the board has had its initial shaping, trace Figure 3-W-4-a onto the board; turn the diagram over and trace it again onto the board. Cut out the two pieces which are the left and right back legs.

(C) CHAIR CREST (Cut 1): 1/8" × 7/16" × 1". See Figure 3-W-6 for the shape. Carve the area above the broken line recessed from the front edge.

(D) SLAT (Cut 1): 1/16" × 1/8" × 1 1/8". See Figure 3-W-7 for the shape.

(E) FRONT LEGS (Cut 2): 1/4" × 1/4" × 1 7/16". See Figure 3-W-5-a for the shape. Figure 3-W-5-b shows

how each leg must be traced onto the wood. Refer to 1-C-3-d for aid in shaping.

ASSEMBLY: Stain all wood before glueing. Refer to Figures 3-W-1 (*front view*) and 3-W-2 (*left side view*) for assembly.

1. Glue the two back legs against the chair crest, with the top and bottom edges flush. See Figure 3-W-1.

2. Glue the slat between the two back legs. See Figure 3-W-1 for position.

3. Glue the front and back legs into the notches in the seat. Be sure the seat is straight and level.

4. Apply a finish coat.

5. Refer to 1-C-4, and upholster the top surface of the chair seat.

VICTORIAN PERIOD
BALLOON-BACK ROCKING CHAIR 3-X

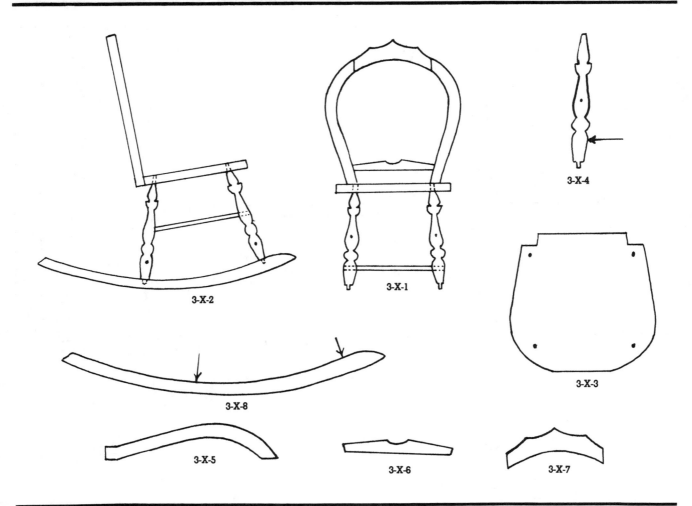

3-X-4

3-X-2

3-X-1

3-X-3

3-X-8

3-X-5

3-X-6

3-X-7

(A) SEAT (Cut 1): 1/8" × 1 1/2" × 1 1/2". See Figure 3-X-3 for the shape. Drill 1/16" diameter holes through the seat at the sites of the black dots in the diagram.

(B) BACK FRAME (Cut 2): 1/8" × 3/16" × 1 13/16". See Figure 3-X-5 for the shape. Round off the front surface edges, with the exception of the top and bottom end edges.

(C) BACK CREST (Cut 1): 1/8" × 7/16" × 1". See Figure 3-X-7 for the shape of the crest. Refer to 1-C-5 for simulated carving. Paint the jewelry finding a color to match the stained wood. Glue the finding to the face of the crest.

(D) BACK SLAT (Cut 1): 1/16" × 1/8" × 1 3/16". See Figure 3-X-6 for the shape.

(E) LEGS (Cut 4): 3/16" diameter wood dowel × 1 7/16". See Figure 3-X-4 for the shape. Drill 1/16" diameter holes through each leg at the sites of the black dot and the arrow.

(F) BACK, FRONT AND SIDE LEG STRETCHERS (Cut 4): 1/16" diameter wood dowel × 1 3/4".

(G) ROCKERS (Cut 2): 1/8" × 3/8" × 3 3/8". See Figure 3-X-8 for the shape. Drill 1/16" diameter holes 1/16" deep into the top edge of the rockers at the sites of the arrows.

ASSEMBLY: Stain all wood before glueing. Refer to Figures 3-X-1 (*front view*) and 3-X-2 (*left side view*) for the assembly.

1. Glue the back frame (**B**) — rounded surface forward — against the back crest (**C**) — "carving" forward — with the top and bottom edges flush. Refer to Figure 3-X-1. Glue the back slat between the two sections of frame. Glue this assembly into the back side notches of the chair seat. The bottom and side edges will be flush. See Figure 3-X-2.

2. Glue the top pegs of the chair legs into the holes in the chair seat and the bottom pegs of the legs into the holes in the rockers. See Figure 3-X-2.

3. Glue the back, front and side leg stretchers between the legs. Be sure the chair is squared. Sand off the excess length of any stretchers.

4. Apply a finish coat.

5. Refer to **1-C-4**. Leave a margin around the seat and apply a piece of upholstery to the top surface of the chair seat. Our chair is upholstered with an old piece of black silk.

EARLY AMERICAN CHAIR-TABLE 3-Y

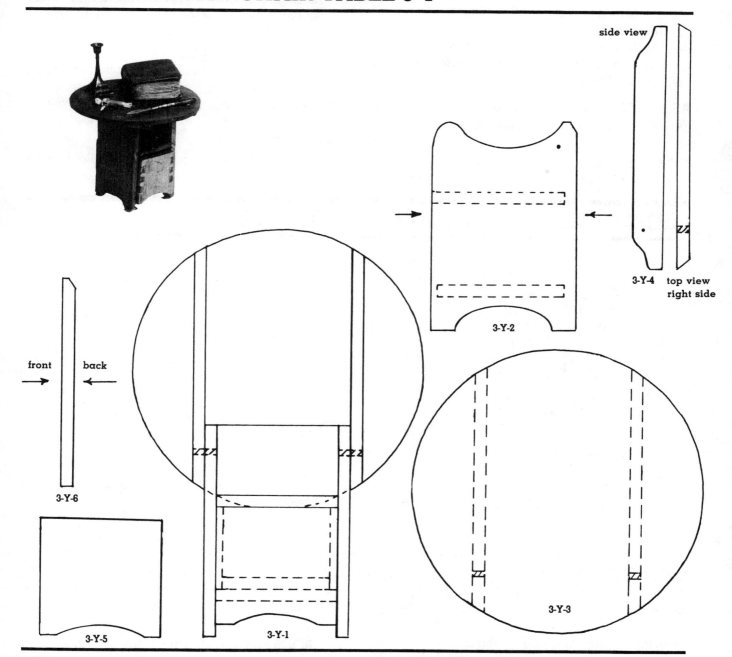

(A) BACK (Cut 1): 1/8″ × 1 1/4″ × 2 1/8″. See Figure **3-Y-6** for a side view showing the angle at the top back edge.

(B) SIDES (Cut 2): 1/8″ × 1 1/2″ × 2 1/4″. See Figure **3-Y-2** for the shape of the side. The black dot represents a 1/16″ diameter hole to be drilled through each board.

(C) SEAT (Cut 1): 1/8″ × 1 1/4″ × 1 3/8″.

(D) BOTTOM (Cut 1): 1/8″ × 1 1/4″ × 1 5/16″.

(E) TOP BRACES (Cut 2): 1/8″ × 5/16″ × 2 5/8″. See Figure **3-Y-4** for a side view and a top view of the shape. The black dot in the diagram (*side view*) represents a 1/16″ diameter hole to be drilled through each board.

(F) TOP (Cut 1): 1/8″ thick × 3″ diameter circle. See Figure **3-Y-3** for the shape.

(G) PEGS (Cut 2): 1/16″ diameter wood dowel × 1/4″.

(H) DRAWER (One)

    (1) **FRONT** (Cut 1): 1/16″ × 1 1/4″ × 1 1/4″. See Figure 3-**Y**-5 for the shape.

    (2) **BACK** (Cut 1): 1/16″ × 7/8″ × 1 1/4″.

    (3) **SIDES** (Cut 2): 1/16″ × 7/8″ × 1 1/4″.

    (4) **BOTTOM** (Cut 1): 1/8″ × 1 1/8″ × 1 1/4″.

Refer to 2-**E**-2 for assembly. Note that the front board is flush with the top edges of the side and back boards. See Figure 3-**Y**-1.

ASSEMBLY: Stain all wood before glueing. See Figures 3-**Y**-1 and 3-**Y**-2 for assembly.

1. The side boards are glued against the side edges of the back board. Be sure that the angle at the top edge of the back matches the angle at the top back edge of each side board.

2. The broken line areas in Figure 3-**Y**-2 show the placement of the seat and bottom boards. Glue in place.

3. The broken line areas in Figure 3-**Y**-3 show the placement of the two brace boards. Glue in place.

4. Place a dot of glue in each hole in the two side boards. Using Figure 3-**Y**-1 as your guide, place the top board with the braces behind the chair and align the holes. Push a peg through the holes, from the outside inward. The glue will hold the peg firmly in the side boards, but will allow the top to fold downward, making a table.

5. Apply a finish coat to the chair-table and its drawer.

CHILD'S ROCKING CHAIR c. 1800-1850 3-Z

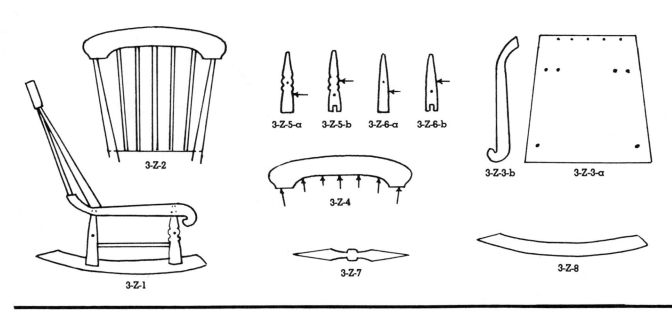

(A) SEAT (Cut 1): 5/16″ × 1 3/8″ × 1 3/8″. See Figure 3-**Z**-3-a (*top view*) and 3-**Z**-3-b (*left side view*) for the shape. The five black dots (*in a row*) in the diagram represent 1/16″ diameter holes to be drilled 1/16″ deep into the top back edge of the seat. The remaining six dots represent 1/16″ diameter holes to be drilled through the seat.

(B) BACK LEGS (Cut 2): 1/8″ diameter wood dowel × 5/8″. Drill 1/16″ diameter holes through each leg at the sites of the black dot and the arrow in Figures 3-**Z**-6-a (*side view of shape*) and 3-**Z**-6-b (*front view of shape*).

(C) FRONT LEGS (Cut 2): 1/8″ diameter wood dowel × 5/8″. See Figures 3-**Z**-5-a (*side view*) and

3-**Z**-5-b (*front view*) for the shape. Drill 1/16″ diameter holes through each leg at the sites of the black dot and the arrow in the diagram. Refer to 1-**C**-3-a.

(D) ROCKERS (Cut 2): 1/16″ × 5/16″ × 1 13/16″. See Figure 3-**Z**-8 for the shape.

(E) SIDE LEG STRETCHERS (Cut 2): 1/16″ diameter wood dowel × 1″.

(F) BACK LEG STRETCHER (Cut 1): 1/16″ diameter wood dowel × 3/4″.

(G) FRONT LEG STRETCHER (Cut 1): 1/8″ diameter wood dowel × 1 1/4″. See Figure 3-**Z**-2 for the shape. Refer to 1-**C**-3-a.

(H) TOP-BACK (Cut 1): 1/8″ × 5/16″ × 1 1/2″. See Figure **3-Z-4** for the shape. Drill 1/16″ diameter holes into the bottom edge 1/16″ deep at the sites of the arrows.

(I) BACK BRACE SPINDLES (Cut 2): 1/8″ diameter wood dowel × 1 7/16″. Leave a 1/16″ diameter peg at each end. Taper the spindle, as shown in Figure **3-Z-1**.

(J) BACK SPINDLES (Cut 5): 1/16″ diameter wood dowel × 1 1/8″.

ASSEMBLY: Stain all wood before glueing. Refer to **3-Z-1**.

1. Glue the top ends of the back and front legs into the holes in the seat (*the back legs fit into the center side holes of each rear pair of holes*).

2. Glue the back, side and front leg stretchers between the legs. Glue the rockers between the bottom edge notches of the front and back legs. See the diagram in Figure **3-Z-1**.

3. Glue the five back spindles into the bottom edge of the top back board (**H**). Glue the two back brace spindles (**I**) into the left and right holes on the bottom edge of the top back board. Glue the lower ends of all of these spindles into the holes in the chair seat.

4. Apply a finish coat.

CORNER WASHSTAND 4-A

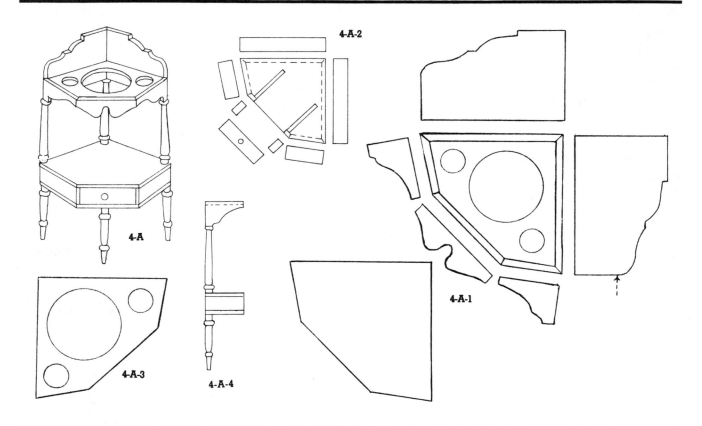

4-A-2

4-A

4-A-1

4-A-3

4-A-4

(A) SPLASH BACK (Cut 2): 1/16″ × 15/16″ × 1 1/2″. See Figure **4-A-1** for the shape. The high back edge of each board is mitred with a 45° angle cut. See the top view assembly diagram for this angle. The right board diagram shows the height of a mitre cut on the front edge of each board. See the top view assembly for the angle of each cut.

(B) WASHSTAND TOP (Cut 1): 1/16″ × 1 5/16″ × 1 5/16″. Trace the diagram in Figure **4-A-3**. Cut out the three circles first, then the outside edges.

(C) SIDE APRON (Cut 2): 1/16″ × 7/16″ × 11/16″. See Figure **4-A-1** for the shape (*side front pieces*). The top view diagram shows the angles for each end edge.

(D) FRONT APRON (Cut 1): 1/16″ × 5/16″ × 1 1/16″. See Figure **4-A-1** for the shape (*front center piece*). The top view diagram shows the angles for each end edge.

(E) DRAWER CHEST

　　(1) **TOP AND BOTTOM** (Cut 2): 1/16″ × 1 1/2″ × 1 1/2″. See Figure **4-A-1** for the shape.

　　(2) **BACK SIDES** (Cut 2): 1/16″ × 1/4″ × 1 1/2″. See Figure **4-A-2** (*top view*) for the angles at each end of each board.

　　(3) **FRONT SIDES** (Cut 2): 1/16″ × 1/4″ × 5/8″.

See Figure **4-A-2** (*top view*) for the angles at the ends of each board.

　　(4) **FRONT** (Cut 2): 1/16″ × 1/8″ × 1/4″. See Figure **4-A-2** (*top view*) for the left edge angle of the left board and the right edge angle of the right board.

　　(5) **DRAWER RUNNERS** (Cut 2): 1/16″ × 1/16″ × 11/16″.

(F) DRAWER

　　(1) **FRONT** (Cut 1): 1/16″ × 1/4″ × 7/8″.

　　(2) **SIDES** (Cut 2): 1/16″ × 1/4″ × 11/16″.

　　(3) **BACK** (Cut 1): 1/16″ × 1/4″ × 3/4″.

　　(4) **BOTTOM** (Cut 1): 1/16″ × 5/8″ × 11/16″.

　　(5) **DRAWER PULL** (One): Refer to **1-B-6**.

Refer to **2-E-2** for drawer assembly.

(G) UPPER LEG (Cut 3): 3/16″ diameter wood dowel × 1 3/16″. See the left front elevation for the shape. Refer to **1-C-3-a**.

(H) LOWER LEG (Cut 4): 3/16″ diameter wood dowel × 1″. See the left front elevation for the shape. Refer to **1-C-3-a**.

ASSEMBLY: Stain all wood before glueing.

DRAWER CHEST: Refer to Figure **4-A-2** (*top view).*

1. Glue the back sides, front sides and front boards

atop the bottom board, with mitred edges meeting and side edges flush with the edges of the bottom board.

2. Place the drawer in the opening (*for placement only*) and glue a drawer runner atop the bottom board and against the inside surface of the front board. See the diagram. Remove the drawer. Glue the top board atop this assembly, with all outside edges flush.

3. Glue the four lower legs in place. See Figure **4-A**. Glue a leg beneath each of the three back corners and the fourth leg centered under the drawer opening.

UPPER ASSEMBLY: Refer to Figures **4-A** and **4-A-1**.

4. Glue the splash back boards with the long mitred

edges together. See Figure **4-A**.

5. Glue the three apron pieces to the front three edges of the washstand top board, with top edges flush. Glue this assembly into the splash back assembly, with the lower mitred edges of the side apron pieces glued against the lower mitred edges of the splash back boards.

6. Refer to Figure **4-A**. Glue the upper legs beneath the back three corners of the upper assembly and atop the back three corners of the lower assembly. Be sure the washstand stands straight and level. Let the glue dry.

7. Apply a finish coat to the drawer and the washstand.

8. Attach the drawer pull.

DUNCAN PHYFE STYLE DRESSING TABLE WITH CURVED SUPPORTS AND STRETCHER c. 1830 4-B

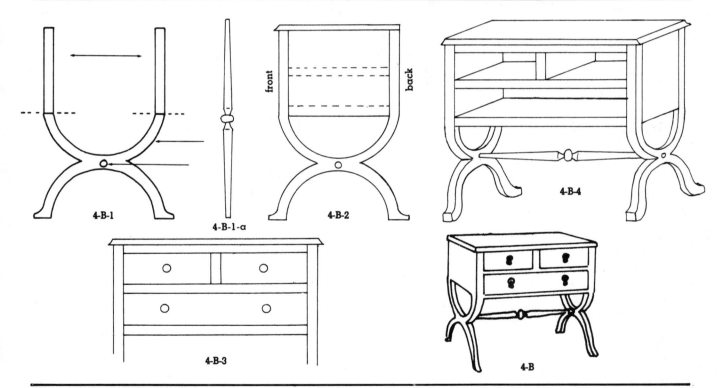

4-B-1

4-B-1-α

4-B-2

4-B-4

4-B-3

4-B

(A) LARGE DRAWER (One)

   (1) **DRAWER BACK AND FRONT** (Cut 2): 1/16″ × 3/8″ × 2 1/4″.

   (2) **DRAWER SIDES** (Cut 2): 1/16″ × 3/8″ × 1 1/4″.

   (3) **DRAWER BOTTOM** (Cut 1): 1/8″ × 1 1/4″ × 2 1/8″.

(B) SMALL DRAWERS (Two)

   (1) **DRAWER BACK AND FRONT** (Cut 4):

1/16″ × 3/8″ × 1 1/16″.

   (2) **DRAWER SIDES** (Cut 4): 1/16″ × 3/8″ × 1 1/4″.

   (3) **DRAWER BOTTOM** (Cut 2): 1/8″ × 15/16″ × 1 1/4″.

TABLE

(C) TABLE BOTTOM AND TWO HORIZONTAL DRAWER DIVIDERS (Cut 3): 1/8″ × 1 3/8″ × 2 1/4″.

(D) END BOARDS (Cut 2): 1/8″ × 1 1/8″ × 1 1/4″.

(E) VERTICAL DRAWER DIVIDER (Cut 1): 1/8″ × 3/8″ × 1 3/8″.

(F) TABLE BACK (Cut 1): 1/8″ × 1 1/8″ × 2 1/4″.

(G) SHAPED END PIECES FORMING LEGS (Cut 4): 1/8″ × 1/8″ × 1 3/32″. See **4-B-1** for the exact sizes of pieces to be traced and cut out.

(H) LEG STRETCHER (Cut 1): 1/8″ diameter wood dowel × 2 1/2″. See **4-B-1** for the shape of the piece, and refer to **1-C-3-a** for aid in turning.

(I) TABLE TOP (Cut 1): 1/16″ × 1 9/16″ × 2 5/8″. Bevel the front and side edges. See Figures **4-B-2** and **4-B-3**.

ASSEMBLY: Stain all wood before glueing.

1. Refer to **2-F-1** for the assembly of the three drawers.

2. Assemble the end boards as shown in Figure **4-B-2**.

3. The back board is glued against the edges of the horizontal drawer dividers, the vertical drawer divider is glued (*centered*) between the upper two dividers. The end assembly is glued against the end edges of these boards. See Figure **4-B-4**.

4. The leg stretcher is glued into the holes in the legs and between these legs. See Figure **4-B-4**.

5. The top board is glued atop the assembled table, with the back edges flush and the beveled edges at the front and sides. See Figure **4-B-3**.

6. Finish according to your preference.

7. Attach the four drawer pulls to the three drawers. See Figure **4-B-3**.

EMPIRE DRESSING TABLE c. 1805 4-C

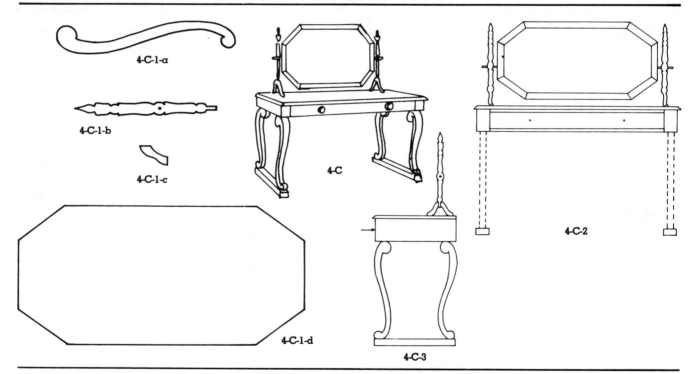

4-C-1-a

4-C-1-b

4-C-1-c

4-C-1-d

4-C

4-C-2

4-C-3

(A) DRESSING TABLE TOP (Cut 1): 1/16″ × 1 9/16″ × 3 7/8″. Bevel the front and side edges. See Figures **4-C-2** and **4-C-3**.

(B) DRESSING TABLE BOTTOM (Cut 1): 1/16″ × 1 7/16″ × 3 5/8″.

(C) SIDES (Cut 2): 1/16″ × 7/16″ × 1 1/2″.

(D) FRONT INNER FRAME (Cut 2): 1/16″ × 3/16″ × 3/8″.

(E) FRONT FACING (Cut 2): 1/16″ × 1/4″ × 7/16″.

(F) DRESSING TABLE LEGS (Cut 4): 1/8″ × 5/8″ × 1 7/8″. Shape these legs as shown in Figure **4-C-1-a**.

(G) LEG SUPPORTS (Cut 2): 1/8″ × 1/4″ × 1 1/2″.

(H) MIRROR POSTS (Cut 2): 1/8″ diameter wood dowel × 1 1/2″. Turn, as shown in Figure **4-C-1-b**. Drill a 1/32″ diameter hole in each post as indicated by the black dot in the diagram. Refer to **1-C-3-a** for aid in carving the post.

(I) MIRROR POST LEGS (Cut 4): Cut from 1/16″ wood. See Figure **4-C-1-c** for the shape.

(J) MIRROR BACK (Cut 1): 1/8″ × 1 1/2″ × 3″. See Figure **4-C-1-d** for the shape to be cut.

(K) MIRROR FRAME MOULDING: The thickness

of these pieces of moulding will be determined by the thickness of the piece of mirror which you choose.

    (1) **MOULDING** (Cut 2): 1/8″ × 2″.

    (2) **MOULDING** (Cut 2): 1/8″ × 3/4″.

    (3) **MOULDING** (Cut 4): 1/8″ × 5/8″.

Mitre the ends of these pieces as indicated in Figure **4-C-2** (*front elevation*).

(L) DRAWER BOTTOM (Cut 1): 1/16″ × 15/8″ × 3 1/8″.

(M) DRAWER FRONT AND BACK (Cut 2): 1/16″ × 5/16″ × 3 1/4″. Drill holes in the drawer front board at the sites indicated by the black dots in Figure **4-C-2**.

(N) DRAWER SIDES (Cut 2): 1/16″ × 5/16″ × 1 5/16″.

(O) UPPER FRONT FRAME OF DRESSING TABLE (Cut 1): 1/16″ × 1/16″ × 3 1/4″.

(P) MIRROR (Cut 1): Select as thin a piece of mirror as you can find. See Figure **4-C-1-e** for the shape. Trace this shape on a piece of paper and glue to the surface of the mirror with rubber cement. Use a glass cutter to cut the mirror to the shape. You may choose to use a thin piece of metal *(such as aluminum)* to simulate the mirror effect; if so, cut the metal to shape.

(Q) DRESSING TABLE BACK (Cut 1): 1/16″ × 7/16″ × 3 5/8″.

(R) MIRROR PEGS (Cut 2): Cut the heads away from two small wire brads.

(S) DRAWER PULLS (Two): You can purchase drawer pulls from your local miniature dealer or from many mail-order lists.

ASSEMBLY

1. Refer to **2-B-2** for assembly of the dressing table.

2. Refer to **2-E-1** for assembly of the drawer.

COLONIAL PERIOD DRESSING TABLE 4-D

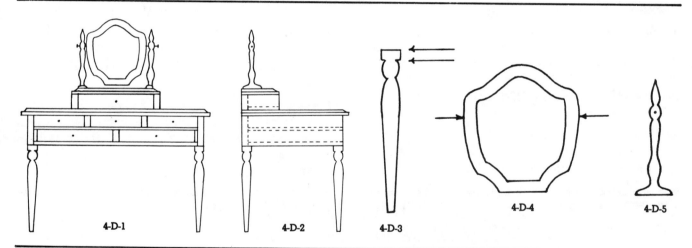

4-D-1   4-D-2   4-D-3   4-D-4   4-D-5

(A) TOP BASE (Cut 1): 1/16″ × 2 1/8″ × 3 3/4″.

(B) TOP MOULDING (Cut 1): 1/16″ × 2 1/16″ × 3 5/8″. Bevel the two side edges and the front edge.

(C) DRAWER BASE AND BOTTOM (Cut 2): 1/16″ × 1 7/8″ × 3 1/4″.

(D) SIDES (Cut 2): 1/8″ × 5/8″ × 2″.

(E) BACK (Cut 1): 1/8″ × 5/8″ × 3 1/4″.

(F) LEGS (Cut 4): 3/16″ × 3/16″ × 1 3/4″. See Figure **4-D-3** for the shape. The area between the two arrows in the diagram remains squared. Refer to **1-C-3-a**.

(G) DRAWER SEPARATOR (Cut 3): 1/8″ × 1/4″ × 1 7/8″.

(H) LOWER DRAWER GUIDES (Cut 2): 1/16″ × 1/4″ × 1 7/8″.

(I) UPPER DRAWERS (Three)

    (1) **FRONT AND BACK** (Cut 6): 1/16″ × 1/4″ × 1″.

    (2) **SIDES** (Cut 6): 1/16″ × 1/4″ × 1 3/4″.

    (3) **BOTTOM** (Cut 3): 1/16″ × 7/8″ × 1 3/4″.

Refer to **2-E-1** for assembly.

(J) LOWER DRAWERS (Two)

    (1) **BACK** (Cut 2): 1/16″ × 1/4″ × 1 1/2″.

    (2) **FRONT** (Cut 2): 1/16″ × 1/4″ × 1 5/8″.

    (3) **SIDES** (Cut 4): 1/16″ × 1/4″ × 1 7/8″.

    (4) **BOTTOM** (Cut 2): 1/16″ × 1 3/8″ × 1 7/8″.

Refer to **2-E-2** for assembly.

(K) TOP DRAWER CHEST ((One)

    (1) **TOP BASE** (Cut 1): 1/16″ × 3/4″ × 1 3/4″.

    (2) **TOP MOULDING** (Cut 1): 1/16″ × 11/16″ × 1 5/8″. Bevel the two side edges and the front edge.

    (3) **BACK** (Cut 1): 1/8″ × 5/16″ × 1 1/2″.

(4) **BOTTOM** (Cut 1): 1/16" × 5/8" × 1 3/8".
(5) **SIDES** (Cut 2): 1/16" × 5/16" × 3/4".

(L) MIRROR POSTS (Cut 2): 3/8" × 3/8" × 1 1/4". See Figure **4-D-5** for a side view of the shape. The black dot in the diagram represents a tiny diameter hole to be drilled through each post. Refer to **1-C-3-a.**

(M) MIRROR FRAME (Cut 1): 1/8" × 1 3/16" × 1 3/8". See Figure **4-D-4** for the shape. Drill holes into the side of the frame (*the diameter of a pin*) at the sites of the arrows in the diagram. Cut a thin piece of mirror which will later glue behind the frame.

(N) TOP CHEST DRAWER (One)
(1) **BACK** (Cut 1): 1/16" × 5/16" × 1 1/2".
(2) **BOTTOM** (Cut 1): 1/16" × 9/16" × 1 3/8".
(3) **SIDES** (Cut 2): 1/16" × 5/16" × 9/16".
(4) **FRONT** (Cut 1): 1/16" × 5/16" × 1 5/8". Bevel all edges.
Refer to **2-E-2** for assembly.

(O) DRAWER PULLS (Six): Refer to **1-B-6.**

ASSEMBLY: Stain all wood before glueing. Refer to Figures **4-D-1** and **4-D-2.**

1. Glue the top moulding (**B**) atop the top base (**A**) with the beveled edge forward and the back edges flush. This will now appear as a shaped board and will be known as the top board. Repeat this procedure with the top base (**K-1**) and the top moulding (**K-2**) pieces for the top drawer chest.

2. Glue the bottom board butted against the lower front edge of the back board. Glue the sides against the upright end edges of the back board and against the end edges of the bottom board, with the back edges flush. Glue the top board atop the top edges of the sides and back board, with the back edges flush. Repeat this assembly for the assembly of the top drawer chest.

3. Glue a lower drawer guide board against the inside surface of the left side board and resting atop the bottom board. Repeat on the right interior side for the second board.

4. Place a lower drawer inside the table opening, against the left side (*for measurement only*). Glue a drawer separator atop the bottom board and against the back board. Place the second lower drawer in the table. Glue the drawer base inside the table against the sides and back (*resting only on the drawers for measurement*). Place an upper drawer in the table against the left side. Repeat the installation of the drawer separator boards until both have been installed. Remove all of the drawers.

5. Glue the upper drawer chest atop the dressing table with side spaces equal and the back edges flush. Glue a mirror support atop the top surface of the upper drawer chest, with the outside edges flush. See Figures **4-D-1** and **4-D-2.**

6. Apply a finish coat to all the drawers, the dressing table and mirror frame.

7. Glue the previously cut piece of mirror behind the mirror frame. Push a tiny pin through the hole in the left mirror support and into the left side hole in the mirror frame. Repeat for the right side.

8. Attach the six drawer pulls.

VICTORIAN PERIOD THREE DRAWER BUREAU WASHSTAND WITH SPLASH BACK 4-E

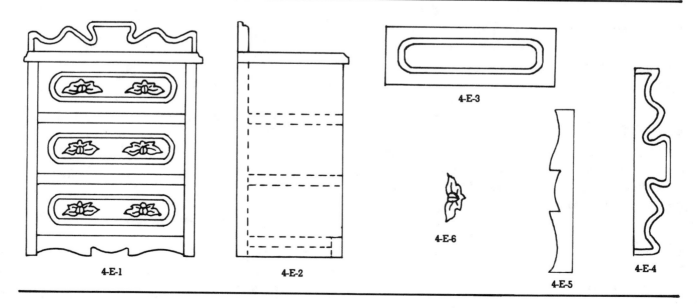

4-E-1   4-E-2   4-E-3   4-E-6   4-E-5   4-E-4

(A) BACK (Cut 1): 1/8″ × 1 3/4″ × 2 3/8″.

(B) SIDES (Cut 2): 1/8″ × 1 1/4″ × 2 3/8″.

(C) BOTTOM (Cut 1): 1/8″ × 1″ × 1 3/4″.

(D) TOP (Cut 1): 1/8″ × 1 5/16″ × 2 1/8″. See Figures **4-E-1** and **4-E-2** for the shape of the two side edges and the front edge.

(E) SPLASH BACK (Cut 1): 1/8″ × 3/8″ × 2″. See Figure **4-E-4** for the shape. The top and side front surfaces are cut back 1/16″ between the inside black line and the outside edges, as indicated in this diagram.

(F) FRONT APRON (Cut 1): See Figure **4-E-5** for the shape.

(G) DRAWER SEPARATORS (Cut 2): 1/8″ × 1 1/8″ × 1 3/4″.

(H) DRAWERS (Three)

(1) **FRONT** (Cut 3): 1/8″ × 5/8″ × 1 3/4″. See Figure **4-E-3**. The center double line moulding in this diagram is raised by carving away the back-

ground inside and outside of the moulding 1/16″. You will then have a 1/16″ thick board with a raised moulding 1/16″ high.

(2) **BACK** (Cut 3): 1/16″ × 5/8″ × 1 3/4″.

(3) **SIDES** (Cut 6): 1/16″ × 5/8″ × 1″.

(4) **BOTTOM** (Cut 3): 1/8″ × 1″ × 1 5/8″.

Refer to **2-E-1** for the drawer assembly.

(I) DRAWER PULLS (Cut 6): 1/8″ × 3/16″ × 1/2″. See Figure **4-E-6** for the shape. The angle is at the top of the pull, and the thickness will recede from the bottom edge, back to the top point. You may also find similar pulls which are cast from a composition, which can be stained, at your local miniature dealer.

ASSEMBLY: Stain all wood before glueing. Refer to Figures **4-E-1** and **4-E-2**. Refer to **2-C-1** for assembly.

1. When the chest is assembled, glue the splash back atop the top board, with back edges flush.

2. Glue the drawer pulls in place.

3. Apply a finish coat.

VICTORIAN PERIOD COMMODE WASHSTAND WITH "MARBLE" TOP AND SPLASH BACK 4-F

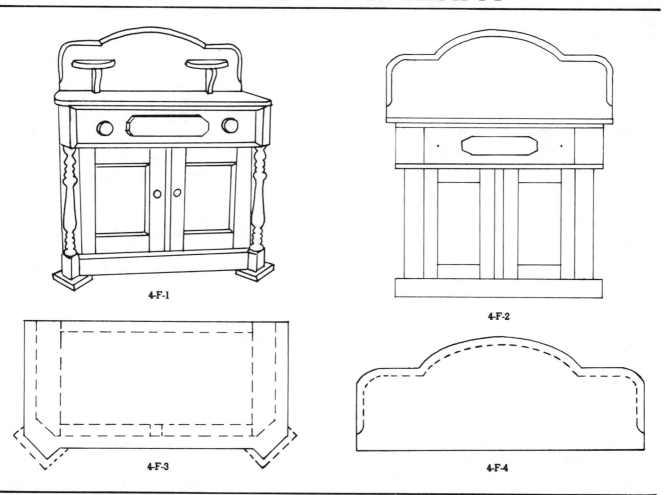

4-F-1

4-F-2

4-F-3

4-F-4

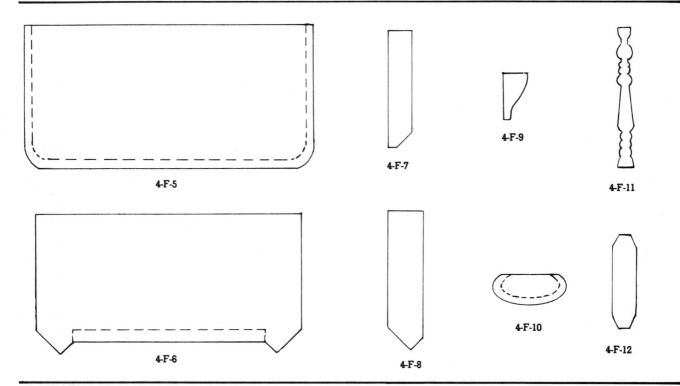

4-F-5

4-F-7

4-F-9

4-F-11

4-F-6

4-F-8

4-F-10

4-F-12

(A) UPPER BACK (Cut 1): 1/8″ × 1/2″ × 2″.

(B) UPPER SIDES (Cut 2): 3/8″ × 1/2″ × 1 1/2″. See Figure **4-F-8** for the top view of the shape. The diagram shows the left side, which would be reversed for the right side.

(C) UPPER BOTTOM AND TOP (Cut 2): 1/16″ × 1 1/2″ × 2 3/4″. See Figure **4-F-6** for the shape. The area in this diagram which is set apart by a broken line is beveled.

(D) LOWER BACK (Cut 1): 1/8″ × 1 1/2″ × 2″.

(E) LOWER SIDES (Cut 2): 1/4″ × 1 1/4″ × 1 1/2″. See Figure **4-F-7** for a top view of the shape. The diagram shows the right side, which would be reversed for the left side.

(F) LOWER BOTTOM (Cut 1): 1/4″ × 1 1/2″ × 2 3/4″. See Figure **4-F-6** for the shape. The area in this diagram which is set apart by a broken line is beveled from a depth of 1/16″.

(G) "MARBLE" TOP (Cut 1): 1/16″ × 1 9/16″ × 3″. See Figure **4-F-5** for the shape. This piece is beveled on the sides and front, from the outside edge to the broken line in the diagram.

(H) "MARBLE" SPLASH BACK (Cut 1): 1/16″ × 1 1/4″ × 3″. See Figure **4-F-4** for the shape. This piece is beveled on the upper sides and top, from the outside edge to the broken line in the diagram.

(I) "MARBLE" SHELF (Cut 2): 1/16″ × 5/16″ × 3/4″. See Figure **4-F-10** for the shape. These pieces are beveled on the rounded edge, from the outside edge

to the broken line in the diagram.

(J) "MARBLE" SHELF SUPPORT (Cut 2): 1/16″ × 1/4″ × 1/2″. See Figure **4-F-9** for the shape. *Note:* Refer to **1-C-9** for all "marble" pieces.

(K) FEET (Cut 4): 1/16″ × 3/8″ × 1/2″.

(L) DRAWER FRONT MOULDING (Cut 1): 1/16″ × 1/4″ × 1″. See Figure **4-F-12** for the shape.

(M) POSTS (Cut 2): 3/16″ diameter wood dowel × 1 1/2″. See Figure **4-F-11** for the shape. Refer to **1-C-3-a**.

(N) POSTS (Cut 4): 1/16″ × 3/8″ × 1/2″.

(O) CENTER FRONT SUPPORT (Cut 1): 1/8″ × 1/8″ × 1 1/2″.

(P) DOORS (Two)
　　(1) **CENTER PANEL** (Cut 2): 1/16″ × 9/16″ × 1 1/8″.
　　(2) **SIDE MOULDING** (Cut 4): 1/8″ × 3/16″ × 1 1/2″.
　　(3) **TOP AND BOTTOM MOULDING** (Cut 4): 1/8″ × 3/16″ × 9/16″.

(Q) DRAWER (One)
　　(1) **FRONT AND BACK** (Cut 2): 1/16″ × 1/2″ × 2″.
　　(2) **SIDES** (Cut 2): 1/16″ × 1/2″ × 1 1/4″.
　　(3) **BOTTOM** (Cut 1): 1/8″ × 1 1/4″ × 1 7/8″.
Refer to **2-E-1** for assembly. When assembled, glue the front moulding (**L**) centered against the drawer front. See Figures **4-F-1** and **4-F-2**.

(R) DRAWER AND DOOR PULLS (Two each):

Refer to **1-B-6**.

(S) HINGES (Two pair): Refer to **1-B-4**.

ASSEMBLY: Stain all wood before glueing, and apply a "marble" finish to the pieces which represent marble. Refer to Figures **4-F-1** and **4-F-2**. Refer to Figure **4-F-3** for a top view of the assembly of the lower portion of the washstand.

1. Glue the upper sides (**B**) against the upright edges of the upper back (**A**) with the back edges flush. Glue the upper bottom and top boards (**C**) atop and beneath the above assembly with the side and back edges flush. The beveled edge will go downward on the top board and upward on the bottom board.

2. Glue the "marble" top centered atop the upper top board, with the back edges flush. Glue the splash back board atop the "marble" top, with the back edges flush. See Figure **4-F-2**.

3. See Figure **4-F-3**. Glue the lower sides (**E**) against the upright edges of the lower back board (**D**) with the back edges flush. Glue the lower bottom board (**F**) beneath this assembly with the side edges equal. The beveled edge will go upward and the back edges will be flush.

4. Glue the front feet beneath the lower bottom board at the angle shown in Figure **4-F-3**. Glue the back feet beneath this board with the back edges flush.

5. Glue a post atop each of the two front side angles. See Figure **4-F-1**.

6. Glue the upper assembly atop the top edges of the lower assembly and the posts with the back edges flush. See Figures **4-F-1** and **4-F-2**.

7. Glue the top and bottom door moulding boards against the top and bottom edges of the center panel. Glue the side moulding boards against the side edges of this assembly. Repeat for the second door.

8. Insert a door in the lower opening (*for measurement only*) and glue the center front support board in place, with front edges flush. See Figure **4-F-2**. Remove the door.

9. See Figure **4-F-1**. Glue the "marble" shelves and their supports together, with the back edges flush. Glue these assembled shelves evenly spaced against the splash back and atop the "marble" top.

10. Apply a finish coat to the wood portion of this washstand, the drawer and the two doors.

11. Hinge the two doors to the lower side boards. Refer to **1-B-4**. Attach the door and drawer pulls.

OAK WASHSTAND 4-G

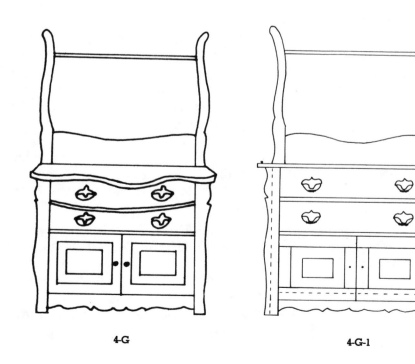

4-G

4-G-1

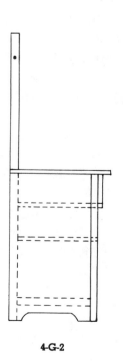

4-G-2

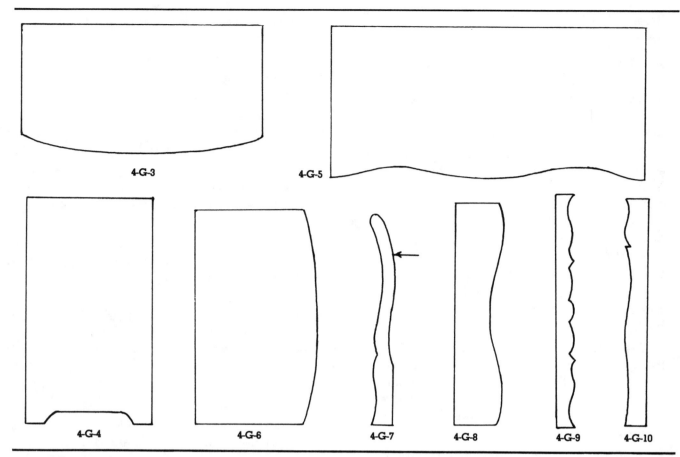

4-G-3

4-G-5

4-G-4

4-G-6

4-G-7

4-G-8

4-G-9

4-G-10

(A) BACK (Cut 1): 1/8″ × 2 3/16″ × 2 1/2″.

(B) SIDES (Cut 2): 1/8″ × 1 5/16″ × 2 7/16″. See Figure **4-G-4** for the shape.

(C) BOTTOM (Cut 1): 1/8″ × 1 3/16″ × 2 1/2″.

(D) TOP (Cut 1): 1/16″ × 1 5/8″ × 3 1/4″. See Figure **4-G-5** for the shape.

(E) UPPER DRAWER SEPARATOR (Cut 1): 1/16″ × 1 3/8″ × 2 1/2″. See Figure **4-G-3** for the shape.

(F) LOWER DRAWER SEPARATOR (Cut 1): 1/16″ × 1 5/16″ × 2 1/2″.

(G) FRONT SIDE FACING (Cut 2): 1/8″ × 1/4″ × 2 7/16″. See Figure **4-G-10** for the shape.

(H) APRON (Cut 1): 1/16″ × 1/4″ × 2 1/2″. See Figure **4-G-9** for the shape.

(I) SPLASH BACK (Cut 1): 1/16″ × 1/2″ × 2 3/8″. See Figure **4-G-8** for the shape.

(J) UPRIGHT BACK FRAME (Cut 2): 1/8″ × 5/16″ × 2 1/4″. See Figure **4-G-7** for the shape. Drill a 1/16″ diameter hole through each piece at the site of the arrow in the diagram.

(K) POLE (Cut 1): 1/16″ diameter wood dowel × 2 3/4″.

(L) LOWER CABINET DOORS (Two)
    (1) **CENTER PANEL** (Cut 2): 1/16″ × 11/16″ × 7/8″.

    (2) **TOP AND BOTTOM** (Cut 4): 1/8″ × 3/16″ × 1 1/4″.

    (3) **SIDES** (Cut 4): 1/8″ × 3/16″ × 11/16″.

    (4) **CENTER MOULDING** (Cut 2): 1/16″ × 5/16″ × 1/2″. Bevel all edges.

(M) UPPER DRAWER (One)
    (1) **BACK** (Cut 1): 1/16″ × 1/2″ × 2 7/16″.

    (2) **FRONT** (Cut 1): 1/16″ × 1/2″ × 2 1/2″. *Note:* This piece will be steamed to allow it to bend for application (*see* **1-C-6**) when using wood, or it can be cut from 1/16″ thick cardboard which would have to be painted to match the other wood.

    (3) **SIDES** (Cut 2): 1/16″ × 1/2″ × 1 3/16″. Sand an angle on the front upright surface to match the shaped front.

    (4) **BOTTOM** (Cut 1): 1/8″ × 1 1/4″ × 2 5/16″. See Figure **4-G-6** for the shape.

(N) LOWER DRAWER (One)
    (1) **FRONT AND BACK** (Cut 2): 1/16″ × 1/2″ × 2 7/16″.

    (2) **SIDES** (Cut 2): 1/16″ × 1/2″ × 1 1/8″.

    (3) **BOTTOM** (Cut 1): 1/8″ × 1 1/8″ × 2 5/16″.
Note: Refer to **2-E-1** for assembly of both drawers.

(O) DRAWER PULLS (Four): Refer to **1-B-6** for drawer pulls with bail.

(P) DOOR KNOBS (Two): Refer to **1-B-6**.

(Q) HINGES (Two pair): Refer to **1-B-4.**

ASSEMBLY: Stain all wood before glueing.

1. Refer to **2-C-1** for the general assembly. Use Figures **4-G, 4-G-1** and **4-G-2** as your guides.

2. Glue the front side facing boards against the upright front edges of the side boards with center edges flush.

3. Glue the apron below the bottom board with the front edges flush.

4. Glue the splash back board between the two upright frame boards with back and bottom edges flush. See Figure **4-G-1.** Glue the pole between the frame boards and in the drilled holes. Sand the out-side ends flush with the outside surfaces of these boards.

5. Glue the above unit atop the top board, with back edges flush. See Figures **4-G-1** and **4-G-2.**

6. Assemble the top and bottom and side boards around the center door panel. See Figure **4-G-1.** Glue the center moulding board centered against the front surface of the center panel. Repeat these directions for the second door.

7. Apply a finish coat to the chest, drawers and doors.

8. Attach the drawer and door pulls. Hinge the doors to the side front facing boards.

OAK DRESSING TABLE 4-H

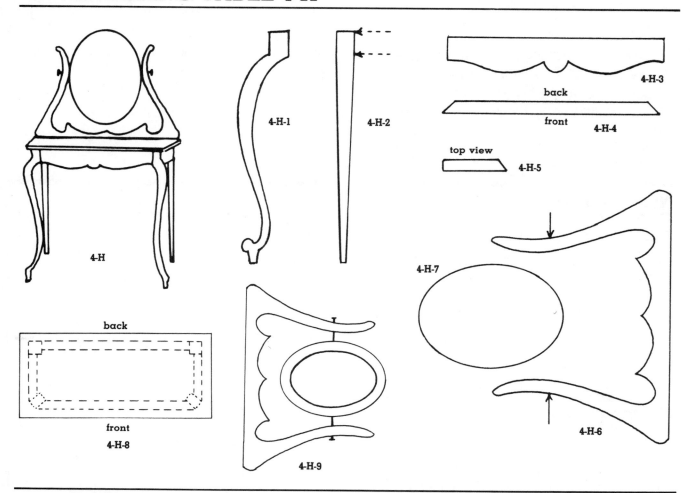

(A) TABLE TOP (Cut 1): 1/16″ × 1 1/4″ × 2 3/4″.

(B) FRONT LEGS (Cut 2): 1/8″ × 9/16″ × 2 1/2″. See Figure **4-H-1** for the shape.

(C) BACK LEGS (Cut 2): 3/16″ × 3/16″ × 2 1/2″. See Figure **4-H-2** for the tapered shape. There are two arrows in this diagram; the area between them re-mains square, and the legs are tapered on all four surfaces below the arrow.

(D) FRONT APRON (Cut 1): 1/8″ × 3/8″ × 2 1/4″. See Figure **4-H-3** for the shape. Figure **4-H-4** is a top view of this board showing the angles to be cut at each end.

(E) END APRON (Cut 2): 1/8″ × 1/4″ × 11/16″. See Figure **4-H-5** for a top view of the left end board showing a 45° angle to be cut into the front edge of the board, while the back edge remains a straight cut. *Note:* The right end board will have an angle (45°) at the front edge, but it will be the reverse of the angle on the left board. See Figure **4-H-8**.

(F) BACK APRON (Cut 1): 1/8″ × 1/4″ × 2 1/8″.

(G) MIRROR SUPPORT (Cut 1): 1/8″ × 1 7/8″ × 2 3/4″. See Figure **4-H-6** for the shape. Drill a hole (*to accommodate a pin*) through the side surface of the two supports at the sites of the arrows in this diagram.

(H) MIRROR FRAME (One): Figure **4-H-7** shows an approximate size and shape of a frame which can be made of wood, metal or plastic. As shown in Figure **4-H-9**, the width of the mirror can be as much as 1 5/16″. When you have found the appropriate frame, you will want to cut a thin piece of mirror to be attached behind at the time of assembly. Metal or plastic frames can be painted with an oak color acrylic paint after the metal or plastic has first been sealed with an acrylic spray.

(I) JEWELRY FINDINGS: The mirror support and front apron can have simulated carving with the use of jewelry findings which are first sprayed with a sealer, painted an oak color and then glued into place.

ASSEMBLY: Stain all wood before glueing. Refer to **4-H** and **4-H-8**.

1. Figure **4-H-8** shows a top view of the assembly of the front and back legs; the front, back and side apron pieces are shown in relation to the top board. Glue these pieces together as shown. Glue the top board in place.

2. Refer to Figure **4-H-9,** which shows the assembly of the mirror supports and the mirror frame. If the mirror frame is metal or plastic it should be sealed and then painted an oak color. Tiny holes will have to be drilled into the sides of the metal or plastic frame at the sites indicated in the diagram. Cut two straight pins to a length of 3/8″. Insert the pin in the hole in the left support and push it on through the hole in the left side of the mirror frame. Repeat this for the right side. The mirror frame will now tilt.

3. Glue the assembled frame and supports atop the top board with back edges flush.

4. Apply the painted jewelry findings to simulate carving on the apron and mirror supports. Refer to **1-C-5**.

5. Apply a finish coat to the piece of furniture.

6. Attach the mirror behind the frame.

WASHSTAND 4-I

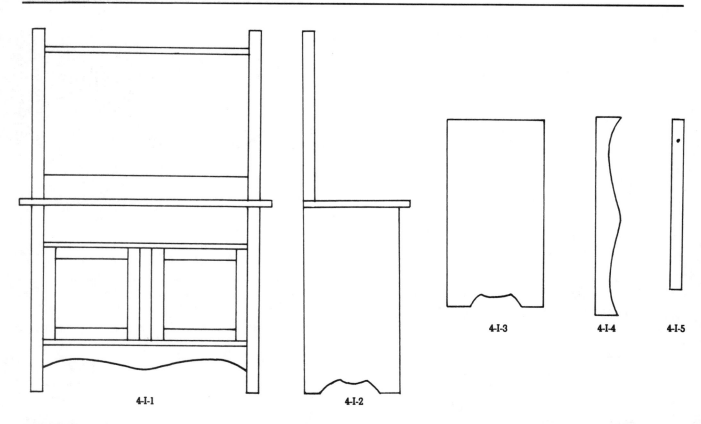

4-I-1

4-I-2

4-I-3

4-I-4

4-I-5

(A) BACK (Cut 1): 1/8″ × 2″ × 2 1/8″.

(B) SIDE (Cut 2): 1/8″ × 1″ × 2″. See Figure **4-I-3** for the shape.

(C) CUPBOARD TOP AND BOTTOM (Cut 2): 1/16″ × 7/8″ × 2 1/8″.

(D) TABLE TOP (Cut 1): 1/16″ × 1 1/8″ × 2 5/8″.

(E) APRON FRONT (Cut 1): 1/8″ × 1/4″ × 2 1/8″. See Figure **4-I-4** for the shape.

(F) UPRIGHT POSTS (Cut 2): 1/8″ × 1/8″ × 1 13/16″. Drill a 1/16″ diameter hole at the site of the black dot in Figure **4-I-5**.

(G) SPLASHER BACK (Cut 1): 1/16″ × 1/4″ × 2 1/8″.

(H) ROD (Cut 1): 1/16″ diameter wood dowel × 2 1/8″.

(I) DRAWER

    (1) FRONT AND BACK (Cut 2): 1/16″ × 3/8″ × 2 1/8″.

    (2) SIDES (Cut 2): 1/16″ × 3/8″ × 3/4″.

    (3) BOTTOM (Cut 1): 1/8″ × 3/4″ × 2″.

Refer to **2-E-1** for drawer assembly. Two drawer pulls are required. We suggest drop pulls. Refer to **1-B-6**.

(J) CUPBOARD DOOR (Cut 2): 1/16″ × 1″ × 1″.

(K) DOOR MOULDING - SIDE (Cut 4): 1/16″ × 1/8″ × 1″.

(L) DOOR MOULDING - TOP AND BOTTOM (Cut 4): 1/16″ × 1/8″ × 3/4″.

(M) DOOR DIVIDER (Cut 1): 1/8″ × 1/8″ × 1″.

(N) HINGES (Two pair): Refer to **1-B-4** for identification of hinge, and to **1-B-4-c** for installation of a butt hinge.

ASSEMBLY

1. Refer to **2-C-2** for assembly of the lower cupboard and doors.

2. Glue an upright post in line with the sides, atop the top board of the lower cabinet, at each side. Glue the splasher back between these two posts and atop the cabinet top, with back edges flush.

3. Glue the ends of the rod into the holes in the upright boards.

4. Apply the finish coat to the washstand.

5. Attach the drawer pulls and the hinges to the cupboard doors.

SAWBUCK TABLE 5-A

(A) TABLE TOP (Cut 3): 1/8″ × 1″ × 7″. Sand the top ends of the boards rounded. See Figure **5-A-1**. Drill 1/16″ diameter holes at the sites of the black dots in the diagram.

(B) TOP LEG BRACE (Cut 2): 1/8″ × 3/8″ × 2 7/16″. See Figure **5-A-2** for the shape.

(C) LEGS (Cut 4): 1/8″ × 3/8″ × 2 13/16″. See Figure **5-A-3** for the shape. See Figure **5-A-4** for notches to be cut into the "facing" surfaces of each pair of legs, and the hole which is to be cut into each leg (*shaded area*).

(D) TABLE STRETCHER (Cut 1): 1/8″ × 3/8″ × 6 1/4″. See Figure **5-A-5** for the shape to be cut into each end. Drill a hole at each end 1/8″ in diameter. See the shaded area in the diagram for placement.

(E) WEDGE (Cut 2): 3/32″ × 3/32″ × 5/16″. See Figure **5-A-6** for the shape.

(F) PEGS (Cut 8): 1/16″ diameter wood dowel × 1/4″.

ASSEMBLY: Stain all pieces before glueing. Refer to **2-B-3**.

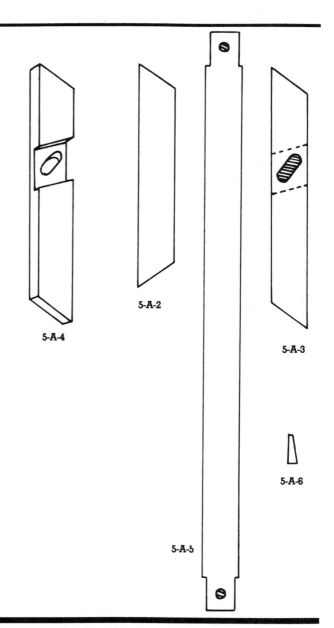

5-A-2

5-A-4

5-A-3

5-A-6

5-A-5

SWEDISH TYPE TRESTLE AND BOARD 5-B

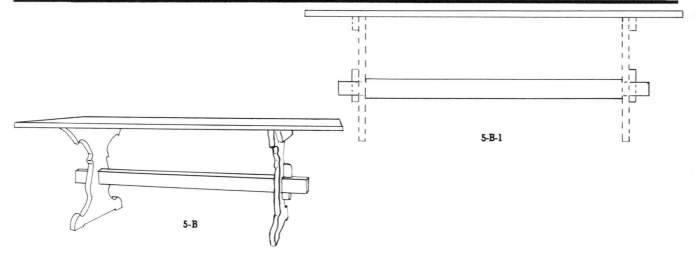

5-B-1

5-B

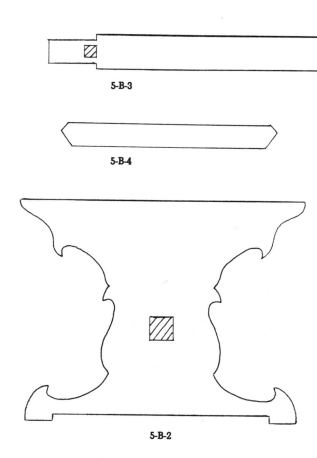

5-B-3

5-B-4

5-B-2

(A) TABLE TOP (Cut 1): 1/8″ × 3″ × 7″.

(B) TABLE LEGS (Cut 2): 1/8″ × 2 3/8″ × 3″. See Figure **5-B-2**. Cut the shaded area away.

(C) STRETCHER (Cut 1): 3/8″ × 3/8″ × 5 3/4″. See Figure **5-B-3** for the shape (*top view*) and shape (*side view*). When this board has been shaped, cut a square hole (*shaded area*) through the board at the sites indicated in the diagram.

(D) TABLE TOP BRACE (Cut 2): 1/8″ × 1/4″ × 2 1/4″. See Figure **5-B-4** for the shape.

(E) PEGS (Cut 2): 1/8″ × 1/8″ (*square*) × 5/8″.

ASSEMBLY: Stain all wood before glueing. Refer to **5-B** and **5-B-1**.

1. Glue the stretcher board through the holes in the legs. Glue the pegs into the holes in the stretcher and against the outside surfaces of the legs. See Figures **5-B** and **5-B-1**.

2. Glue the table top atop the top edges of the legs, with equal overhang at the ends and at the sides. Glue the table to braces against the underside of the top board and the outside surfaces of the legs. See Figures **5-B** and **5-B-1**.

3. Apply a finish coat to the table.

TAVERN TABLE 5-C

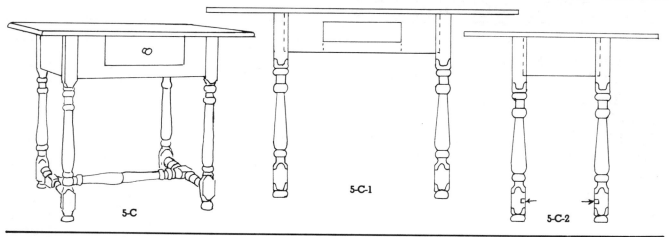

5-C

5-C-1

5-C-2

(A) TOP (Cut 1): 1/16″ × 2 1/2″ × 4″.

(B) LEGS (Cut 4): 3/16″ × 3/16″ (*square*) × 2 7/16″. See Figure **5-C-5** for the shape. Refer to **1-C-3-a** for aid in shaping. The arrow in the diagram indicates a 1/16″ hole to be drilled into the one side of each leg. The shaded area indicates a mortise cut; and another mortise cut (*like the first one*) is to be cut in the same area of the leg, but on the side of the leg in which you drilled the hole.

(C) TABLE BACK (Cut 1): 1/16″ × 1/2″ × 2″.

(D) TABLE FRONT (Cut 1): 1/16″ × 1/2″ × 2″. See Figure **5-C-8** for the area (*shaded*) to be cut away.

(E) TABLE SIDE (Cut 2): 1/16″ × 1/2″ × 1″.

(F) CENTER LEG STRETCHER (Cut 1): 3/16″ diameter wood dowel × 2 1/16″. See Figure **5-C-7** for the shape. Refer to **1-C-3-a**.

(G) SIDE STRETCHERS (Cut 2): 3/16″ diameter

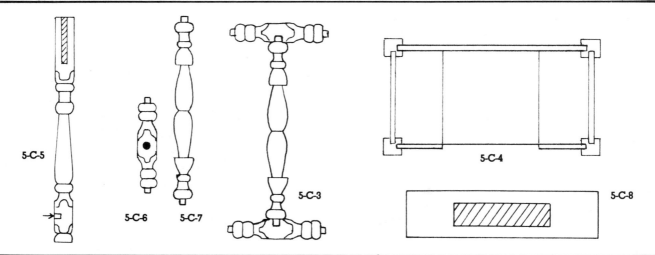

5-C-5

5-C-6

5-C-7

5-C-3

5-C-4

5-C-8

wood dowel × 1 1/16". See Figure **5-C-6** for the shape. Refer to **1-C-3-a**. Drill a 1/16" diameter hole 1/16" deep at the site of the black dot in the diagram.

(H) DRAWER BASE (Cut 1): 1/8" × 1" × 1".

(I) DRAWER (One)
    (1) **BACK** (Cut 1): 1/16" × 1/4" × 1".
    (2) **SIDES** (Cut 2): 1/16" × 1/4" × 1 1/16".
    (3) **BOTTOM** (Cut 1): 1/16" × 7/8" × 1".
    (4) **FRONT** (Cut 1): 1/16" × 3/8" × 1 1/8".
Refer to **2-E-2** for assembly.

(J) DRAWER PULL (One): Refer to **1-B-6**.

ASSEMBLY: Stain all wood before glueing.

1. Refer to Figure **5-C-4**. Glue the front, back and side boards into the mortise cuts in the upper legs.

2. Refer to Figure **5-C-3**. Assemble the stretchers as shown. Glue this assembly into the drilled holes in the table legs.

3. Glue the drawer base between the front and back boards and below the front opening, with the bottom edges flush. See Figure **5-C-1**.

4. Glue the table top atop the above assembly, with equal front and back and side overhang.

5. Apply a finish coat to the table and the drawer.

6. Attach a drawer pull to the front of the drawer.

MAPLE OBLONG TABLE 5-D

(A) TOP (Cut 1): 1/16" × 2" × 3".

(B) FRONT AND BACK APRON (Cut 2): 1/16" × 1/2" × 2 1/4". See Figure **5-D-1** for the shape.

(C) SIDE APRON (Cut 2): 1/16" × 1/2" × 1 1/4". See Figure **5-D-2** for the shape.

(D) LEG (Cut 4): 3/8" × 3/8" × 2 7/16". See Figure **5-D-3** for cabriole shape to trace onto the wood. Refer to **1-C-3-d** for shaping instructions.

ASSEMBLY: Stain all wood before glueing. Refer to **2-B-1** for instructions.

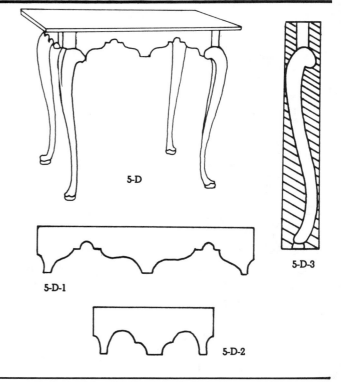

5-D

5-D-1

5-D-2

5-D-3

WILLIAM AND MARY TYPE OF TABLE WITH CUP-TURNED LEGS AND STRETCHERS c. 1700-20 5-E

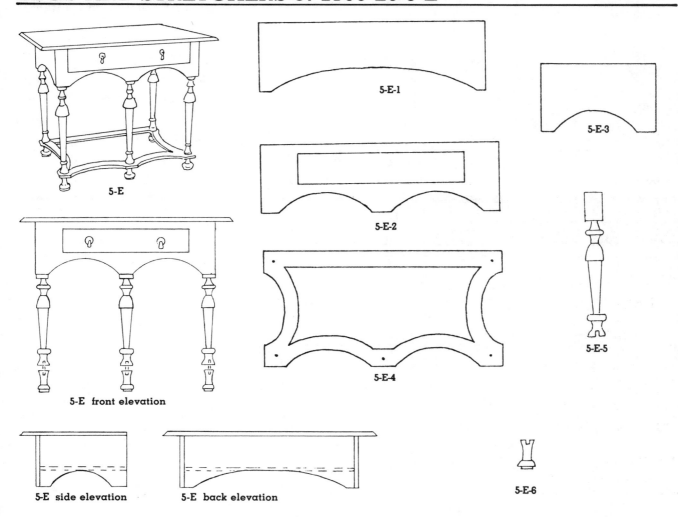

5-E

5-E-1

5-E-3

5-E-2

5-E-4

5-E-5

5-E front elevation

5-E side elevation

5-E back elevation

5-E-6

(A) TABLE FRONT (Cut 1): 1/16″ × 3/4″ × 2 1/2″. See Figure **5-E-2** for the shape. Cut away the oblong area in the diagram.

(B) TABLE BACK (Cut 1): 1/16″ × 3/4″ × 2 3/8″. See Figure **5-E-1** for the shape.

(C) SIDES (Cut 2): 1/16″ × 3/4″ × 1 3/16″. See Figure **5-E-3** for the shape.

(D) TABLE BOTTOM (Cut 1): 1/16″ × 1 3/16″ × 2 3/8″.

(E) TABLE TOP (Cut 1): 1/16″ × 1 1/2″ × 3″. See the front and side elevation diagrams. Bevel the top edge of the front and sides of this board.

(F) TOP PORTION OF LEGS (Cut 5): 3/16″ × 3/16″ × 1 9/16″. See Figure **5-E-5** for the shape. Refer to **1-C-3-a** for aid in turning. Drill a 1/16″ diameter hole 1/16″ deep up into the bottom surface of each leg.

(G) LOWER PORTION OF LEGS (Cut 5): 3/16″ diameter wood dowel × 5/16″. See Figure **5-E-6** for

the shape. Refer to **1-C-3-a** for aid in turning. Drill a 1/16″ diameter hole 1/16″ deep down into the top of each of these legs.

(H) LEG PEGS (Cut 5): 1/16″ diameter wood dowel × 3/16″.

(I) LEG STRETCHER FRAME (Cut 1): 1/16″ × 1 1/4″ × 2 1/2″. Trace the diagram in Figure **5-E-4** onto the piece of wood. Drill 1/16″ diameter holes at the sites of the black dots through the piece of wood. Cut away the center section first, then the outside edges. If the piece should break, stain before glueing it back together.

(J) DRAWER

    (1) **FRONT AND BACK** (Cut 2): 1/16″ × 5/16″ × 1 3/4″.

    (2) **SIDES** (Cut 2): 1/16″ × 5/16″ × 1 1/8″.

    (3) **BOTTOM** (Cut 1): 1/8″ × 1 1/8″ × 1 5/8″.
Refer to **2-E-1** for assembly.

(K) DRAWER PULLS (Two): Refer to **1-B-6**.

ASSEMBLY: Stain all wood before glueing.

1. Refer to the right side elevation and back elevation diagrams. Glue the sides against the upright end edges of the back, with back edges flush.

2. Glue the front board against the front of this assembly, with top and side edges flush.

3. Refer to the back elevation. Glue the bottom board (*with the top surface*) 7/16" below the top edge of the back, front and sides.

4. Glue the top board atop this assembly, with side overhang equal and back edges flush. See the front elevation diagram.

5. See Figure **5-E** and the front elevation diagram. Glue the five legs in place resting inside against the front, side and back boards, with the top surfaces glued to the bottom surface of the bottom board. Glue a peg up into the hole in the bottom of each leg.

6. The pegs will go through the holes in the leg stretcher frame (*see Figure* **5-E**) and will be glued into the holes in the top of the lower legs. See front elevation.

7. Apply a finish coat to the drawer and the table.

8. Attach the two drawer pulls.

OAK KITCHEN TABLE WITH TWO DRAWERS c. EARLY 1900's 5-F

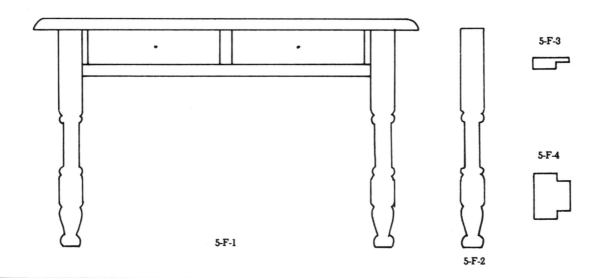

Note: Wood used in this project can be oak or bass or pine which is stained to represent oak.

(A) TABLE TOP (Cut 1): 1/8" × 2 1/2" × 4". Round off the top of all edges.

(B) LEG (Cut 4): 1/4" × 1/4" × 2 3/8". See Figure **5-F-2** for the shape. Refer to **1-C-3-a** for aid in carving.

(C) DRAWER BASE (Cut 1): 1/8" × 1 7/8" × 3".

(D) TABLE SIDE (Cut 2): 1/8" × 3/4" × 1 1/2".

(E) SHAPED DRAWER RUNNER (Cut 2): 1/8" × 3/8" × 1 7/8". See Figure **5-F-3** for the shape.

(F) SHAPED DRAWER DIVIDER (Cut 1): 3/8" × 1/2" × 1 7/8". See Figure **5-F-4** for the shape.

(G) DRAWER FRONT (Cut 2): 1/16" × 3/8" × 1 3/8". Drill a hole in each board at the site indicated by a black dot in Figure **5-F-1**.

(H) DRAWER BACK (Cut 2): 1/16" × 3/8" × 1 1/8".

(I) DRAWER SIDES (Cut 4): 1/16" × 3/8" × 1 11/16".

(J) DRAWER BOTTOM (Cut 2): 1/16" × 1" × 1 3/4".

(K) DRAWER RUNNERS (Cut 4): 1/16" × 1/8" × 1 13/16".

(L) LEG STRETCHERS (Cut 2): 1/8" × 1/4" × 1 1/2".

(M) TABLE BACK (Cut 1): 1/8" × 3/4" × 3".

(N) DRAWER PULLS (Two): Tiny brass drawer pulls can be purchased through your miniature dealer or through many mail-order lists.

ASSEMBLY: Stain all wood before glueing.

1. See **2-B-4** for table assembly.

2. See **2-E-3** for drawer assembly.

3. When the table is assembled, apply the finish coat and drawer pulls.

COUNTRY SIDE TABLE 5-G

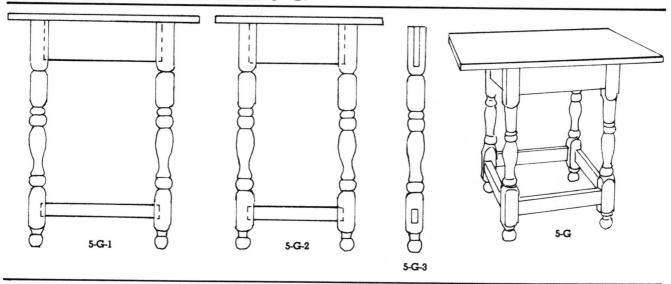

5-G-1

5-G-2

5-G-3

5-G

(A) LEG (Cut 4): 3/16″ × 3/16″ × 2 7/16″. See Figure **5-G-3** for the shape. Refer to **1-C-3-a.** A 1/16″ deep mortise cut is made at the top side and lower side of each leg, as indicated in the diagram. These same cuts are to be made on the side at right angles to this side of each leg.

(B) FRONT AND BACK APRON (Cut 2): 1/16″ × 7/16″ × 1 1/4″.

(C) SIDE APRON (Cut 2): 1/16″ × 7/16″ × 1″.

(D) FRONT AND BACK LEG STRETCHERS (Cut 2): 1/16″ × 1/8″ × 1 1/4″.

(E) SIDE LEG STRETCHERS (Cut 2): 1/16″ × 1/8″ × 1″.

(F) TABLE TOP (Cut 1): 1/16″ × 1 3/4″ × 2″.

ASSEMBLY: Stain all wood before glueing. Refer to Figures **5-G-1** and **5-G-2.**

1. Glue the front, back and side apron and leg stretchers in place. Be sure this assembly is squared.

2. Glue the table top atop this assembly, with equal overhang at the sides and front and back.

3. Apply a finish coat.

VICTORIAN PARLOR TABLE WITH PEDESTAL AND "MARBLE" TOP 5-H

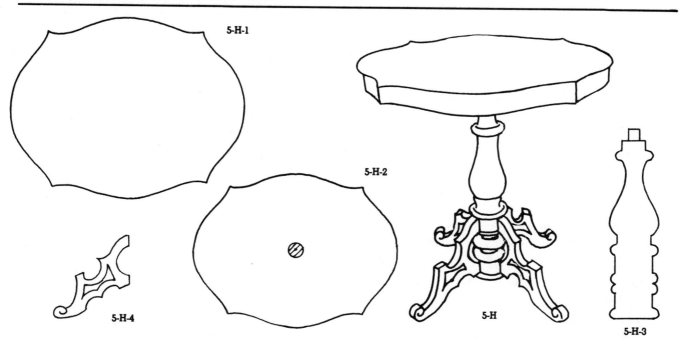

5-H-1

5-H-2

5-H-4

5-H

5-H-3

(A) "MARBLE" TOP (Cut 1): 1/16" × 2" × 2 1/2". See Figure **5-H-1** for the shape. Refer to **1-C-9**.

(B) TABLE TOP (Cut 1): 1/8" × 1 5/8" × 2 1/8". See Figure **5-H-2** for the shape. Drill a 1/8" diameter hole in the center of this board, as indicated by the shaded area in the diagram.

(C) PEDESTAL (Cut 1): 1/2" diameter wood dowel × 2". Refer to **1-C-3-a**. See Figure **5-H-3** for the shape.

(D) LEGS (Cut 4): 1/8" × 1/2" × 1 1/4". See Figure

5-H-4 for the shape. Cut out the inside area.

ASSEMBLY: Stain all wood before glueing.

1. Glue the pedestal into the hole in the table top, with the top edges flush. Be sure that it is straight and level.

2. Refer to **5-H**. Glue the legs against the pedestal evenly spaced around the pedestal.

3. Apply a finish coat to the table.

4. Glue the "marble" top atop the table top, with equal overhang on all sides.

VICTORIAN PERIOD SIDE TABLE WITH SPOOL-TURNED LEGS 5-I

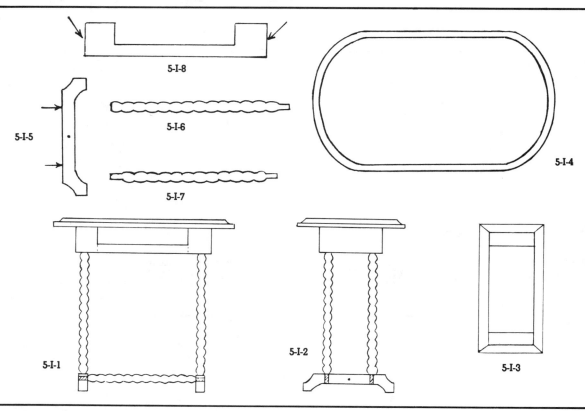

(A) TOP (Cut 1): 1/16" × 1 1/2" × 2 1/2". See Figure **5-I-4** (*outside oval*) for the shape.

(B) TABLE TOP MOULDING (Cut 1): 1/16" × 1 3/8" × 2 3/8". See Figure **5-I-4** (*inside oval*) for the shape. Bevel the top edge.

(C) FRONT APRON (Cut 1): 1/8" × 3/8" × 1 7/8". See Figure **5-I-8** for the shape. Mitre cut each end (*indicated by an arrow*) with a 45° angle cut.

(D) BACK APRON (Cut 1): 1/8" × 3/8" × 1 7/8". Mitre each end, as you did in **(C)**.

(E) SIDE APRON (Cut 2): 1/8" × 3/8" × 7/8". Mitre each end, as you did in **(C)**.

(F) DRAWER SUPPORT (Cut 1): 1/8" × 5/8" × 1 1/4".

(G) LEGS (Cut 4): 1/8" diameter wood dowel × 1 7/8". See Figure **5-I-6** for the shape. Refer to **1-C-3-a**.

(H) LEG STRETCHER (Cut 1): 1/8" diameter wood dowel × 1 3/4". See Figure **5-I-7** for the shape. Refer to **1-C-3-a**.

ASSEMBLY: Stain all wood before glueing.

1. Refer to Figure **5-I-3** for the assembly of the apron front, back and sides. The mitred edges are glued together. Be sure it is squared. Glue the drawer support (**F**) between the front and back apron boards (*even with the drawer opening*) with the bottom edges flush. See Figure **5-I-1** (*the dotted lines in this diagram*).

2. See Figure **5-I-2.** Glue the peg end of the legs into the holes in the top of the two feet. Glue the leg stretcher in the hole in the side of each foot. Glue this assembly beneath the four corners of the apron.

3. Glue the top moulding centered atop the top surface of the table top. Glue this assembly centered atop the top edges of the apron.

4. Apply a finish coat to the table and the drawer. Let dry. Attach the drawer pull.

OAK PARLOR STAND 5-J

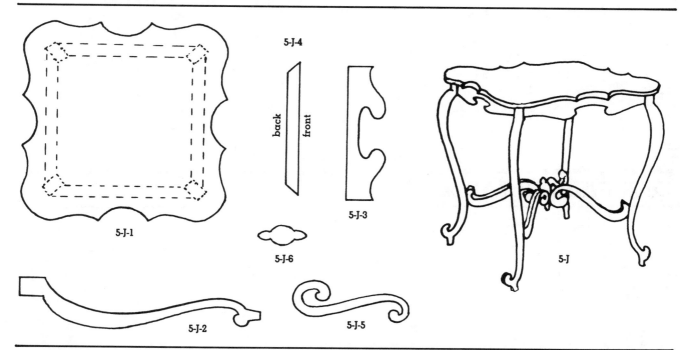

(A) TOP (Cut 1): 1/16" × 2 1/8" × 2 1/8". See Figure **5-J-1** for the shape.

(B) LEGS (Cut 4): 1/8" × 5/8" × 2 1/2". See Figure **5-J-2** for the shape.

(C) APRON (Cut 4): 1/8" × 1/2" × 1 7/16". See Figure **5-J-3** for the shape. See Figure **5-J-4** for a top view of this board showing the angles to be cut at each end.

(D) ORNAMENTAL LEG BRACES (Cut 4): 1/16" × 1/2" × 1 1/4". See Figure **5-J-5** for the shape.

(E) CENTRAL BRACE ORNAMENT (Cut 1): 3/16" diameter wood dowel × 1/2". See Figure **5-J-6** for the shape. Refer to **1-C-3-a.**

ASSEMBLY: Stain all wood before glueing. Refer to Figures **5-J** and **5-J-1.**

1. The broken lines in Figure **5-J-1** represent a top view of the assembly of the four legs and the four apron pieces. Glue these pieces together as indicated.

2. Glue the top board atop the top edges of the apron pieces and the legs, with equal overhang.

3. Glue the ornamental leg braces against the inside surface of each leg 3/4" above the floor line. The opposite ends of the leg braces are glued against the central brace ornament. Be sure the table stands straight and level.

4. Apply a finish coat.

OAK JARDINIERE STAND 5-K

(A) TOP (Cut 1): 1/16" × 1 1/4" × 1 1/4". See Figure **5-K-1** for the shape.

(B) LEGS (Cut 6): 1/16" × 9/16" × 1 3/4". See Figure **5-K-2** for the shape. Drill 1/16" diameter holes through the wood at the sites of the two circles in the diagram. Figure **5-K-3** shows a top view of this piece of wood with angles at each side. As you see, the angles go toward the back.

ASSEMBLY: Stain all wood before glueing. Refer to Figures **5-K** and **5-K-4.**

1. Glue the six legs together, with the mitred edges joining.

2. Glue the top atop the top edge of the six legs, with a 1/16" overhang on all edges.

3. Apply a finish coat.

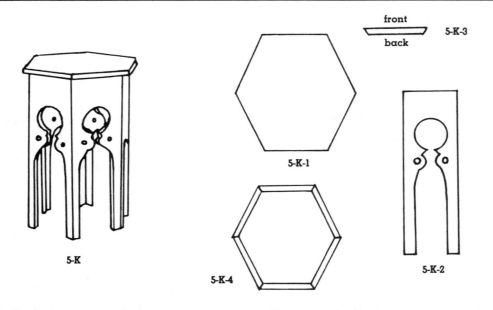

5-K 5-K-1 5-K-2 5-K-3 5-K-4

front
back

OAK PARLOR TABLE 5-L

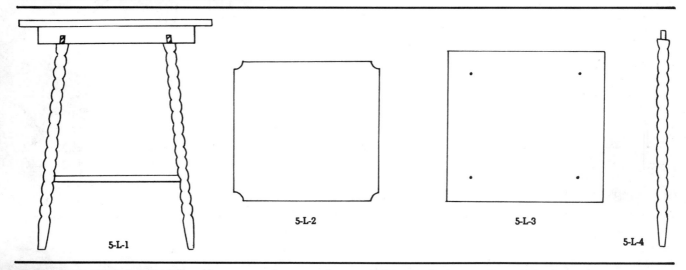

5-L-1 5-L-2 5-L-3 5-L-4

(A) TABLE TOP BASE (Cut 1): 3/16″ × 1 5/8″ × 1 5/8″. Drill four 1/16″ diameter holes at the sites of the black dots in Figure **5-L-3**. Drill these holes at the angles of the legs in Figure **5-L-1**.

(B) TABLE TOP (Cut 1): 1/16″ × 2″ × 2″.

(C) LEGS (Cut 4): 1/8″ diameter wood dowel × 2 3/8″. See Figure **5-L-4** for the shape. Refer to **1-C-3-a**.

(D) SHELF (Cut 1): 1/16″ × 1 1/2″ × 1 1/2″. See Figure **5-L-2** for the shape.

ASSEMBLY: Stain all wood before glueing.

1. Glue the legs up into the holes drilled into the table top base. Refer to **5-L-1**. Glue the shelf between the legs at the level indicated in this diagram. Be sure that this assembly sits straight and level.

2. Glue the table top atop the top base, with equal overhang on all sides.

3. Apply a finish coat.

OAK PILLAR TABLE 5-M

(A) LOWER DISC (Cut 2): 1/4″ × 1 3/4″ × 3 1/2″. See Figure **5-M-1** for the shape. Stain the wood and glue the two pieces butted together to form a circular disc.

(B) TOP (Cut 2): 1/16″ × 2″ × 4″. See Figure **5-M-2** for the shape. Stain the wood and glue the two pieces butted together to form a circular disc.

(C) PILLAR (Cut 1): 1/4″ × 1/4″ × 1 5/8″.

(D) PILLAR FACING (Cut 1): 1/16″ thick × 3/8″ diameter disc.

(E) PILLAR ORNAMENT (One): Wooden collar

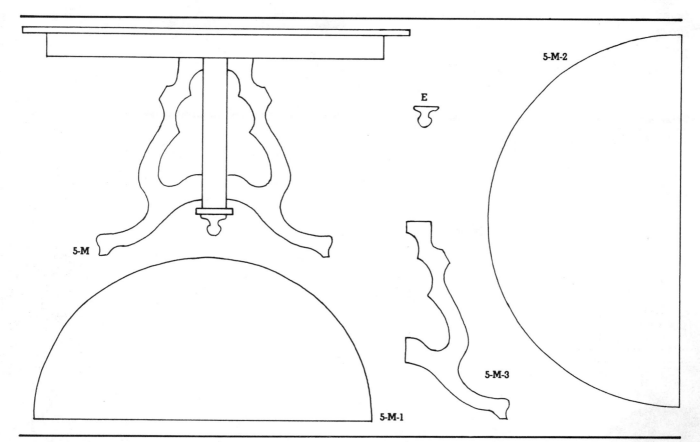

button or similar shaped ornament.

(F) LEG (Cut 4): 1/8″ × 1 1/8″ × 2 1/8″. See Figure **5-M-3** for the shape.

ASSEMBLY: Stain all wood before glueing.

1. Glue the lower disc centered on the reverse side of the top, with all overhang equal.

2. Glue the pillar facing centered on the bottom end of the pillar. Glue the pillar ornament centered on the bottom surface of the pillar facing. Glue this pillar assembly centered on the bottom surface of the lower disc.

3. Glue a leg against each side surface of the pillar, with the top edge of each leg glued against the bottom surface of the lower disc.

4. Apply a finish coat to the table.

PARLOR TABLE 5-N

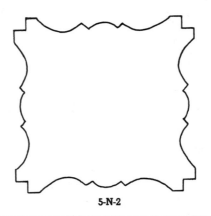

(A) TABLE TOP (Cut 1): 1/8″ × 2″ × 2″. Refer to Figure **5-N-1** for the shaping of the edges.

(B) LEGS (Cut 4): 1/8″ × 5/16″ × 1 7/8″. Refer to Figure **5-N-3** for the shape and **1-C-3-d** for aid in carving.

(C) SHELF (Cut 1): 1/16″ × 1 7/8″ × 1 7/8″. Refer to Figure **5-N-2** for the shape.

ASSEMBLY: Stain all wood before glueing.

1. The shelf is placed between the four legs at the

85

point indicated in Figure **5-N-1**. The legs fit into the notches in the four corners of the shelf.

2. The table top is glued against the top edges of the four legs. Be sure that they are equally spaced between the edges of the table and that the table is level before glueing.

3. Apply a finish coat to the table.

PIER TABLE c. 1870 5-O

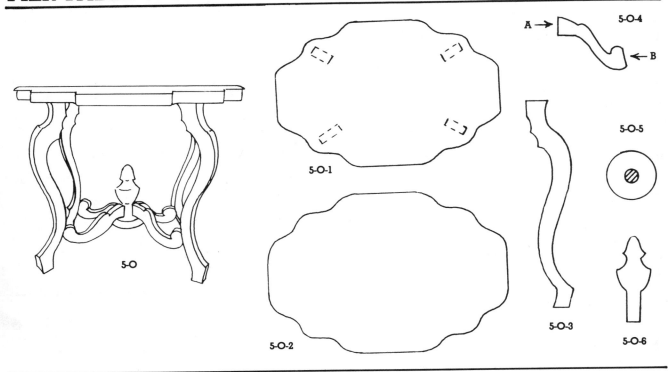

(A) TABLE TOP (Cut 1): 1/8″ × 1 9/16″ × 2 3/8″. See Figure **5-O-1** for the shape.

(B) "MARBLE" TOP (Cut 1): 1/16″ × 1 3/4″ × 2 1/2″. See Figure **5-O-2** for the shape. Bevel the top edge. Refer to **1-C-9**.

(C) LEGS (Cut 4): 1/8″ × 1/2″ × 2 1/4″. See Figure **5-O-3** for the shape.

(D) LEG SUPPORTS (Cut 4): 1/8″ × 3/8″ × 1″. See Figure **5-O-4** for the shape. As shown in this diagram, edge A fits against the center post and edge B fits against the leg.

(E) CENTER DISC (Cut 1): 1/8″ thick × 1/2″ diameter circle. Round off the top and bottom edges. Drill a 1/8″ diameter hole through the center of the disc. Refer to Figure **5-O-5**.

(F) CENTER FINIAL (Cut 1): 3/8″ diameter wood dowel × 1″. See Figure **5-O-6** for the shape. Refer to 1-C-3-a.

ASSEMBLY: Stain all wood before glueing. Paint the "marble" top.

1. Figure **5-O-1** shows the locations where the four legs are glued against the undersurface of the table top. Refer to **5-O**, which shows how the legs are placed.

2. Glue the center finial (**F**) into the hole in the center disc (**E**) with the bottom edges flush.

3. End A of each leg support is glued atop the center disc and against the post of the center finial. End B of each leg support is glued (*at the same level*) against the center surface of each leg. Refer to Figure **5-O**.

4. Glue the "marble" top atop the top surface of the table top.

5. Apply a finish coat.

EARLY AMERICAN TIP-TOP TABLE 5-P

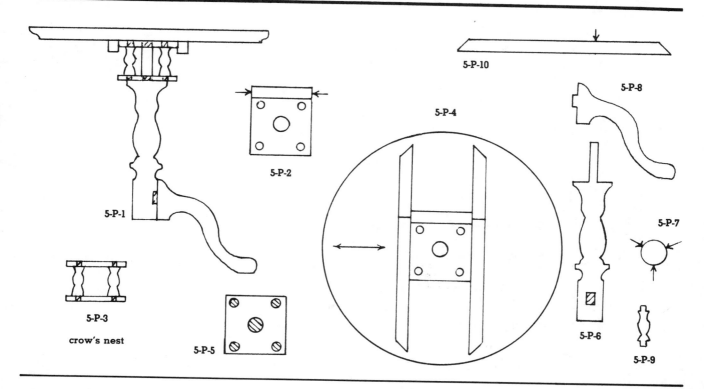

(A) TOP (Cut 1): 1/8″ thick × 2 1/2″ diameter. See Figure **5-P-4**. See Figure **5-P-1** for the shaping of the edge.

(B) PEDESTAL (Cut 1): 3/8″ diameter wood dowel × 1 15/16″. See Figure **5-P-6** for the shape. Refer to **1-C-3-a** for aid in shaping. The shaded area in this diagram represents a mortise hole 1/16″ deep. See Figure **5-P-7**. The arrows in this diagram show the three points where the three mortise holes must be cut.

(C) LEGS (Cut 3): 1/8″ × 1″ × 1 1/8″. See Figure **5-P-8** for the shape. Round off the front edges.

(D) CROW'S NEST—TOP AND BOTTOM (Cut 2): 1/16″ × 5/8″ × 5/8″. See Figure **5-P-5**. Drill four 1/16″ diameter holes and one 5/32″ diameter hole in the center. These holes are drilled through each piece of wood.

(E) PIVOTING BLOCK (Cut 1): 1/8″ × 1/8″ × 5/8″. Round off one top side edge.

(F) POSTS (Cut 4): 1/8″ diameter wood dowel × 7/16″. See Figure **5-P-9** for the shape. Refer to **1-C-3-a**.

(G) TABLE TOP BRACES (Cut 2): 1/8″ × 1/8″ × 2 1/4″. See Figure **5-P-10** for the shape. The arrow in the diagram indicates the area where a tiny pin will be pushed through the side of each board.

ASSEMBLY: Stain all wood before glueing.

1. Glue the posts (**F**) in the 1/16″ diameter holes in the crow's nest top and bottom boards, with the top and bottom edges flush. See Figure **5-P-3**.

2. Glue the pivoting block (**E**) against an edge of the top crow's nest board, with the top edges flush and the rounded edge toward the outside and at the top. See Figure **5-P-2**.

3. Glue the three legs into the mortise holes in the lower portion of the pedestal.

4. Apply a finish coat to the pedestal assembly, the top braces, the crow's nest and the table top board.

5. See Figure **5-P-4**. Using this diagram as a placement guide, place the crow's nest (*top surface downward*) and the top brace boards atop the diagram. Push a tiny sequin pin through the outside surface of the brace board and into the end surface of the pivoting block. Repeat for the other side.

6. Again, using Figure **5-P-4** as your guide, glue the top surfaces of the two braces against the table top. *Do not glue any part of the crow's nest to the table top.*

7. Drop the crow's nest over the top portion of the pedestal. *Do not glue.* The table top will now tip and turn around.

COLONIAL HIGH POST BED 6-A

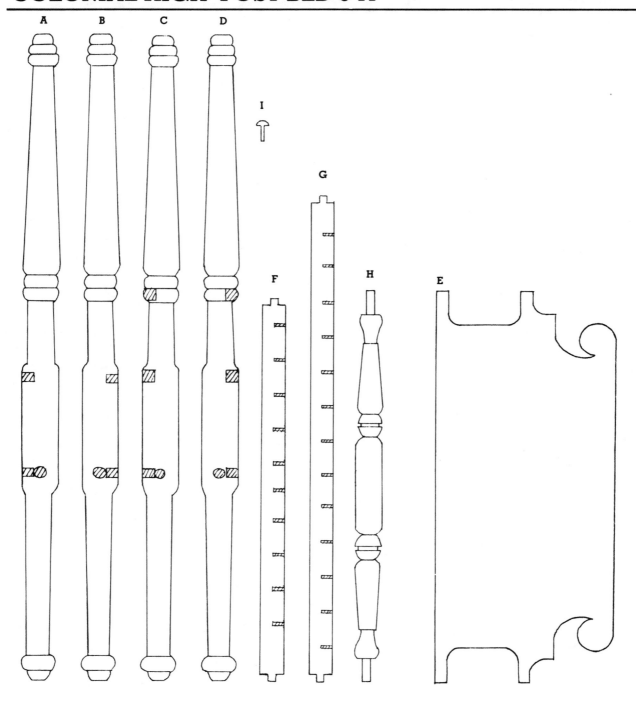

(A) POSTS (Cut 4): 3/8" × 3/8" × 7". See Figure **A** for the shape. Refer to **1-C-3-a.**

    (1) **POSTS A AND B:** The shaded circle indicates a 1/8"diameter hole to be drilled 1/8" deep. The shaded areas on the side of the post indicate 1/8" diameter holes to be drilled 1/8" deep. See Figures **A** and **B.**

    (2) **POSTS C AND D:** The shaded circle indicates a 1/8" diameter hole to be drilled 1/8" deep. The shaded top and middle areas indicate mortise cuts to be made in these locations 1/8" × 1/8" × 1/8" in-

to the posts. The lower side shaded area indicates a 1/8" diameter hole to be drilled 1/8" deep. See Figures **C** and **D.**

(B) BLANKET ROLL (Cut 1): 1/4" diameter wood dowel × 4 1/4". See Figure **H** for the shape. Refer to **1-C-3-a.**

(C) HEADBOARD (Cut 1): 1/8" × 1 7/8" × 4 1/4". See Figure **E** for the shape.

(D) HEAD AND FOOT RAIL (Cut 2): 1/4" × 1/4" × 4 3/16". See Figure **F** for the shape. Drill 1/32" diameter holes 1/8″ deep at the sites indicated by the shaded areas in the diagram.

(E) SIDE RAILS (Cut 2): 1/4″ × 1/4″ × 5 5/16″. See Figure **G** for the shape. Drill 1/32″ diameter holes 1/8″ deep at the sites indicated by the shaded areas in the diagram.

(F) PEGS (Cut 46): 1/8″ diameter wood dowel ×

1/4″. See Figure **I** for the shape. Refer to **1-C-3-a**.

ASSEMBLY: Stain all wood before glueing.

1. Refer to **2-D** for assembly.

2. Glue the pegs in the holes drilled in the top surface of the bed rails. Apply a finish coat.

3. Rope the bed. Refer to **1-C-10**.

FIELD BED 6-B

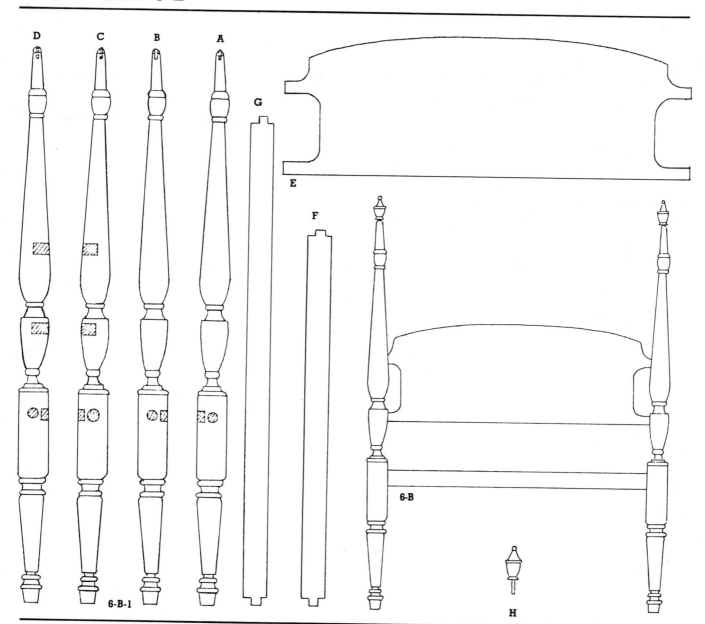

(A) POSTS (Cut 4): 5/16″ diameter wood dowel × 6″. See Figure **6-B-1-A** for the shape. Refer to **1-C-3-a**.

(1) **POSTS A AND B:** Drill a 1/8″ diameter hole 1/16″ deep at the site of the shaded circle in the diagrams. Drill a 1/8″ diameter hole 1/16″ deep at the sites of the shaded areas in the side of each post. Drill

a 1/32″ diameter hole 1/8″ deep in the top of each post. See Figures **A** and **B**.

(2) **POSTS C AND D:** Drill a 1/8″ diameter hole 1/16″ deep at the site of the shaded circle. Drill a 1/8″ diameter hole 1/16″ deep at the site of the lower shaded side area. Cut two mortise cuts (*upper and middle shaded area*) into the posts 1/8″ × 1/8″ × 1/8″. Drill

a 1/32" diameter hole 1/8" deep in the top of each post. See Figures **C** and **D**.

(B) HEADBOARD (Cut 1): 1/8" × 1 1/2" × 4 1/4". See Figure **E** for the shape.

(C) SIDE RAILS (Cut 2): 1/4" × 1/4" × 4 1/16". See Figure **G** for the shape.

(D) HEAD AND FOOT RAILS (Cut 2): 1/4" × 1/4" × 5 5/16". See Figure **F** for the shape.

(E) FINIALS (Cut 4): 3/16" diameter wood dowel × 1/2". See Figure **H** for the shape. *Note:* Two sized beads glued together could be used in place of each finial.

(F) SIDE SLAT SUPPORTS (Cut 2): 1/8" × 1/8" × 5".

(G) BED SLATS (Cut 5): 1/16" × 1/4" × 3 3/4".

ASSEMBLY: Stain all wood before glueing.

1. Refer to **2-D**.

2. Glue the slat supports against the inside surface of the side rails, with the bottom edges flush. Glue the five slats evenly spaced atop the slat support boards.

3. Glue the finials into the holes in the top surface of the bed posts. *Note:* If you choose to use a bead assembly, these beads will have to be painted a color to match the wood in the bed before glueing in place.

4. Apply a finish coat to the bed.

LOW POST SINGLE BED 6-C

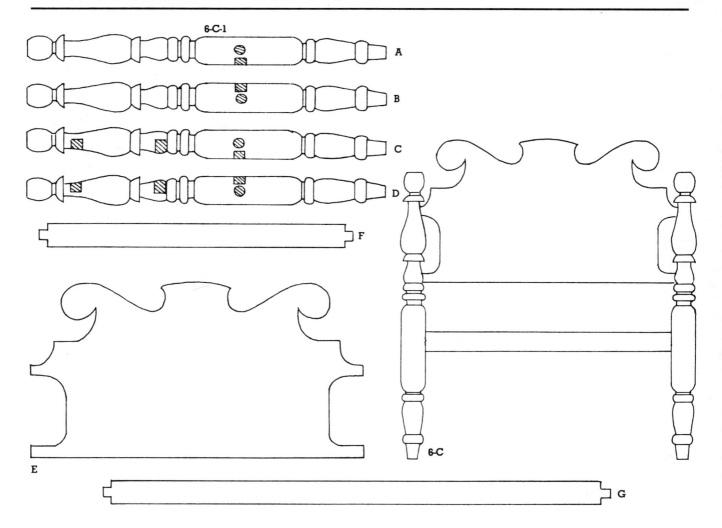

(A) POSTS (Cut 4): 5/16" diameter wood dowel × 3 3/4". See Figure **6-C-1** for the shape. Refer to **1-C-3-a**.

    (1) **POSTS A AND B:** Drill a 1/8" diameter hole 1/16" in depth at the site of the shaded circle in the diagram. Drill a 1/8" diameter hole 1/16" in depth at the site of the shaded side area of the diagram.

    (2) **POSTS C AND D:** Drill a 1/8" diameter hole 1/16" in depth at the site of the shaded circle in the diagram. Drill a 1/8" diameter hole 1/16" in depth at

the site of the shaded side area (*by circle*) in the diagram. Cut 1/8″ × 1/8″ × 1/8″ mortise cuts at the sites of the upper and middle shaded areas in the diagram.

(B) HEADBOARD (Cut 1): 1/8″ × 1 7/8″ × 3 1/2″. See Figure **E** for the shape.

(C) HEAD AND FOOT RAILS (Cut 2): 1/4″ × 1/4″ × 3 5/16″. See Figure **F** for the top and side view of these boards.

(D) SIDE RAILS (Cut 2): 1/4″ × 1/4″ × 5 5/16″. See

Figure **G** for the top and side view of these boards.

(E) SLAT SUPPORTS (Cut 2): 1/8″ × 1/8″ × 5″.

(F) SLATS (Cut 5): 1/16″ × 1/4″ × 3 1/8″.

ASSEMBLY: Stain all wood before glueing.

1. Refer to **2-D**.

2. Glue the slat supports against the inside surfaces of the side rails, with bottom edges flush. Glue the slats atop these supports, evenly spaced.

3. Apply a finish coat to the bed.

JENNY LIND TYPE SPOOL BED 6-D

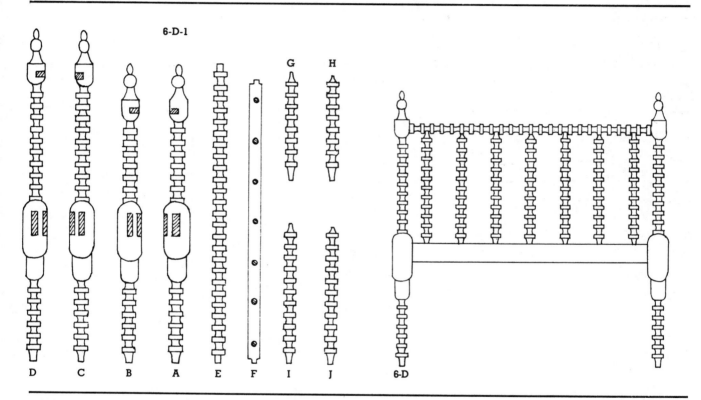

6-D-1

D C B A E F I J   6-D

There are two methods of accomplishing the spool turnings:

1. Turning the wood. Refer to **1-C-3-a**.

2. Stringing wooden beads on stiff wire to the diameter and length of each section of the turnings. The ends of the stiff wire would then be anchored in the turned portions of the posts.

The following measurements are for the turned pieces of wood. If you prefer to use beads, you will make your adjustments to fit.

(A) FOOT POSTS (Cut 2): 1/4″ × 1/4″ × 3 1/4″. See Figures **6-D-1-A** and **6-D-1-B** for the shape. Refer to **1-C-3-a** for turning. The shaded area in the upper post represents a 1/16″ diameter hole to be drilled 1/8″ in depth. The shaded area at the front and side of the lower post represents a mortise cut to be made at each site 1/16″ × 1/16″ × 1/4″.

(B) HEAD POSTS (Cut 2): 1/4″ × 1/4″ × 3 5/8″. See

Figures **6-D-1-C** and **6-D-1-D** for the shape. Refer to **1-C-3-a** for turning. Follow the directions in section **(A)** for the holes and mortise cuts in these posts.

(C) TOP RAIL (Cut 2): 1/8″ diameter wood dowel × 3 1/4″. Refer to **1-C-3-a** for turning.

(D) BOTTOM RAIL (Cut 2): 1/8″ × 1/4″ × 3 1/8″. See Figure **F** for a top view of the shape. Drill seven 1/16″ diameter holes 1/16″ deep at the sites of the shaded circles in this diagram.

(E) SPINDLES FOR HEADBOARD (Cut 3): 1/8″ diameter wood dowel × 1 1/2″. See Figure **J** for the shape.

(F) SPINDLES FOR HEADBOARD (Cut 4): 1/8″ diameter wood dowel × 1 9/16″. See Figure **I** for the shape.

(G) SPINDLES FOR FOOTBOARD (Cut 3): 1/8″ diameter wood dowel × 1 1/8″. See Figure **H** for the shape.

(H) SPINDLES FOR FOOTBOARD (Cut 4): 1/8″ diameter wood dowel × 1 3/16″. See Figure **G** for the shape.

(I) SIDE RAILS (Cut 2): 1/16″ × 1/4″ × 5 5/16″.

(J) SLAT SUPPORTS (Cut 2): 1/8″ × 1/8″ × 5″.

(K) SLATS (Cut 5): 1/8″ × 1/4″ × 3 1/8″.

ASSEMBLY: Stain all wood before glueing. Refer to **6-D.**

1. HEADBOARD: Glue the spindles into the holes in the top surface of the bottom rail as follows — I, J, I, J, I, J, I. Refer to Figure **6-D.** Glue the top rail atop the top surfaces of these spindles. *Note:* The longer spindles fit up between the turnings. Glue this assembly into the two head posts, with the lower mortise cuts forward.

2. FOOTBOARD: Glue the spindles into the holes in the top surface of the bottom rail as follows — G, H, G, H, G, H, G. Follow the directions in the preceding Step 1 to complete this assembly.

3. Glue the side rails into the mortise cuts (*lower*) in the head and footboard posts. Glue the slat supports against the inside surfaces of the side rails, with bottom edges flush.

4. Glue the five slats evenly spaced atop the slat support boards.

5. Apply a finish coat to the bed.

QUEEN ANNE STYLE DAYBED 6-E

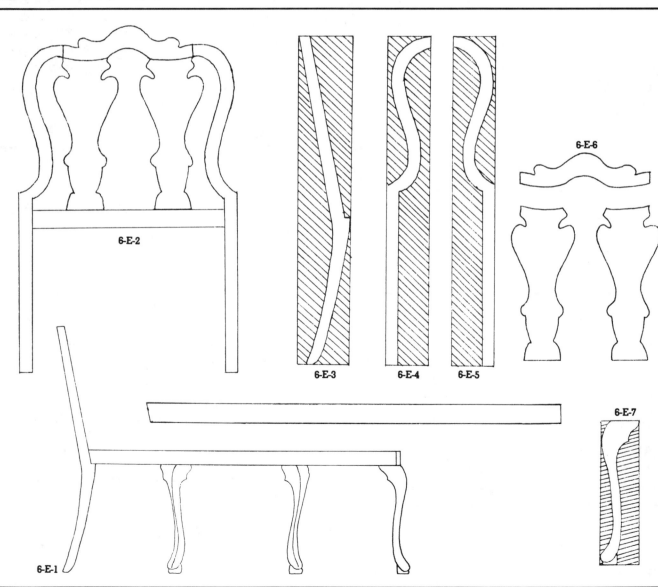

(A) HEADBOARD POSTS (Cut 2): 7/16″ × 9/16″ × 3 9/16″. See Figure **6-E-3** (*side view*) for the initial shaping of each board.

    (1) **LEFT POST:** See Figure **6-E-4** (*front view*) for the final shaping of this post.

    (2) **RIGHT POST:** See Figure **6-E-5** (*front view*) for the final shaping of this post.

(B) CENTER-TOP HEADBOARD (Cut 1): 1/8″ × 3/8″ × 1 3/8″. See the top diagram in Figure **6-E-6** for the shape.

(C) BACK BANNISTERS (Cut 2): 1/16″ × 11/16″ × 1 11/16″. See the lower diagrams in Figure **6-E-6** for the shape.

(D) HEADBOARD BRACE (Cut 1): 1/8″ × 3/16″ × 2″.

(E) LEGS (Cut 6): 7/16″ × 7/16″ × 1 9/16″. See Figure **6-E-7** for the shape. Refer to **1-C-3-d** for aid in carving. *Note:* Most miniature supply stores carry pre-cut wood cabriole legs. You may choose to use these commercially made legs; if so, adjust the length of the headboard posts to correspond to the length of the commercial legs.

(F) SIDE BED FRAME (Cut 2): 1/8″ × 3/16″ × 4 5/16″. See Figure **6-E-6** for the side view of this board. Cut the angle at one end of each board.

(G) END BED FRAME (Cut 1): 1/16″ × 3/16″ × 2 5/16″.

(H) BED SLAT SUPPORTS (Cut 2): 1/16″ × 1/16″ × 4 1/8″.

(I) BED SLATS (Cut 5): 1/16″ × 1/4″ × 2″.

ASSEMBLY: Stain all wood before glueing. Refer to Figures **6-E-1** and **6-E-2**.

1. Refer to Figure **6-E-2**. Assemble the headboard, as shown in this diagram. Glue the center-top piece between the two side posts. Let the glue dry. Glue the bannisters atop the headboard brace, and glue this assembly in place. Let dry.

2. Refer to Figure **6-E-1**. Glue the angled ends of the side frame boards in place against the headboard posts. Glue the end bed frame board across the two ends of the side frame boards.

3. Glue the slat support boards against the inside surfaces of the side frame boards, with bottom edges flush. Glue the five slats atop the support boards, evenly spaced. Be sure this assembly is squared.

4. Glue a leg at the corner of the foot of the bed, beneath the bed frame, and pointing angled out to the corner. Repeat for the second leg. Glue the remaining four legs (*two each side, evenly spaced*) beneath the bed frame and pointing forward from the side. See Figure **6-E-1**.

5. Apply a finish coat to the daybed.

WAGON CHAIR TYPE DAYBED
c. MID EIGHTEENTH CENTURY 6-F

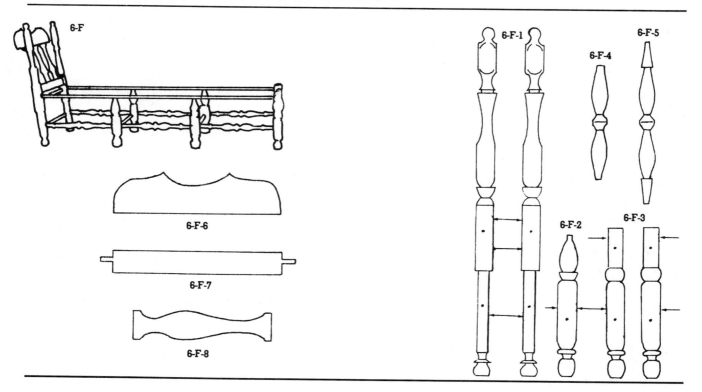

6-F

6-F-6

6-F-7

6-F-8

6-F-1

6-F-4

6-F-5

6-F-2

6-F-3

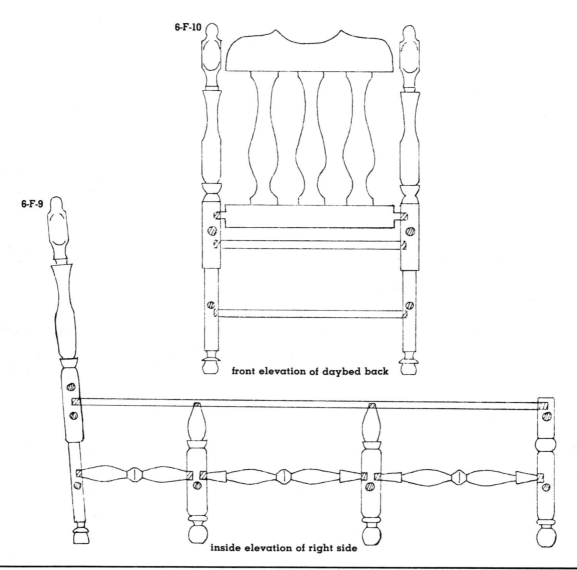

6-F-10

6-F-9

front elevation of daybed back

inside elevation of right side

(A) BACK POSTS (Cut 2): 3/16″ diameter wood dowel × 3 3/4″. See Figure **6-F-1** for the shape. Drill 1/16″ diameter holes 1/16″ deep at the sites of the black dots and arrows in the diagram. Refer to **1-C-3-a** for aid in shaping.

(B) FRONT POSTS (Cut 2): 3/16″ diameter wood dowel × 1 5/8″. See Figure **6-F-3** for the shape. Drill 1/16″ diameter holes 1/16″ deep at the sites of the black dots and arrows in the diagram. Refer to **1-C-3-a** for aid in shaping.

(C) CENTER POSTS (Cut 4): 3/16″ diameter wood dowel × 1 1/2″. See Figure **6-F-2** for the shape. Drill 1/16″ diameter holes 1/16″ deep at the sites of the two arrows and black dot in the diagram. Refer to **1-C-3-a**.

(D) LONG SIDE LEG STRETCHERS (Cut 4): 3/16″ diameter wood dowel × 1 3/4″. See Figure **6-F-5** for the shape. Refer to **1-C-3-a**.

(E) SHORT SIDE LEG STRETCHERS (Cut 2): 3/16″ diameter wood dowel × 1 1/4″. See Figure **6-F-4** for the shape. Refer to **1-C-3-a**.

(F) CENTER STRETCHERS (Cut 6): 1/16″ diameter wood dowel × 2″.

(G) SIDE FRAME (Cut 2): 1/8″ × 3/16″ × 5″ long (*including 1/16″ × 1/16″ × 1/16″ shaped peg carved into each end of the board*). Drill a 1/16″ diameter hole 1/16″ deep 1 5/16″ from the extreme end of the board, and another 3 1/8″ from the same end of the board.

(H) TOP BACK SLAT (Cut 1): 1/8″ × 7/16″ × 1 3/4″. See Figure **6-F-6** for the shape.

(I) LOWER BACK SLAT (Cut 1): 1/8″ × 1/4″ × 2 1/16″. See Figure **6-F-7** for the shape.

(J) BACK BANNISTERS (Cut 3): 1/8″ × 5/16″ × 1 7/16″. See Figure **6-F-8** for the shape.

(K) BED SLATS (Cut 4): 1/8″ × 1/4″ × 1 7/8″.

ASSEMBLY: Stain all wood before glueing. See Figures **6-F**, **6-F-9** and **6-F-10** for aid in the assembly.

1. Refer to Figure **6-F-10**. Glue the three back bannisters between the upper and lower back slats. Lay your pieces on top of the diagram for correct placement.

2. Refer to Figure **6-F-10**. Slip the above assembly (*do not glue*) into the upper inside hole in each long post. Glue two center stretchers into the remaining two inside holes in these posts. Be sure the assembly is squared.

3. For assembly of bed frame, refer to Figure **6-F-9**. Glue the two long side stretchers into the end post and two side posts. Lay the second set of end and side posts down with the lower hole on your work area (*this is the reverse position of your first assembly*) and glue the side stretchers in place. Glue the three center stretchers into the lower holes of all three posts; glue the opposite ends into the holes in the other assembly. Glue a center stretcher into the inside top hole of each end post, joining the two.

4. Glue an end of the side frame board into the remaining hole in the end post; glue the top pegs of the side posts into the holes in this board; glue the pegged end into the hole in the front of the back post. Repeat for the second side frame board. Be sure that this assembly is straight and level before the glue is dry.

5. Apply a finish coat to the bed.

6. Clip four brads to the desired length. Push a brad into the back (*top*) board near each edge. Tie a piece of fine twine around the head of the brad. Touch a dot of glue to each knot. Push a second brad into the back of each long post (*at the same level*). Loop the twine around the head of the second brad. The daybed back can be raised or lowered in this manner.

7. Glue the four bed slats evenly spaced between the side frame boards, with top edges flush.

WALNUT DAYBED c. LATE SEVENTEENTH CENTURY 6-G

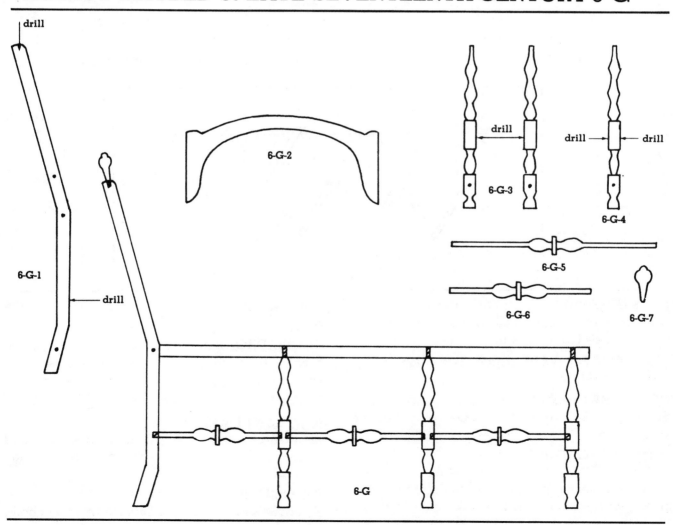

6-G-2

6-G-3

6-G-4

6-G-5

6-G-6

6-G-7

6-G-1

6-G

drill

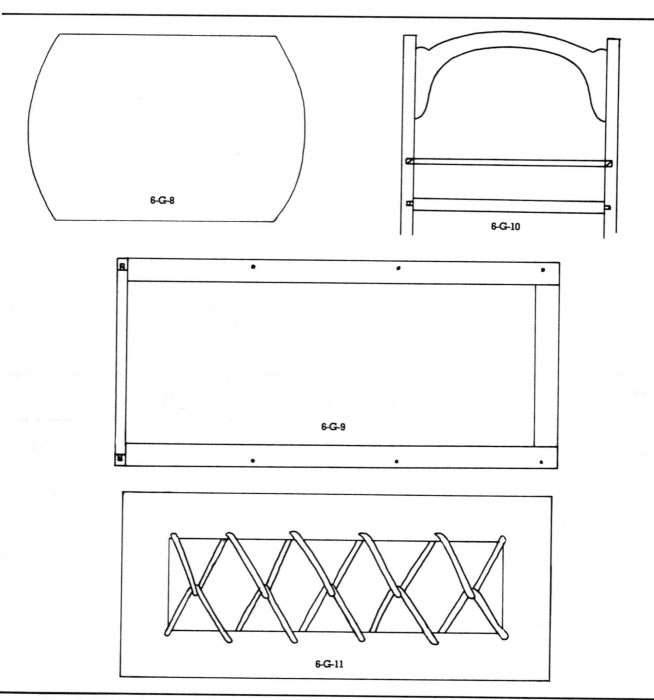

6-G-8

6-G-10

6-G-9

6-G-11

(A) **FRAME SIDE** (Cut 2): 1/8″ × 1/4″ × 4 1/2″. Drill 1/16″ diameter holes at the sites of the black dots in the diagram. See Figure **6-G-9**.

(B) **FRAME FOOT END** (Cut 1): 1/8″ × 1/4″ × 1 3/4″. See Figure **6-G-9**.

(C) **FRAME HEAD END** (Cut 1): 1/8″ × 1/8″ × 2 1/8″. See Figure **6-G-10** for the shaped ends forming pegs.

(D) **HEAD POSTS** (Cut 2): 1/8″ × 1/8″ × 3 1/2″. See Figure **6-G-1** for the shape to be cut. Drill 1/16″ diameter holes on the inside surfaces of these two posts. The black dots indicate these holes. Drill 1/16″

diameter holes at the sites of the two arrows in the diagram.

(E) **HEADBOARD** (Cut 1): See Figure **6-G-2** for the shape to be cut from a board 1/8″ in thickness.

(F) **UPHOLSTERY STRETCHER - IN HEADBOARD** (Cut 1): 1/16″ diameter wood dowel × 2 1/8″.

(G) **FRONT LEGS** (Cut 2): 1/8″ × 1/8″ × 1 3/4″. See Figure **6-G-3** for the shape. Drill 1/16″ diameter holes at the sites of the black dots and arrows in the diagram.

(H) **CENTER LEGS** (Cut 4): 1/8″ × 1/8″ × 1 3/4″. See Figure **6-G-4** for the shape. Drill 1/16″ diameter holes at the sites of the black dots and arrows in the diagram.

(I) LEG STRETCHERS

(1) **LEG STRETCHERS** (Cut 4): 1/8" diameter wood dowel × 2 1/8". See Figure **6-G-5** for the shape.

(2) **LEG STRETCHERS** (Cut 4): 1/8" diameter wood dowel × 1 1/2". See Figure **6-G-6** for the shape.

(3) **LEG STRETCHERS** (Cut 2): 1/8" diameter wood dowel × 1 3/8". See Figure **6-G-6** for the shape.

(J) FINIAL (Cut 2): 3/16" diameter wood dowel × 3/8". See Figure **6-G-7** for the shape.

(K) CLOTH UPHOLSTERY FOR BACK: See Figure **6-G-8** for the shape.

(L) CLOTH UPHOLSTERY FOR "SPRING": See Figure **6-G-11** for the shape.

ASSEMBLY: Be sure to stain all wood before glueing.

1. Figure **6-G-9** shows the top elevation of the assembly of pieces forming the frame. Glue the side and foot end pieces together as shown.

2. The legs are inserted into the holes in the frame. The side stretchers insert into the sides of the legs and the four long stretchers join the legs at both sides.

3. The headboard piece is glued between the head posts; the upholstery stretcher is glued into the two holes beneath the headboard. The finials are glued into the holes at the top of these posts. See Figures **6-G** and **6-G-10**.

4. The rounded end of the cloth upholstery glues against the front of the headboard, around the upholstery stretcher, and up against the reverse side of the headboard.

5. The cloth upholstery for the spring is glued atop the frame. When the glue is thoroughly dry, lace the inside cut-out area together, as shown in Figure **6-G-11**. *Note:* This piece and the back upholstery piece are applied after the piece of furniture has had its finish coat.

VICTORIAN PERIOD SPOOL CRIB c. 1865-1870 6-H

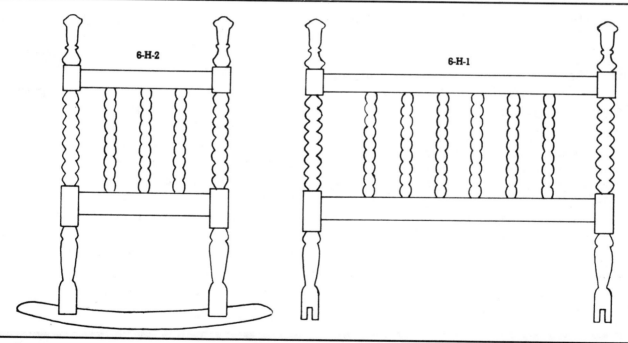

6-H-2

6-H-1

(A) POST (Cut 2): 3/16" × 3/16" × 3 1/4". See Figure **6-H-3** for the shape. Refer to **1-C-3-a**. The shaded areas in the post represent mortise cuts 1/16" × 1/16" × 1/8". The notches in the side of the post represent mortise cuts of the same dimension and in the same position in this side of the post.

(B) POST (Cut 2): 3/16" × 3/16" × 3 1/4". See Figure **6-H-4**. Follow directions for mortise cuts in (**A**).

(C) TOP SIDE RAILS (Cut 2): 1/8" × 3/16" × 3". Drill

1/16" diameter holes 1/16" deep at the sites of the arrows in Figure **6-H-6**, which also shows the shape.

(D) BOTTOM SIDE RAILS (Cut 2): 1/8" × 1/4" × 3". Follow directions for drilling holes in (**C**). See Figure **6-H-5** for the shape.

(E) TOP END RAILS (Cut 2): 1/8" × 3/16" × 1 1/2". See Figure **6-H-7** for the shape. Follow directions for drilling holes in (**C**).

(F) BOTTOM END RAILS (Cut 2): 1/8" × 1/4" × 1

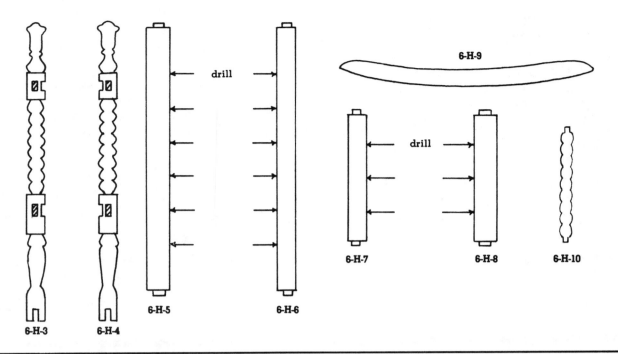

6-H-3   6-H-4   6-H-5   6-H-6   6-H-9   6-H-7   6-H-8   6-H-10

1/2". See Figure **6-H-8** for the shape. Follow directions for drilling holes in (**C**).

(G) SPINDLES (Cut 18): 1/8" diameter wood dowel × 1 1/4". See Figure **6-H-10** for the shape. Refer to 1-C-3-a.

(H) ROCKERS (Cut 2): 1/16" × 1/4" × 2 11/16" (*with the grain*). See Figure **6-H-9** for the shape.

(I) SLAT SUPPORTS (Cut 2): 1/8" × 1/8" × 2 7/8".

(J) SLATS (Cut 3): 1/16" × 1/4" × 1 1/2".
Note: The spool-turning portions of this crib can be accomplished with an alternate method. Select wood beads approximately the size of the turnings, string them on a stiff wire to the various lengths of the turnings. The ends of the stiff wire will insert into the carved portions of the posts.

ASSEMBLY: Stain all wood before glueing.

1. SIDE RAILS: Refer to Figure **6-H-1**. Glue six spindles into the holes in the bottom rail. Glue the ends of the spindles into the holes in the top rail. Be sure this assembly is squared. Repeat for the second side rail.

2. END RAILS: Refer to Figure **6-H-2**. Glue three spindles into the bottom rail. Glue the ends of the spindles into the top rail. Be sure this assembly is squared. Repeat for the second end rail.

3. Glue an end rail assembly into a set of posts: one **6-H-3** and one **6-H-4**. Repeat this process for the second end assembly.

4. Glue a side rail assembly between the two end assemblies. Repeat for the second side rail assembly. Be sure that the assembled bed sits straight and is squared.

5. Glue a slat support against the inside surface of each bottom side rail, with bottom edges flush. Glue the three slats atop the slat supports evenly spaced.

6. Glue a rocker up into the slot at the bottom of each set of end posts. See Figure **6-H-2**.

7. Apply a finish coat to the crib.

VICTORIAN YOUTH BEDSTEAD 6-I

(A) HEADBOARD (Cut 1): 1/16" × 2 1/2" × 3 3/16". See Figure **6-I-3** for the shape.

(B) HEADBOARD MOULDING

(1) **TOP** (Cut 1): 1/16" × 7/8" × 3". See Figure **6-I-4** for the shape.

(2) **SIDE** (Cut 2): 1/16" × 1/4" × 1 5/8". See Figure **6-I-5** for a 45° angle cut at one end.

(3) **BOTTOM** ((Cut 1): 1/16" × 1/4" × 3". See Figure **6-I-6** for 45° angle cuts at either end.

(4) **CENTER** (Cut 1): 1/16" × 1/4" × 1 5/8".

(5) **DECORATION** (Cut 1): 1/16" × 3/8" × 1/2". See Figure **6-I-15** for the shape.

(6) **BONNET** (Cut 1): 1/16" × 1/4" × 2 3/8". *Note:* This piece will be steamed and bent just prior to its assembly.

(C) HEADPOSTS (Cut 2): 3/16" diameter wood

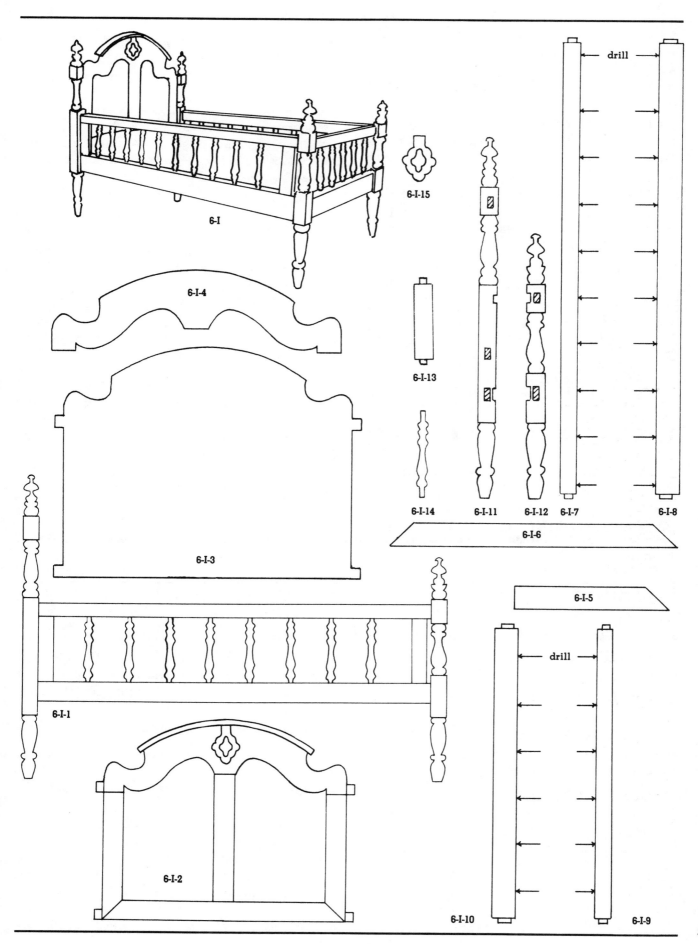

6-I

6-I-15

6-I-4

6-I-13

6-I-3

6-I-14   6-I-11   6-I-12   6-I-7   6-I-8

6-I-6

6-I-5

drill

drill

6-I-1

6-I-2

6-I-10   6-I-9

dowel × 3 7/8". See Figure **6-I-11** for the shape. Refer to **1-C-3-a**. The shaded areas represent mortise cuts 1/16" × 1/16" × 1/8" to be made at these sites in each post. The notched side of the post represents two similar cuts on one side only. Reverse these cuts for the second post.

(D) FOOTPOSTS (Cut 2): 3/16" diameter wood dowel × 2 7/8". Refer to **1-C-3-a** for shaping. See Figure **6-I-12** for the shape. Follow the directions in **(C)** for cutting the mortise holes in these posts.

(E) TOP SIDE RAILS (Cut 2): 1/8" × 3/16" × 4 15/16". See Figure **6-I-7** for the shape. The arrows in the diagram indicate sites of 1/16" diameter holes to be drilled 1/16" in depth.

(F) BOTTOM SIDE RAILS (Cut 2): 1/8" × 1/4" × 4 15/16". See Figure **6-I-8** for the shape. Follow directions in **(E)**.

(G) TOP END RAIL (Cut 1): 1/8" × 3/16" × 3 3/16". See Figure **6-I-9** for the shape. Follow directions in **(E)**.

(H) BOTTOM END RAIL (Cut 1): 1/8" × 1/4" × 3 3/16". See Figure **6-I-10** for the shape. Follow directions in **(E)**.

(I) SIDE POSTS (Cut 4): 1/8" × 3/16" × 15/16". See Figure **6-I-13** for the shape.

(J) SPINDLES (Cut 22): 1/8" diameter wood dowel × 15/16". See Figure **6-I-14** for the shape. Refer to **1-C-3-a**.

(K) SLAT SUPPORTS (Cut 2): 1/16" × 1/16" × 4 3/4".

(L) SLATS (Cut 4): 1/16" × 1/4" × 3 1/8".

ASSEMBLY: Stain all wood before glueing.

1. **HEADBOARD:** Figure **6-I-2** shows the assembled headboard. Refer to **1-C-6**. Steam the bonnet piece (**B-6**) while assembling the headboard. Glue the moulding pieces against the headboard. When the bonnet piece can be bent without breaking, glue atop the top arched edge of the headboard, with back edges flush. Secure with sequin pins (*to hold only while drying*) and rubber bands.

2. **SIDE RAILS:** See Figure **6-I-1**. Glue a side post into each end hole. Glue eight spindles into the remaining holes in the bottom rail. Glue the side posts and spindles into the top rail. Repeat this assembly for the second side rail. Be sure this assembly remains squared.

3. **END RAILS:** Refer to Figure **6-I-1** as your guide. Glue six spindles into the holes in the bottom rail. Glue the top ends of the spindles into the top rail. Be sure this assembly remains squared.

4. Refer to **2-D**.

5. Glue the slat supports against the inside surface of each side rail, with bottom edges flush. Glue the slats atop these support boards evenly spaced.

6. When the bonnet portion of the headboard is dry and is glued securely, remove the pins. Cut the rubber bands and remove them.

7. Apply a finish coat.

OAK BED 6-J

(A) HEAD POST (Cut 2): 1/4" × 1/4" × 5 7/8". Round off the top surface.

(B) APPLIED MOULDING (Cut 6): 1/8" × 1/4" × 4".

(C) APPLIED MOULDING (Cut 5): 1/16" × 1/2" × 4".

(D) APPLIED MOULDING (Cut 1): 1/16" × 3/4" × 4".

(E) HEADBOARD TOP (Cut 1): 1/16" × 2" × 4". See Figure **6-J-3** for the shape.

(F) FOOT POST (Cut 2): 1/4" × 1/4" × 2 3/4".

(G) SIDE BOARD (Cut 2): 1/8" × 1" × 5 1/2". See Figure **6-J-4** for the shape.

(H) BRACE (Cut 2): 1/8" × 1/8" × 4". This piece faces onto the inside surface of the headboard and the footboard, with bottom edges flush.

(I) BRACE (Cut 2): 1/8" × 1/8" × 5 3/8". This piece faces onto the inside surface of the side board, with bottom edges flush.

(J) FOOTBOARD TOP FINISH (Cut 1): 1/16" × 3/8" × 4 7/8". Round off all four top edges.

(K) SLAT (Cut 5): 1/8" × 1/4" × 4".

(L) CARVED TRIM FOR HEADBOARD: This carved trim will be simulated with jewelry findings of your choice to represent the carving. Refer to **1-C-5** for preparation and application.

ASSEMBLY: Stain all wood before glueing.

1. Refer to **2-D** for the general assembly of the bed after the specialized assembly has been completed.

2. **HEADBOARD ASSEMBLY:** Using Figure **6-J-1** as your guide, glue the headboard top (**E**) butted against a piece of the applied moulding (**B**), with back edges flush. Glue this assembly butted against a piece of applied moulding (**C**), with back edges flush. Continue in this manner, glueing board (**B**), then board (**C**), then board (**B**), then board (**D**) and finally board (**C**) — all with back edges flush. Let this assembly dry thoroughly. Glue a brace (**H**)

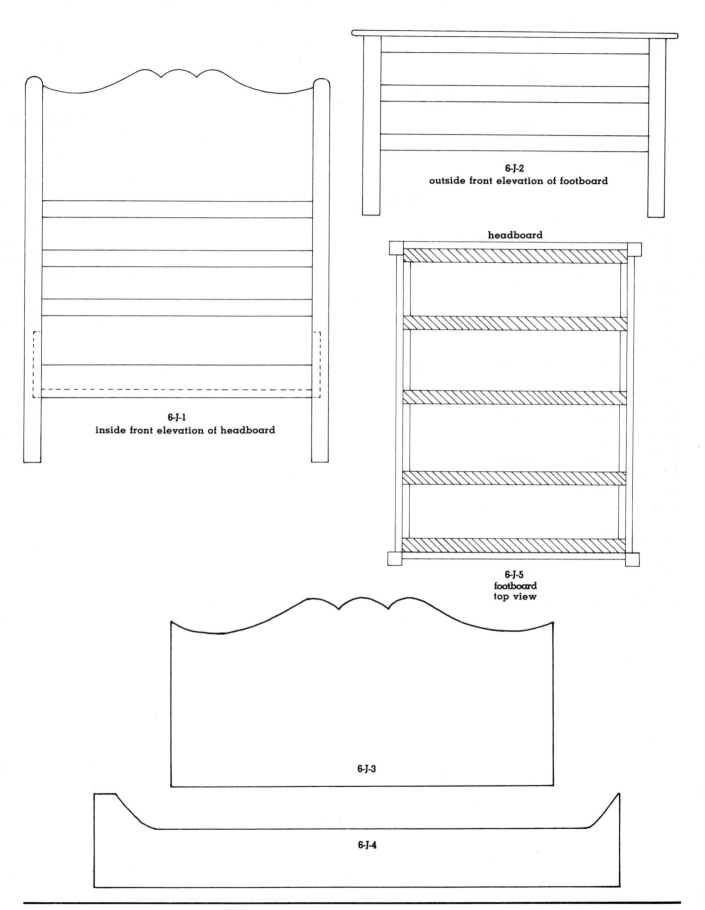

6-J-2
outside front elevation of footboard

headboard

6-J-1
inside front elevation of headboard

6-J-5
footboard
top view

6-J-3

6-J-4

against the front surface of the lower board (C), with bottom edges flush.

3. FOOTBOARD ASSEMBLY: Using Figure 6-J-2 as your guide, glue an applied moulding board (B) butted against board (C). Glue this assembly butted against another board (B), and then board (C), and then board (B) — all with back edges flush. Let this assembly dry. Glue a brace (H) against the back surface of the last board (B), with bottom edges flush. Glue the footboard top finish board (J) atop the top edge of the first board (B), with 1/8" overhang at the front and back and at both ends.

Note: The flat surface (*back edges flush*) of the headboard will be the side that would turn to the wall; the front surface will appear like applied moulding. The flat surface (*back edges flush*) of the footboard will be the back surface of this piece; the front surface will appear like applied moulding.

4. Prepare the jewelry findings as instructed in 1-C-5 and glue in place against the front surface of the headboard.

5. Glue a brace (I) against the inside surface of the two side boards (G). These will be flush with the bottom edge of the side board. The braces will support the bed slats.

6. Glue a head post (A) on either side of the assembled headboard. Refer to Figure 6-J-1.

7. Glue a foot post (F) on either side of the assembled footboard. Refer to Figure 6-J-2.

8. Refer to 2-D for the completion of the bed assembly.

9. Apply a finish coat to the bed.

10. Figure 6-J-5 shows a top view of the assembly of the bed. The shaded areas represent the bed slats.

WELSH DRESSER 7-A

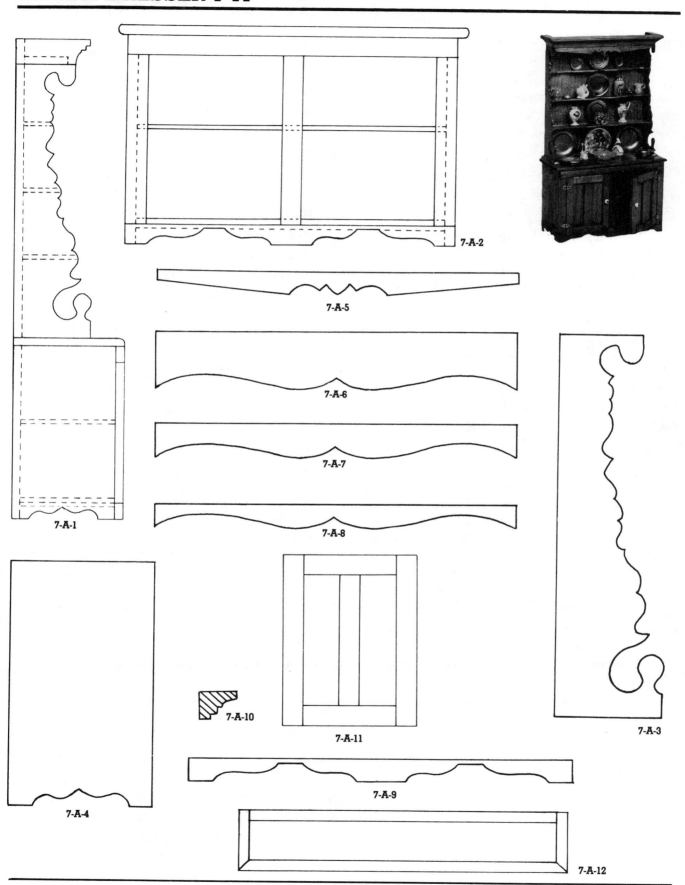

7-A-2

7-A-5

7-A-6

7-A-7

7-A-8

7-A-1

7-A-3

7-A-10

7-A-11

7-A-4

7-A-9

7-A-12

UPPER SECTION

(A) UPPER BACK (Cut 2)): 1/8″ × 1 7/8″ × 4 1/2″. Glue the two pieces butted together so the width will measure 3 3/4″.

(B) UPPER SIDES (Cut 2): 1/8″ × 1 1/8″ × 4 1/8″. See Figure **7-A-3** for the shape.

(C) TOP SHELF (Cut 1): 1/16″ × 1/4″ × 3 3/4″. See Figure **7-A-8** for the shape.

(D) MIDDLE SHELF (Cut 1): 1/16″ × 3/8″ × 3 3/4″. See Figure **7-A-7** for the shape.

(E) LOWER SHELF (Cut 1): 1/16″ × 5/8″ × 3 3/4″. See Figure **7-A-5** for the shape.

(F) TOP BOARD (Cut 1): 1/8″ × 5/8″ × 3 3/4″.

(G) TOP MOULDING: Figure **7-A-10** shows an end view of a piece of moulding which I used for this piece of furniture. It measure 1/8″ at the lower edge × 5/16″ high × 3/8″ deep. If you choose a different size moulding, allow for differences in the following measurements.

(1) **SIDES** (Cut 2): 1 1/8″ long. Mitre the front with a 45° angle. Refer to **7-A-12**.

(2) **FRONT** (Cut 1): 4 1/2″ long. Mitre both corners with a 45° angle. Refer to Figure **7-A-12**.

(H) TOP FRONT FACING (Cut 1): 1/16″ × 1/4″ × 3 3/4″. See Figure **7-A-5** for the shape.

ASSEMBLY: Refer to Figures **7-A-1** and **7-A-12**.

1. Glue the sides butted against the back, with the back edges flush.

2. Glue the top moulding side pieces atop the top surface of the side boards, and against the remainder of the back board. Glue the top board against the back board, with the lower edges flush with the lower edges of the side moulding. Glue the front moulding between the side moulding pieces and against the front edge of the top board, with bottom edges flush. Refer to Figure **7-A-12**.

3. Note the dotted lines in the top section of Figure **7-A-1**. These show the location of the top, middle and lower shelves. Glue in place. Glue the top front facing board below the lower surface of the top front moulding and between the two sides.

LOWER SECTION

(I) BACK (Cut 2): 1/8″ × 1 7/8″ × 2 5/8″. Glue the two pieces butted together so the width will measure 3 3/4″.

(J) SIDES (Cut 2): 1/8″ × 1 1/2″ × 2 5/8″. See Figure **7-A-4** for the shape.

(K) TOP (Cut 1): 1/8″ × 1 5/8″ × 4 1/4″. Sand the front and two side edges rounded.

(L) TOP FRONT FACING (Cut 1): 1/8″ × 1/4″ × 4″.

(M) SIDE FRONT FACING AND CENTER DIVIDER (Cut 3): 1/8″ × 1/4″ × 2 1/8″.

(N) BOTTOM BOARD (Cut 1): 1/8″ × 1 3/8″ × 3 3/4″.

(O) SHELF (Cut 1): 1/16″ × 1 3/8″ × 3 3/4″.

(P) LOWER FRONT FACING (Cut 1): 1/8″ × 1/4″ × 4″. See Figure **7-A-9** for the shape.

(Q) DOORS (Two)

(1) **CENTER PANEL** (Cut 2): 1/16″ × 1 1/8″ × 1 5/8″.

(2) **SIDE FRAME** (Cut 4): 1/8″ × 1/4″ × 2 1/8″.

(3) **TOP AND BOTTOM FRAME** (Cut 4): 1/8″ × 1/4″ × 1 1/8″.

(4) **CENTER MOULDING** (Cut 2): 1/16″ × 1/4″ × 1 5/8″.

(R) HINGES (Two pair): Refer to **1-B-4-d** or **1-B-4-e**.

(S) DOOR PULLS (Two): Refer to **1-B-6-d**.

ASSEMBLY: Refer to **2-C-5** and Figures **7-A-1**, **7-A-2** and **7-A-11**.

1. When the assembly has been completed for the two sections, glue the top section atop the top of the lower cabinet evenly spaced, with the back edges flush.

2. Apply the finish coat. When the finish is dry, attach the hinges to the two doors and the lower front side facing boards. Attach the two door pulls.

CHEST ON STAND 7-B

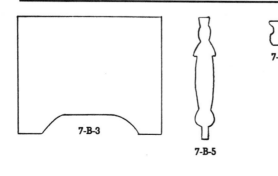

7-B-3

7-B-5

7-B-6

CHEST

(A) BACK (Cut 1): 1/8″ × 2 3/4″ × 2 7/8″.

(B) SIDES (Cut 2): 1/8″ × 1 1/2″ × 2 7/8″.

(C) TOP (Cut 1): 1/8″ × 1 1/2″ × 3″.

(D) LOWER TOP MOULDING (Cut 1): 1/8″ × 1 5/8″ × 3 1/4″. Bevel the lower side and front edges.

(E) TOP MOULDING (Cut 1): 1/16″ × 1 11/16″ × 3 3/8″. Bevel the lower side and front edges.

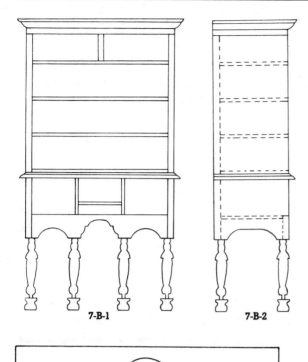

7-B-1   7-B-2

7-B-4

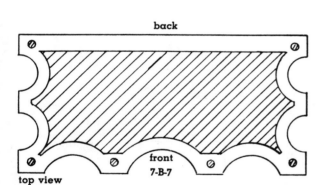

back

front
7-B-7

top view

(2) NARROW DRAWERS (Two)

    a. **FRONT AND BACK** (Cut 4): 1/16″ × 1/2″ × 1 5/16″.

    b. **SIDES** (Cut 4): 1/16″ × 1/2″ × 1 1/4″.

    c. **BOTTOM** (Cut 2): 1/8″ × 1 3/16″ × 1 1/4″.

Refer to **2-E-1** for assembly.

(I) DRAWER PULLS (Eleven): Refer to **1-B-6**.

STAND

(J) BACK (Cut 1): 1/8″ × 1 1/4″ × 2 3/4″.

(K) SIDES (Cut 2): 1/8″ × 1 1/4″ × 1 1/2″. See Figure **7-B-3** for the shape.

(L) FRONT APRON (Cut 1): 1/8″ × 1/2″ × 2 3/4″. See Figure **7-B-4** for the shape.

(M) FRONT PANEL (Cut 1): 1/8″ × 3/16″ × 7/8″.

(N) BOTTOM (Cut 1): 1/16″ × 1 1/4″ × 2 3/4″.

(O) TOP (Cut 1): 1/16″ × 1 5/8″ × 3 1/4″. Bevel the top side and front edges.

(P) TOP MOULDING (Cut 1): 1/16″ × 1 9/16″ × 3 1/8″. Bevel the top side and front edges.

(Q) LEGS (Cut 6): 1/4″ diameter wood dowel × 1 5/16″. See Figure **7-B-5** for the shape. Refer to **1-C-3-a**.

(R) FEET (Cut 6): 1/4″ diameter wood dowel × 1/4″. See Figure **7-B-6** for the shape. Refer to **1-C-3-a**. Drill a 1/16″ diameter hole 1/16″ deep into the top of each foot.

(S) FRAME (Cut 1): 1/8″ × 1 1/2″ × 3″. See Figure **7-B-7** for the shape. The shaded area in this diagram is cut out. Six 1/16″ diameter holes are drilled through the frame. *Note:* Drill the six holes before cutting the center section away.

(T) DRAWERS

    (1) SIDE DRAWERS (Two)

        a. **FRONT AND BACK** (Cut 4): 1/16″ × 3/4″ × 7/8″.

        b. **SIDES** (Cut 4): 1/16″ × 3/4″ × 1 1/4″.

        c. **BOTTOM** (Cut 2): 1/8″ × 3/4″ × 1 1/4″.

Refer to **2-E-1** for assembly.

    (2) CENTER DRAWER (One)

        a. **BACK AND FRONT** (Cut 2): 1/16″ × 1/2″ × 7/8″.

        b. **SIDES** (Cut 2): 1/16″ × 1/2″ × 1 1/4″.

        c. **BOTTOM** (Cut 1): 1/8″ × 3/4″ × 1 1/4″.

Refer to **2-E-1** for assembly.

(U) DRAWER SEPARATORS (Cut 2): 1/16″ × 3/4″ × 1 3/8″.

(V) DRAWER DIVIDER (Cut 1): 1/16″ × 7/8″ × 1 3/8″.

(F) DRAWER DIVIDERS AND CHEST BOTTOM (Cut 4): 1/16″ × 1 3/8″ × 2 3/4″.

(G) DRAWER SEPARATOR (Cut 1): 1/8″ × 9/16″ × 1 3/8″.

(H) DRAWERS

    (1) WIDE DRAWERS (Three)

        a. **FRONT AND BACK** (Cut 6): 1/16″ × 5/8″ × 2 3/4″

        b. **SIDES** (Cut 6): 1/16″ × 5/8″ × 1 1/4″.

        c. **BOTTOM** (Cut 3): 1/8″ × 1 1/4″ × 2 5/8″.

Refer to **2-E-1** for assembly.

ASSEMBLY: Stain all wood before glueing. Refer to Figures **7-B-1** (*front view*) and **7-B-2** (*left side view*) for the assembly diagrams. Refer to **2-C-1** for the general assembly directions for the upper chest and stand, with the following additions.

STAND

1. The bottom board (**N**) is flush with the top edge of the front apron (**L**). See Figure **7-B-1**.

2. Place the left side drawer into the stand (*for measurement only*). Glue a drawer separator (**U**) into the stand, resting against the right side of this drawer, and glued against the bottom and back boards.

3. Glue the front panel (**M**) atop the bottom board and against the right edge of the drawer separator. See Figure **7-B-1**.

4. Glue the drawer divider (**V**) atop the front panel (*front edges flush*) and against the right edge of the separator and the back board. See Figure **7-B-1**.

5. Place the center drawer in the opening (*for measurement only*) and glue the second separator (**U**) resting against the right edge of this drawer and glued against the right edge of the center panel, atop the bottom board and against the back board. See Figure **7-B-1**.

6. Remove the drawers. Glue the chest centered atop the stand, with back edges flush.

7. Refer to Figure **7-B-1** and **7-B-2**. Glue the six legs in place against the bottom surfaces of the apron, side boards and back board. Place the peg ends of the legs through the holes in the frame, and glue the ends of the pegs into the six feet (**R**).

8. Apply a finish coat to the cabinet and eight drawers.

9. Attach two drawer pulls to each wide drawer, and one drawer pull to each remaining drawer.

CHEST OF DRAWERS 7-C

7-C

7-C-5

7-C-6

7-C-1   7-C-2

7-C-3   7-C-4

(A) FRONT LEGS (Cut 2): 5/16″ × 5/16″ × 11/16″. Trace the patterns in Figures **7-C-1** and **7-C-2** on the two blocks of wood. Refer to **1-C-3-d** for aid in carving.

(B) BACK LEGS (Cut 2): 1/8″ × 5/16″ × 11/16″. Trace the pattern in Figure **7-C-4** on the two blocks of wood and carve.

(C) SIDES (Cut 2): 1/8″ × 1 3/8″ × 3 1/8″.

(D) TOP (Cut 1): 1/8″ × 1 1/2″ × 2 7/8″.

(E) BOTTOM (Cut 1): 1/16″ × 1 1/2″ × 2 7/8″. Round the top edge of the front and side surfaces of this board. See Figure **7-C**.

(F) BACK (Cut 1): 1/8″ × 2 1/2″ × 3 1/8″.

(G) DRAWER SPACERS (Cut 5): 1/16″ × 1 1/4″ × 2 1/2″.

(H) DRAWER DIVIDER (Cut 1): 1/8″ × 3/4″ × 1 1/4″.

(I) FRONT APRON (Cut 1): 1/8″ × 1/4″ × 2 1/2″. See Figure **7-C-5** for the shape.

(J) SIDE APRON (Cut 2): 1/8″ × 1/4″ × 1 1/8″. See Figure **7-C-6** for the shape.

(K) LOWER DRAWERS (Three)
   (1) **FRONT AND BACK** (Cut 6): 1/16″ × 9/16″ × 2 1/2″.
   (2) **SIDES** (Cut 6): 1/16″ × 9/16″ × 1 1/8″.
   (3) **BOTTOM** (Cut 3): 1/8″ × 1 1/8″ × 2 3/8″.

(L) CENTER DRAWERS (Two side by side)
   (1) **FRONT AND BACK** (Cut 4): 1/16″ × 3/4″ × 1 3/16″.
   (2) **SIDES** (Cut 4): 1/16″ × 3/4″ × 1 1/8″.
   (3) **BOTTOM** (Cut 2): 1/8″ × 1 1/8″ × 1 3/16″.

(M) TOP DRAWER
   (1) **FRONT AND BACK** (Cut 2): 1/16″ × 3/8″ × 2 1/2″.
   (2) **SIDES** (Cut 2): 1/16″ × 3/8″ × 1 1/8″.
   (3) **BOTTOM** (Cut 1): 1/8″ × 1 1/8″ × 2 3/8″.

ASSEMBLY OF DRAWERS: Refer to **2-E-1** for the assembly of all drawers. Drill holes in the drawer front boards at the sites indicated by the black dots in Figure **7-C**.

ASSEMBLY OF CHEST: Refer to **2-C-1**.

THREE DRAWER CHEST c. 1750 7-D

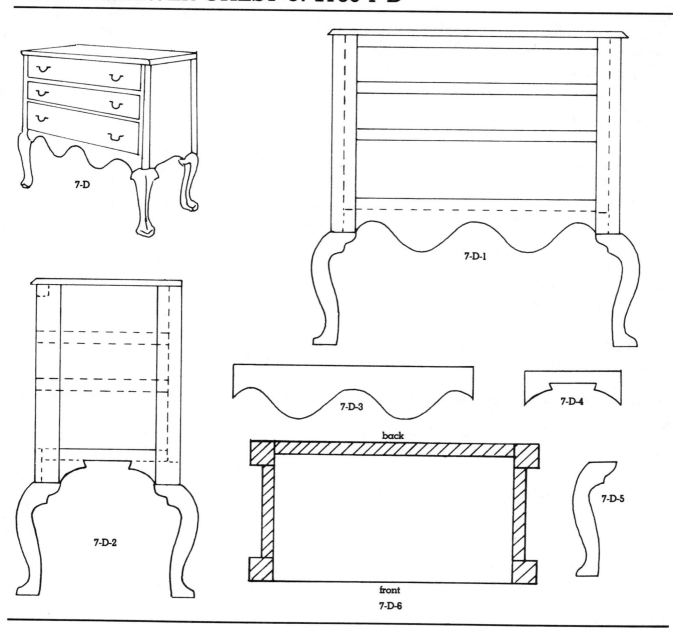

7-D

7-D-1

7-D-2

7-D-3

7-D-4

7-D-5

back

front
7-D-6

(A) BACK (Cut 1): 1/8″ × 1 7/8″ × 2 1/2″.

(B) CORNER POSTS (Cut 4): 1/4″ × 1/4″ × 2 1/8″.

(C) SIDES (Cut 2): 1/8″ × 1″ × 1 3/4″.

(D) TOP (Cut 1): 1/16″ × 1 9/16″ × 3 1/8″. See Figures 7-D-1 and 7-D-2. Bevel the front and side edges of this board.

(E) UPPER FRONT (Cut 1): 1/8″ × 1/8″ × 2 1/2″.

(F) DRAWER DIVIDERS (Cut 2): 1/8″ × 1 3/8″ × 2 1/2″.

(G) CHEST BOTTOM (Cut 1): 1/8″ × 1 5/16″ × 2 1/2″.

(H) FRONT APRON (Cut 1): 1/16″ × 9/16″ × 2 1/2″. See Figure 7-D-3 for the shape.

(I) SIDE APRON (Cut 2): 1/8″ × 3/8″ × 1″. See Figure 7-D-4 for the shape.

(J) LEGS (Four): Purchase two packages of pre-shaped cabriole legs (*two per package*) measuring 1 3/16″ in height. Most miniature supply shops have these legs for sale. If you wish to carve these legs, see Figure 7-D-5 for the shape. Refer to **1-C-3-d**.

(K) DRAWERS (Two small)
    (1) **FRONT AND BACK** (Cut 4): 1/16″ × 3/8″ × 2 1/2″.
    (2) **SIDES** (Cut 4): 1/16″ × 3/8″ × 1 1/4″.
    (3) **BOTTOM** (Cut 2): 1/8″ × 1 1/4″ × 2 3/8″.
Refer to **2-E-1** for assembly.

(L) DRAWER (One large)
    (1) **FRONT AND BACK** (Cut 2): 1/16″ × 5/8″ × 2 1/2″.
    (2) **SIDES** (Cut 2): 1/16″ × 5/8″ × 1 1/4″.
    (3) **BOTTOM** (Cut 1): 1/8″ × 1 1/4″ × 2 3/8″.
Refer to **2-E-1** for assembly.

(M) DRAWER PULLS (Three pair): Bail-type. Refer to **1-B-6**.

ASSEMBLY: Stain all wood before glueing. Refer to Figures **7-D-1, 7-D-2** and **7-D-6** for a top view of the assembly.

1. Glue a corner post atop the top surface of each of the four legs, with the left and right back edges flush.

2. Refer to Figures **7-D-2** and **7-D-6**. Glue the back board between two side posts. The legs will face to the back, with the top and back edges flush.

3. Refer to Figure **7-D-6**. Glue the left and right side boards between the rear side posts and the front side posts (*the front legs will face forward*), with the inside surfaces and top edges flush.

4. Refer to Figures **7-D-1** and **7-D-2**. Glue the bottom board between the sides and against the back board, with the bottom edge 1/4″ above the bottom edge of the side posts and the rear bottom edge flush with the bottom edge of the back board. Be sure this board is level.

5. Glue the top front board between the side posts, with the front edges flush. Glue the top board atop the top edges of the chest, with equal side overhang and the back edges flush.

6. Place the large drawer into the chest frame, resting on the bottom board (*for measurement only*). Glue a drawer separator against the inside surfaces of the side boards and the back board while resting on the drawer. Insert a small drawer. Follow the same procedure and glue the remaining drawer separator in place. Remove the drawers.

7. Glue the front apron between the front side posts and legs and glued against the front edge of the chest bottom board, with these top edges flush. See Figure **7-D-1**.

8. Glue the side apron pieces between the side posts and legs, butted against the bottom edge of the side board, with these front surfaces flush. See Figure **7-D-2**.

9. Apply a finish coat to the chest and drawers.

10. Attach the drawer pulls.

CHEST ON FRAME 7-E

(A) BACK (Cut 1): 1/16″ × 2 1/8″ × 3 5/8″.

(B) SIDES (Cut 2): 1/16″ × 1 3/8″ × 2 1/8″.

(C) CHEST BOTTOM AND SEPARATORS (Cut 3): 1/16″ × 1 11/16″ × 3 3/4″. See Figure **7-E-3** for the shape.

(D) TOP (Cut 1): 1/16″ × 1 7/8″ × 4 1/4″. Round off the top edge of the front and sides of this board. See Figures **7-E-1** and **7-E-2**.

(E) LEGS (Cut 4): 3/16″ × 3/16″ × 4″. See Figure **7-E-4** for the shape. Refer to **1-C-3-a**. When all four of the legs have been shaped, drill a hole 1/16″ in diameter and 1/16″ deep at the site of the black dot in the diagram. Drill a second hole 1/16″ in diameter and 1/16″ deep into the two legs at the site of the left arrow, and repeat this hole for the remaining two legs at the site of the right arrow in the diagram.

(F) FRONT HORIZONTAL MOULDING (Cut 2): 1/16″ × 1/4″ × 3 5/8″.

(G) FRONT VERTICAL MOULDING (Cut 1): 1/16″ × 1/4″ × 7/16″.

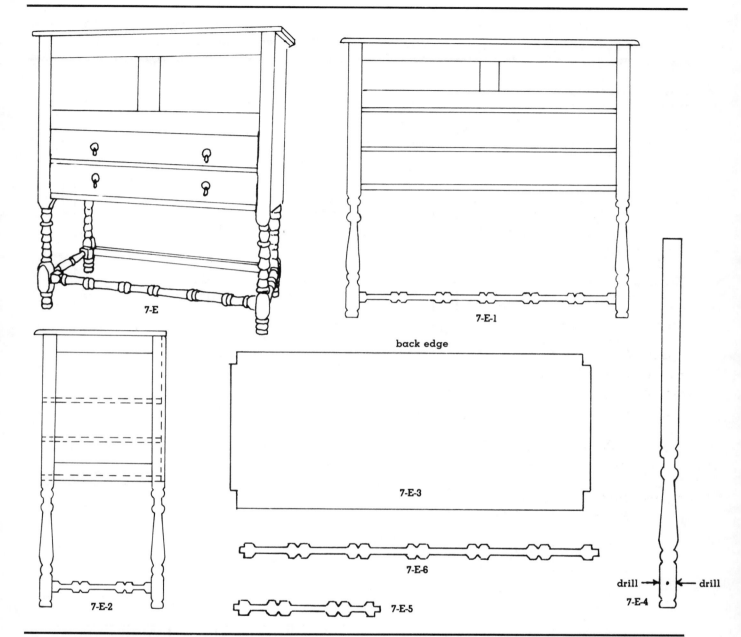

7-E

7-E-1

back edge

7-E-3

7-E-6

7-E-2

7-E-5

7-E-4

drill → • ← drill

(H) UPPER FRONT BOARD (Cut 1): 1/16″ × 15/16″ × 3 5/8″.

(I) HORIZONTAL SIDE MOULDING (Cut 4): 1/16″ × 1/4″ × 1 3/8″.

(J) FRONT LEG STRETCHER (Cut 1): 1/8″ diameter wood dowel × 3 3/4″. See Figure **7-E-6** for the shape. Refer to **1-C-3-a**.

(K) BACK LEG STRETCHER (Cut 1): 1/8″ × 1/8″ × 3 3/4″. Shape a 1/16″ × 1/16″ × 1/16″ peg at each end of this board.

(L) SIDE LEG STRETCHERS (Cut 2): 1/8″ diameter wood dowel × 1 9/16″. See Figure **7-E-5** for the shape. Refer to **1-C-3-a**.

(M) CLEAT HINGE (Cut 2): 1/16″ × 1/8″ × 1 3/4″.

(N) DRAWERS (Two)

   (1) FRONT AND BACK (Cut 4): 1/16″ × 1/2″ × 3 5/8″.

   (2) SIDES (Cut 4): 1/16″ × 1/2″ × 1 9/16″.

   (3) BOTTOM (Cut 2): 1/8″ × 1 9/16″ × 3 1/2″.

Refer to **2-E-1** for assembly.

(O) DRAWER PULLS (Four): Refer to **1-B-6**.

ASSEMBLY: This chest can be finished natural and will require staining of all wood before glueing. It can also be painted and you will find a color print marked **7-E** on the color insert page to apply on the chest.

1. Assemble the moulding pieces on the upper front board as shown in Figure **7-E-1**.

2. Assemble the side moulding pieces on the two side boards as shown in Figure **7-E-2**.

3. Refer to **2-C-3** for final assembly.

4. After this piece of furniture has been assembled either apply a finish coat for the natural wood or refer to **1-C-2** for application of the color print.

DRY SINK 7-F

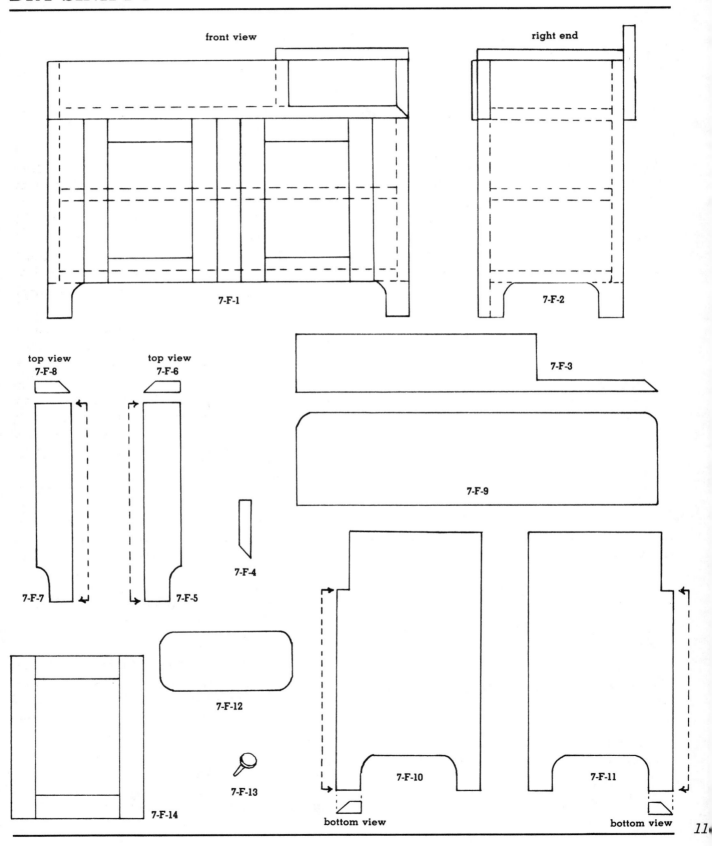

front view

7-F-1

right end

7-F-2

top view
7-F-8

top view
7-F-6

7-F-7

7-F-5

7-F-4

7-F-3

7-F-9

7-F-12

7-F-13

7-F-14

7-F-10

7-F-11

bottom view

bottom view

(A) WELL FRONT (Cut 1): 1/8″ × 5/8″ × 3 3/4″. See Figure **7-F-3** for the shape. The right lower edge is mitre cut with a 45° angle.

(B) RIGHT SIDE OF WELL FRONT (Cut 1): 1/8″ × 1/8″ × 5/8″. See Figure **7-F-4** for the 45° angle mitre cut at the bottom edge.

(C) LEFT SIDE FRONT FACING (Cut 1): 1/8″ × 3/8″ × 2 1/8″. See Figure **7-F-5** for the shape to be cut. See Figure **7-F-6** for a top view diagram of the top edge of this board, showing a 45° angle to be cut into the left edge of this board for mitring.

(D) RIGHT SIDE FRONT FACING (Cut 1): 1/8″ × 3/8″ × 2 1/8″. See Figure **7-F-7** for the shape to be cut. See Figure **7-F-8** for a top view diagram of the top edge of this board, showing a 45° angle to be cut into the right edge of this board for mitring.

(E) BACK (Cut 1): 1/8″ × 2 3/8″ × 3 1/2″.

(F) TOP BACK (Cut 1): 1/8″ × 1″ × 3 3/4″. See Figure **7-F-9** for the shape.

(G) RIGHT END (Cut 1): 1/8″ × 1 1/2″ × 2 3/4″. See Figure **7-F-10** for the shape. The arrows in the diagram indicate the area of a 45° angle to be cut into the front edge of the board for mitring.

(H) LEFT END (Cut 1): 1/8″ × 1 1/2″ × 2 3/4″. See Figure **7-F-11** for the shape. The arrows in the diagram indicate the area of a 45° angle to be cut into the front edge of the board for mitring.

(I) SHELF, FLOOR OF WELL AND BOTTOM BOARD (Cut 3): 1/8″ × 1 1/8″ × 3 1/2″.

(J) TOP OF DRAWER ENCLOSURE (Cut 1): 1/8″ × 1 3/8″ × 1 1/2″.

(K) SIDE OF DRAWER ENCLOSURE (Cut 1): 1/8″ × 1/2″ × 1 1/8″.

(L) DOORS (Two)
    (1) **DOOR PANEL** (Cut 2): 1/16″ × 7/8″ × 1 1/4″.
    (2) **DOOR SIDES AND CENTER DIVIDER** (Cut 5): 1/8″ × 1/4″ × 1 3/4″.
    (3) **TOP AND BOTTOM BOARDS** (Cut 4): 1/8″ × 1/4″ × 7/8″.

(M) DRAWER (One)
    (1) **DRAWER FRONT** (Cut 1): 1/16″ × 5/8″ × 1 3/8″. See Figure **7-F-12** for the shape. The black dot in the diagram indicates a 1/16″ diameter hole to be drilled through this board.
    (2) **DRAWER BACK** (Cut 1): 1/16″ × 1/2″ × 1 1/8″.
    (3) **DRAWER SIDES** (Cut 2): 1/16″ × 1/2″ × 1 7/16″.
    (4) **DRAWER BOTTOM** (Cut 1): 1/8″ × 1″ × 1 7/16″. Refer to **2-E-2** for the drawer assembly.
    (5) **DRAWER KNOB** (Cut 1): 1/8″ diameter

wood dowel × 1/4″. See Figure **7-F-13** for the shape. The peg end will be 1/16″ in diameter to fit into the hole in the drawer front.

(N) HINGES (Two pair): Refer to **1-B-4**.

ASSEMBLY: Stain all wood before glueing. Refer to Figures **7-F-1** and **7-F-2** for assembly.

1. Refer to Figure **7-F-14** for the assembly of the two doors. Glue the sides, top and bottom boards against the center panel, with the back and side edges flush.

2. Glue the sides (*with mitred edges forward*) against the side edges of the back board, with the back and top edges flush.

3. Glue the well front board (**A**) into the upper notch in the left side board, with the front and top edges flush. Glue the right side of the well front (**B**) into the upper notch in the right side board, with the left mitred end fitting against the right mitred end of the well front board and the front and top edges flush.

4. Glue one board (**I**) into the space between the well front board, the back board and the side boards, with bottom edges flush with the well front board. Be sure this board is level.

5. Glue a shelf (**I**) with the lower edge of this board 7/8″ above the lower edge of the back board and between the two end boards. Be sure this board is straight and level.

6. Glue the bottom board (**I**) between the two end boards and against the back board, with the bottom edges of this board and the back board flush. Be sure this board is straight and level.

7. Glue the left and right side front facing boards in place, with the mitred edges fitting against the front mitred edges of the two end boards. These boards will butt against the lower edge of the well front board.

8. Refer to Figure **7-F-1**. Place a door against each of the side front facing boards, and glue the center divider board between the two doors against the front edges of the bottom board and shelf, and butted against the bottom edge of the well front board.

9. Refer to Figure **7-F-1**. Glue the side of the drawer enclosure (**K**) atop the well bottom board and between the well front board and the back board, with the right edge flush with the right edge of the well front board. This will make the left side of the drawer enclosure. Glue the top of the drawer enclosure atop the top edges of the drawer enclosure side boards and butted against the back board.

10. Glue the top back board (**F**) against the back surface of the back board. See Figure **7-F-2** for placement.

11. Paint the interior walls and floor of the well a moss green, or line it with thin copper. Our antique dry sink still has the old moss green paint on the boards in the well.

12. Apply a finish coat.

13. Attach the hinges and drawer pull.

HUNT BOARD 7-G

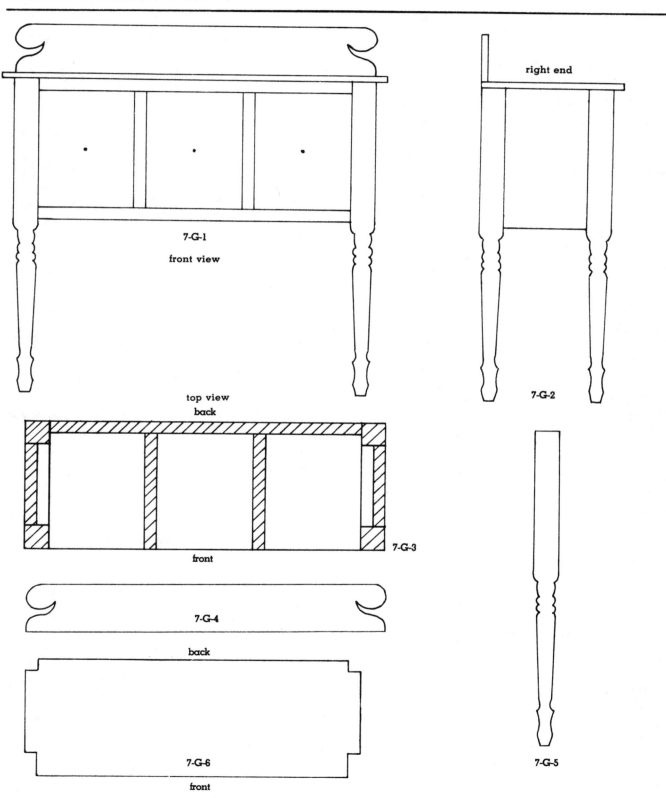

7-G-1

front view

right end

7-G-2

top view

back

front

7-G-3

7-G-4

back

7-G-6

front

7-G-5

(A) BACK (Cut 1): 1/8" × 1 1/2" × 3 1/4".

(B) SIDES (Cut 2): 1/8" × 7/8" × 1 1/2".

(C) TOP BASE AND BOTTOM (Cut 2): 1/8" × 1 1/4" × 3 1/2". See Figure **7-G-6** for the shape.

(D) TOP (Cut 1): 1/16" × 1 1/2" × 4".

(E) SHAPED TOP BACK (Cut 1): 1/16" × 1/2" × 3 3/4". See Figure **7-G-4** for the shape.

(F) DRAWER SPACERS (Cut 2): 1/8" × 1 1/4" × 1 1/4".

(G) DRAWER GUIDES (Cut 2): 1/8" × 1/8" × 7/8".

(H) LEGS (Cut 4): 1/4" × 1/4" × 3 3/8". See Figure **7-G-5** for the shape. The upper 1 1/2" remains square and the remainder is shaped. Refer to **1-C-3-a**.

(I) DRAWERS (Three)

    (1) **FRONT AND BACK** (Cut 6): 1/16" × 1" × 1 1/4". Drill 1/16" diameter holes centered in the three drawer fronts.

    (2) **SIDES** (Cut 6): 1/16" × 1 1/8" × 1 1/4".

    (3) **BOTTOM** (Cut 3): 1/8" × 7/8" × 1 1/8".

    (4) **DRAWER KNOBS** (Three): Refer to **1-B-6-d**. The knobs on the antique piece are white porcelain.

Refer to **2-E-1** for the drawer assembly.

ASSEMBLY: Stain all wood before glueing. Refer to Figures **7-G-1**, **7-G-2** and **7-G-3**.

1. Glue a side board between two legs, with the top and outside edges flush. Refer to Figures **7-G-2** and

7-G-3. Repeat for the second side.

2. Glue the back board between the two back legs, with the top and back edges flush. See Figure **7-G-3**.

3. Glue the bottom board butted against the inside surfaces of the back and side boards, with the bottom edges flush. See Figure **7-G-3**.

4. Glue the drawer guides atop the top side edges of the bottom board and between the leg posts and against the inside surfaces of the side boards. See Figure **7-G-3**.

5. Glue the top base board against the inside surfaces of the back and side boards, with the top edges flush.

6. Insert a drawer (*for measurement only*). Glue a drawer spacer atop the bottom board, against the back board and the undersurface of the top base board. Insert a second drawer and repeat this procedure. Remove the drawers.

7. Glue the top board atop the top base board, with equal side overhang and the back edges flush.

8. Glue the shaped top back board centered atop the top board with the back edges flush.

9. Apply a finish coat to the hunt board and the three drawers.

10. Attach the three drawer pulls.

QUEEN ANNE STYLE OAK SIDEBOARD 7-H

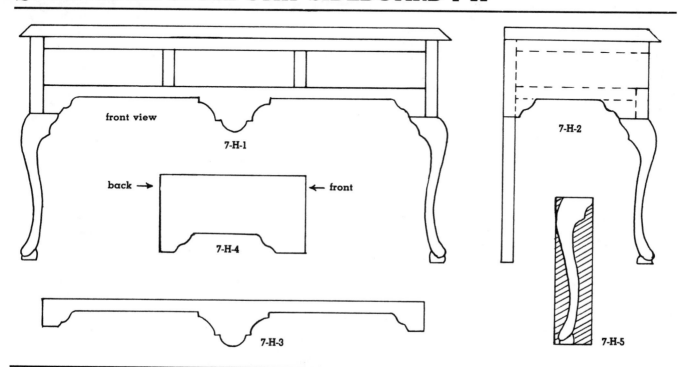

front view

7-H-1

back →   ← front

7-H-4

7-H-2

7-H-3

7-H-5

(A) BACK (Cut 1): 1/8″ × 13/16″ × 4″.

(B) SIDES (Cut 2): 1/8″ × 13/16″ × 1 1/2″. See Figure **7-H-4** for the shape.

(C) TOP (Cut 1): 1/8″ × 1 3/8″ × 4″.

(D) BOTTOM (Cut 1): 1/8″ × 1 1/4″ × 4″.

(E) TOP MOULDING (Cut 1): 1/8″ × 1 5/8″ × 4 1/2″. Bevel the side and front top edges.

(F) APRON (Cut 1): 1/8″ × 1/2″ × 4″. See Figure **7-H-3** for the shape.

(G) DRAWER SEPARATORS (Cut 2): 1/8″ × 3/8″ × 1 3/8″.

(H) FRONT CABRIOLE LEGS (Cut 2): 3/8″ × 3/8″ × 1 9/16″. See Figure **7-H-5** for the shape. Refer to **1-C-3-d** for aid in carving.

(I) BACK LEGS (Cut 2): 1/8″ × 1/8″ × 1 9/16″.

(J) DRAWERS (Three)

(1) **BACK AND FRONT** (Cut 6): 1/16″ × 3/8″ × 1 1/4″.

(2) **SIDES** (Cut 6): 1/16″ × 3/8″ × 1 1/4″.

(3) **BOTTOM** (Cut 3): 1/8″ × 1 1/8″ × 1 1/4″.

Refer to **2-E-1** for assembly.

(K) DRAWER PULLS (Six): Refer to **1-B-6-b**.

ASSEMBLY: Stain all wood before glueing. Refer to Figures **7-H-1** (*front view*) and **7-H-2** (*left side view*) for the assembly diagrams.

1. Refer to **2-C-1-a** (*general chest assembly*). *Note:* The chest bottom board is glued between the back board and the front apron, with the top surface flush with the top edge of the apron.

2. When the assembly is complete, apply a finish coat.

3. Attach the drawer pulls.

VICTORIAN SIDEBOARD 7-I

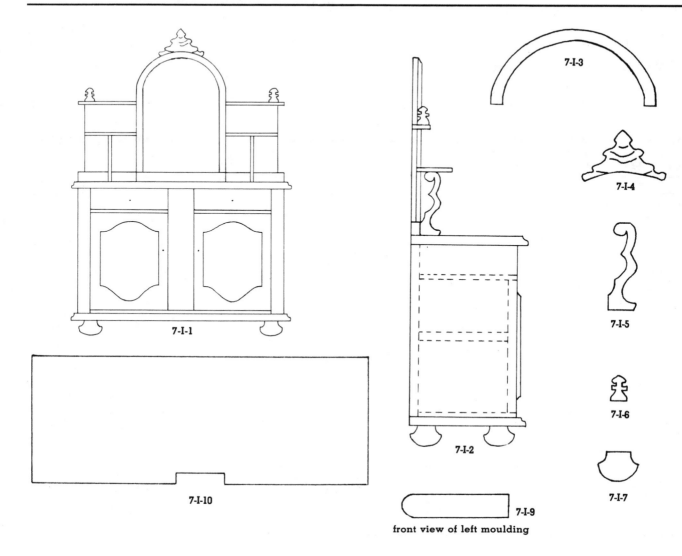

7-I-1

7-I-10

7-I-2

7-I-9

front view of left moulding

7-I-3

7-I-4

7-I-5

7-I-6

7-I-7

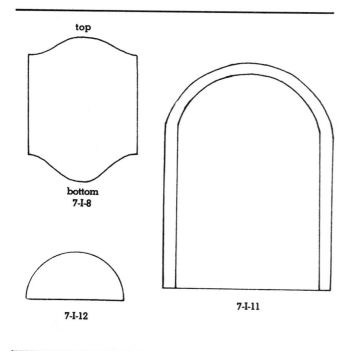

top

bottom
7-I-8

7-I-12

7-I-11

LOWER CABINET

(A) BACK (Cut 1): 1/8″ × 2 7/16″ × 3 1/2″.

(B) BOTTOM (Cut 1): 1/16″ × 1 3/8″ × 3 1/2″.

(C) SIDES (Cut 2): 1/4″ × 1 1/2″ × 2 1/2″. Round off one side edge.

(D) BASE AND TOP (Cut 2): 1/8″ × 1 5/8″ × 4 1/4″. See Figures **7-I-1** and **7-1-2** for the shaping of the front and side edges of these boards.

(E) DRAWER BASE (Cut 1): 1/16″ × 1 3/8″ × 3 1/2″. See Figure **7-I-10** for the shape.

(F) INSIDE SHELF (Cut 1): 1/8″ × 1 1/4″ × 3 1/2″.

(G) DOORS (Cut 2): 1/8″ × 1 1/2″ × 1 15/16″.

(H) DOOR PANELS (Cut 2): 1/16″ × 1 1/8″ × 1 9/16″. See Figure **7-I-8** for the shape.

(I) CENTER DIVIDER (Cut 1): 1/8″ × 1/2″ × 2 7/16″.

(J) FEET (Cut 4): 1/2″ diameter wood dowel × 5/16″. See Figure **7-I-7** for the shape. Refer to **1-C-3-a**.

(K) DRAWERS (Two)

    (1) **BACK AND FRONT** (Cut 4): 1/16″ × 7/16″ × 1 1/2″.

    (2) **SIDES** (Cut 4): 1/16″ × 7/16″ × 1 1/4″.

    (3) **BOTTOM** (Cut 2): 1/8″ × 1 1/4″ × 1 3/8″. Refer to **2-E-1** for assembly.

    (4) **DRAWER AND DOOR PULLS** (Four): Refer to **1-B-6**.

TOP ASSEMBLY

(L) SIDE BACK (Cut 2): 1/16″ × 1″ × 1 3/8″.

(M) CENTER BACK (Cut 1): 1/16″ × 1 3/4″ × 2 7/16″. See Figure **7-I-11** (*outside line*) for the shape.

(N) TOP SIDE MOULDING (Cut 2): 1/16″ × 1/4″ × 1 1/8″. See Figure **7-I-9** for a top view diagram.

(O) SHELF (Cut 2): 1/16″ × 1/2″ × 1″. See Figure **7-I-12** for the shape.

(P) SHELF BRACE (Cut 2): 1/16″ × 5/16″ × 15/16″. See Figure **7-I-5** for the shape.

(Q) UPPER SIDE BASE (Cut 2): 1/8″ × 3/16″ × 1 1/8″. Round off one end.

(R) UPPER CENTER BASE (Cut 1): 3/16″ × 1/4″ × 1 3/4″.

(S) TOP MIRROR FRAME (Cut 1): 1/8″ × 13/16″ × 1 3/4″. See Figure **7-I-3** for the shape. Bevel the outside edge.

(T) SIDE MIRROR FRAME (Cut 2): 1/8″ × 1/8″ × 1 5/8″. Bevel one side edge of each board.

(U) FINIAL (Cut 2): 3/16″ diameter wood dowel × 5/16″. See Figure **7-I-6** for the shape. Refer to **1-C-3-a**.

(V) MIRROR CREST (Cut 1): 1/8″ × 9/16″ × 7/8″. See Figure **7-I-4** for the shape. The lines in the diagram indicate a simple carved shaping to this piece.

(W) MIRROR (Cut 1): 1/8″ or less in thickness × 1 1/2″ × 2 5/16″. See Figure **7-I-11** (*inside line*) for the shape.

ASSEMBLY: Stain all wood before glueing.

1. Glue the mirror top frame (**S**) atop the top edges of the side frame (**T**), being sure that the beveled edges match. Glue this assembled frame (*beveled edges forward*) against the center back (**M**) with all edges flush.

2. Glue the side back pieces (**L**) butted against the center section, with the back and bottom edges flush.

3. Glue the upper side base boards (**Q**) butted against the center base (**R**), with the rounded ends to the outside and the back edges flush. Glue the upper back assembly centered atop this base assembly, with the back edges flush. See Figures **7-I-1** and **7-I-2**.

4. Glue the top side moulding pieces (**N**) atop the top surfaces of the sides (**L**), with the rounded end to the outside and the back edges flush. See Figures **7-I-1** and **7-I-2**.

5. Glue a finial (**U**) atop the top surface of the top side moulding (**N**). Glue the mirror crest (**V**) centered atop the mirror frame, with the back edges flush. See Figure **7-I-1**.

6. See Figures **7-I-1** and **7-I-2**. Glue a shelf brace (**P**) centered against the bottom surface of each shelf (**O**), with the back edges flush. Glue these shelves

and braces in place against the upper side back boards and resting against the front surface of the upper side base, with bottom edges flush.

7. Glue the lower side boards (**C**) against the upright edges of the back board (**A**), with the back edges flush and the rounded front side edges to the outside.

8. Glue the bottom board (**B**) between the sides and against the lower front edge of the back, with the bottom edges flush.

9. Insert the two drawers in the cabinet (*for measurement only*) and glue the drawer base (**E**) against the back and sides (*the notched edge will be forward*). See Figure **7-I-1**. Remove the drawers.

10. Glue the center divider (**I**) into the notch in the front of the drawer base board and atop the bottom board.

11. See Figure **7-I-2**. The center double broken line in this diagram represents the placement of the interior shelf (**F**). Glue it in place.

12. Place the doors in the cabinet. Refer to **1-B-4-a** (*pin hinge*). Push a pin down through the drawer base board and into the top edge of the door. Push a second pin up through the bottom board and into the bottom edge of the door. Repeat for the second door.

13. Glue the top and base boards (**D**) centered above and below this assembled cabinet, with the back edges flush.

14. Refer to Figure **7-I-1**. Glue the two door panels centered against the doors.

15. Refer to Figures **7-I-1** and **7-I-2**. Glue the four feet in place.

16. Glue the two sections together, with back edges flush.

17. Apply a finish coat. Attach the door and drawer pulls.

EARLY AMERICAN PINE THREE-PART CUPBOARD 7-J

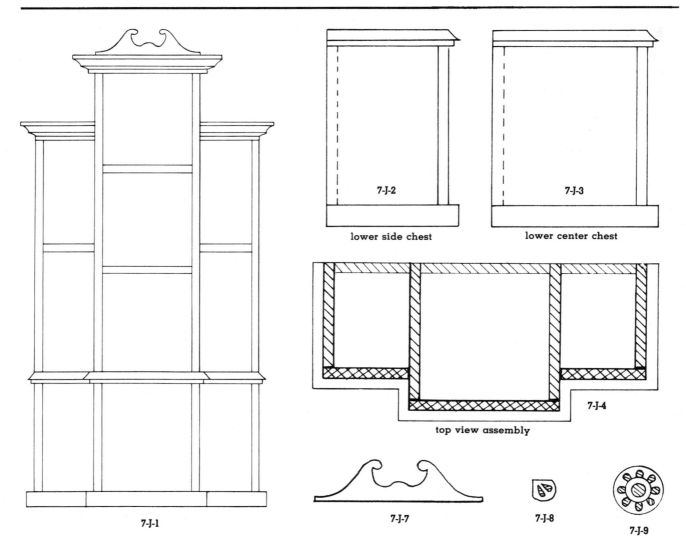

7-J-1

7-J-2 lower side chest

7-J-3 lower center chest

7-J-4 top view assembly

7-J-7

7-J-8

7-J-9

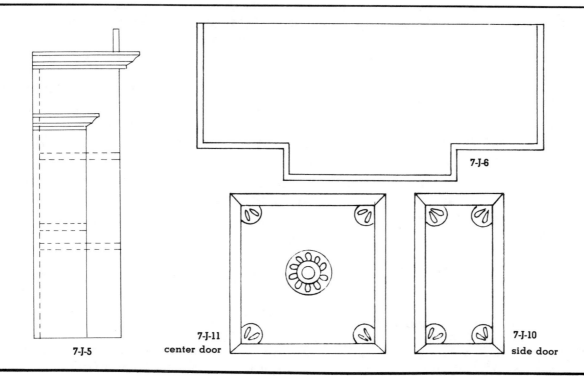

7-J-6

7-J-5

7-J-11 center door

7-J-10 side door

LOWER CABINET

(A) BASE (Cut 1): 1/4″ × 1 7/8″ × 4″. See Figure **7-J-6** (*outside black line*) for the shape.

(B) CENTER SIDES (Cut 2): 1/8″ × 1 5/8″ × 1 7/8″.

(C) CENTER BACK (Cut 1): 1/8″ × 1 1/2″ × 1 7/8″.

(D) SIDES (Cut 2): 1/8″ × 1 1/4″ × 1 7/8″.

(E) SIDE BACK (Cut 2): 1/8″ × 7/8″ × 1 7/8″.

(F) TOP (Cut 1): 1/16″ × 1 13/16″ × 3 7/8″. See Figure **7-J-6** (*inside black line*) for the shape.

(G) TOP MOULDING (Cut 1): 1/8″ × 1 7/8″ × 4″. See Figure **7-J-6** (*outside black line*) for the shape. Bevel the side edges and all front edges.

(H) SIDE DOORS (Two)

    (1) **CENTER PANEL** (Cut 2): 1/16″ × 3/4″ × 1 5/8″.

    (2) **SIDE MOULDING** (Cut 4): 1/8″ × 1/8″ × 1 7/8″. Mitre each end with a 45° angle cut.

    (3) **TOP AND BOTTOM MOULDING** (Cut 4): 1/8″ × 1/8″ × 1″. Mitre each end with a 45° angle cut.

(I) CENTER DOOR (One)

    (1) **CENTER PANEL** (Cut 1): 1/16″ × 1 1/2″ × 1 5/8″.

    (2) **SIDE MOULDING** (Cut 2): 1/8″ × 1/8″ × 1 7/8″. Mitre each end with a 45° angle cut.

    (3) **TOP AND BOTTOM MOULDING** (Cut 2): 1/8″ × 1/8″ × 1 3/4″. Mitre each end with a 45° angle cut.

    (4) **CORNER DECORATIONS** (Cut 12): 1/16″ × 1/4″ × 1/4″. See Figure **7-J-8** for the shape. The

shaded areas in the diagram are carved down into the wood.

    (5) **CENTER MEDALLION** (Cut 1): 1/16″ × 1/2″ × 1/2″. See Figure **7-J-9**. The shaded areas in the diagram are carved down into the wood.

(J) DOOR STOPS (Cut 2): 1/8″ × 1/8″ × 1 7/8″.

(K) DOOR PULLS (Three): Refer to **1-B-6**.

UPPER CABINET

(L) CENTER SIDES (Cut 2): 1/8″ × 1 5/8″ × 5 1/8″.

(M) CENTER BACK (Cut 1): 1/8″ × 1 1/2″ × 5 1/8″.

(N) OUTSIDE SIDES (Cut 2): 1/8″ × 1″ × 4″.

(O) OUTSIDE BACKS (Cut 2): 1/8″ × 7/8″ × 4″.

(P) CENTER TOP (Cut 1): 1/16″ × 1 3/4″ × 2″.

(Q) CENTER TOP MOULDING

    (1) **CENTER TOP MOULDING** (Cut 1): 1/16″ × 1 7/8″ × 2 1/4″. Bevel the lower front and side edges.

    (2) **CENTER TOP MOULDING** (Cut 1): 1/8″ × 2″ × 2 1/2″. Bevel the lower front and side edges.

    (3) **CENTER TOP MOULDING** (Cut 1): 1/16″ × 2″ × 2 1/2″. Stain all pieces of wood and glue together, as shown in Figures **7-J-1** and **7-J-5**.

(R) SIDE TOP MOULDING

    (1) **SIDE TOP MOULDING** (Cut 2): 1/16″ × 1 1/8″ × 1 1/8″. Bevel the lower front edges of both boards, the lower left side of one board and the lower right side of the second board.

    (2) **SIDE TOP MOULDING** (Cut 2): 1/8″ × 1 1/4″ × 1 1/4″. Finish these boards as you did in the above directions.

117

(3) **SIDE TOP MOULDING** (Cut 2): 1/8″ × 1 1/4″ × 1 1/4″. Stain all pieces of wood and glue together, as shown in Figures **7-J-1** and **7-J-5**, with back edges and either the right or left edges flush.

(S) **SIDE SHELVES** (Cut 2): 1/8″ × 7/8″ × 7/8″.

(T) **CENTER SHELVES** (Cut 2): 1/8″ × 1 1/2″ × 1 1/2″.

(U) **TOP DECORATION** (Cut 1): 1/8″ × 7/16″ × 1 3/4″. See Figure **7-J-7** for the shape.

ASSEMBLY: Stain all wood before glueing.

1. See Figures **7-J-10** (*side doors*) and **7-J-11** (*center door*). Glue the side, top and bottom pieces of moulding around the corresponding center panels. Glue the corner decorations (I-4) into the four inside corners of each door. Glue the center medallion (I-5) centered against the front surface of the center door.

2. Refer to **7-J-4** (*top view diagram of the lower cabinet assembly*). Glue the sides and backs together, as shown in this diagram. Glue this assembly atop the base, with back edges flush and side spaces equal. Glue the top (**F**) atop the top edges of this assembly, with back edges flush and side spaces equal.

3. Glue the door stops (**J**) against the outside surfaces of the center sides and recessed from the front edge so that each side door will rest against a stop.

4. Place the doors against the side and center openings. Refer to **1-B-4-a** (*pin hinge*). Pin hinge the left side of the left door and the right side of the center and right doors. Push the pins down through the top board and into the top edge of the door and up through the baseboard and into the bottom edge of each door.

5. Glue the top moulding (**G**) atop the top board with the back edges flush and side spaces equal.

6. Refer to Figure **7-J-4** (*top view*). Use this diagram (*ignoring the front cross hatched shaded areas*) as your guide to assemble the upper cabinet.

7. The assembled upper cabinet sides and backs are glued atop the lower base top moulding, with back edges flush and side spaces equal.

8. Refer to Figures **7-J-1** and **7-J-5**. Glue the top moulding assemblies atop the top boards. Glue these assembled top sections atop the center cupboard and the two side cupboards.

9. Glue the top decoration centered atop the center cupboard. See Figures **7-J-1** and **7-J-5**.

10. Figures **7-J-5** (*broken lines — side view*) and **7-J-1** (*front view*) show the placement of the shelves in the upper side and center cupboards. Glue in place.

11. Apply a finish coat. Attach the door pulls.

EMPIRE STYLE WARDROBE c. 1830 7-K

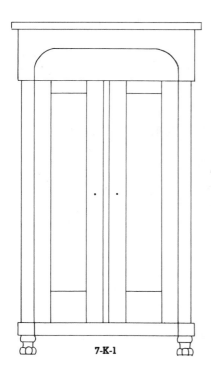

7-K-1

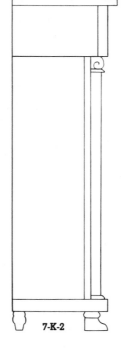

7-K-2

(A) **UPPER BACK AND FRONT** (Cut 2): 1/8″ × 1″ × 3 1/8″.

(B) **UPPER SIDES** (Cut 2): 1/8″ × 1″ × 1 5/8″.

(C) **UPPER BOTTOM** (Cut 1): 1/8″ × 1 3/8″ × 3 1/8″.

(D) **WARDROBE TOP** (Cut 1): 1/8″ × 2″ × 3 5/8″.

(E) **UPPER FRONT MOULDING** (Cut 1): 3/16″ × 1″ × 3 3/8″. See Figure **7-K-5** for the shape.

(F) **LOWER BACK** (Cut 1): 1/8″ × 3″ × 4 3/4″.

(G) **LOWER SIDES** (Cut 2): 1/8″ × 1 3/8″ × 4 3/4″.

(H) **LOWER TOP, BOTTOM AND SHELF** (Cut 3): 1/8″ × 1 1/4″ × 3″.

(I) **LOWER SIDE FRONT FACING** (Cut 2): 1/8″ × 1/4″ × 4 3/4″.

(J) **CENTER DIVIDER** (Cut 1): 1/8″ × 1/8″ × 4 3/4″.

(K) **CENTER BASE** (Cut 1): 1/4″ × 1 1/2″ × 2 3/4″.

(L) **SIDE BASE** (Cut 2): 1/4″ × 5/16″ × 1 13/16″.

(M) **FRONT FOOT TOP** (Cut 2): 1/8″ thick × 5/16″ diameter circle. See Figure **7-K-8**. Round off the top and bottom edges.

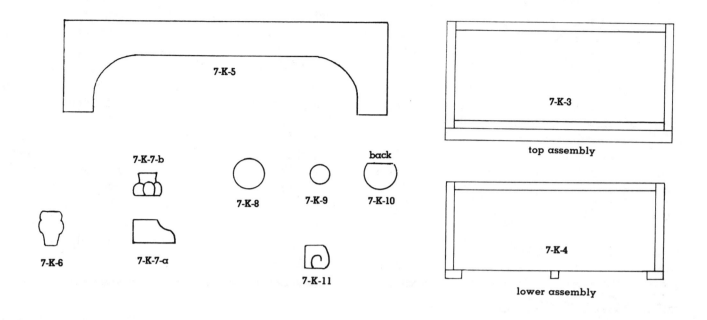

7-K-5

7-K-7-b

back

7-K-8   7-K-9   7-K-10

7-K-6   7-K-7-a

7-K-11

7-K-3

top assembly

7-K-4

lower assembly

(N) FRONT FEET (Cut 2): 1/4″ × 5/16″ × 7/16″. See Figures **7-K-7-a** (*left side view*) and **7-K-7-b** (*front view*) for the shape to be carved.

(O) BACK FEET (Cut 2): 1/4″ diameter wood dowel × 3/8″. See Figure **7-K-6** for the shape. Refer to **1-C-3-a**.

(P) SIDE PILLAR TOP ORNAMENT (Cut 2): 1/4″ × 1/4″ × 1/4″. See Figure **7-K-11** for a left side view of the shape to be carved.

(Q) SIDE PILLAR BASE AND TOP (Cut 4): 1/16″ thickness. See Figure **7-K-10** for the shape. Bevel the front edges.

(R) SIDE PILLARS (Cut 2): 3/16″ diameter wood dowel × 4 1/8″. See Figure **7-K-9**.

(S) DOORS (Two)

(1) **CENTER PANEL** (Cut 2): 1/16″ × 11/16″ × 3 13/16″.

(2) **SIDE MOULDING** (Cut 4): 1/8″ × 5/16″ × 4 11/16″.

(3) **TOP MOULDING** (Cut 2): 1/8″ × 1/4″ × 11/16″.

(4) **BOTTOM MOULDING** (Cut 2): 1/8″ × 5/8″ × 11/16″.

(T) DOOR PULLS (Two): Refer to **1-B-6**.

ASSEMBLY: Stain all wood before glueing. Refer to Figures **7-K-1** (*front view*), **7-K-2** (*left side view*), **7-K-3** (*top view of top assembly*) and **7-K-4** (*top view of lower assembly*).

TOP SECTION ASSEMBLY

1. Glue the bottom board (**C**) against the back (**A**)

with the bottom edges flush. Glue the front (**A**) against the front edge of the bottom board with the bottom edges flush. See Figure **7-K-3**.

2. Glue the sides (**B**) against the side edges of the back, front and bottom boards, with all edges flush. Glue the upper front moulding (**E**) — arch at the top — against the front board with all edges flush. See Figures **7-K-3** and **7-K-1**.

CUPBOARD ASSEMBLY

3. Glue the bottom board (**H**), top board (**H**), sides (**G**) and back board (**F**) together as you did in preceding Steps 1 and 2. See Figure **7-K-4**.

4. Glue the lower front facing (**I**) against the front edges of the side boards, with the side and bottom edges flush. See Figure **7-K-4**.

DOOR ASSEMBLY

5. Refer to Figure **7-K-1**. Glue the side (**S-2**), top (**S-3**) and bottom (**S-4**) moulding pieces against the center panel (**S-1**) as shown in this diagram, with the back edges flush. Repeat for the second door.

6. Glue the shelf (**H**) inside the lower assembly, with the top edge of the shelf 3 7/8″ above the top surface of the bottom board.

7. Glue the top section of this wardrobe centered atop the top surface of the cupboard top, with the back edges flush.

8. Glue the center base (**K**) and the side base (**L**) pieces butted together with the back edges flush. Glue this assembly centered beneath the lower cupboard, with the back edges flush.

INSTALLATION OF DOORS

9. Refer to **1-B-4-a** (*pin hinge*). Place the left door in the opening and against the upright edge of the side facing, the front edges of the top, shelf and bottom boards. Push a pin down through the bottom board of the top assembly into the top left edge of the door. Push a second pin up through the lower base into the lower left edge of the door. Glue the center divider (**J**) into the opening, resting against the right edge of the left door. Follow the above instructions and install the right door, pushing the pins into the right edges of the door.

10. Glue the wardrobe top (**D**) centered atop the top assembly with the back edges flush.

11. Glue a front foot top (**M**) centered atop each of the front feet (**N**). Glue a front foot assembly under

each of the front corners of the wardrobe, with the toes pointed forward. Glue the back legs beneath each of the corners of the wardrobe. See Figures **7-K-1** and **7-K-2**.

12. Glue the pillar top ornament (**P**) against each front side of the wardrobe and under the front overhang. See Figure **7-K-2**. Glue a side pillar top (**Q**) — beveled edge downward — against the lower surface of the top ornament, with the straight edge against the front of the wardrobe. Glue the pillar base (**Q**) — beveled edge upward — atop the side base and against the front of the wardrobe. Glue the side pillar between the base and top. See Figure **7-K-2**.

13. Apply a finish coat to the wardrobe. Let dry.

14. Attach the door pulls.

DOUGH BIN 7-L

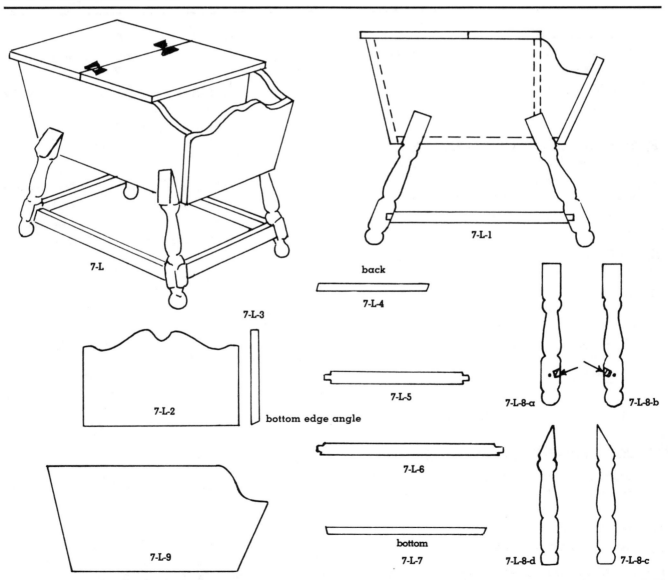

7-L

7-L-1

back
7-L-4

7-L-3

7-L-2

bottom edge angle

7-L-5

7-L-8-a

7-L-8-b

7-L-6

7-L-9

bottom
7-L-7

7-L-8-d

7-L-8-c

(A) SIDES (Cut 2): 1/16″ × 1 1/8″ × 2 5/16″. See Figure **7-L-9** for the shape.

(B) FRONT (Cut 1): 1/16″ × 1 1/16″ × 1 5/8″. See Figure **7-L-2** for the shape. Note the angle at the bottom edge of this board as shown in the right edge diagram.

(C) BACK (Cut 1): 1/16″ × 1 3/16″ × 1 1/2″. Figure **7-L-4** shows an edge view with the angle cuts at both ends.

(D) BOTTOM (Cut 1): 1/16″ × 1 1/2″ × 1 11/16″. See Figure **7-L-7** showing an edge view with angles at both ends.

(E) TOP
    (1) **BACK TOP** (Cut 1): 1/16″ × 1 1/8″ × 1 5/8″.
    (2) **FRONT TOP** (Cut 1): 1/16″ × 3/4″ × 1 5/8″.

(F) LEGS (Cut 4): 3/16″ × 3/16″ × 1 1/2″. See Figure **7-L-8** for the shape. Refer to **1-C-3-a** for aid in turning. When the four legs have been shaped, refer to Figure **7-L-8-a** and drill 1/16″ diameter holes 1/16″ deep in each of these two legs in the direction of the arrow and at the site of the black dot. With each leg facing you as it is in the diagram, angle to the left side as shown in **7-L-8-d**. Follow Figures **7-L-8** and **7-L-8-c** for the remaining two legs.

(G) END LEG STRETCHERS (Cut 2): 1/8″ × 1/8″ × 1 1/2″. See Figure **7-L-5**. Shape a 1/16″ × 1/16″ × 1/16″ peg at each end of each of these boards.

(H) SIDE LEG STRETCHERS (Cut 2): 1/8″ × 1/8″ × 1 15/16″. See Figure **7-L-6**. Shape a 1/16″ × 1/16″ × 1/16″

peg at each end of each of these boards.

(I) FRONT INSIDE WALL (Cut 1): 1/16″ × 1 1/16″ × 1 1/2″.

(J) PEGS (Cut 4): 1/16″ diameter wood dowel × 3/16″.

ASSEMBLY: Stain all wood before glueing. Refer to Figures **7-L** and **7-L-1**.

1. Glue the back board against the rear edge of the bottom board, with bottom edges flush. Glue the side boards against the side edges of the bottom and back board, with bottom and rear edges flush. Refer to Figure **7-L-1**. The forward series of dotted lines in this diagram shows the position of the front inside wall. It is glued against the bottom board and the inside surfaces of the side boards.

2. The front board is glued against the forward edges of the bottom board and side boards. See Figure **7-L-1**.

3. Refer to Figure **7-L**. Glue the side and end stretchers into the drilled holes in the lower legs. *Note:* The top flat side of each leg is glued against the side board and the angled top side edge faces outward. Glue the four legs in place. Be sure that the bin sits straight and level. Let the glue dry.

4. Attach the hinges to the two top boards. Glue the smaller board atop the top edges of the sides, just behind the curved shape of this board.

5. Apply a finish coat.

OAK KITCHEN CABINET c. EARLY 1900's 7-M

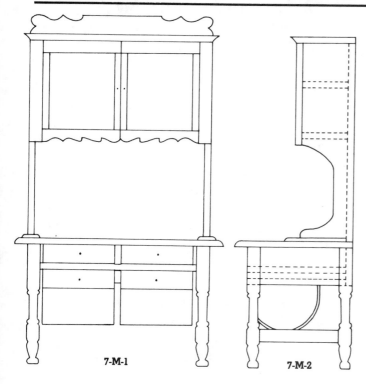

7-M-1   7-M-2

Use oak or bass or pine which is stained to represent oak. You will also need two pairs of tiny hinges, aluminum (such as a soft drink can which has been cut and flattened) and four tiny brass drawer pulls. The hinges and drawer pulls can be purchased from many mail-order lists or from your miniature dealer.

LOWER CABINET

(A) TABLE TOP (Cut 1): 1/8″ × 2 1/4″ × 4″. Round the front and side top edges. See Figure **7-M-4**.

(B) LEG (Cut 4): 1/4″ × 1/4″ × 2 3/8″. See Figure **7-M-5** for the shape. Refer to **1-C-3-a** for aid in carving.

(C) DRAWER BASE (Cut 1): 1/8″ × 1 7/8″ × 3″.

(D) TABLE SIDE (Cut 2): 1/8″ × 3/4″ × 1 1/2″.

(E) SHAPED DRAWER RUNNER (Cut 2): 1/8″ × 3/8″ × 1 7/8″. See Figure **7-M-11**. *Note:* This shaping runs the length of the board.

(F) SHAPED DRAWER DIVIDER (Cut 1): 3/8″ × 1/2″ × 1 7/8″. See Figure **7-M-12**. *Note:* This shaping runs the length of the board.

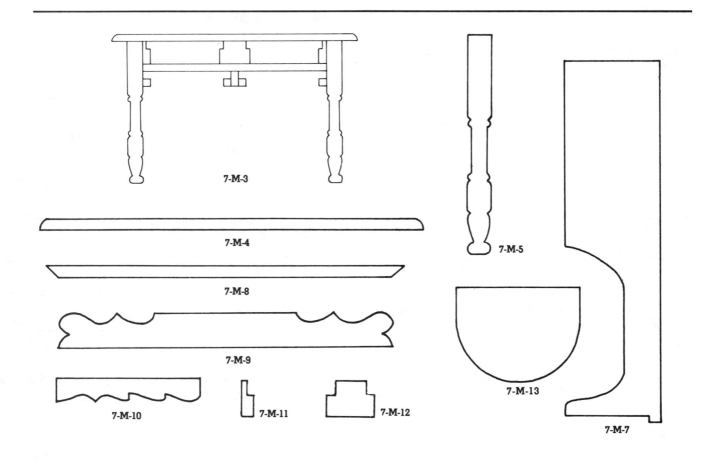

7-M-3

7-M-4

7-M-8

7-M-9

7-M-10

7-M-11

7-M-12

7-M-5

7-M-13

7-M-7

(G) BIN DRAWER RUNNERS (Cut 2): 1/8″ × 1/8″ × 1 7/8″.

(H) BIN DRAWER DIVIDERS

(1) **BIN DRAWER DIVIDERS** (Cut 2): 1/8″ × 1/8″ × 1 7/8″.

(2) **BIN DRAWER DIVIDER** (Cut 1): 1/8″ × 1/4″ × 1 7/8″.

(I) BIN SIDE (Cut 4): 1/8″ × 1″ × 1 5/16″. See Figure **7-M-6** for the shape.

(J) BIN DRAWER FRONT AND BACK

(1) **BIN DRAWER FRONT** (Cut 2): 1/16″ × 3/8″ × 1 7/16″. Drill holes in the drawer fronts at the sites indicated by the black dots in Figure **7-M-1**.

(2) **BIN DRAWER BACK** (Cut 2): 1/16″ × 3/8″ × 15/16″.

(K) BIN DRAWER RUNNERS (Cut 4): 1/8″ × 1/8″ × 1 3/4″.

(L) BIN DRAWER OUTSIDE SURFACE (Cut 2): Cut from thin aluminum. 1 1/8″ × 2 1/2″.

(M) CABINET DRAWER FRONT (Cut 2): 1/16″ × 3/8″ × 1 3/8″. Drill a hole to accept a drawer pull at the site indicated by a black dot in Figure **7-M-1**.

(N) CABINET DRAWER BACK (Cut 2): 1/16″ × 3/8″ × 1 1/8″.

(O) CABINET DRAWER SIDES (Cut 4): 1/16″ × 3/8″ × 1 11/16″.

(P) CABINET DRAWER RUNNERS (Cut 4): 1/16″ × 1/8″ × 1 13/16″.

(Q) CABINET DRAWER BOTTOM (Cut 2): 1/16″ × 1″ × 1 3/4″.

(R) LEG STRETCHER (Cut 2): 1/8″ × 1/4″ × 1 1/2″.

(S) TABLE BACK (Cut 1): 1/8″ × 3/4″ × 3″.

UPPER CABINET

(T) UPPER BACK Cut 2): 1/8″ × 1 5/8″ × 3 7/8″. Stain the wood and glue butted together to achieve a width of 3 1/4″.

(U) UPPER SIDES (Cut 2): 1/8″ × 1″ × 3 7/8″. See Figure **7-M-7** for the shape.

(V) UPPER TOP (Cut 1): 1/8″ × 1 1/4″ × 3 3/4″. The front and side edges are beveled downward. See Figure **7-M-8**.

(W) UPPER FRONT SIDE FACING (Cut 2): 1/8″ × 1/4″ × 2″.

(X) SIDE BASES (Cut 2): 1/16″ × 3/8″ × 1 1/8″. Round the top front and side edges.

(Y) UPPER CABINET TOP DECORATION (Cut 1): 1/8″ × 3/8″ × 3 1/2″. See Figure **7-M-9** for the shape.

(Z) SHELVES (Cut 2): 1/8″ × 7/8″ × 3 1/4″.

CUPBOARD DOORS

(AA) TOP (Cut 2): 1/8″ × 1/4″ × 1 1/2″.

(BB) BOTTOM (Cut 2): 1/8″ × 1/4″ × 1 1/2″. See Figure **7-M-10** for the shape.

(CC) SIDES (Cut 4): 1/8″ × 1/8″ × 1 1/2″.

(DD) CENTER PANEL (Cut 2): 1/16″ × 1 1/4″ × 1 1/2″.

ASSEMBLY

1. **CABINET DRAWER ASSEMBLY:** See **2-E-3**.

2. **BIN DRAWER ASSEMBLY:** See **2-E-4**.

3. **LOWER CABINET ASSEMBLY:** See **2-B-4** for assembly of the table. *Note this exception:* The lower cabinet top is flush with the back edge of the table. See Figure **7-M-3** which is the front view of this lower cabinet for the assembly of the runners and their placement for the bin drawers.

4. **UPPER CABINET ASSEMBLY:** See **2-C-5** for the assembly of the cabinet and doors. Glue the top decoration centered at the top of the cabinet.

5. When the assembly of both sections has been completed, glue them together. Apply the finish coat. After the finish coat is thoroughly dry, attach the drawer pulls and place the drawers in the cabinet.

CABINET DESK 7-N

(A) BACK (Cut 2): 1/8″ × 2 3/4″ × 5 1/2″. Stain the wood and glue butted together, making one piece measuring 1/8″ × 5 1/2″ × 5 1/2″.

DESK

(B) RIGHT SIDE (Cut 1): 1/8″ × 1 3/8″ × 4 3/8″. See Figure **7-N-3** for the shape. Drill a hole at the site of the black dot.

(C) LEFT SIDE (Cut 1): 1/8″ × 1 3/8″ × 3 1/2″. See Figure **7-N-5** for the shape. Drill a hole at the site of the black dot.

(D) BASE (Cut 1): 1/8″ × 1 1/4″ × 3 1/4″.

(E) LEFT BASE FACING (Cut 1): 1/8″ × 1/8″ × 1 1/4″.

(F) DESK TOP (Cut 1): 1/8″ × 1/2″ × 1 7/8″.

(G) TABLE TOP (Cut 1): 1/8″ × 1 1/8″ × 1 3/4″.

(H) SPACER (Cut 1): 1/16″ × 1/16″ × 1 3/4″.

(I) UPPER DESK FRONT (Cut 1): 1/8″ × 1 3/4″ × 1 13/16″. See Figure **7-N-4** for a side view of the shape. Drill a hole on each side at the site of the black dot.

(J) SPACER (Cut 1): 1/8″ × 1 3/8″ × 1 3/4″.

(K) LOWER FRONT FACING (Cut 1): 1/8″ × 1/4″ × 3 1/2″.

INTERIOR DESK COMPARTMENT

(L) COMPARTMENT SIDE (Cut 2): 1/16″ × 3/8″ × 1 1/8″. See Figure **7-N-7** for the shape.

(M) COMPARTMENT SPACER (Cut 2): 1/16″ × 3/8″ × 1″. See Figure **7-N-7-a** for the shape.

(N) COMPARTMENT SPACER (Cut 2): 1/16″ × 3/8″ × 11/16″. See Figure **7-N-6** for the shape.

(O) SPACER (Cut 1): 1/16″ × 3/8″ × 1″.

(P) BASE (Cut 1): 1/16″ × 3/8″ × 1 5/8″.

(Q) INTERIOR DRAWER
    (1) **FRONT** (Cut 1): 1/16″ × 1/4″ × 1″.
    (2) **BOTTOM** (Cut 1): 1/16″ × 1/4″ × 7/8″.
    (3) **SIDES** (Cut 2): 1/16″ × 3/16″ × 1/4″.
    (4) **BACK** (Cut 1): 1/16″ × 3/16″ × 1″.
Refer to **2-E-2** for assembly. *Note:* The front overhang will only be at the top.

(R) DESK DRAWER
    (1) **FRONT** (Cut 1): 1/8″ × 1/2″ × 1 3/4″.
    (2) **BOTTOM** (Cut 1): 1/8″ × 1 1/8″ × 1 1/2″.
    (3) **SIDES** (Cut 2): 1/8″ × 3/8″ × 1 1/8″.
    (4) **BACK** (Cut 1): 1/8″ × 3/8″ × 1 3/4″.
Refer to **2-E-2** for assembly. *Note:* The front overhang will only be at the top.

(S) LOWER CUPBOARD DOOR (Cut 1): 1/8″ × 1″ × 1 3/4″.

SIDE CABINET

(T) CABINET SIDE
    (1) **CABINET SIDE** (Cut 2): 1/8″ × 1 3/8″ × 5″.
    (2) **LEFT CABINET SIDE** (Cut 1): 1/8″ × 1 3/8″ × 5″. See Figure **7-N-1** for the shape.

(U) RIGHT CABINET SIDE (Cut 1): 1/8″ × 1 3/8″ × 4 7/8″. See Figure **7-N-2** for the shape.

(V) SHELF (Cut 4): 1/8″ × 1 1/4″ × 1 1/4″.

(W) SIDE DOOR FRAME (Cut 2): 1/16″ × 1/8″ × 4 3/8″.

(X) UPPER AND LOWER DOOR FRAME (Cut 2): 1/16″ × 1/8″ × 1″.

(Y) DOOR GLASS (Cut 1): Cut from a piece of thin plastic, such as a greeting card box top. 1 1/4″ × 4 3/8″.

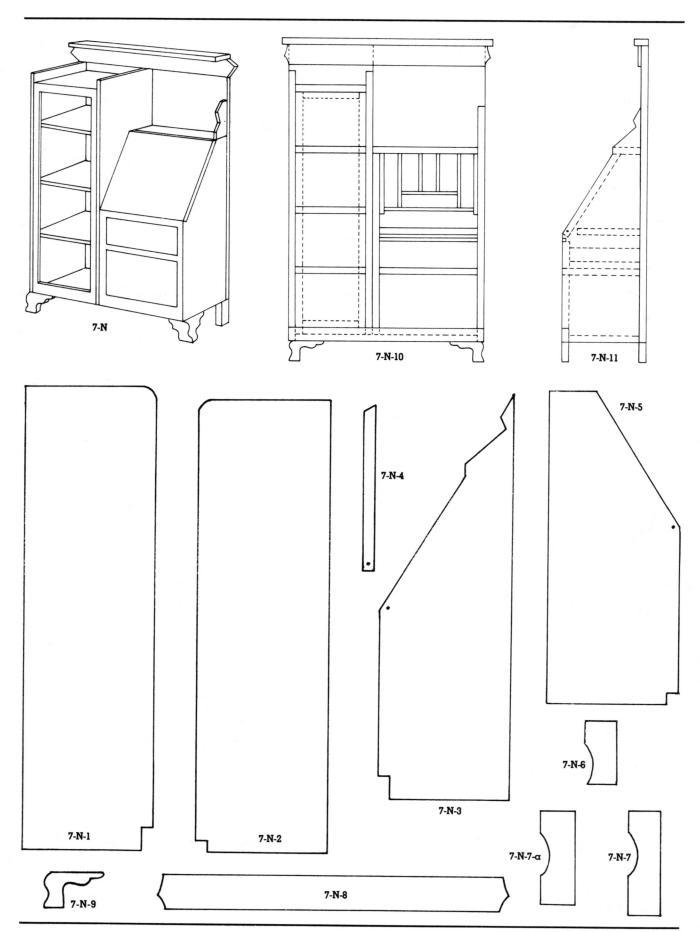

7-N

7-N-10

7-N-11

7-N-1

7-N-2

7-N-4

7-N-3

7-N-5

7-N-6

7-N-7-α

7-N-7

7-N-9

7-N-8

(Z) TOP FACING (Cut 1): 1/16" × 3/8" × 3 3/4". See Figure **7-N-8** for the shape.

(AA) TOP MOULDING (Cut 1): 1/8" × 1/4" × 3 3/4".

(BB) REAR LEGS (Cut 2): 1/8" × 1/8" × 3/8".

(CC) FRONT LEGS (Cut 2): 1/8" × 3/8" × 5/8". See Figure **7-N-9** for the shape. Refer to **1-C-3-d** for aid in carving.

ASSEMBLY: Stain all wood before glueing.

1. Glue the top moulding atop the top edge of the back board, with the back edges flush and equal overhang on both sides.

2. Glue the top facing directly beneath the top moulding and against the back board.

3. Glue the left cabinet side along the left front edge of the back board. Glue the right desk side along the right front edge of the back board. These boards will be flush with the bottom edge of the back board. Glue the base (**D**) between the left cabinet side and the right desk side, along the lower front edge of the back, with the lower edges flush.

4. Glue the left base facing (**E**) along the top left inside edge of the base, against the depth of the left cabinet wall.

5. Lay the table top (**G**) and spacer (**H**) against the right desk side (*these are being used as spacing guides only*). Glue the left desk side against the back board and the base, with the right surface against these guide boards. When the glue begins to set, remove these spacing guide boards.

6. Lay the cabinet shelves against the left cabinet side (*as you did in Step 5*) and glue the right cabinet side against the back, the left desk side and the base. When the glue begins to set, remove these spacing guide boards.

7. Glue spacer (**J**) with the bottom surface 1 1/8" above the base board and between the desk sides. See Figures **7-N-10** and **7-N-11**.

8. Glue spacer (**H**) with the bottom surface 1/2" above the previous spacer (**J**), between the desk sides and flush with the front edges of the boards.

9. Glue the table top (**G**) with the bottom surface 5/8" above piece (**J**), against the back board and between the desk sides.

10. Glue the lower front facing (**K**) along the front

edge of the base board and in the notches of the side boards. See Figures **7-N-10** and **7-N-11**.

11. Glue the desk top (**F**) resting atop the top edge of the left side board and level across the back board, and against the inside surface of the right desk side. See Figure **7-N-10**.

12. See Figure **7-N-11** for the side view of the desk. Place the upper desk front board between the two desk side boards, aligning the drilled holes. Push a brad through the holes on the right side of the desk and on into the front board. Push a brad, at the same height, through the right cabinet wall — through the left desk wall — and on into the front board. These brads will act as hinges for the desk front board (*pin hinge*).

13. Glue the cabinet shelves in place between the left and right cabinet sides. Use Figure **7-N-10** as your placement guide.

14. Glue the two side door frames to the end edges of the upper and lower door frames. Be sure that this unit is kept squared. Apply a finish coat to this unit when the glue is thoroughly dry. Glue the "glass" (**Y**) to the back edges of these boards.

15. Construct the interior desk compartment, as shown in Figure **7-N-10**. This unit will be glued inside the desk, between the side walls and against the underneath surface of the desk top.

16. Construct the small drawer and the large drawer as directed in **2-E-2**.

17. Glue the front and back legs in place as indicated in Figures **7-N-10** and **7-N-11**.

18. Attach the lower cupboard door in the desk portion, using the pin hinge method. Brad down through board (**J**) into the upper right edge of the door; brad up through the base and into the lower right edge of the door.

19. Attach the cupboard door (*using the pin hinge method*). Brad down through the top shelf of the cupboard and into the left top edge of the door frame. Brad up through the facing board (**K**) into the lower left edge of the door frame.

20. Apply a finish coat to this piece of furniture. Be careful to avoid getting it on the plastic which you used for the door glass.

21. Attach a door pull. Use brass nails (*cut off*) as the interior and exterior drawer pulls.

SIDEBOARD 7-O

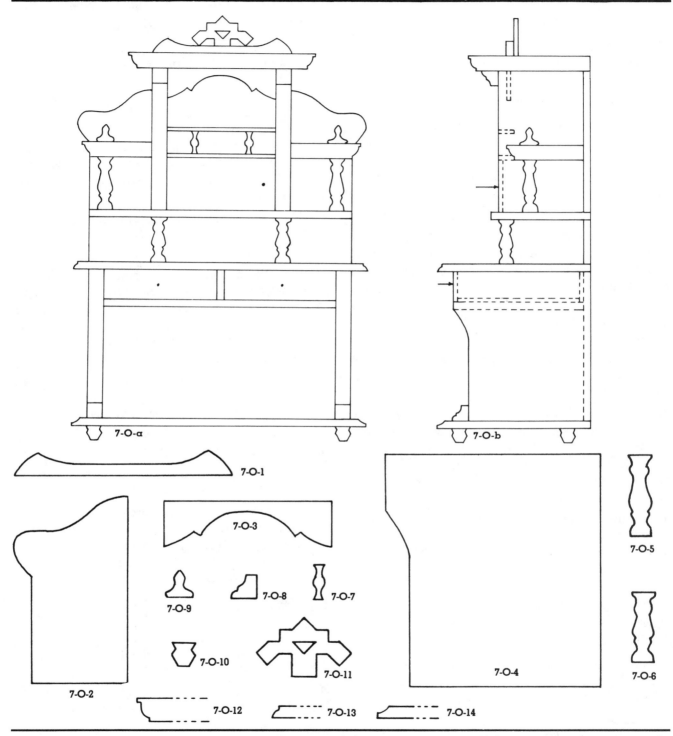

7-O-a

7-O-b

7-O-1

7-O-2

7-O-3

7-O-9

7-O-8

7-O-7

7-O-10

7-O-11

7-O-4

7-O-5

7-O-6

7-O-12

7-O-13

7-O-14

LOWER CABINET

(A) BASE (Cut 1): 1/8″ × 2 1/2″ × 4 3/4″. See Figure **7-O-14** for a side view of the edge shaping for the front and side edges.

(B) LOWER BACK (Cut 1): 1/8″ × 2 1/2″ × 3 3/4″.

(C) LOWER SIDES (Cut 2): 1/4″ × 2 1/4″ × 2 1/2″. See Figure **7-O-4** for the shape.

(D) TOP OF LOWER CABINET (Cut 1): 1/8″ × 2 1/2″ × 4 3/4″. See Figure **7-O-13** for a side view of the edge shaping for the front and side edges.

(E) DRAWER BASE (Cut 1): 1/8″ × 2 1/8″ × 3 3/4″.

(F) DRAWERS (Two)

　　(1) **FRONT AND BACK** (Cut 4): 1/16″ × 1/2″ × 13/16″.

(2) **SIDES** (Cut 4): 1/16″ × 1/2″ × 2″.

(3) **BOTTOM** (Cut 2): 1/16″ × 11/16″ × 2″.
Refer to **2-E-1** for assembly.

(G) DRAWER DIVIDER (Cut 1): 1/8″ × 1/2″ × 2 1/8″.

(H) TOP FRONT AND BASE FRONT DECORATIONS (Cut 4): 1/4″ × 1/4″ × 1/4″. See Figure **7-O-8** for the front shape.

(I) FEET (Cut 4): 1/4″ × 1/4″ × 1/4″. See Figure **7-O-10** for the shape on all sides.

(J) DRAWER PULLS (Two): Refer to **1-B-6**.

UPPER CABINET

(K) CENTER-UPPER BACK (Cut 1): 1/8″ × 2 1/4″ × 2 3/8″.

(L) SIDE-UPPER BACK (Cut 2): 1/8″ × 1 3/16″ × 2″. See Figure **7-O-2** for the shape.

(M) LOWER SHELF (Cut 1): 1/8″ × 1 5/8″ × 4 1/4″.

(N) LOWER BACK (Cut 1): 1/8″ × 3/4″ × 4 1/4″.

(O) UPPER SIDE SHELVES (Cut 2): 1/4″ × 1 1/8″ × 1 1/4″. See Figure **7-O-12** for a side view of the edge shaping for the front and one side edge. The side shaping is on the left for the left shelf, and on the right for the right shelf.

(P) UPPER CENTER SHELF (Cut 1): 1/16″ × 1 3/8″ × 1 3/4″.

(Q) UPPER CENTER SHELF RAIL (Cut 1): 1/16″ × 1/16″ × 1 3/4″.

(R) UPPER SIDE PANELS (Cut 2): 1/4″ × 1 3/8″ × 2 3/8″.

(S) UPPER CABINET TOP (Cut 1): 1/4″ × 2″ × 3 1/16″. See Figure **7-O-12** for a side view of the edge shaping for the front and side edges.

(T) UPPER CABINET FACING (Cut 1): 1/16″ × 1/2″ × 1 3/4″. See Figure **7-O-3** for the shape.

(U) TOP DECORATIONS

(1) **FRONT PIECE** (Cut 1): 1/8″ × 1/4″ × 2 1/4″. See Figure **7-O-1** for the shape.

(2) **BACK PIECE** (Cut 1): 1/16″ × 1/2″ × 1″. See Figure **7-O-11** for the shape.

(V) SPINDLES (Cut 2): 1/8″ diameter wood dowel × 3/8″. See Figure **7-O-7** for the shape.

(W) POSTS

(1) **POSTS** (Cut 2): 1/4″ diameter wood dowel × 3/4″. See Figure **7-O-6** for the shape.

(2) **POSTS** (Cut 2): 1/4″ diameter wood dowel × 7/8″. See Figure **7-O-5** for the shape.
Refer to **1-C-3-a** for aid in shaping the posts and spindles.

(X) UPPER SHELF ORNAMENT (Cut 2): 5/16″ diameter wood dowel × 1/4″. See Figure **7-O-9** for

the shape. *Note:* A wooden collar button or like ornament can be used instead of carving them.

(Y) CUPBOARD DOOR (Cut 1): 1/16″ × 7/8″ × 1 3/4″.

(Z) DOOR PULL (One): Refer to **1-B-6**.

ASSEMBLY: Stain all wood before glueing. Be sure that the shaped edges are assembled according to the diagrams. Refer to **7-O-a** and **7-O-b**.

LOWER CABINET

1. The back is glued centered atop the base, with the back edges flush.

2. The sides are glued against the upright side edges of the back and atop the base.

3. The lower cabinet top is glued atop the top edges of the sides and the back. There will be a 1/4″ overhang at the front and sides.

4. Place a drawer beneath the cabinet to use as a spacer. Glue the drawer base beneath the drawer against the sides and back board. Place the drawer divider into this opening and against the drawer. It will be glued against the drawer base board and against the back board. Remove the drawer.

5. Glue the four feet in place. See Figures **7-O-a** and **7-O-b**.

UPPER CABINET ASSEMBLY

6. Glue the two side-upper back boards against the center-upper back board. See Figure **7-O-a**. Glue this assembly atop the lower shelf, with the back edges flush.

7. Glue the above assembly atop the top edge of the lower back, with back edges flush.

8. Glue the two upper side panels against the assembled back with the outside edges flush with the joints in the back, and atop the shelf. See Figures **7-O-a** and **7-O-b**.

9. Place the cupboard door between the two side panels and against the back (*for measurement only*). Glue the center shelf above the door and against the side panels and back board. Remove the door.

10. Glue the two spindles atop the above shelf, and glue the rail above the spindles and between the side panels. Refer to **7-O-a**.

11. Pin hinge the cupboard door in the opening below the above assembled shelf. Refer to **1-B-4**. Push one pin down through the upper shelf and the other up through the lower shelf into the left side of the cupboard door.

12. Glue a 7/8″ long post atop each side of the lower shelf (*see Figure* **7-O-a**) and glue the upper side shelves atop the posts and against the upper side panels and back board. See Figure **7-O-a.**

13. Glue the upper cabinet top (*centered*) in place atop the top edges of the upper side panels and the center back, with the back edges flush.

14. Refer to Figures **7-O-a** and **7-O-b.** Glue the top decoration in place atop the upper cabinet top.

15. Glue the upper shelf decorations in place. See Figure **7-O-a.**

16. Glue the top front and base front decorations in place. See Figure **7-O-b.**

17. Glue the upper cabinet atop the top board of the lower cabinet, with the side spaces equal and back edges flush. Glue the remaining posts (*3/4"*) beneath the shelf and atop the top of the lower cabinet (*these are in line with the upper side boards*). See Figure **7-O-a.**

18. Apply a finish. When the finish is completely dry, attach the door and drawer pulls.

DRESSER 7-P

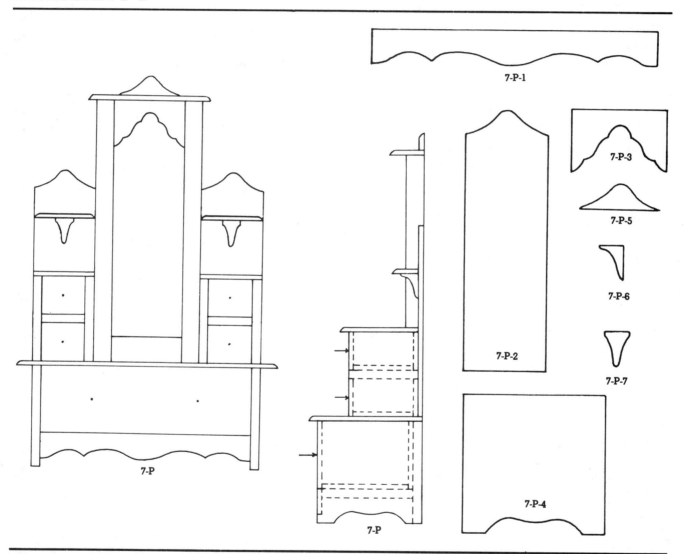

UPPER SECTION

(A) CENTER BACK (Cut 1): 1/16" × 1" × 3 7/8".

(B) SIDE BACK (Cut 2): 1/16" × 7/8" × 2 7/8". See Figure **7-P-2** for the shape. Glue the sides butted against the upright sides of the center back, with the lower edges and back edges flush.

(C) UPPER CHEST (Two)

(1) **SIDES** (Cut 4): 1/8" × 1" × 1 1/4".

(2) **TOP** (Cut 2): 1/16" × 7/8" × 1 1/8". Round off the top surface of the front edge of this board.

(3) **DRAWER SEPARATORS** (Cut 2): 1/8" × 5/8" × 1".

(D) UPPER CHEST DRAWERS (Four)

(1) **FRONT AND BACK** (Cut 8): 1/16" × 9/16" × 5/8".

(2) **SIDES** (Cut 8): 1/16" × 9/16" × 7/8".

(3) **BOTTOM** (Cut 4): 1/16" × 1/2" × 3/4".
Refer to **2-E-1** for assembly of all drawers.

(E) **SIDE SHELVES** (Cut 2): 1/16" × 3/8" × 7/8". Bevel the front and side edges. See the front and side elevation diagrams.

(F) **SHELF BRACE** (Cut 2): 1/4" × 1/4" × 3/8". See Figure **7-P-6** for a side view of the shaping and Figure **7-P-7** for a front view of the shaping.

(G) **MIRROR FRAME SIDES** (Cut 2): 1/4" × 1/4" × 3 7/8".

(H) **MIRROR FRAME BOTTOM** (Cut 1): 1/16" × 3/8" × 1".

(I) **MIRROR FRAME TOP** (Cut 1): 1/16" × 11/16" × 1". See Figure **7-P-3** for the shape.

(J) **TOP SHELF** (Cut 1): 1/16" × 1/2" × 1 3/4". Bevel the top surfaces of the front and side edges.

(K) **TOP ORNAMENT** (Cut 1): 1/16" × 1/4" × 7/8". See Figure **7-P-5** for the shape.

LOWER CHEST

(L) **BACK** (Cut 1): 1/8" × 1 1/2" × 3".

(M) **SIDES** (Cut 2): 1/8" × 1 1/2" × 1 1/2". See Figure **7-P-4** for the shape.

(N) **BOTTOM** (Cut 1): 1/8" × 1 5/16" × 3".

(O) **TOP** (Cut 1): 1/16" × 1 5/8" × 3 3/4". Bevel the top surfaces of the front and side edges.

(P) **APRON** (Cut 1): 1/16" × 3/8" × 3". See Figure **7-P-1** for the shape.

(Q) **LOWER DRAWER** (One)
(1) **FRONT AND BACK** (Cut 2): 1/16" × 1" × 3".

(2) **SIDES** (Cut 2): 1/16" × 1" × 1 1/4".

(3) **BOTTOM** (Cut 1): 1/16" × 1 1/4" × 2 7/8".
Refer to **2-E-1** for assembly.

(R) **DRAWER PULLS** (Six): Refer to **1-B-6**.

(S) **MIRROR** (Cut 1): As thin as possible × 1 × 3 7/8".

ASSEMBLY: Stain all wood before glueing.

1. Glue the mirror frame sides against the center back board, with the outside edges along the edges of the center back board and the bottom edges flush.

2. Glue a small chest side board against the outside surfaces of the mirror frame side board and against the back, with the bottom edges flush. Glue the second chest side board against the back board, with the side and bottom edges flush. Repeat for the second chest. See the front elevation.

3. Insert a drawer between the two sides, with the bottom edges flush (*for measurement only*). Glue a drawer separator against the back and side boards (*this separator will only rest on the drawer for measurement and placement*). Remove the drawer. Repeat for the second chest.

4. Glue a chest top atop the two sides and against the back board. Repeat for the second chest.

5. See the front elevation for placement of the side shelves. Glue the bracket centered beneath each shelf, with back edges flush. Glue the two shelf assemblies in place.

6. Glue the top shelf atop the top edges of the center back board and side mirror frame boards. Glue the ornament centered atop this shelf, with the back edges flush.

LOWER CHEST ASSEMBLY

7. Glue the sides against the upright end edges of the back board.

8. Glue the top atop the top edges of the sides and back board, with the back edges flush and with equal overhang at both sides.

9. Insert the drawer for measurement only. Glue the bottom board against the back and inside surfaces of the side boards. See the side elevation.

10. Glue the apron against the front edge of the bottom board and between the two side boards. Remove the drawer. See the front and side elevations.

11. Glue the top assembly atop the top surface of the lower chest, with back edges flush and with equal spacing at each side.

12. Apply a finish coat to the assembled chest, the five drawers and the top and bottom pieces of the mirror frame.

13. Glue the mirror between the side pieces of the mirror frame and against the center back board. Glue the upper and lower pieces of the mirror frame in place against the mirror. See the front elevation.

14. Attach the six drawer pulls and place the drawers in the dresser.

OAK PARLOR WALL CABINET 7-Q

(A) **BACK** (Cut 1): 1/16" × 1 3/4" × 2 1/2". See Figure **7-Q-5** for the shape. The shaded areas are cut out.

(B) **TOP-SIDE SHELVES** (Cut 2): 1/16" × 11/16" × 13/16". See Figures **7-Q-6** (*right shelf*) and **7-Q-7** (*left*

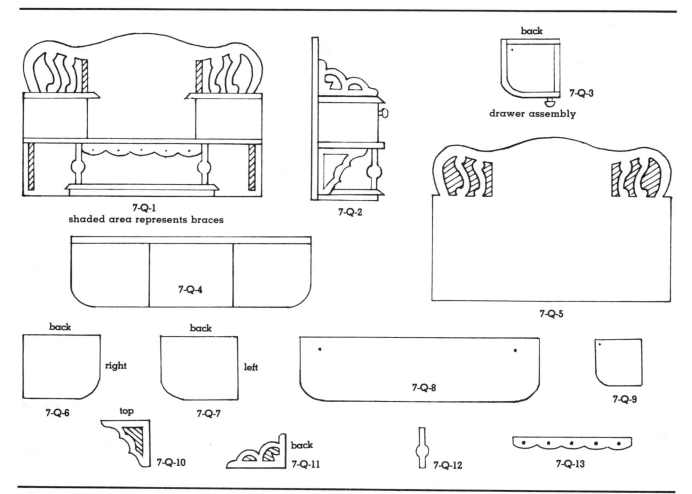

7-Q-1
shaded area represents braces

7-Q-2

back
7-Q-3
drawer assembly

7-Q-4

7-Q-5

back
right
7-Q-6

back
left
7-Q-7

7-Q-8

7-Q-9

top
7-Q-10

back
7-Q-11

7-Q-12

7-Q-13

shelf) for the shape of the shelves. Bevel the top edges of the sides and front of both shelves.

(C) MIDDLE SHELF (Cut 1): 1/16″ × 11/16″ × 2 1/2″. See Figure **7-Q-8** for the shape. Drill pin-sized holes through the wood at the sites of the black dots in the diagram.

(D) BOTTOM SHELF (Cut 1): 1/16″ × 5/8″ × 1 1/2″.

(E) BOTTOM SHELF TOP MOULDING (Cut 1): 1/16″ × 11/16″ × 1 5/8″. Bevel the top edges of the sides and front.

(F) APRON (Cut 1): 1/16″ × 1/8″ × 1 1/4″. See Figure **7-Q-13** for the shape. The black dots in this diagram represent tiny holes to be drilled through the board.

(G) POSTS (Cut 2): 1/8″ diameter wood dowel × 7/16″. See Figure **7-Q-12** for the shape. Refer to **1-C-3-a**.

(H) TOP SHELF DECORATION (Cut 2): 1/16″ × 3/8″ × 5/8″. See Figure **7-Q-11** for the shape. The shaded areas are cut out.

(I) SHELF SUPPORTS (Cut 2): 1/16″ × 1/2″ × 1/2″. See Figure **7-Q-10** for the shape. The shaded area is cut out.

(J) DRAWERS (Two)

(1) **BACK** (Cut 2): 1/16″ × 7/16″ × 9/16″.

(2) **SIDES** (Cut 2): 1/16″ × 7/16″ × 1/2″.

(3) **FRONT** (Cut 2): 1/16″ × 7/16″ × 1 1/8″.

(4) **BOTTOM** (Cut 2): 1/8″ × 1/2″ × 1/2″. See Figure **7-Q-9** for the shape. The black dot in the diagram represents a pin-sized hole to be drilled through the board.

(K) DRAWER PULLS (Two): Refer to **1-B-6**.

ASSEMBLY: Stain all wood before glueing. Refer to Figures **7-Q-1** (*front view*) and **7-Q-2** (*left side view*).

DRAWER ASSEMBLY: Refer to Figure **7-Q-3** which is the drawer assembly for the left drawer. You will reverse the diagram for the right drawer. The directions will be for the left drawer; reverse them for the right drawer.

1. Glue the side against the right edge of the drawer bottom, with bottom edges flush. See Figure **7-Q-3**.

2. Glue the back against the back edge of the bottom board and against the back upright edge of the side, with all edges flush.

3. Refer to **1-C-6**. When the wood will bend easily, glue it against the left and front edges of the bottom

board and the edges of the back and side boards. All edges are flush. See Figure **7-Q-3**.

4. Reverse the placement of the side board and the shape of the bottom board for the right drawer. Set the assembled drawers aside until called for.

WALL CABINET ASSEMBLY

5. Refer to Figure **7-Q-1**. The top side shelves (**B**) are glued against the back, with the top edge at the bottom line of the cut-out area in the back. See Figure **7-Q-4** for the placement of the left and right shelves.

6. Place the left drawer beneath the left shelf (*for measurement only*). Repeat for the right drawer. Glue the middle shelf against the back board and resting against the bottom surfaces of the two drawers. Remove the drawers.

7. Glue the top shelf decorations (**H**) atop the center side edge of each top shelf and against the back. See Figure **7-Q-1**. The two upper shaded areas represent these decorations.

8. Glue the bottom shelf moulding atop the top surface of the shelf, with the back edges flush. Glue this assembled shelf centered against the back board, with the bottom edges flush.

9. Glue a post at each front corner of the bottom shelf and beneath the middle shelf. Glue the apron against the bottom of the middle shelf (*flush with the front edge*) and against the inside top edges of the two posts.

10. Apply a finish coat to the wall cabinet, the two drawers, the two shelf supports and the drawer pulls.

11. Insert the left and right drawers in their respective openings. Cut two pins, measuring 1/2" long with the heads snipped off. Push a pin up through the hole in the middle shelf, through the hole in the drawer, and up into the corner of the top side shelf. The bottom edge of the pin will be flush with the bottom surface of the middle shelf. Repeat for the second drawer. The drawers will now swing open to the side.

12. Glue the middle shelf supports (**I**) against the bottom surface of the middle shelf (*against the site of the pin hole*) and against the back board. Attach the two drawer pulls. Refer to Figure **7-Q-1**.

OAK SIX DRAWER CHEST WITH SHAVING MIRROR 7-R

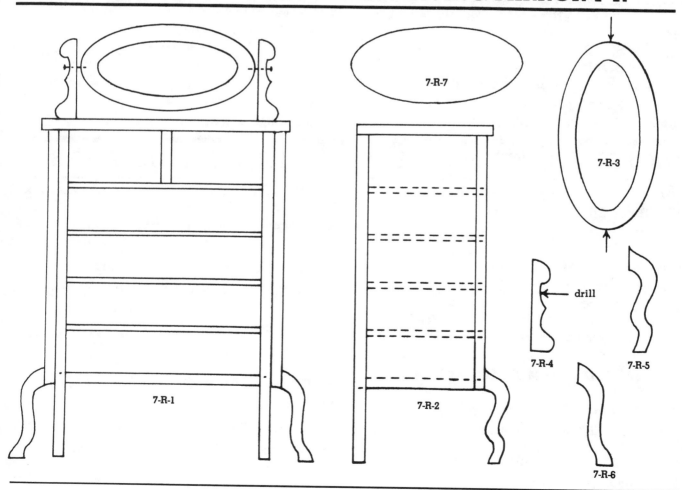

(A) BACK (Cut 1): 1/8″ × 2 1/4″ × 3″.

(B) SIDES (Cut 2): 1/16″ × 1 3/8″ × 3″.

(C) TOP (Cut 1): 1/8″ × 1 9/16″ × 2 7/8″.

(D) BOTTOM (Cut 1): 1/8″ × 1 3/8″ × 2 1/4″.

(E) DRAWER SPACERS (Cut 4): 1/16″ × 1 3/8″ × 2 1/4″.

(F) DRAWER DIVIDER (Cut 1): 1/8″ × 5/8″ × 1 1/4″.

(G) CORNER MOULDING (Cut 4): 1/8″ × 1/8″ × 3″.

(H) BACK LEGS (Cut 2): 1/8″ × 3/8″ × 1 1/8″. See Figure **7-R-6** for the shape.

(I) FRONT LEGS (Cut 2): 1/8″ × 5/16″ × 1 1/8″. See Figure **7-R-5** for the shape.

(J) MIRROR FRAME (Cut 1): 1/8″ × 1″ × 2″. See Figure **7-R-3** for the shape. The inside area is cut away. The arrows indicate the location where two pins will be inserted.

(K) MIRROR (Cut 1): As thin as possible × 13/16″ × 1 13/16″. See Figure **7-R-7** for the shape.

(L) MIRROR POSTS (Cut 2): 1/8″ × 1/4″ × 15/16″. See Figure **7-R-4** for the shape. The arrow indicates a pin-sized hole to be drilled through each post.

(M) SMALL DRAWERS (Two)
  (1) **FRONT AND BACK** (Cut 4): 1/16″ × 5/8″ × 1″.
  (2) **SIDES** (Cut 4): 1/16″ × 5/8″ × 1 1/8″.
  (3) **BOTTOM** (Cut 2): 1/8″ × 7/8″ × 1 1/8″.

(N) LARGE DRAWERS (Four)
  (1) **FRONT AND BACK** (Cut 8): 1/16″ × 1/2″ × 2 1/4″.

  (2) **SIDES** (Cut 8): 1/16″ × 1/2″ × 1 1/4″.
  (3) **BOTTOM** (Cut 4): 1/8″ × 1 1/4″ × 2 1/8″.
See **2-E-1** for assembly.

(O) DRAWER PULLS (Ten): Refer to **1-B-6-b**.

ASSEMBLY: Stain all wood before glueing.

1. Glue the mirror centered behind the mirror frame after a finish coat has been applied to the frame.

2. Each back leg and each front leg is glued against a piece of corner moulding (**G**). See Figure **7-R-1** for a view of the back legs and **7-R-2** for a view of the front legs.

3. The front leg moulding assembly is glued against the front edge of each side board, with the top and inside edges flush. See Figure **7-R-2**.

4. Refer to **2-C-1** for the general assembly of the chest. You will note that the front edges of the drawer spacers are flush with the front edge of the side moulding. The drawers and drawer divider are all recessed from the front.

5. Glue the back leg side moulding against the side, with the top and back edges flush. See Figures **7-R-1** and **7-R-2**.

6. Glue the two mirror support posts (**L**) atop the top of the chest, with space between them for the mirror, the back edges flush, and equal side spaces. Apply a finish coat to the chest and drawers.

7. Push a sequin pin through the hole in each post and on into the mirror frame. Be sure the mirror is level. Repeat for the second side. See Figure **7-R-1**.

8. Attach the drawer pulls.

VICTORIAN PERIOD PIE SAFE WITH PIERCED METAL 7-S

(A) BACK (Cut 1): 1/8″ × 3 1/4″ × 3 7/8″.

(B) UPPER SIDES (Cut 2): 1/8″ × 1″ × 1″.

(C) SIDE METAL (Cut 2): 1/16″ thick aluminum or tin × 3/4″ × 2 1/2″. Refer to Figure **7-S-6** for the design to be pierced in the metal. Trace this design onto a piece of tracing paper. Tape the metal securely behind the paper. Place the metal on a piece of scrap wood which is a bit larger than the metal. Using a tiny nail and hammer, pierce a hole through the metal at the site of each black dot in the design.

(D) VERTICAL SIDE MOULDING (Cut 4): 1/8″ × 1/8″ × 2 1/2″.

(E) HORIZONTAL SIDE MOULDING
  (1) **HORIZONTAL SIDE MOULDING** (Cut 2): 1/8″ × 1/4″ × 1″.
  (2) **HORIZONTAL SIDE MOULDING** (Cut 4): 1/16″ × 1/8″ × 3/4″.

(F) DRAWER BASE BOARD (Cut 1): 1/8″ × 1 1/8″ × 3″. See Figure **7-S-9** for the shape.

(G) CHEST BOTTOM BOARD (Cut 1): 1/8″ × 1 1/8″ × 3 1/4″. See Figure **7-S-8** for the shape.

(H) SHELVES (Cut 2): 1/8″ × 1″ × 3″.

(I) TOP (Cut 1): 1/8″ × 1 3/8″ × 3 1/2″. Bevel the bottom edge of the sides and front. See Figures **7-S-1** and **7-S-2**.

(J) SIDE FRONT FACING (Cut 2): 1/8″ × 1/4″ × 4 3/8″.

(K) BACK LEGS (Cut 2): 1/8″ × 1/4″ × 1/2″.

(L) DRAWER DIVIDER (Cut 1): 1/4″ × 1/2″ × 1 1/8″.

(M) TOP FRONT (Cut 1): 1/8″ × 1/8″ × 2 3/4″.

(N) DRAWER RUNNERS (Cut 2): 1/8″ × 1/8″ × 1″.

(O) DRAWERS (Two)

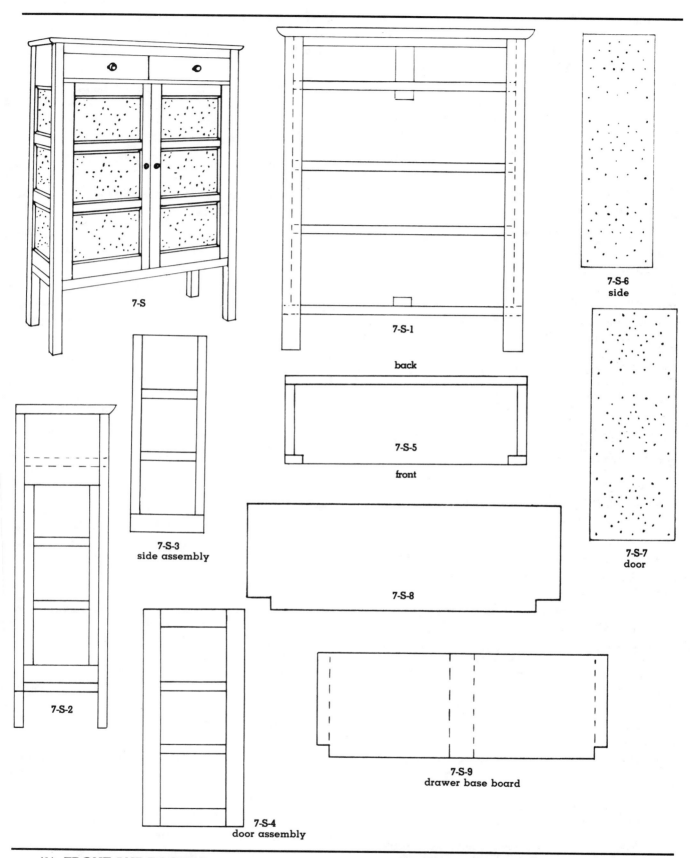

7-S

7-S-1

back

7-S-5

front

7-S-3
side assembly

7-S-2

7-S-4
door assembly

7-S-8

7-S-9
drawer base board

7-S-6
side

7-S-7
door

(1) **FRONT AND BACK** (Cut 4): 1/16″ × 1/2″ × 1 1/4″.

(2) **SIDES** (Cut 4): 1/16″ × 1/2″ × 1″.

(3) **BOTTOM** (Cut 2): 1/8″ × 1″ × 1 1/8″.

(4) **PULLS** (Two drawer and two door): Refer to 1-B-6. Refer to 2-E-1 for assembly.

(P) **DOORS** (Two)

(1) **DOOR METAL** (Cut 2): 1/16″ thick

133

aluminum or tin × 7/8″ × 2 1/2″. Refer to Figure **7-S-7** for the design to be pierced into the metal. Pierce the metal as you did for the sides.

    (2) **VERTICAL MOULDING** (Cut 4): 1/8″ × 1/4″ × 3″.

    (3) **HORIZONTAL MOULDING**
        (a) **HORIZONTAL MOULDING** (Cut 4): 1/8″ × 1/4″ × 7/8″.
        (b) **HORIZONTAL MOULDING** (Cut 4): 1/16″ × 1/8″ × 7/8″.

(Q) DOOR STOPS (Cut 2): 1/8″ × 1/8″ × 1/4″.

ASSEMBLY: Stain all wood before glueing.

1. Refer to Figure **7-S-3** for the side assembly. Glue the vertical moulding pieces against each side of the metal, with back edges flush. Glue the lower horizontal moulding piece against the bottom edges of this assembly, with back edges flush. Glue the upper side (**B**) against the top edges of this assembly, with back edges flush. Glue the two horizontal moulding pieces against the metal, between the side moulding boards. Repeat for the other side.

2. Refer to Figure **7-S-4** for the door assembly. The two doors are assembled as the sides were.

3. Glue the assembled sides butted against the back board, with side and top edges flush. See Figure **7-S-2** for a left side view.

4. Glue the top board atop the top edges of the back and sides, with back edges flush and equal side overhang. Refer to Figures **7-S-1** and **7-S-2**.

5. Glue the bottom board butted against the back board and beneath the side board assembly, with bottom and side edges flush. *Note:* The notched edge of this board is forward.

6. Glue the drawer base board between the sides and butted against the back, with the top surface 5/8″ below the top. The notched edge will be forward.

7. Refer to Figure **7-S-1**. Glue the upper shelf in place, with the top surface 1″ below the bottom surface of the drawer base board. Glue the lower shelf in place, with the bottom surface 1″ above the top surface of the bottom board.

8. Glue the two side front facing boards against the front edges of the side boards and in the notches in the bottom board and the drawer base board, with the side and top edges flush.

9. Glue the top front board (**M**) butted against the bottom surface of the top and between the side facing boards.

10. Glue the drawer divider centered in the drawer opening (*insert a drawer as your guide*) and atop the drawer base, with front edges flush. Remove the drawer.

11. Glue a door stop centered atop the bottom board, with the front edges flush. Glue the second door stop centered beneath the drawer base and recessed 1/8″ from the front edge.

12. Glue the back legs (*1/4″ wide*) beneath the bottom board, with the back and side edges flush. See Figure **7-S-2**.

13. Apply a finish coat to the cabinet, two doors and two drawers.

14. Refer to **1-B-4-a** (*pin hinge*). Attach the doors, pinning through the drawer base board and the bottom board.

15. Attach the door and drawer pulls.

VICTORIAN PERIOD THREE DRAWER DRESSER WITH WISHBONE MIRROR AND TWO DRAWER DECK 7-T

(A) BACK (Cut 1): 1/8″ × 2 1/4″ × 2 3/4″.

(B) SIDES (Cut 2): 1/16″ × 1 1/4″ × 2 3/8″. See Figure **7-T-3** for the shape.

(C) TOP (Cut 1): 1/8″ × 1 5/8″ × 3 1/4″. See Figures **7-T-1** and **7-T-2** for the shape of the front and side edges.

(D) BOTTOM (Cut 1): 1/16″ × 1 5/16″ × 2 3/4″.

(E) WISHBONE BASE (Cut 1): 3/16″ thick × 1/2″ diameter disc. See Figure **7-T-5-a** for a side view of the shape and Figure **7-T-5-b** showing a 1/8″ diameter hole to be drilled through the base.

(F) WISHBONE (Cut 1): 1/8″ × 1 7/16″ × 1 5/8″. See Figure **7-T-4** for the shape. The arrows indicate the sites of pin-sized holes to be drilled through each "arm".

(G) MIRROR FRAME (Cut 1): 1/8″ × 1 1/8″ × 1 1/2″. See Figure **7-T-6** for the shape. The inside area is cut away. Round off the top surface. The arrows indicate the location of pin insertion.

(H) MIRROR (Cut 1): As thin as possible × 7/8″ × 1 1/8″. See Figure **7-T-7** for the shape.

(I) DECK DRAWER CABINETS (Two)
    (1) **SIDES** Cut 4): 1/16″ × 3/8″ × 1 1/8″.
    (2) **BACK** (Cut 2): 1/16″ × 3/8″ × 5/8″.
    (3) **TOP** (Cut 2): 1/16″ × 7/8″ × 1 5/16″. Bevel the top edge of the sides and front.

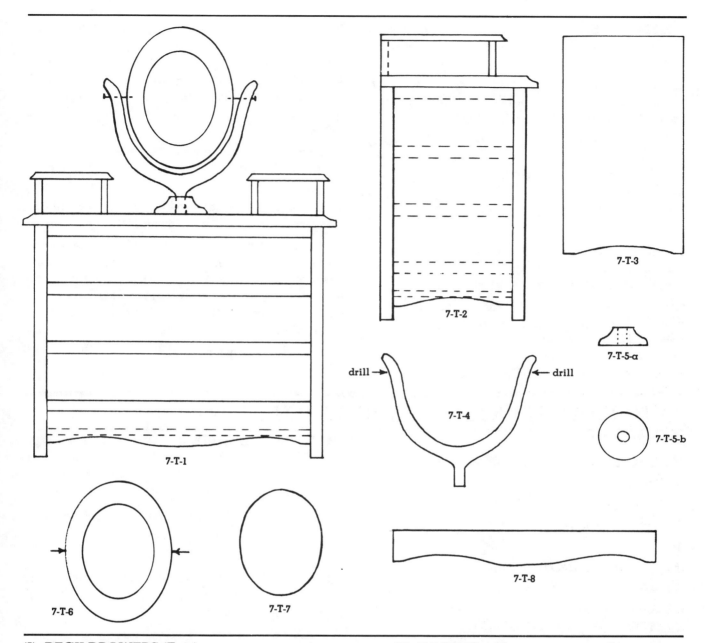

7-T-1

7-T-2

7-T-3

7-T-5-α

drill → ← drill

7-T-4

7-T-5-b

7-T-6

7-T-7

7-T-8

(J) DECK DRAWERS (Two)

   (1) **FRONT** (Cut 2): 1/16″ × 3/8″ × 3/4″.

   (2) **BACK** (Cut 2): 1/16″ × 3/8″ × 5/8″.

   (3) **SIDES** (Cut 4): 1/16″ × 3/8″ × 1 1/16″.

   (4) **BOTTOM** (Cut 2): 1/16″ × 1/2″ × 1 1/16″.

Refer to **2-E-2** (*overhang at each side*) for drawer assembly.

(K) LARGE DRAWERS (Three)

   (1) **FRONT AND BACK** (Cut 6): 1/16″ × 1/2″ × 2 3/4″.

   (2) **SIDES** (Cut 6): 1/16″ × 1/2″ × 1 1/4″.

   (3) **BOTTOM** (Cut 3): 1/8″ × 1 1/4″ × 2 5/8″.

Refer to **2-E-1** for assembly.

(L) APRON DRAWER (One)

   (1) **FRONT APRON** (Cut 1): 1/16″ × 3/8″ × 2 3/4″. See Figure **7-T-8** for the shape.

   (2) **BACK** (Cut 1): 1/16″ × 3/16″ × 2 3/4″.

   (3) **SIDES** (Cut 2): 1/16″ × 3/16″ × 1 1/4″.

   (4) **BOTTOM** (Cut 1): 1/16″ × 1 1/4″ × 2 5/8″.

Refer to **2-E-2** (*overhang at lower front*) for assembly. *Note:* The double broken lines in Figure **7-T-1** indicate the location of the chest bottom board. The drawer bottom would rest on the top broken line and would glue against the back of the apron board at this location.

(M) DRAWER SPACERS (Cut 3): 1/8″ × 1 3/8″ × 2 3/4″.

(N) SIDE MOULDING (Cut 4): 1/8″ × 1/8″ × 2 1/2″.

(O) TOP FRONT FACING (Cut 1): 1/8″ × 1/8″ × 2 3/4″.

(P) DRAWER PULLS (Eight): Refer to **1-B-6**.

ASSEMBLY: Stain all wood before glueing and refer to Figures **7-T-1** (*front view*) and **7-T-2** (*left side view*).

1. Glue a piece of side moulding against both of the upright edges of each side board with the top and back edges flush.

2. Glue these assembled sides (*moulding sides out*) against the upright side edges of the back board, with the back and top edges flush.

3. Glue the top board atop the top edges of this assembly, with the back edges flush and equal side overhang.

4. Glue the top front facing (O) between the sides and against the undersurface of the top board, flush with the front surfaces of the sides.

5. Refer to **2-C-1** for further assembly of the main dresser. You will note that the apron drawer, at the bottom, forms a secret drawer. This dresser is an exact copy of our great-grandmother's dresser. She hid her silverware in the secret drawer.

6. Glue the small chest sides against the upright edges of the back board. Glue a top board atop this assembly, with the back edges flush and equal side overhang. Repeat for the second chest. Glue a small chest on each side of the dresser, atop the top board and with the back edges flush. See Figures **7-T-1** and **7-T-2**.

7. Glue the wishbone base centered atop the top board and between the two small chests. See Figure **7-T-1**.

8. Apply a finish coat to the dresser, wishbone frame, mirror frame and drawers.

9. Glue the mirror centered behind the mirror frame. Push a sequin pin through each hole in the wishbone frame and on into the mirror frame. Be sure that the mirror is level. Place the end of the wishbone frame in the hole in the base. The mirror will now tilt and turn. See Figure **7-T-1**.

10. Attach the drawer pulls.

VICTORIAN PERIOD WARDROBE 7-U

LOWER CHEST

(A) BACK (Cut 1): 1/8" × 1 1/8" × 3 3/4".

(B) SIDES (Cut 2): 1/8" × 1 3/8" × 1 3/8".

(C) BOTTOM (Cut 1): 1/8" × 1 1/4" × 3 3/4".

(D) DRAWER RUNNERS (Cut 2): 1/8" × 1/8" × 1 1/4".

(E) FRONT FACING (Cut 2): 1/8" × 1/4" × 1 3/8".

(F) APRON (Cut 1): 1/8" × 5/16" × 3 1/2". See Figure **7-U-8** for the shape.

(G) TOP (Cut 1): 1/8" × 1 1/2" × 4".

(H) DRAWER DIVIDER (Cut 1): 1/4" × 1" × 1 3/8".

(I) DRAWERS (Two)
    (1) **FRONT AND BACK** (Cut 4): 1/8" × 1" × 1 5/8".
    (2) **SIDES** (Cut 4): 1/8" × 1" × 1 1/8".
    (3) **BOTTOM** (Cut 2): 1/8" × 1 1/8" × 1 3/8".
Refer to **2-E-1** for assembly.

(J) DRAWER AND DOOR PULLS (Six): Refer to **1-B-6**.

UPPER CHEST

(K) BACK (Cut 1): 1/4" × 4" × 5 5/8". See Figure **7-U-6** for the notches to be cut into the top corners.

(L) TOP FRONT BOARD (Cut 1): 1/8" × 1/2" × 4". Cut 45° angles at each end for mitring. See Figure **7-U-4** for a top view diagram.

(M) TOP SIDE BOARDS (Cut 2): 1/8" × 1/2" × 1 1/2". Cut a 45° angle at the front edge of each board for mitring. See Figure **7-U-4** for a top view diagram.

(N) FRONT CORNERS (Cut 2): 1/4" × 1/4" × 5 1/8".

(O) SIDE PANELS (Cut 2): 1/16" × 1" × 5 1/8".

(P) LOWER SIDE MOULDING (Cut 2): 1/16" × 3/8" × 1".

(Q) UPPER SIDE MOULDING (Cut 4): 1/16" × 7/8" × 1". See Figure **7-U-9** for the shape. *Note:* Two of these will be used for the doors.

(R) TOP (Cut 1): 1/8" × 1 1/8" × 3 3/4".

(S) BOTTOM AND SHELF (Cut 2): 1/8" × 1 1/8" × 3 3/4". See Figure **7-U-11** for the shape.

(T) SHELF SUPPORTS (Cut 2): 1/8" × 1/8" × 1". See Figure **7-U-12** for a top view of the shape.

(U) CORNICE MOULDING: Select a pre-shaped moulding which is approximately 3/8" high. The moulding which is shown in Figure **7-U-10** is just an example of the type which is needed and similar to those which can be purchased from miniature supply stores or from mail-order lists. Cut the moulding to fit the top front and side corners of the cabinet, with 45° angle mitre cuts at the front corners.

(V) TOP DECORATION (Cut 1): 1/8" × 1/2" × 4". See Figure **7-U-7** for the shape.

(W) DOORS (Two)

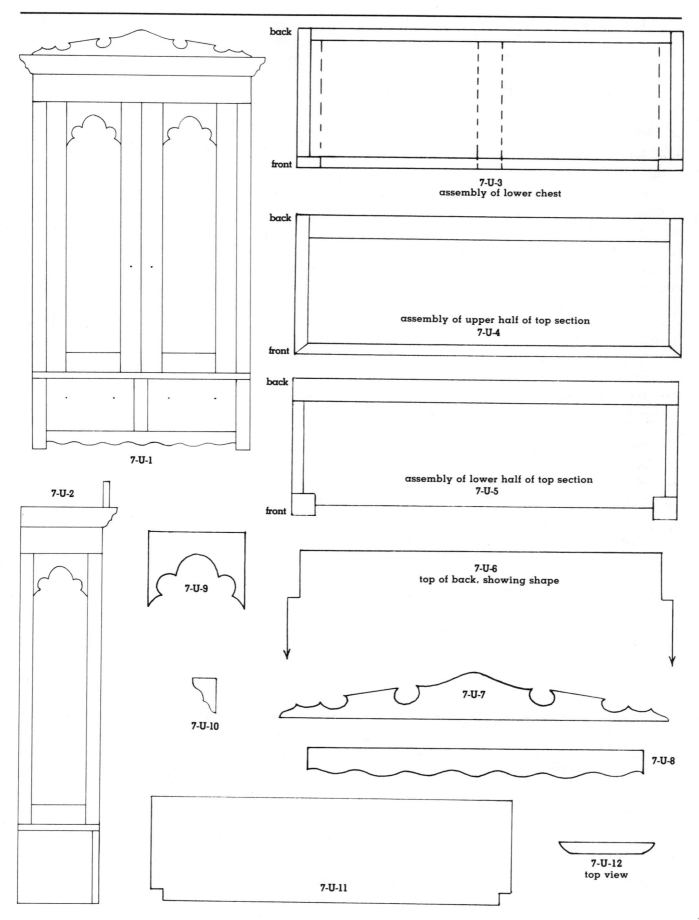

7-U-1

7-U-2

back
front
7-U-3
assembly of lower chest

back
front
assembly of upper half of top section
7-U-4

back
front
assembly of lower half of top section
7-U-5

7-U-6
top of back, showing shape

7-U-9

7-U-10

7-U-7

7-U-8

7-U-11

7-U-12
top view

(1) **CENTER PANELS** (Cut 2): 1/16" × 1" × 5 1/8".

(2) **VERTICAL SIDE MOULDING** (Cut 4): 1/8" × 3/8" × 5 1/8".

(3) **LOWER MOULDING** (Cut 2): 1/16" × 3/8" × 1".

ASSEMBLY: Stain all wood before glueing.

ASSEMBLY OF LOWER CHEST

1. Glue the sides against the upright side edges of the back, with back edges flush.

2. Glue the top edge of the bottom board 3/8" above the bottom edge of the back, between the side boards, and against the back board.

3. Glue the front facing boards (**E**) against the front edge of each side board, with outside side edges flush. Glue the apron between the side facing boards, with the top edge flush with the top edge of the bottom board.

4. Glue the top board atop the top edges of this assembly, with all edges flush.

5. Glue the drawer divider (**H**) centered atop the bottom board and against the back board. The front edge will be flush with the front edge of the top and the apron. See Figure **7-U-3**. Glue the drawer runners (**D**) atop the bottom board and against the inside surface of the side boards. See Figure **7-U-3**.

ASSEMBLY OF UPPER CHEST

1. **SIDE PANELS:** Glue an upper and lower side moulding piece against the face of each side panel (**O**) with top and bottom edges flush. See Figure **7-U-2**.

2. **UPPER HALF TOP SECTION:** Refer to Figure **7-U-4** which is a top view diagram. Glue the top side boards (**M**) and the top front board (**L**) together as shown. Glue this assembly into the notch in each side of the upper back. (*See Figure* **7-U-6**.) Glue the top board (**R**) inside of this assembly, with the top edges flush.

3. Glue an assembled side panel (*moulding side facing outward*) against the back board, beneath the upper assembly, with edges flush. Glue a front corner (**N**) against the front edge of the side panel and beneath the upper assembly, with the outside edges flush. See Figures **7-U-5** (*top view*) and **7-U-2** (*left side view*). Repeat for the second side.

4. Glue the bottom board (**S**) inside of the lower portion of this assembly, with the bottom edges flush. See Figure **7-U-5**.

5. Glue the shelf (**S**) inside of the chest, with the top surface 4" above the top surface of the bottom board. Glue a shelf support (**T**) beneath each side of the shelf and against the inside surface of the side panels.

6. **DOORS:** Glue the upper (**Q**) and lower (**W-3**) moulding pieces against the center panels, with the top and bottom edges flush. Glue a vertical side moulding board (**W-2**) against each side of each door panel, with the back edges flush.

7. Glue the upper cabinet atop the top surface of the lower cabinet, with the back and side edges flush.

8. Refer to **1-B-4-a** (*pin hinge*). Place the left door in position in the upper cabinet. Push a pin down through the top front board (**L**) and into the top left edge of the left door. Push a second pin up through the top board of the lower cabinet and into the lower left edge of this door. Repeat for the right door.

9. Glue the cornice moulding pieces (**U**) together and glue atop the top surface of the upper cabinet. See Figure **7-U-I** and **7-U-2**. Glue the top decoration (**V**) centered atop the front portion of the cornice, with the back edges flush.

10. Apply a finish coat to the assembled cabinet and the two drawers. Attach the door pulls and the drawer pulls.

VICTORIAN PERIOD BOOKCASE 7-V

(A) CHEST BOTTOM BOARDS (Cut 2): 1/8" × 1 1/4" × 4".

(B) CHEST BOTTOM MOULDING (Cut 1): 1/8" × 1 3/8" × 4 3/8". Round off the top edge of the sides and front.

(C) LOWER CHEST BACK (Cut 1): 1/8" × 3/4" × 4".

(D) LOWER CHEST SIDES AND CENTER DIVIDER (Cut 3): 1/4" × 3/4" × 1 1/8".

(E) FEET

(1) **FRONT** (Cut 2): 1/8" × 1/2" × 1/2". Round off the top edge of two adjoining sides.

(2) **BACK** (Cut 2): 1/8" × 1/8" × 1/8".

(F) UPPER BACK (Cut 2): 1/8" × 2" × 5 1/8". Stain the wood. Glue the two boards butted together, making one board measuring 4" × 5 1/8".

(G) SIDE PANELS (Cut 2): 1/16" × 3/4" × 5 1/8".

(H) UPPER SIDE MOULDING (Cut 2): 1/16" × 3/4" × 3/4". See Figure **7-V-6** for the shape.

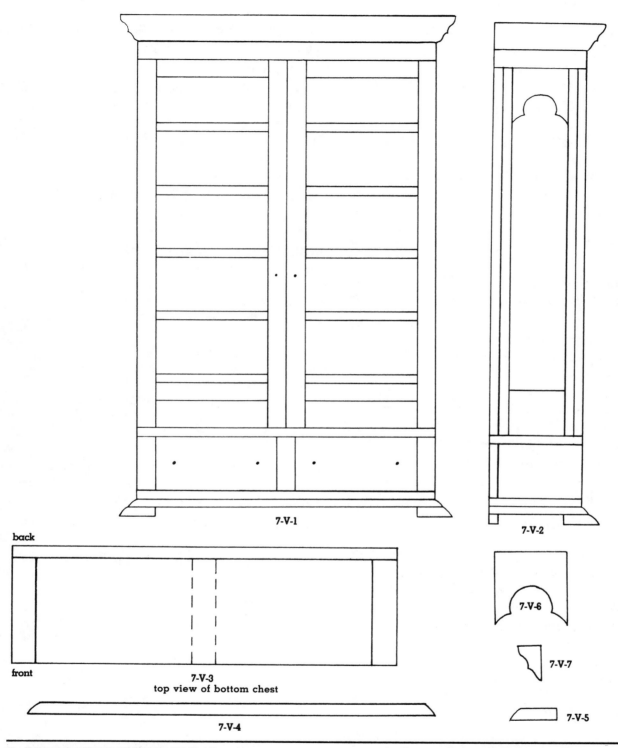

7-V-1

7-V-2

back

front

7-V-3
top view of bottom chest

7-V-4

7-V-6

7-V-7

7-V-5

(I) LOWER SIDE MOULDING (Cut 2): 1/16″ × 5/8″ × 3/4″.

(J) VERTICAL SIDE MOULDING (Cut 4): 1/8″ × 1/8″ × 5 1/8″.

(K) CABINET TOP (Cut 1): 1/4″ × 1 1/4″ × 4″.

(L) SHELVES (Cut 5): 1/8″ × 1″ × 3 3/4″.

(M) DOOR STOPS (Cut 2): 1/8″ × 1/8″ × 1/2″.

(N) CORNICE MOULDING: Select a pre-shaped moulding which is approximately 3/8″ high. The moulding which is shown in Figure **7-V-7** is just an example of the type which is needed and is similar to those which can be purchased from miniature supply stores or from mail-order lists. Cut the moulding to fit the top front and side corners of the cabinet, with 45° angle mitre cuts at the front corners.

(O) DRAWERS (Two)

    (1) **FRONT AND BACK** (Cut 4): 1/8″ × 3/4″ × 1 5/8″.

    (2) **SIDES** (Cut 4): 1/8″ × 3/4″ × 7/8″.

    (3) **BOTTOM** (Cut 2): 1/8″ × 7/8″ × 1 3/8″.

Refer to **2-E-1** for assembly.

(P) DRAWER PULLS (Four drop pulls) **AND DOOR PULLS** (Two knobs): Refer to **1-B-6**.

(Q) DOORS (Two)

    (1) **SIDE MOULDING** (Cut 4): 1/8″ × 1/4″ × 5 1/8″.

    (2) **TOP MOULDING** (Cut 2): 1/8″ × 1/4″ × 1 1/2″.

    (3) **BOTTOM MOULDING** (Cut 2): 1/8″ × 3/8″ × 1 1/2″.

    (4) **GLASS** (Cut 2): 1/16″ or 1/8″ thick glass or Plexiglas × 1 1/2″ × 4 1/2″.

ASSEMBLY: Stain all wood before glueing. Refer to Figures **7-V-1** (*front view*) and **7-V-2** (*left side view*).

1. Glue the upper side moulding (**H**) and the lower side moulding (**I**) pieces against the side panel (**G**) with the top and bottom edges flush. Repeat for the second panel.

2. Glue each side panel (*moulding surface toward the outside*) butted against the front edge of the upper back board (**F**) with side edges flush.

3. Glue the top (**K**) and the bottom (**A**) against the top and bottom edges of this assembly, with the back and side edges flush. Refer to Figures **7-V-1** and **7-V-2**.

4. Glue the five shelves between the sides and against the back board. See Figure **7-V-1** for a guide for placement. Glue the top and bottom door stops centered and recessed 1/8″ against the inside surfaces of the top and bottom boards.

5. **DOOR ASSEMBLY:** Glue the side moulding boards (**Q-1**) against the end edges of the top moulding (**Q-2**) and bottom moulding (**Q-3**) with top and bottom edges flush. Apply a finish coat and let dry. Glue the glass or Plexiglas inside the door frame. Repeat for the second door.

6. Apply a finish coat to the upper cabinet.

7. Refer to **1-B-4-a** (*pin hinge*). Place the left door inside the cabinet opening. Push a pin down through the cabinet top into the upper left corner of the door. Push another pin up through the cabinet bottom into the lower left corner of the door. Repeat for installation of the right door.

8. Glue the cornice moulding together. Apply a finish coat. Glue the cornice atop the front and side edges of the cabinet top board.

9. **ASSEMBLY OF LOWER CHEST**

    a. Glue the back (**C**) atop the top back edge of the bottom board (**A**) with the back edges flush. Refer to Figure **7-V-3**.

    b. Glue the sides (**D**) atop the bottom board and butted against the back board with side edges flush. Refer to Figure **7-V-3**.

    c. Glue this assembly atop the chest bottom moulding (**B**) with the back edges flush.

    d. Glue the center divider (**D**) centered atop the bottom board and against the back board. Refer to Figure **7-V-3**.

    e. Glue the front feet beneath the front corners of the lower chest, with the shaped edges forward and to the outside. Glue the back feet beneath the back corners of the lower chest with edges flush.

10. Apply a finish coat to the lower chest and the two drawers.

11. Glue the upper chest atop the top edges of the lower chest with all edges flush.

12. Install the drawer and door pulls.

STENCILLED SIDE CHAIR —
MODIFIED HITCHCOCK TYPE 8-A

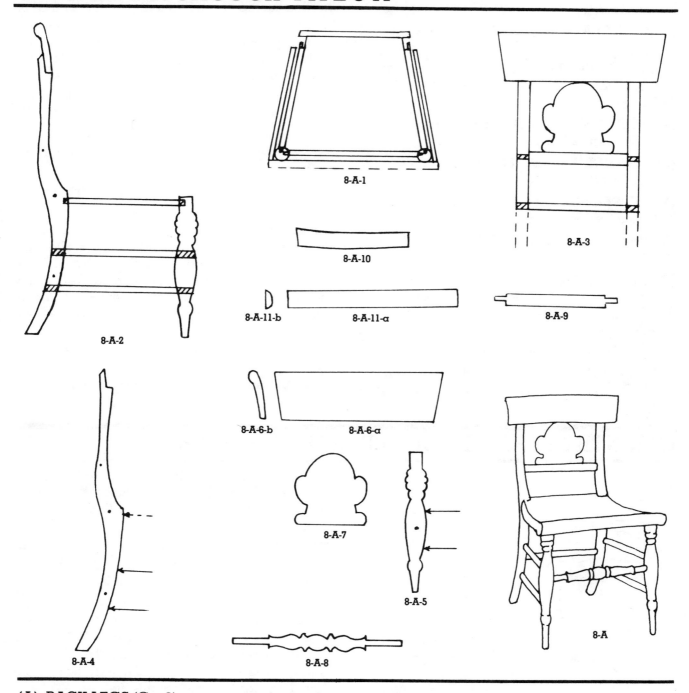

8-A-1

8-A-10

8-A-11-b   8-A-11-a   8-A-9

8-A-3

8-A-2

8-A-6-b   8-A-6-a

8-A-7

8-A-5

8-A-4

8-A-8

8-A

(A) BACK LEGS (Cut 2): 1/8″ × 1/2″ × 3 1/16″. See Figure **8-A-4** for the shape. Drill 1/16″ diameter holes through each leg at the sites of the black dots and un-broken arrows in the diagram. Drill a 1/16″ diameter hole 1/16″ deep at the site of the broken arrow in the diagram.

(B) FRONT LEGS (Cut 2): 1/4″ diameter wood dowel × 1 1/2″. See Figure **8-A-5** for the shape. Refer to **1-C-3-a**.

(C) TOP BACK (Cut 1): 3/16″ × 1/2″ × 1 3/4″. See Figure **8-A-6-a** for a front view and **8-A-6-b** for a left end view of the shape to be carved.

(D) BACK SLAT (Cut 1): 1/8″ × 1/8″ × 1 9/32″. See Figure **8-A-9** for the shape.

(E) BACK SLAT DECORATION (Cut 1): 1/16″ × 3/4″ × 3/4″. See Figure **8-A-7** for the shape.

(F) BACK SEAT RAIL (Cut 1): 1/16″ diameter wood dowel × 1 1/4″.

(G) FRONT SEAT RAIL (Cut 1): 1/16″ diameter wood dowel × 1 7/16″.

(H) SIDE SEAT RAIL (Cut 2): 1/16″ diameter wood dowel × 1 1/4″.

(I) BACK SEAT FACING (Cut 1): 1/16″ × 3/16″ × 1 3/16″.

(J) FRONT SEAT FACING (Cut 1): 1/16″ × 3/16″ × 1 3/4″. See Figure **8-A-11-a** (*front view*) and **8-A-11-b** (*left end view*) for the shape.

(K) SIDE SEAT FACING (Cut 2): 1/16″ × 1/4″ × 1 3/16″. See Figure **8-A-10** for the shape.

(L) TOP-SIDE LEG STRETCHERS (Cut 2): 1/16″ diameter wood dowel × 1 1/2″.

(M) LOWER-SIDE LEG STRETCHERS (Cut 2): 1/16″ diameter wood dowel × 1 9/16″.

(N) BACK LEG STRETCHER (Cut 1): 1/16″ diameter wood dowel × 1 5/16″.

(O) FRONT LEG STRETCHER (Cut 1): 3/16″ diameter wood dowel × 1 3/4″. See Figure **8-A-8** for the shape. Refer to **1-C-3-a**.

ASSEMBLY: This chair will be painted and therefore does not have to be stained.

1. Figures **8-A**, **8-A-2** (*side view*) **8-A-3** (*chair back*) and **8-A-1** (*top view of seat assembly*) show the construction of the chair.

2. Glue the side stretchers, side seat rail, back and front legs together, as shown in Figure **8-A-2**. Repeat for the second side.

3. Glue the top back (**C**) into the front top notch of the back legs (**A**). Glue the back slat (**D**), back seat rail (**F**), back leg stretcher (**N**) in place. Glue the back slat decoration (**E**) atop the back slat and beneath the top back board. See Figure **8-A-3**.

4. Glue the front seat rail (**G**) and the front leg stretcher (**O**) in place.

5. At this time, be sure that the chair sits straight and level. Let the glue dry thoroughly, for several days to one week.

6. Paint the chair frame and the seat facing boards black.

7. Refer to **1-C-7** to rush the seat, or **1-C-7-a** for the alternate rush seat. If you choose the alternate method, trace the inside area of Figure **8-A-1**. Cut a piece of wood to fit into the seat opening. Refer to the color insert sheet and cut a print marked **1-C-7-a** to fit the top of the seat and around the top of the front legs. Glue it in place.

8. Again refer to the color insert sheet, and cut out the prints marked **8-A**. Glue them in place against the back boards. Refer to **1-C-2** for finishing.

COUNTRY TYPE STENCILLED SIDE CHAIR 8-B

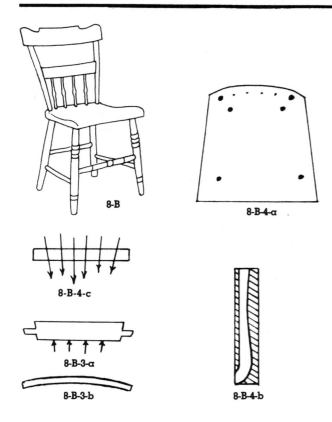

8-B

8-B-4-a

8-B-4-c

8-B-3-a

8-B-3-b

8-B-4-b

(A) TOP BACK (Cut 1): 1/4″ × 3/8″ × 1 5/8″. See Figure **8-B-2-a** for the shape. Figure **8-B-2-b** shows the curve to the board. Refer to **1-C-3-c** for aid in shaping.

(B) BACK SLAT (Cut 1): 3/16″ × 3/16″ × 1 3/16″. See Figure **8-B-3-a** for the shape. Figure **8-B-3-b** shows the curve to the board. Refer to **1-C-3-c** for aid in shaping.

(C) BACK POSTS (Cut 2): 3/16″ × 5/16″ × 1 5/8″. See Figure **8-B-5-a** for the shape. Figure **8-B-5-b** shows the side view of the initial shaping. The arrows in Figure **8-B-5-a** show a 1/16″ diameter hole to be drilled through the board at this site.

(D) BACK SPINDLES (Cut 4): 1/16″ diameter wood dowel × 3/4″. See Figure **8-B-7** for the shape. Refer to **1-C-3-a**.

(E) SEAT (Cut 1): 1/4″ × 1 1/4″ × 1 1/4″. See Figure **8-B-4-a** for a top view of the shape, and Figure **8-B-4-b** for a left side view of the shaping of the seat. Refer to **1-C-3-e** for aid in shaping the "dished" portion of the seat. The small black dots (*four*) in the diagram represent the 1/16″ diameter holes to be

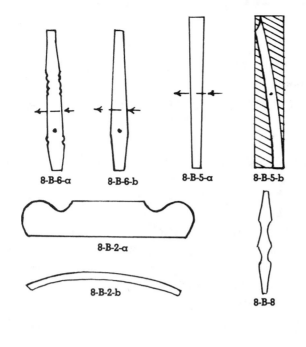

8-B-6-α   8-B-6-b   8-B-5-α   8-B-5-b

8-B-2-α

8-B-2-b

8-B-8

8-B-7

8-B-1

drilled at these sites, while the larger black dots represent 3/32" diameter holes to be drilled. Figure **8-B-4-c** shows a back view of the seat, showing the angles for drilling the six rear holes.

(F) LEGS (Cut 4): 3/16" diameter wood dowel × 1 1/8". Shape two legs as shown in Figure **8-B-6-a**. Shape two legs as shown in Figure **8-B-6-b**. Drill 1/16" diameter holes through each leg at the sites of the black dots and arrows in the diagram.

(G) FRONT LEG STRETCHER (Cut 1): 1/8" diameter wood dowel × 1 1/8". See Figure **8-B-8** for the shape. Refer to **1-C-3-a**.

(H) BACK AND SIDE LEG STRETCHERS (Cut 3): 1/16" diameter wood dowel × 1 1/8".

ASSEMBLY

1. Refer to Figures **8-B** and **8-B-1** (*back view of back and seat assembly*).

2. Refer to **2-A-2** for general assembly.

3. You will find color prints marked **8-B** on the color insert sheet which will allow you to make a set of four chairs.

4. Paint the chair a brown color to match the background in the color print. Refer to **1-C-2** for application of the color print. Paint a fine gold line around the legs and front stretcher at the "valleys" of the shaping.

5. Apply an acrylic sealer coat to the completed chair.

STENCILLED ARM CHAIR c. 1810 8-C

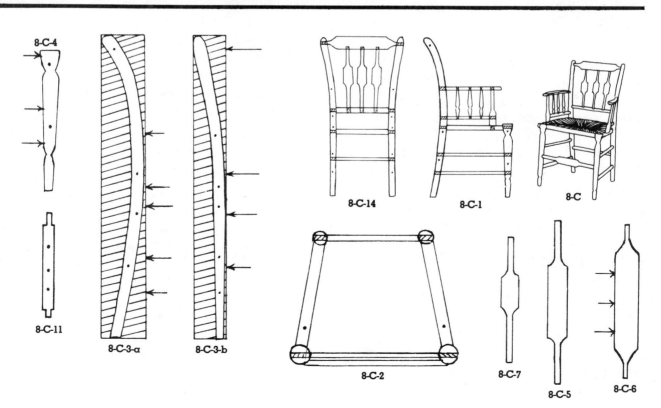

8-C-4

8-C-11

8-C-3-α   8-C-3-b

8-C-14

8-C-1

8-C

8-C-2

8-C-7

8-C-5   8-C-6

143

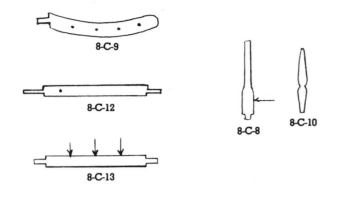

8-C-9

8-C-12

8-C-13

8-C-8   8-C-10

(A) LEFT BACK LEG (Cut 1): 3/8" × 1/2" × 3 1/4". See Figure **8-C-3-a** for a side view of the initial shaping. Figure **8-C-3-b** shows the front view of the final shaping. Drill 1/16" diameter holes through the leg at the sites of the black dots and arrows in diagram **8-C-3-b**. Refer to **1-C-3-b** for aid in carving.

(B) RIGHT BACK LEG (Cut 1): 3/8" × 1/2" × 3 1/4". Trace Figures **8-C-3-a** and **8-C-3-b**. Reverse these diagrams for the right leg. Follow the directions for **(A)** in finishing this leg.

(C) LEFT AND RIGHT FRONT LEGS (Cut 2): 1/4" diameter wood dowel × 1 1/2". See Figure **8-C-4** for the shape. Refer to **1-C-3-a**. Drill 1/16" diameter holes through each leg at the sites of the black dots and arrows in the diagram.

(D) FRONT SEAT RAIL (Cut 1): 1/8" diameter wood dowel × 1 3/4". Shape a peg at each end 3/16" long.

(E) BACK SEAT RAIL (Cut 1): 1/8" diameter wood dowel × 1 1/4". Shape a peg at each end 1/8" long.

(F) SEAT SIDE RAILS (Cut 2): 1/8" diameter wood dowel × 1 7/16". Shape a peg at each end 3/16" long. See Figure **8-C-12**. Drill a hole 1/16" in diameter through each rail at the site of the black dot in the diagram.

(G) BACK TOP RAIL (Cut 1): 1/8" × 1/4" × 1 11/16". See Figure **8-C-6** for the shape. Drill 1/16" diameter holes 1/16" deep into the bottom edge of this rail at the sites of the three arrows in this diagram.

(H) BACK BOTTOM RAIL (Cut 1): 1/8" diameter wood dowel × 1 5/16". See Figure **8-C-13** for the shape. Drill 1/16" diameter holes through the rail at the sites of the three black arrows.

(I) BACK BANNISTERS (Cut 3): 1/16" × 3/16" × 1 5/16". See Figure **8-C-7** for the shape.

(J) BACK LEG STRETCHER (Cut 1): 1/16" diameter wood dowel × 1 5/16".

(K) SIDE LEG STRETCHERS (Cut 4): 1/16" diameter wood dowel × 1 1/2".

(L) FRONT LEG STRETCHER (Cut 1): 1/16" × 1/4" × 1 3/4". See Figure **8-C-5** for the shape.

(M) ARM (Cut 2): 1/16" × 5/16" × 1 5/16". See Figure **8-C-9** (*right arm*) for the shape. Reverse the diagram for the left arm. Drill 1/16" diameter holes through each board at the sites of the black dots in the diagram.

(N) BOTTOM ARM RAIL (Cut 2): 1/16" × 1/8" × 1 1/8". See Figure **8-C-11** for the shape. Drill 1/16" diameter holes through each board at the sites of the black dots in the diagram.

(O) ARM SPINDLES (Cut 6): 1/8" diameter wood dowel × 3/4". See Figure **8-C-10** for the shape. Refer to **1-C-3-a**.

(P) ARM POST (Cut 2): 1/8" diameter wood dowel × 7/8". See Figure **8-C-8** for the shape. Refer to **1-C-3-a**. Drill a 1/16" diameter hole through each post at the site of the black arrow in the diagram.

ASSEMBLY: Stain all wood before glueing.

1. Refer to Figure **8-C-1**. Assemble the left and right arms as shown.

2. Refer to Figure **8-C-1**. Assemble the left back leg, the left arm assembly, the seat side rail, the front leg and the two side leg stretchers, as shown. Repeat for the right side.

3. Glue the back top rail (**G**) at the top between the back posts. Glue the back bannisters, back bottom rail, back seat rail and back leg stretchers in place. See Figure **8-C-14**.

4. Glue the front seat rail and front leg stretcher in place.

5. Be sure the chair sits straight and level. Let the glue dry for several days.

6. Paint the chair a flat black.

7. Refer to **1-C-7** to rush the seat. If you do not choose to rush the seat, cut a piece of wood 1/16" × 1 3/16" × 1 7/16". See Figure **8-C-2** (*the inside line of the wood pieces*) for the shape. Glue this piece inside the seat frame. Refer to the color insert sheet and cut out a rush seat print (**1-C-7-a**) and glue it atop the board. See **1-C-7-a**.

8. Refer to the color insert sheet and cut out the prints marked **8-C**. Glue the prints to the front of the top back rail, the three back bannisters and the front leg stretcher.

9. Apply a finish coat of acrylic sealer.

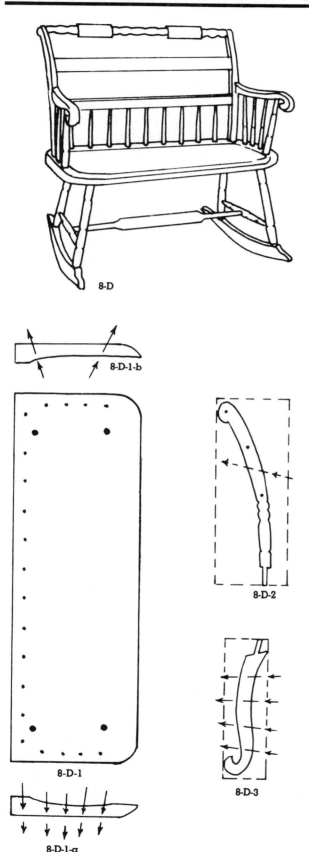

8-D

8-D-1-b

8-D-1

8-D-1-α

8-D-2

8-D-3

(A) SEAT (Cut 1): 3/16″ × 1 5/16″ × 3 15/16″. See Figure **8-D-1** for the shape. Figure **8-D** shows the "dishing" of the seat. Figure **8-D-1-a** shows the angles of 1/16″ diameter holes (*small black dots in the diagram*) to be drilled through the left side of the seat. Reverse these angles for the right side of the seat. The holes at the back of the seat (*small black dots in the diagram*) are drilled at right angles with the seat. Figure **8-D-1-b** shows the angles of 1/16″ diameter holes (*large black dots in the diagram*) to be drilled through the right side of the seat. Reverse these angles for the left side of the seat. The legs will fit into these holes.

(B) BACK POSTS (Cut 2): 3/8″ × 5/8″ × 2″. See Figure **8-D-2** for the side view of the shape. Refer to **1-C-3-b** for aid in carving. Drill 1/16″ diameter holes through the side of each post at the sites of the three black dots in the diagram. Drill a 1/16″ diameter hole through the front of each post at the site and angle of the arrow in this diagram.

(C) ARM RESTS (Cut 2): 3/16″ × 7/16″ × 1 1/2″. See Figure **8-D-3** for the shape. Round off the top edges of each arm. The arrows in the diagram show the angle of four 1/16″ diameter holes to be drilled through the top surface of each arm.

(D) ARM POST (Cut 2): 3/16″ diameter wood dowel × 1 3/16″. See Figure **8-D-7** for the shape. Refer to **1-C-3-a**.

(E) ARM SPINDLE (Cut 6): 1/8″ diameter wood dowel × 1 3/16″. See Figure **8-D-6** for the shape. Refer to **1-C-3-a**.

(F) TOP BACK SLAT (Cut 1): 3/16″ × 1/4″ × 3 11/16″. See Figure **8-D-9** for the shape. Refer to **1-C-3-a**. The two oblong areas in this turned piece are flat.

(G) MIDDLE BACK SLAT (Cut 1): 1/8″ × 1/4″ × 3 11/16″. *Do not drill holes in this board.* See Figure **8-D-8** for the shape.

(H) LOWER BACK SLAT (Cut 1): 1/8″ × 1/4″ × 3 11/16″. See Figure **8-D-8** for the shape. Drill 1/16″ diameter holes 1/16″ up into the bottom of this board. See the ten arrows.

(I) BACK SPINDLES (Cut 10): 1/8″ diameter wood dowel × 7/8″. See Figure **8-D-10** for the shape. Refer to **1-C-3-a**.

(J) BACK LEGS (Cut 2): 3/16″ diameter wood dowel × 1 9/16″. Drill a 1/16″ diameter hole through the leg

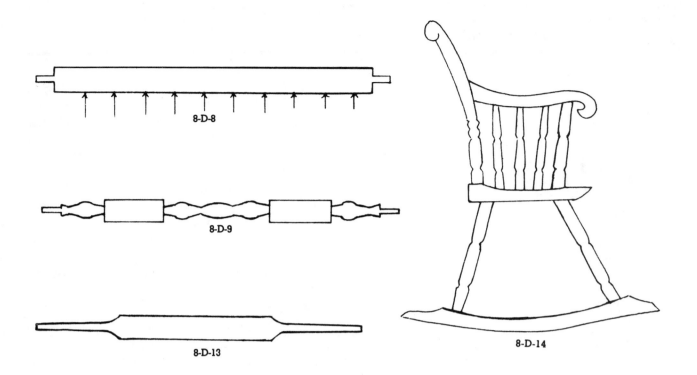

8-D-8

8-D-9

8-D-13

8-D-14

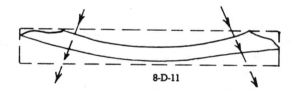

8-D-11

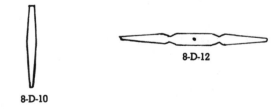

8-D-10

8-D-12

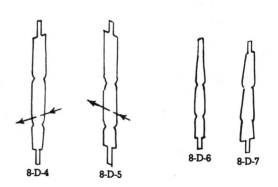

8-D-4

8-D-5

8-D-6

8-D-7

at the angle of the arrow in the diagram. See Figure **8-D-4** for the shape. Refer to **1-C-3-a**.

(K) FRONT LEGS (Cut 2): 3/16″ diameter wood dowel × 1 9/16″. Drill a 1/16″ diameter hole through the leg at the angle of the arrow in the diagram. See Figure **8-D-4** for the shape. Refer to **1-C-3-a**.

(L) SIDE LEG STRETCHERS (Cut 2): 1/8″ diameter wood dowel × 1 9/16″. See Figure **8-D-12** for the shape. Refer to **1-C-3-a**. Drill a 1/16″ diameter hole through the stretcher at the site of the black dot in the diagram.

(M) CENTER LEG STRETCHER (Cut 1): 1/8″ × 1/4″ × 3 3/8″. See Figure **8-D-13** for the shape. The oblong area in this turned piece remains flat.

(N) ROCKERS (Cut 2): 1/8″ × 3/8″ × 2 3/4″. See Figure **8-D-11** for the shape. Figure **8-D-11** is a side view of the rocker. The two sets of arrows in this diagram show the direction of 1/16″ diameter holes to be drilled through these boards.

ASSEMBLY: Refer to Figures **8-D** and **8-D-14**.

1. Refer to **2-A-2** and **2-A-3** for general assembly.

2. Find the color prints marked **8-D** on the color insert sheet. Paint the bench a red-brown color (*as close to the print background as possible*). Refer to **1-C-2** for the application of the color print.

3. Spray or coat the completed piece of furniture with several coats of a good acrylic sealer.

STENCILLED HITCHOCK TYPE SIDE CHAIR WITH EAGLE SLAT 8-E

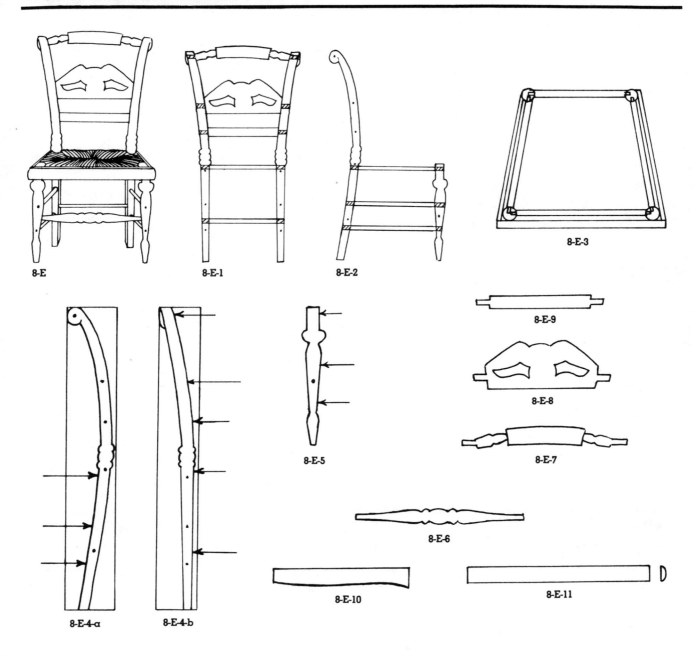

8-E

8-E-1

8-E-2

8-E-3

8-E-9

8-E-8

8-E-7

8-E-5

8-E-6

8-E-4-a

8-E-4-b

8-E-10

8-E-11

(A) LEFT BACK LEG (Cut 1): 1/2" × 7/16" × 3 1/4". See Figure **8-E-4-a** for a side view of the initial shaping. Figure **8-E-4-b** shows the front view of the final shaping. Refer to **1-C-3-b** for aid in shaping this leg with splay.

(B) RIGHT BACK LEG (Cut 1): 1/2" × 7/16" × 3 1/4". Trace Figures **8-E-4-a** and **8-E-4-b**. Turn **8-E-4-b** over when tracing onto the wood (*reversing the splay for the right side*). Shape the wood, using **8-E-4-a** first, and then shape according to the reversed tracing of **8-E-4-b**. Refer to **1-C-3-b** for aid in shaping this leg with splay. Note the dots and arrows in both diagrams, and drill 1/16" diameter holes through the wood at the various sites in both legs.

(C) UPPER BACK SLAT (Cut 1): 1/8" × 1/4" × 1 3/4". See Figure **8-E-7** for the shape. The extreme end pegs will measure 1/16" diameter when the piece is completed.

(D) EAGLE BACK SLAT (Cut 1): 1/16" × 1/2" × 1 7/16". See Figure **8-E-8** for the shape.

(E) LOWER BACK SLAT (Cut 1): 1/16" × 1/8" × 1 3/8". See Figure **8-E-9** for the shape.

(F) BACK SEAT FRAME (Cut 1): 1/16" diameter wood dowel × 1 1/16". Narrow down a 1/16" length peg at each end.

(G) SIDE SEAT FRAME (Cut 2): 1/16" diameter wood dowel × 1 1/4". Narrow down a 1/16" length peg at each end.

(H) FRONT SEAT FRAME (Cut 1): 1/16" diameter wood dowel × 1 7/16". Narrow down a 1/16" length peg at each end.

(I) FRONT LEGS (Cut 2): 1/4" diameter wood dowel × 1 1/2". See Figure **8-E-5** for the shape. The black dots and lower arrows in the diagram indicate 1/16" diameter holes to be drilled through each leg. The top arrow indicates a 1/32" diameter hole to be drilled into the right side of the left leg and the left side of the right leg, 1/16" deep.

(J) FRONT LEG BRACE (Cut 1): 3/16" diameter wood dowel × 1 3/4". See Figure **8-E-6** for the shape. Refer to **1-C-3-a**.

(K) SIDE LEG BRACES (Cut 4): 1/16" diameter wood dowel × 1 1/2".

(L) BACK LEG BRACE (Cut 1): 1/16" diameter wood dowel × 1 1/4".

(M) SIDE SEAT FACING (Cut 2): 1/16" × 1/4" × 1 3/8". See Figure **8-E-10** for the shape.

(N) FRONT SEAT FACING (Cut 1): 1/16" × 3/16" × 1 7/8". See Figure **8-E-11** for the shape. The small end view diagram at the right shows how the top and bottom front edges of this board should be rounded off.

ASSEMBLY: Do not stain, as this chair will be painted. Figure **8-E** shows an overall view of the chair, Figure **8-E-1** shows a back view of the assembly and Figure **8-E-2** shows a side view of the assembly. Figure **8-E-3** shows the back assembly.

1. Figure **8-E-1** shows a top view of the seat assembly. The circles represent the top edge of the four legs. The front, back and side frame dowels are pegged into the legs. There is a clear space around this inner frame (*allowing for rushing*) and the three outer boards are the seat facing boards.

2. Refer to **2-A-3** for general assembly of the chair.

3. Paint the chair black. Paint a fine gold line in the "valley" of each turning.

4. Rush the seat. Refer to **1-C-7** *or* trace the seat frame in Figure **8-E-1**, notching the corners to fit around the four legs, onto 1/8" thick wood. Find a piece of seat rushing color print (*marked 1-C-7 on the color insert sheet*) and cut to fit this solid seat blank. Glue this seat in place of the seat frame.

5. Paint the seat facing boards black and glue against the two sides and front of the seat.

6. Find the color prints marked **8-E** on the color insert sheet. Glue the eagle print against the front surface of the eagle slat. Glue the small print on the flat surface of the top back slat. Refer to **1-C-2**.

7. Apply an acrylic sealer finish to the completed chair.

STENCILLED SHIELD-BACK SIDE CHAIR OF GREEK REVIVAL TYPE 8-F

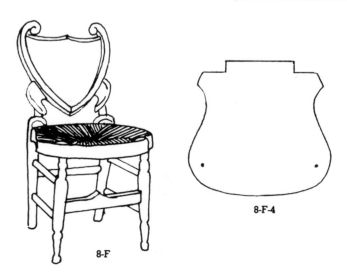

8-F

8-F-4

(A) SEAT (Cut 1): 1/8" × 1 7/16" × 1 1/2". See Figure **8-F-4** for the shape. Drill 1/16" diameter holes through the seat at the sites of the black dots in the diagram.

(B) BACK FRAME (Cut 2): 1/8" × 1/2" × 1 1/2". See Figure **8-F-6-a** for the shape of the left side, and **8-F-6-b** for the shape of the right side.

(C) SHIELD-BACK (Cut 1): 1/16" × 1 1/16" × 1 1/8". See Figure **8-F-5** for the shape. This back can be cut from 1/16" wood or 1/16" cardboard. Apply airplane cement to the cut edges of the cardboard to prevent separation.

(D) BACK LEGS (Cut 2): 1/4" × 5/16" × 2 3/16". See Figure **8-F-8** (*front view of left leg*) and **8-F-9** (*left side view of left leg*). Reverse the diagrams for the

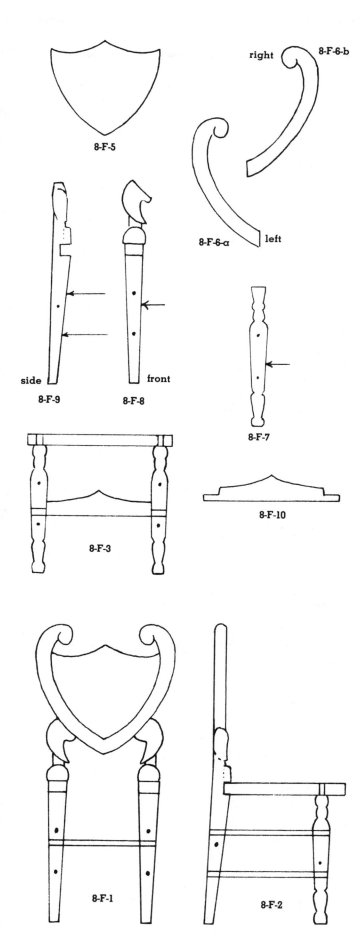

8-F-5

right 8-F-6-b

8-F-6-a left

side front

8-F-9 8-F-8

8-F-7

8-F-3

8-F-10

8-F-1

8-F-2

shape of the right leg. Drill 1/16" diameter holes through each leg at the sites of the black dots and arrow in Figure 8-F-8. See Figure 8-F for another view of the legs.

(E) FRONT LEGS (Cut 2): 3/16" diameter wood dowel × 1 1/2". See Figure **8-F-7** for the shape. Drill 1/16" diameter holes through each leg at the sites of the black dots and arrow in the diagram. Refer to **1-C-3-a**.

(F) FRONT LEG STRETCHER (Cut 1): 1/16" × 5/16" × 1 7/16". See Figure **8-F-10** for the shape.

(G) BACK LEG STRETCHER (Cut 1): 1/16" diameter wood dowel × 1 1/8".

(H) SIDE LEG STRETCHER (Cut 4): 1/16" diameter wood dowel × 1 1/4".

ASSEMBLY: Stain all wood before glueing.

1. Glue the back frame together at the lower center edge. Glue the shield-back in the frame, with back edges flush. See Figures **8-F** and **8-F-1**.

2. Glue the front leg stretcher between the front legs. Glue this assembly into the holes at the front of the seat. See Figure **8-F-3**.

3. Glue the seat into the notches in the fronts of the two back legs. Glue two leg stretchers on each side of the chair. See Figure **8-F-2**.

4. Glue the shield-back frame between the two wings at the top of the back legs. See Figures **8-F 8-F-1**. Be sure that the chair sits straight and level. Let the glue dry.

5. Paint the legs, all stretchers, back and the wings black. Paint the round area at the top of the notch in each back leg gold. Add gold line highlights to the knobs and "valleys" in the front legs and touches of gold on the wings.

6. Refer to **1-C-2**. Cut out the color prints marked **8-F** on the color insert sheet. Glue the shield prints against the front and back surfaces of the shield-back. Glue the "rush" seat print atop the seat. Glue the print against the front surface of the front leg stretcher. Glue the long print onto a piece of file card and cut out. Touch the top and bottom edges with a brown felt-tip pen. Glue this cardboard edging around the sides and front of the chair seat.

7. Refer to **1-C-2**. Finish the chair.

BLANKET CHEST 8-G

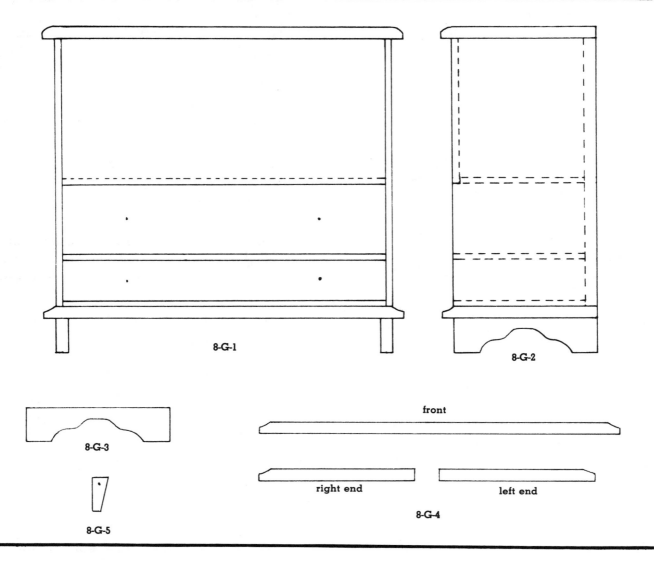

8-G-1

8-G-2

8-G-3

8-G-5

front

right end

left end

8-G-4

(A) BACK (Cut 1): 1/8″ × 2 7/8″ × 3 3/8″. These measurements can be accomplished by cutting one board 1/8″ × 1 3/8″ × 2 7/8″ and one board 1/8″ × 2″ × 2 7/8″. Glue butted together after staining.

(B) SIDES (Cut 2): 1/16″ × 1 1/2″ × 2 7/8″.

(C) UPPER FRONT (Cut 1): 1/16″ × 1 9/16″ × 3 3/8″.

(D) UPPER CHEST BOTTOM (Cut 1): 1/16″ × 1 5/16″ × 3 3/8″.

(E) TOP (Cut 1): 1/8″ × 1 5/8″ × 3 3/4″. Round off the top surface of the front and side edges.

(F) BASE (Cut 1): 1/8″ × 1 5/8″ × 3 3/4″. Figure **8-G-4** shows the edge shaping for the front and side edges of this board.

(G) DRAWER BASE (Cut 2): 1/16″ × 1 3/8″ × 3 3/8″.

(H) LEGS (Cut 2): 1/8″ × 3/8″ × 1 1/2″. See Figure **8-G-3** for the shape.

(I) TOP DRAWER
   (1) **FRONT AND BACK** (Cut 2): 1/16″ × 3/4″ × 3 3/8″.
   (2) **SIDES** (Cut 2): 1/16″ × 3/4″ × 1 1/4″.
   (3) **BOTTOM** (Cut 1): 1/8″ × 1 1/4″ × 3 1/4″.
Refer to **2-E-1** for assembly.

(J) BOTTOM DRAWER
   (1) **FRONT AND BACK** (Cut 2): 1/16″ × 7/16″ × 3 3/8″.
   (2) **SIDES** (Cut 2): 1/16″ × 7/16″ × 1 1/4″.
   (3) **BOTTOM** (Cut 1): 1/8″ × 1 1/4″ × 3 1/4″.
Refer to **2-E-1** for assembly.

(K) CLEAT HINGE (Cut 2): 1/16″ × 1/8″ × 3/8″. See Figure **8-G-5** for the shape. *Do not* drill a hole at the dot in the diagram.

(L) DRAWER PULLS (Four): Refer to **1-B-6**.

ASSEMBLY

1. Glue the sides butted against the side edges of the back board, with back edges flush.

2. Glue this assembly atop the base, with equal side overhang and the back edges flush.

3. Refer to Figures **8-G-1** and **8-G-2**. Glue the legs beneath the base.

4. Glue a drawer base board inside the chest and glued atop the base board. Insert the bottom drawer (*for measurement only*). Glue the second drawer base board (*resting atop the drawer*) against the side and back boards.

5. Insert the top drawer (*for measurement only*). Glue the upper chest bottom board (*resting on the drawer*) against the side and back boards. Glue the upper front board between the two side boards and against the forward edge of the upper chest bottom board. Remove the drawers.

6. Place the top board atop the assembled chest (*do not glue*) with the back edges flush and equal side overhang. Glue a cleat hinge against the undersurface of this board (*resting but not glued against the outside surface of each side board*). Refer to **1-B-4**.

7. Find the color print marked **8-G** on the color insert sheet. Select a color that will accent the color print, and paint the chest. Glue the color prints in place. Refer to **1-C-2**. Apply a finish coat.

8. Push a sequin pin through each cleat hinge and into each side of the chest, attaching the top board. Attach the drawer pulls.

DOWER CHEST 8-H

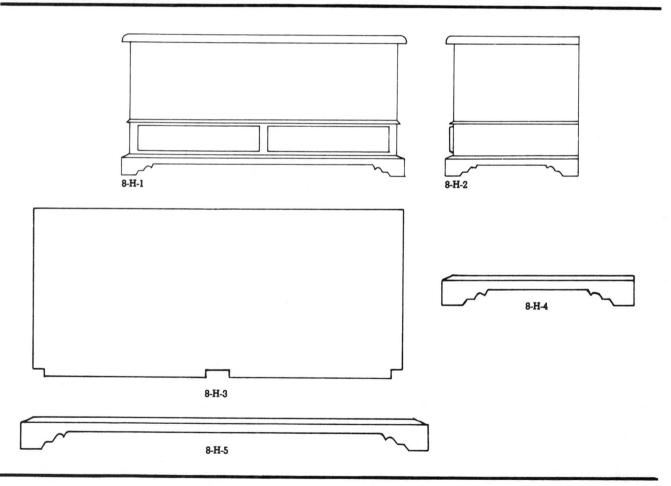

8-H-1

8-H-2

8-H-4

8-H-3

8-H-5

(A) BACK (Cut 1): 1/16″ × 1 3/4″ × 4″.

(B) UPPER FRONT (Cut 1): 1/16″ × 1 5/16″ × 4″.

(C) SIDES (Cut 2): 1/16″ × 1 3/4″ × 1 3/4″.

(D) TOP (Cut 1): 1/8″ × 1″ × 4 1/4″. Round off the top edge of the front and sides of this board.

(E) BOTTOM (Cut 1): 1/8″ × 1 3/4″ × 3 7/8″.

(F) DRAWER SPACER (Cut 1): 1/16″ × 1 3/4″ × 3 7/8″.

(G) LOWER FRONT SIDE FACING (Cut 2): 1/16″ × 3/16″ × 7/16″.

151

(H) LOWER FRONT CENTER FACING (Cut 1): 1/16″ × 1/4″ × 7/16″.

(I) FRONT BASE FRAME (Cut 1): 1/4″ × 3/8″ × 4 1/4″. See Figure **8-H-5** for the shape. Mitre each end with a 45° angle cut.

(J) SIDE BASE FRAME (Cut 2): 1/4″ × 3/8″ × 2″. See Figure **8-H-4** for the shape of the left side piece. Reverse this pattern when tracing it onto the second piece of wood for the right side piece. Mitre each front end with a 45° angle cut.

(K) DRAWERS (Two)
    (1) **FRONT** (Cut 2): 1/16″ × 3/8″ × 1 13/16″.
    (2) **BACK** (Cut 2): 1/16″ × 5/16″ × 1 11/16″.
    (3) **SIDES** (Cut 4): 1/16″ × 5/16″ × 1 3/4″.
    (4) **BOTTOM** (Cut 2): 1/8″ × 1 9/16″ × 13/4″.

(L) DRAWER PULLS (Two sets): Use the bail type drawer pulls. Refer to Figure **1-B-6** for an example.

ASSEMBLY: Refer to **2-E-2** for the assembly of the two drawers. Refer to **2-C-4** for the assembly of the dower chest.

1. When the chest is assembled, apply the color print which can be found on the color insert sheet. Refer to **1-C-2** for aid in the application of the print.

2. Using an acrylic (*water base*) paint, match the background color in the color print and paint all portions of the chest prior to the application of the color print. After the print has been applied, spray the completed chest with several coats of decoupage spray.

3. Attach the drawer pulls.

DOWER CHEST 8-I

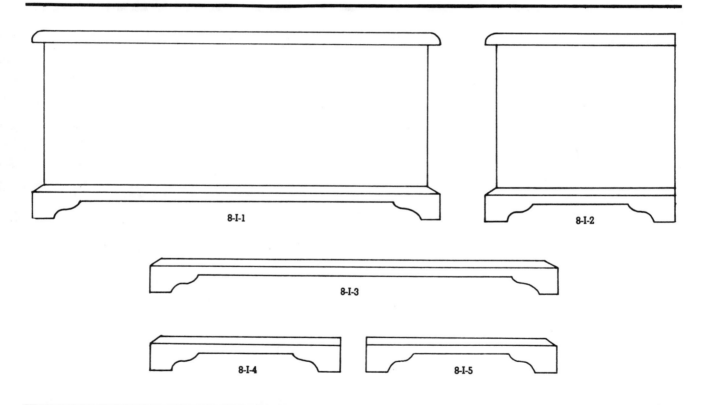

(A) FRONT AND BACK (Cut 2): 1/16″ × 1 1/2″ × 4″.

(B) SIDES (Cut 2): 1/16″ × 1 1/2″ × 1 3/4″.

(C) TOP (Cut 1): 1/8″ × 2″ × 4 1/4″. Round the top edges of the front and side surfaces of this board. See Figures **8-I-1** and **8-I-2**.

(D) BOTTOM (Cut 1): 1/16″ × 2″ × 4 1/4″. Bevel the top edges of the front and side surfaces of this board. See Figures **8-I-1** and **8-I-2**.

(E) FRONT BASE FRAME (Cut 1): 1/4″ × 3/8″ × 4

1/4″. See Figure **8-I-3** for the shape. Mitre each end with a 45° angle cut.

(F) SIDE BASE FRAME (Cut 2): 1/4″ × 3/8″ × 2″. See Figure **8-I-4** for the shape of the right side base. See Figure **8-I-5** for the shape of the left side base. Mitre the front end of each board with a 45° angle cut.

ASSEMBLY: Refer to **2-C-4** for the assembly of the dower chest. *Note:* Disregard the portion of instructions dealing with the lower chest assembly and drawers.

1. When the chest is assembled, apply the color print **8-I** which can be found on the color insert sheet. Refer to **1-C-2** for aid in the application of the print.

2. Using an acrylic paint, match the background color in the color print and paint all portions of the chest prior to the application of the color print. After the print has been applied, spray the completed chest with several coats of decoupage spray.

STENCILLED WASHSTAND — NINETEENTH CENTURY BEDROOM 8-J

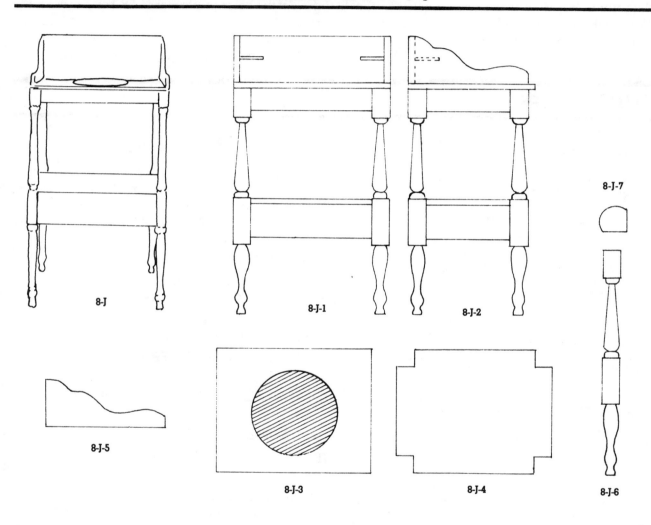

(A) BACK (Cut 1): 1/16″ × 1/2″ × 1 1/2″.

(B) SIDES (Cut 2): 1/16″ × 1/2″ × 1 1/4″. See Figure **8-J-5** for the shape.

(C) WASHSTAND TOP (Cut 1): 1/16″ × 1 5/16″ × 1 5/8″. See Figure **8-J-3**. Cut a hole 7/8″ in diameter at the site indicated by a shaded area in the diagram.

(D) SHELF (Cut 2): 1/32″ thick. See Figure **8-J-7** for the shape.

(E) LEGS (Cut 4): 3/16″ × 3/16″ × 2 7/16″ long. Figure **8-J-6** shows the shape. Refer to **1-C-3-a**.

(F) TOP APRON — FRONT AND BACK (Cut 2): 1/16″ × 1/4″ × 1 1/4″.

(G) TOP APRON — SIDES (Cut 2): 1/16″ × 1/4″ × 7/8″.

(H) LOWER SHELF (Cut 1): 1/16″ × 1 5/16″ × 1 5/8″. See Figure **8-J-4** for the shape.

(I) LOWER APRON — FRONT AND BACK (Cut 2): 1/16″ × 3/8″ × 1 1/4″.

(J) LOWER APRON SIDES (Cut 2): 1/16″ × 3/8″ × 7/8″.

ASSEMBLY

1. Glue the sides against the upright edges of the back, with back edges flush. See Figure **8-J-2**. Glue this assembly atop the washstand top board, with back and side edges flush.

2. Glue the two back legs beneath the washstand top, with back and side edges flush. Glue the top back apron between the back legs and against the underside of the top board.

3. Glue the upper side apron boards between the side legs and against the underside of the top board, with the inside surfaces of the board and upper leg flush. Glue the upper front apron board between the front legs in a like manner. See Figures **8-J-1** and **8-J-2**.

4. Glue the shelf between the four legs (*the notches will fit against the legs*) in the location indicated in Figures **8-J-1** and **8-J-2**. Glue the lower apron pieces in place, as you did the upper apron.

5. Paint the shelves (**D**) and the assembled wash-stand an ivory or cream color.

6. Select the color prints marked **8-J** on the color insert sheet. Refer to **1-C-2**. Glue the color prints in place. Glue shelves (**D**) against the upper side and back walls. Refer to **8-J-1**. Apply a finish coat.

SCHRANK 8-K

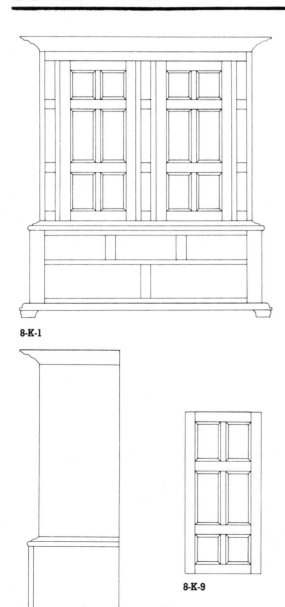

8-K-1

8-K-9

8-K-2

Note: This piece of furniture will be painted and will have color print applied to simulate the antique painted decoration. If you wish to have the painted surface appear old and worn, stain all of the wood with a dark stain before glueing. When you apply the paint, wipe a portion away before it is thoroughly dry and it will appear to be worn.

LOWER CABINET

(A) CABINET BASE (Cut 1): 1/4" × 2 1/8" × 5 1/2". See Figure **8-K-6** for the shape.

(B) DRAWER BASE (Cut 1): 1/8" × 2 1/8" × 5 1/2". See Figure **8-K-6** for the shape.

(C) LOWER DRAWER SEPARATOR (Cut 1): 1/8" × 1/4" × 7/8".

(D) UPPER DRAWER SEPARATOR (Cut 2): 1/8" × 1/4" × 5/8".

(E) DRAWER DIVIDERS (Cut 7): 1/8" × 1/4" × 2".

(F) LOWER CABINET SIDES (Cut 2): 1/8" × 2" × 2 1/8".

(G) LOWER CABINET TOP (Cut 1): 1/8" × 2 5/16" × 5 7/8". Round off the top edges of the front and sides.

(H) LOWER CABINET BACK (Cut 1): 1/8" × 2" × 5 1/2".

(I) LOWER SIDE FRONT FACING (Cut 2): 1/8" × 3/8" × 2".

(J) UPPER FRONT FACING (Cut 1): 1/8" × 1/8" × 5".

(K) UPPER DRAWERS (Three)
    (1) **FRONT AND BACK** (Cut 6): 1/8" × 5/8" × 1 1/2".
    (2) **SIDES** (Cut 6): 1/8" × 5/8" × 1 7/8".
    (3) **BOTTOM** (Cut 3): 1/8" × 1 1/4" × 1 7/8".
See **2-E-1** for assembly.

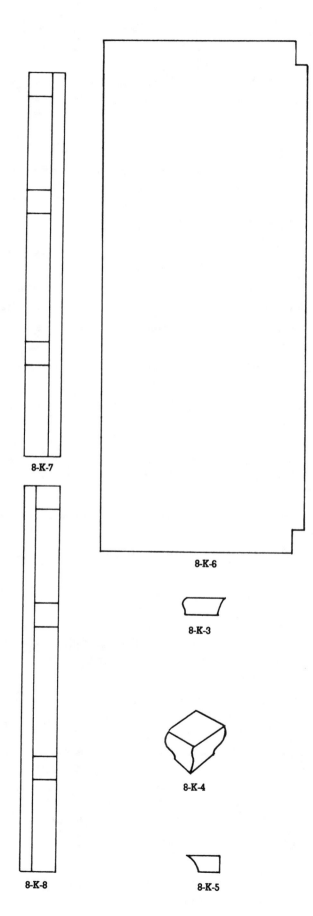

8-K-7

8-K-8

8-K-6

8-K-3

8-K-4

8-K-5

(L) LOWER DRAWERS (Two)

    (1) **FRONT AND BACK** (Cut 4): 1/8" × 7/8" × 2 3/8".

    (2) **SIDES** (Cut 4): 1/8" × 7/8" × 1 7/8".

    (3) **BOTTOM** (Cut 2): 1/8" × 1 7/8" × 2 1/8".

See **2-E-1** for assembly.

Note: You will also need ten Chippendale drawer pulls with bail. Refer to **1-B-6**.

UPPER CABINET

(M) UPPER CABINET BACK (Cut 2): 1/8" × 2 1/2" × 4 1/2". Glue butted together. Final measurement will be 1/8" × 4 1/2" × 5".

(N) UPPER CABINET BASE (Cut 1): 1/8" × 1 7/8" × 5".

(O) UPPER CABINET TOP (Cut 1): 1/4" × 1 7/8" × 5".

(P) UPPER CABINET SIDES (Cut 2): 1/8" × 2" × 4 1/2".

(Q) DOOR DIVIDER BACKING (Cut 1): 1/16" × 1/2" × 4 1/8".

(R) DOOR DIVIDER VERTICAL MOULDING (Cut 2): 1/16" × 1/8" × 4 1/8".

(S) FRONT FACING BACKING (Cut 2): 1/16" × 3/8" × 4 1/8".

(T) FRONT FACING VERTICAL MOULDING (Cut 2): 1/16" × 1/8" × 4 1/8".

(U) HORIZONTAL MOULDING FOR DOOR DIVIDER AND FRONT FACING PIECES (Cut 9): 1/16" × 1/4" × 1/4".

(V) DOORS (Two)

    (1) **CENTER PANEL** (Cut 2): 1/16" × 1 3/8" × 3 5/8".

    (2) **TOP AND BOTTOM** (Cut 4): 1/8" × 1/4" × 1 3/8".

    (3) **SIDES** (Cut 4): 1/8" × 1/4" × 4 1/8".

    (4) **HORIZONTAL MOULDING** (Cut 6): 1/16" × 1/4" × 1 3/8".

    (5) **LOWER VERTICAL MOULDING** (Cut 2): 1/16" × 1/8" × 1".

    (6) **CENTER VERTICAL MOULDING** (Cut 2): 1/16" × 1/8" × 1 3/8".

    (7) **UPPER VERTICAL MOULDING** (Cut 2): 1/16" × 1/8" × 3/4".

(W) DOOR PANEL INNER MOULDING: 1/16" × 1/16" quarter-round; mitre ends.

    (1) **LOWER PANELS**

        (a) **SIDES** (Cut 8): 1" long. 45° mitre cut at each end.

        (b) **TOP AND BOTTOM** (Cut 8): 5/8" long. 45° mitre cut at each end.

(2) CENTER PANELS

(a) **SIDES** (Cut 8): 1 3/8" long. 45° mitre cut at each end.

(b) **TOP AND BOTTOM** (Cut 8): 5/8" long. 45° mitre cut at each end.

(3) UPPER PANELS

(a) **SIDES** (Cut 8): 3/4" long. 45° mitre cut at each end.

(b) **TOP AND BOTTOM** (Cut 8): 5/8" long. 45° mitre cut at each end.

(X) CORNICE: There are many varieties of mouldings which can be purchased from your miniature dealer or from mail-order lists. Choose a piece of moulding which is approximately 3/8" in height. The following measurements are for the bottom edge length:

(1) **FRONT** (Cut 1): 5 1/4". Mitre both ends with a 45° angle cut. See Figure **8-K-1**.

(2) **SIDES** (Cut 2): 2". Mitre one end with a 45° angle cut (*opposite cut for the other side piece*) and the other end is straight cut.

(Y) UPPER CABINET BASE MOULDING: Choose a moulding which is approximately 1/8" high. The measurements are for the back edge (*the mitre cut at each end is added to the length*).

(1) **FRONT** (Cut 1): 5 3/4" plus a 45° angle mitre cut at both ends.

(2) **SIDES** (Cut 2): 2 1/4" plus a 45° angle mitre cut at the front end, with the back end a straight cut.

(Z) LOWER CABINET BASE MOULDING: Choose a moulding that is approximately 3/16" high × 3/8" deep.

(1) **FRONT** (Cut 1): 6 1/4" wide at the front. Mitre both ends with a 45° angle cut.

(2) **SIDES** (Cut 2): 2 1/2" long. Cut the back edge straight and mitre the front end with a 45° angle cut. Reverse the angle of the cut for the other piece.

(AA) FEET

(1) **FRONT FEET** (Cut 2): 3/16" × 1/2" × 1/2". See Figures **8-K-3** and **8-K-4** for the shape to be cut. Refer to **1-C-3-d** for aid in carving.

(2) **BACK FEET** (Cut 2): 3/16" × 1/4" × 3/8". See Figure **8-K-5** for the shape.

(BB) DOOR PULLS (Two): Refer to **1-B-6**.

UPPER CABINET ASSEMBLY

1. See Figures **8-K-7** (*left side*) and **8-K-8** (*right side*). Left side: Glue a piece of the front facing vertical moulding against the front facing backing with the right edges flush. Glue three pieces of the horizontal moulding (1/16" × 1/4" × 1/4") against the backing as shown in **8-K-7**. Reverse the above assembly for the right side piece.

2. Glue the two door divider vertical moulding pieces against the door divider backing (1/16" × 1/2" × 4 1/8") with the left and right edges flush. Glue three pieces of the horizontal moulding against the backing and between the two vertical pieces of moulding as you did for the above assembly. See Figure **8-K-7** for placement.

3. **DOOR ASSEMBLY:** Refer to Figure **8-K-9**.

a. Glue the top and bottom boards against the center panel, with the side edges flush.

b. Glue the side boards against the side edges of the above assembly, with the top and bottom edges flush.

c. Glue the door panel horizontal and vertical moulding pieces in place.

d. Glue the door panel inner moulding pieces in place.

4. Refer to **2-C-2** for the major assembly of the upper cabinet.

5. Glue the three top moulding pieces in place atop the cabinet top board, forming the cornice.

LOWER CHEST ASSEMBLY: Refer to 2-C-1, using Figures **2-C-1-c**, **2-C-1-d**, **2-C-1-e** and **2-C-1-f**.

6. Glue the lower cabinet base moulding pieces together and glue underneath the front and sides of the lower chest, as shown in Figures **8-K-1** and **8-K-2**.

7. Glue the front and back feet in place under the base moulding. Refer to Figures **8-K-1** and **8-K-2**.

8. Glue the upper cabinet atop the top of the lower cabinet, with the side spaces equal and the back edges flush. Glue the upper cabinet base moulding atop the lower cabinet and against the front and side surfaces of the upper cabinet.

9. Turn to the color insert sheet and find the color prints for the schrank. They will be marked 8-K. Refer to **1-C-2**.

10. Paint the schrank your choice of color. We recommend that you choose a color that will compliment the color prints. The insides of the cabinet, drawers and doors should also be painted.

11. Refer to **1-C-2** for application of the color print. These prints are glued in the narrow sections of the side and center facing mouldings, in the door panels and on the front surfaces of the five drawers.

12. Apply an acrylic sealer to the schrank and all of the color prints.

13. Hinge the cupboard doors to the upper cabinet. Attach the door and drawer pulls.

PROVINCIAL CRADLE WITH DECORATED PANELS 8-L

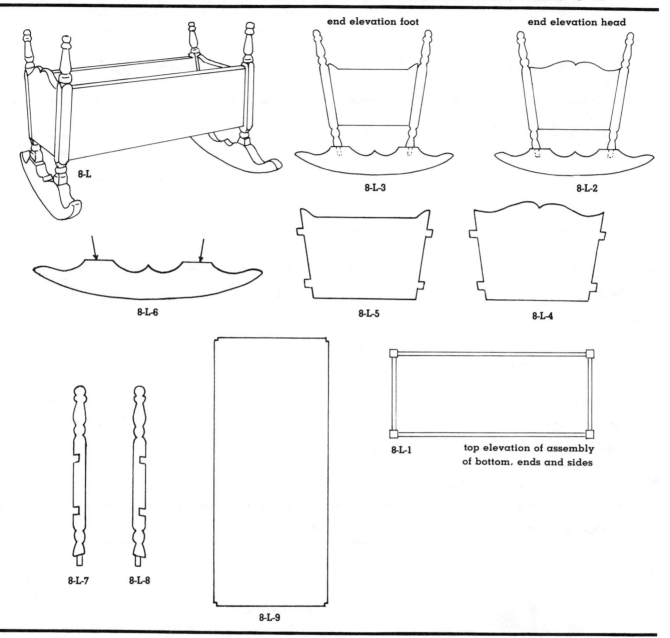

end elevation foot

end elevation head

8-L

8-L-3

8-L-2

8-L-6

8-L-5

8-L-4

8-L-1

top elevation of assembly of bottom, ends and sides

8-L-7   8-L-8

8-L-9

(A) HEADBOARD (Cut 1): 1/16″ × 1 1/16″ × 1 1/2″. See Figure **8-L-4** for the shape.

(B) FOOTBOARD (Cut 1): 1/16″ × 1″ × 1 1/2″. See Figure **8-L-5** for the shape.

(C) SIDES (Cut 2): 1/16″ × 1″ × 2 13/16″.

(D) BOTTOM (Cut 1): 1/16″ × 1 3/16″ × 2 7/8″. See Figure **8-L-9** for notches to be cut from each corner. The side edges will be sanded at an angle to match the angle of the head and footboards.

(E) POSTS

   (1) **LEFT POST** (Cut 2): 1/8″ diameter wood dowel × 1 15/16″. See Figure **8-L-8** for the shape and

mortise cuts in the side of the posts to accept the head and footboards.

   (2) **RIGHT POSTS** (Cut 2): 1/8″ diameter wood dowel × 1 15/16″. See Figure **8-L-7** for the shape and mortise cuts in the side of the posts to accept the head and footboards.

(F) ROCKERS (Cut 2): 1/8″ × 1/2″ × 2 3/8″. See Figure **8-L-6** for the shape. The arrows in the diagram indicate the angle of a 1/16″ diameter hole to be drilled at these sites in each rocker.

ASSEMBLY: Refer to Figure **8-L**. Stain all wood before glueing.

1. Glue the headboard and the footboard into each

pair of posts. Glue the bottom of the cradle against the head and footboards, with the bottom edges flush. Be sure the edge angle follows the angle of these boards. See Figures **8-L-1**, **8-L-2** and **8-L-3**.

2. Glue the side boards between the two posts and against the edge of the bottom board, with the bottom edges flush. See Figure **8-L-1**.

3. Glue the ends of the posts into the drilled holes in the rockers. See Figure **8-L**.

4. Refer to **1-C-2**. Find the cradle print marked **8-L** on the color insert sheet. Glue the color print on the outside surfaces of the ends and sides of the cradle.

5. Apply a finish coat to the cradle.

CANDLE BOX 8-M

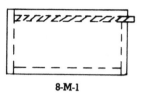

8-M-1

8-M-2

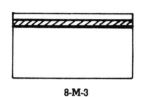

8-M-3

end view

(A) FRONT AND BACK (Cut 2): 1/8″ × 11/16″ × 1 1/4″. See Figure **8-M-3** for a view of the inside surface and the end view of the board showing a 3/32″ high × 1/16″ groove to be cut into the length of the board 1/16″ from the top edge. Repeat for the second board.

(B) BOTTOM (Cut 1): 1/16″ × 5/8″ × 1 1/8″.

(C) LEFT END (Cut 1): 1/16″ × 5/8″ × 11/16″.

(D) RIGHT END (Cut 1): 1/16″ × 17/32″ × 5/8″.

(E) TOP (Cut 1): 1/16″ × 3/4″ × 1 1/4″. Sand the edges and thickness of this board slightly to accommodate a color print and still move easily.

ASSEMBLY: Stain all wood before glueing.

1. Refer to Figures **8-M-1** (*front view*) and **8-M-2** (*right end view*). Glue the two end boards against the end edges of the bottom board. With the notched edges upward and toward the inside, glue the front and back boards against the previous assembly.

2. Refer to the color print sheet and cut out the prints marked **8-M**. Refer to **1-C-2**. Glue the side and end prints against the box. Glue the print against the top board. Apply a finish coat.

FRENCH HARPSICHORD c. 1750 8-N

8-N

The large French harpsichord, of which this is a 1″ = 1′ scale reproduction, is presently being displayed in our Mott Miniature Museum, located at Knott's Berry Farm. It is owned by the Knott family and we are grateful that Russell Knott kindly gave us permission to reproduce it in miniature for this book.

I have designed this piece of furniture so that any miniaturist who has had some experience in building will not be afraid to attempt it. It is such a satisfying experience to hold this tiny harpsichord in your hand and know that you have built it.

This miniature French harpsichord can be made completely of wood (with the exception of the leg brace, which is made of two different thicknesses of cardboard) for the more advanced craftsman, or it can be made in varying degrees of simplicity for the beginning craftsman. In either instance, the finished product will closely resemble the wooden model.

The directions for making the harpsichord are for wood (*with the exception of the leg brace*). The following marks which will appear beside the capital

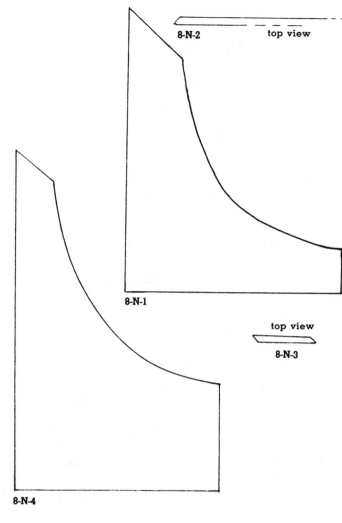

8-N-2 top view

8-N-1

top view
8-N-3

8-N-4

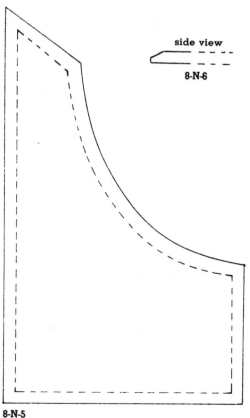

side view
8-N-6

8-N-5

letter identifying the piece will simplify construction:

* This piece may be cut from 1/16" thick cardboard rather than wood. Follow the directions for the wooden piece. When bending or curving cardboard, place the piece on a table top or a book and gently pull downward over the edge, thus beginning the shaping. All cut edges of the cardboard must be coated with a glue, such as airplane cement, to prevent separation of the layers of paper in the cardboard when the piece is painted.

** This piece must be cut from cardboard. Follow directions.

• There is a color print to simulate this construction:

(M) • **KEYBOARD:** Cut only the basic keyboard. Do not score, do not make the black keys. Do not follow the main construction directions for this piece, but choose the alternate color directions.

(K) • **STRINGBOARD:** Cut only the basic stringboard piece of wood. Do not drill holes; do not cut pegs. Do not follow the main construction directions for this piece, but choose the alternate color directions.

* The apron pieces can all be made of 1/16" thick cardboard with the pierced (*open*) sections cut away *or;* these pierced areas are black in the color print, and they need not be cut away in the wood or cardboard. This more simple procedure will be your choice; however, if the apron pieces are pierced, be sure to cut away the black areas in the color prints.

(A) * **TOP BACK PIECE** (Cut 1): 1/16" × 2 1/4" × 3 1/16". See Figure **8-N-1** for the shape.

(B) * **TOP FRONT PIECE** (Cut 1): 1/16" × 3/4" × 2 1/4".

(C) * **LEFT SIDE** (Cut 1): 1/16" × 3/4" × 3 3/4". See Figure **8-N-2** for a top view diagram of the angle at the left end edge.

(D) * **BACK ANGLE END** (Cut 1): 1/16" × 3/4" × 3/4". See Figure **8-N-3** for a top view diagram of the edge angles at the left and right end edges of this board.

(E) * **RIGHT CURVED SIDE** (Cut 1): 1/16" × 3/4" × 4 1/2". *Note:* This piece will eventually be bent. When assembled, the excess length will be removed.

(F) * **RIGHT END** (Cut 1): 1/16" × 3/4" × 1 1/8".

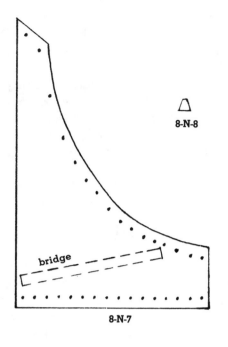

8-N-8

bridge

8-N-7

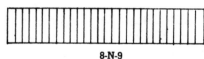

8-N-9

top view

8-N-10

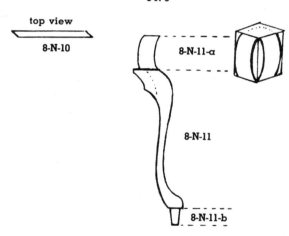

8-N-11-a

8-N-11

8-N-11-b

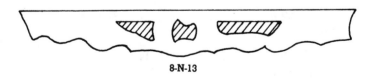

8-N-13

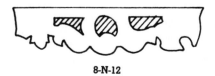

8-N-12

(G) * **FRONT** (Cut 1): 1/16″ × 3/4″ × 2 1/4″.

(H) **BOTTOM** (Cut 1): 1/4″ × 2 1/8″ × 3 21/32″. See Figure **8-N-4** for the shape.

(I) **MOULDING BASE** (Cut 1): 1/8″ × 2 1/2″ × 4 3/16″. See Figure **8-N-5** for the shape. Trace onto the wood. Trace the broken line onto both sides of this piece of wood. Figure **8-N-5** is a top view diagram. Bevel the edges on the top surface of the wood from the broken line downward to the bottom edge of the wood. See Figure **8-N-6** for a side view of this shaping.

(J) * • **STRINGBOARD** (Cut 1): The stringboard should be cut from 1/8″ thick wood if you choose to peg and string it. It can be made of 1/16″ thick cardboard if you choose to use the color print. The other dimensions are 2″ × 3 1/8″. See Figure **8-N-7** for the shape. The black dots in this diagram represent 1/32″ diameter holes to be drilled into the wood.

(K) • **STRING BRIDGE** (Cut 1): Delete this piece if you have chosen to use the color print. 1/8″ × 1/8″ × 1 1/2″. See Figure **8-N-8** for an end view of the shaping.

(L) • **PEGS** (Cut 32): Delete these pegs if you have chosen to use the color print. Use the shaped flat wooden tooth picks. The assembly instructions will tell you how to use them.

(M) * • **KEYBOARD** (Cut 1): If you choose to use the color print, the keyboard can be cut from 1/16″ cardboard; otherwise, it must be cut from wood. The dimensions are: 1/16″ × 3/8″ × 2 1/16″. See Figure **8-N-9**, if you are using wood, for the marked areas to be scored with your knife on the top surface and front edge of this board. This will represent the "white" keys which are actually natural color wood in the antique harpsichord.

(N) • **BLACK KEYS** (Cut 18): Ignore these directions if you have chosen to use the color print. 1/16″ × 1/16″ × 3/16″. Paint each piece black on the top, two sides and one end.

(O) * **SOUND BOARD — BEHIND KEYBOARD** (Cut 1): 1/16″ × 1/2″ × 2 1/8″.

(P) * **MOULDING AROUND TOP FRONT BOARD**
    * (1) **LEFT AND RIGHT SIDE** (Cut 2): 1/16″ × 1/8″ × 3/4″.
    * (2) **FRONT** (Cut 1): 1/16″ × 1/8″ × 2 3/8″.

(Q) * **MOULDING AROUND TOP BACK BOARD**
    * (1) **RIGHT SIDE** (Cut 1): 1/16″ × 1/8″ × 1/2″.
    * (2) **CURVED RIGHT SIDE** (Cut 1): 1/16″ × 1/8″ × 4 1/2″. *Note:* This piece will eventually be bent. When assembled, the excess length will be removed.

1

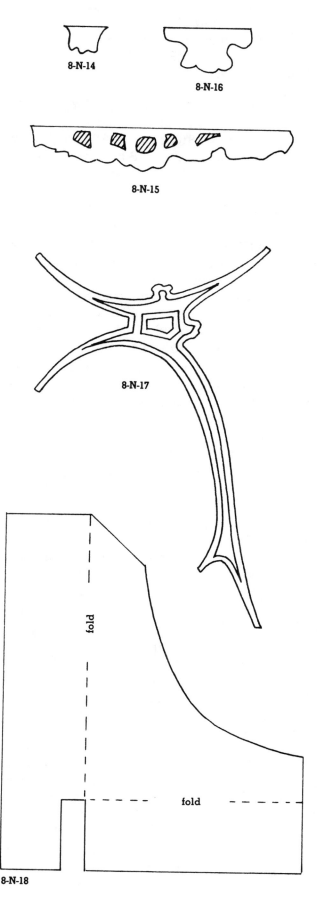

8-N-14

8-N-16

8-N-15

8-N-17

8-N-18

fold

fold

* (3) **ANGLED END** (Cut 1): 1/16" × 1/8" × 7/8". See Figure 8-N-10 for a top view diagram of the angle at each end of this board.

(R) LEGS (Five): There are three methods that can be used to produce the five legs. Figure **8-N-11** shows the shape of the leg which I made for the miniature harpsichord which is pictured. I used method No. 2. Method No. 1 will be the most difficult. No. 2 has carving, but uses the pre-shaped cabriole legs which can be purchased from your miniature dealer. No. 3 uses the same pre-shaped cabriole legs which can be purchased, but with no additional carving. Please read the three methods, and choose one of them to produce the five required legs.

METHOD NO. 1: Refer to Figure 8-N-11. Trace the full leg diagram onto five pieces of wood, each measuring 1/2" × 1/2" × 2 1/8". Follow the instructions in **1-C-3-d** for shaping each leg.

METHOD NO. 2: Purchase three packages of pre-shaped cabriole legs measuring approximately 1 5/8" in length. There are two legs in each package. Cut five pieces of wood measuring 1/4" × 1/4" × 3/8", and glue one piece atop each of the five legs **(8-N-11-a)** with the two back edges flush. Cut five pieces of 1/8" diameter wood dowel measuring 3/16" **(8-N-11-b)**; glue a piece, centered, beneath each of the five feet. Let the glue dry. These legs can now be carved and shaped like the leg shown in Figures **8-N-11-a** and **b**.

METHOD NO. 3: Follow the instructions in Method No. 2, but you need not carve the legs. This leg will not be exactly like the leg pictured, but will be pretty and is quite simple to assemble.

(S) * APRON: The length and end shape of each piece of apron will vary slightly with the shape which is or is not carved into the top portion of each leg. The back surfaces of the end edges of each piece will be beveled to allow the front surface to fit as smoothly as possible. Be sure that the fit is correct before glueing in place.

Refer to the color insert sheet and find the prints marked **8-N**. You will see that there are black areas in the apron prints. These black areas represent the pierced (*cut out*) areas in the pieces of apron. If you choose to have these areas open in either your wood or cardboard pieces, they should be cut out first, before the final shaping of the piece. Likewise, the black areas in these color prints would be cut away. If you choose not to pierce the wood or cardboard, ignore the instructions for piercing and cut only the outside shape. Likewise, the black areas would remain in these prints. Choose one of these methods before you cut the apron pieces.

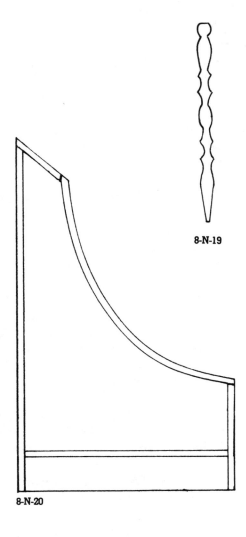

8-N-19

8-N-20

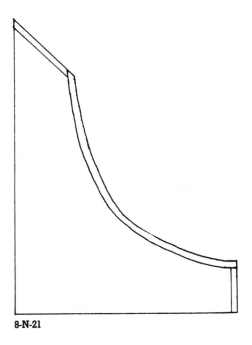

8-N-21

* (1) **FRONT APRON** (Cut 1): 1/16" × 1/2" × 1 15/16". See Figure **8-N-12** for the shape. The shaded areas in this diagram represent the pierced areas.

* (2) **LEFT SIDE APRON** (Cut 1): 1/16" × 1/2" × 3 3/8". See Figure **8-N-13** for the shape. The shaded areas in the diagram represent the pierced areas.

* (3) **ANGLED BACK APRON** (Cut 1): 1/16" × 5/16" × 3/8". See Figure **8-N-14** for the shape.

* (4) **CURVED RIGHT SIDE APRON** (Cut 1): 1/16" × 1/2" × 3 7/8". See Figure **8-N-15** for the shape. The shaded areas in the diagram represent the pierced areas.

* (5) **RIGHT SIDE APRON** (Cut 1): 1/16" × 1/2" × 7/8". See Figure **8-N-16** for the shape.

(T) ** **LEG BRACE:** The leg brace is the only piece which must be cut from cardboard. It is cut in two pieces of two different thicknesses, and is then glued together to simulate a shaped piece. Remember to coat all cut edges of the cardboard with airplane cement (*or a similar glue*) to prevent separation. This piece will eventually be painted.

Figure **8-N-17** shows the shape of this leg brace. Trace the outside black line and the inside shaped area black line in this diagram. Re-trace onto 1/16" thick cardboard. Cut away the inside shaped area first. Using decoupage or curved-end fingernail scissors, cut out this piece of the leg brace.

Trace the inside black line and the outside shaped area black line in the same diagram. Re-trace onto a piece of file card or file folder. Cut away the inside shaped area first; then cut out this piece, as you did the previous piece. Refer to Figure **8-N-17** and glue the thinner piece of cardboard atop the 1/16" thick piece, as shown in this top view diagram.

(U) **HINGES:** I found a gummed paper tape containing fibre reinforcement to be an excellent hinge material. It can be painted (*the plastic fibre tape will not hold paint*), folded without cracking, and does not leave frayed edges as a piece of cloth will do. The size of the hinge for the harpsichord front board (**G**) is 2 3/8" wide × 1 15/16" long. Figure **8-N-18** shows the size and shape of the hinge for the harpsichord top boards. *Note:* This type of tape can be purchased at paper supply houses, paper carton supply houses, or shops that stock supplies for sealing cartons for shipping. You will need to purchase a piece measuring 3 1/8" in width × 6" in length. Some tapes will only come in 3" widths. Adjust this shortage on the left side edge of the hinge pattern for the harpsichord top boards.

(V) **TOP BOARD SPINDLE** (Cut 1): 1/8" diameter wood dowel × 2 1/8". See Figure **8-N-19** for the shape. Refer to **1-C-3-a** for aid in carving.

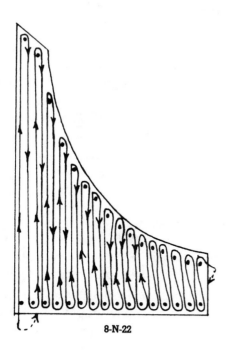

8-N-22

8-N-23

ASSEMBLY: Refer to the picture of the harpsichord.

1. Refer to Figure **8-N-20** showing the assembly of the bottom, sides and soundboard. This is a top view diagram. Glue the left side (**C**) against the left side of the bottom board (**H**) with bottom edges flush. Glue the right end (**F**) against the right side of the bottom board (**H**) with bottom edges flush. Glue the back angled end (**D**) against the angled end of the bottom board (**H**) with left edges and bottom edges flush. Glue the soundboard (**O**) atop the bottom board, between the left and right side boards and with the front edge 3/8" behind the front (*open*) edge of the bottom board.

2. The following directions are for bending the wood piece *or* curving a cardboard piece. You will be referred back to these directions for subsequent wood bending or cardboard curving.

a. Bending the right curved side board (*wood*): Place the piece of wood in a pan of water, bring it to a boil, cover the pan with a lid and reduce the heat but keep the water boiling. My piece of wood took 28 minutes of boiling until it would bend easily. While the wood is boiling, bring your

previous assembly to a work area very near the stove. You will need a prong or spoon to remove the wood from the boiling water. You will need a towel on which to place the wet wood. You will need a quick-set glue such as "Permabond" or "Crazy Glue". When the wood has boiled sufficiently to bend without cracking, place it quickly on a towel and pat "dry". Place it immediately in position against the right curved side, with bottom edges flush and run glue along all joining surfaces. You will note that the board will extend over the two adjoining end boards; this excess will be removed after the glue is thoroughly dry. Hold in place until the glue is dry. Using a small hand saw or a knife, trim the excess length away and sand the ends to follow the angle of each end.

b. Curving the right curved side board (*cardboard*): Place this piece of cardboard on a table top or book, and gently pull down across the edge. Fit the curved edge against the right side curved edge of the bottom board (**H**) with bottom edges flush. Run "Permabond" or "Crazy Glue" into all joining areas. Hold in place until the glue is set. Using a knife, cut the excess length to match the angles at the back and right ends. Paint or stain the inside areas a light brown (*pine, maple or oak color*).

3. Glue the moulding side pieces (**P-1**) against the side of the top front piece (**B**) with top edges flush. Glue the front moulding (**P-2**) against the front edge of this board, with top and side edges flush.

4. Glue the right side moulding (**Q-1**) against the right side of the top back board (**A**), with top edges flush. See Figure **8-N-21**. Glue the back angle moulding in place, with top edges flush. Refer to Step 2-a in these assembly instructions for wood or Step 2-b for cardboard. After the glue is dry, trim to fit, as before.

5. **STRINGBOARD**

a. If you have chosen to use the color print, cut it out at this time and glue it against the top surface of this board. Refer to **1-C-2**. Glue the stringboard inside the rear area of the harpsichord.

b. If you have chosen to simulate the string portion of the harpsichord, follow these instructions: Stain the stringboard (**J**), the bridge (**K**) and the narrow ends of the toothpicks a pine or maple color. Glue the small ends of the toothpicks into the drilled holes in the board. When the glue is dry, clip each toothpick at the height of 1/4". Stain each cut end. Using a single strand of grey embroidery thread or silver thread of that weight, begin to string the board. Refer to Figure **8-N-22**. Glue an end of thread beneath the front left side of the board. Refer to Figure 8-N-7; the broken line indicates the position of the bridge. Glue it in place. Follow the arrows in Figure 8-N-22 and weave the thread forward and back around the pegs. When it is completed, glue the other end of the thread beneath the board. Clip off any excess length. Glue this assembled board inside the rear area of the harpsichord.

6. KEYBOARD

a. If you have chosen to use the color print, cut it out at this time and glue it against the top surface of the keyboard (M), with the front edge glued downward against the front edge of this board. Glue this board atop the bottom board, between the side boards and butted against the front of the soundboard (O). See Figure 8-N-20.

b. If you have chosen to simulate the wooden keyboard, follow these instructions: The scored board (M) must be stained a light pine, maple or oak color. Refer to Figure 8-N-23 for placement of the black keys. Glue in place atop the bottom board, between the side boards and butted against the front of the soundboard (O). See Figure 8-N-20.

7. Glue the hinge against the front surface of the front board (G). The edges will be flush and there will be a length that will extend past the bottom edge. Place this board against the upright front edges of the side boards and the front edge of the bottom board. While holding it in place, glue the hinge against the bottom edge of the front board and the bottom surface of the bottom board. Glue the second hinge (*Figure 8-N-18*) with the front edge atop the top front piece (B) inside the edges of the front and side moulding. Glue the right back portion of this hinge atop the top back board (*it will be butted against the rear edge of the top front board*) inside of the right end moulding, curved side moulding and angled end moulding pieces. Place this assembly atop the previously assembled harpsichord body, with the moulding pieces extending downward over the outside edges of the lower assembly. Glue the remainder of this hinge downward against the left edge of the back top board and against the left side board of the harpsichord. The fold lines in the diagram in Figure 8-N-18 will aid in the placement of this hinge. Let the glue dry. The top front board will now fold upward, allowing the front board to fold downward, and the harpsichord top will lift up to the left. When returning the boards to position, fold the front board upward in place first. While the top front board is still raised, lower the top, then the top front board is lowered and will hold the front board in place.

8. Glue the previous assembly atop the base

moulding piece. It should fit at the top edge of the shaped side edge moulding. Let the glue dry.

9. Turn the above assembly over and glue a leg at each corner in the broken line which was traced on the bottom surface of the base board. Be sure that the top surface of the leg is glued down against this board with the front of the leg against the marked line, and with each leg facing the angle of the corner. Let the glue dry.

10. Fit each piece of apron between each set of legs; shape the ends of the apron pieces if necessary. Bevel the end edges so that the front surface of each piece of apron will fit smoothly against the legs. When the fit meets with your approval, glue the pieces in place. Be sure that you glue the front surface of each apron piece toward the outside of the harpsichord, or the color print will not fit.

11. Adjust the leg brace to fit between the five legs. It was designed so that ends could be clipped to fit varying thicknesses of legs. Be sure that the smooth surface is at the bottom. When the leg brace fits, glue it in place. Let the glue dry.

12. Refer to the color insert sheet and remove all of the prints marked 8-N. Note the greenish-brown background color. This is the color of the antique harpsichord. Using acrylic paints, mix a color that will closely resemble the background color. Paint the edges and inside surface of the front board, the front edges and top edges of all of the side and end boards, all surfaces of the top board moulding pieces, the bottom surface and all side surfaces of the moulding base board, all edges and pierced edges and back surfaces of the apron boards, and all surfaces of the legs and the leg brace.

13. Refer to 1-C-2. Glue the color print against the front surface of the front board. The top board print is glued against both sections of the top board and downward against the left side of the harpsichord. The remaining side print is glued against the right side, the curved right side and the angled end. Glue the two prints on the inside surfaces of the top front and back boards. Glue the prints against the outside surfaces of all of the apron pieces.

14. If you wish, you can decorate the leg brace, legs and moulding pieces with fine brush stroke lines of gilt paint; you can highlight the color print with very fine lines of gilt paint. I would suggest using a .003 to to .005 artist's brush.

15. Follow the instructions in 1-C-2 in applying a sealer coat to all color print and painted surfaces of the harpsichord.

BREAD TRAY 8-O

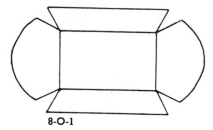

8-O-1

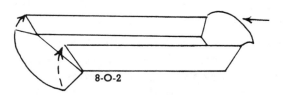

8-O-2

Note: These trays were usually made of papier-mache and painted with a stencilled design.

The materials which will be required are 1/16" thick cardboard, airplane cement, paper glue, black acrylic paint and an acrylic sealer.

1. Trace around the outside black line of the tray. Re-trace onto the cardboard and cut out. Cut-score the inside black lines; fold the edges upward, with the scored surface at the bottom. Gently round the two ends by pulling around a pencil. Glue the four edges together. Apply airplane cement to all cut edges to seal the cardboard for painting. Paint all surfaces of the tray and let dry.

2. Refer to the color insert sheet and cut out the color print marked **8-O**. Glue the print against the inside surfaces of the tray. Apply a touch of black paint to the exposed cut edges of the print. Let dry.

3. Spray all surfaces of the tray with an acrylic sealer.

SWEDISH BOX 8-P

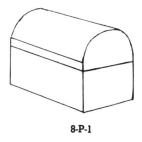

8-P-1

8-P-2

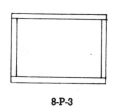

8-P-3

8-P-4

Note: This box can be constructed from 1/16" thick wood or cardboard. The top of the lid will be cut from a file card. If you choose to use cardboard, be sure to apply a line of model airplane cement to all cut edges to prevent separation when painted.

(A) FRONT AND BACK (Cut 2): 1/16" × 1/2" × 1".

(B) ENDS (Cut 2): 1/16" × 1/2" × 5/8".

(C) BOTTOM (Cut 1): 1/16" × 5/8" × 7/8".

(D) BOX LID — FRONT AND BACK (Cut 2): 1/16" × 1/8" × 7/8".

(E) BOX LID — ENDS (Cut 2): 1/16" × 3/8" × 5/8". See Figure **8-P-4** for the shape.

(F) BOX LID — TOP(Cut 1): 1" wide × 1 1/4" long. Cut from a file card.

ASSEMBLY

1. Assemble the front, back, ends and bottom as directed in **2-E-1**. Refer to a top view diagram of this assembly, **8-P-3**.

2. Glue the box lid front and back boards (**D**) between the end boards (**E**) with the bottom edges and side edges flush. See Figure **8-P-2**.

3. Pull the box lid top (**F**) cardboard around a pencil to gently curl it. Glue this "rounded" piece of cardboard against the outside surface of the box

lid front board, atop the top edges of the end boards, and against the back surface of the back board. Let dry.

4. Cut a piece of cotton cloth tape 1″ wide × 2″ in length. Glue the tape over the box lid top and down the back of the box, hinging the two assemblies together.

5. Using a red paint that will closely match the background color of the color print, paint the interior of the box and box lid, all exposed edges and end edges and the ends of the box lid. Paint the cloth hinge at the joint of the two sections, inside and out.

6. Refer to the color insert sheet and cut out the prints marked 8-P. Refer to 1-C-2.

7. Glue the 1/2″ wide color print around the ends and front board of the lower section. Glue the 1″ wide color print against the front surface of the box lid front board, against the box lid top, against the back surface of the box lid back board, and down against the back surface of the back board of the lower assembly.

8. Glue the two remaining prints against the box lid ends.

HARPSICHORD BENCH 8-Q

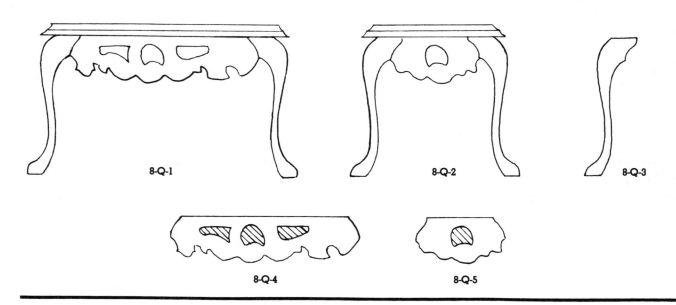

8-Q-1
8-Q-2
8-Q-3
8-Q-4
8-Q-5

(A) LEGS (Cut 4): 9/16″ × 9/16″ × 1 1/2″. See Figure 8-Q-3 for the shape. Refer to 1-C-3-d for aid in shaping.

ALTERNATE LEGS (Four): Commerically carved cabriole legs which are manufactured by X-Acto (*House of Miniatures*) #43112, and are 1 9/16″ in length. These legs may be used as-is or can be further shaped to Figure 8-Q-3. Most miniature dealers stock these legs.

(B) FRONT AND BACK APRON (Cut 2): 1/16″ × 1/2″ × 2″. See Figure 8-Q-4 for the shape. The shaded areas in the diagram can, or need not be, cut out. These pieces can be cut from 1/16″ thick cardboard.

(C) END APRON (Cut 2): 1/16″ × 1/2″ × 15/16″. See Figure 8-Q-5 for the shape. The shaded area in the

diagram can, or need not be, cut out. These pieces can be cut from 1/16″ thick cardboard.

Note: If you have chosen to use the 1/16″ thick cardboard, you must apply airplane cement to all cut edges to seal the layers of cardboard and prevent separation at the time of painting.

(D) TOP (Cut 1): 1/16″ × 1 1/2″ × 2 5/8″. Bevel all top edges.

(E) TOP MOULDING (Cut 1): 1/16″ × 1 3/8″ × 2 1/2″. Bevel all top edges.

ASSEMBLY: Refer to Figures 8-Q-1 and 8-Q-2.

1. Glue the top moulding atop the top board with all spaces equal.

2. Glue the front apron between two legs, with the top edges flush. Repeat for the back apron. See Figure 8-Q-1.

3. Glue the side apron pieces between the front and back legs, with top edges flush.

4. Glue the assembled legs and apron pieces against the undersurface of the assembled top, with equal end and front and back areas.

5. Paint this bench the same color as you did the harpsichord (**8-N**).

6. Refer to the color insert sheet and cut out the prints marked **8-Q**. Do not cut the black areas out if you did not cut out the corresponding areas in the apron pieces. Refer to **1-C-2**. Glue the prints against the four pieces of the apron and bench top.

7. Apply a finish, as instructed in **1-C-2**.

WRITING DESK 8-R

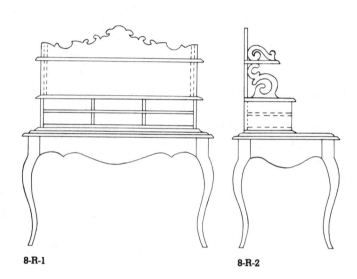

8-R-1   8-R-2

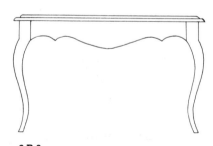

8-R-3

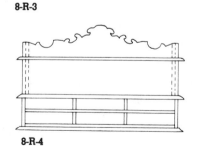

8-R-4

8-R-5

(A) TABLE TOP (Cut 1): 1/16" × 2 1/4" × 4". Round off the top edge of all sides.

(B) TABLE TOP MOULDING (Cut 1): 1/16" × 2" × 3 3/4". Round off the top edge of all sides.

(C) FRONT AND BACK APRON (Cut 2): 1/8" × 5/8" × 3 1/4". See Figure **8-R-6** for the shape.

(D) SIDE APRON (Cut 2): 1/8" × 5/8" × 1 1/2". See Figure **8-R-7** for the shape.

(E) LEGS (Cut 4): 3/8" × 3/8" × 2 3/8". See Figures **8-R-10-a** and **8-R-10-b** for the shape. Refer to **1-C-3-d** for aid in shaping.

(F) DRAWER CABINET BACK (Cut 1): 1/16" × 5/8" × 3 1/8".

(G) DRAWER CABINET SIDES (Cut 2): 1/16" × 5/8" × 1".

(H) DRAWER CABINET — DRAWER SEPARATOR AND BOTTOM (Cut 2): 1/16" × 15/16" × 3 1/8".

(I) DRAWER CABINET — DRAWER DIVIDERS (Cut 4): 1/16" × 1/4" × 15/16".

(J) DRAWERS (Six)
  (1) **FRONT AND BACK** (Cut 12): 1/16" × 1/4" × 1".
  (2) **SIDES** (Cut 12): 1/16" × 1/4" × 13/16".
  (3) **BOTTOM** (Cut 6): 1/16" × 7/8" × 13/16".
Refer to **2-E-1** for assembly.

(K) DRAWER CHEST TOP AND BASE (Cut 2): 1/16" × 1 1/8" × 3 1/2". Round off the top edge of the sides and front.

(L) LOWER SHELF BACK (Cut 1): 1/16" × 3/4" × 3 1/4".

(M) SHELF (Cut 1): 1/16" × 3/4" × 3 1/2". Round off the top edge of the sides and front.

(N) UPPER SHELF BACK (Cut 1): 1/16" × 11/16" × 3 1/4". See Figure **8-R-5** for the shape.

(O) TOP SHELF BRACE (Cut 2): 1/16" × 3/8" × 5/8". See Figure **8-R-9** for the shape.

167

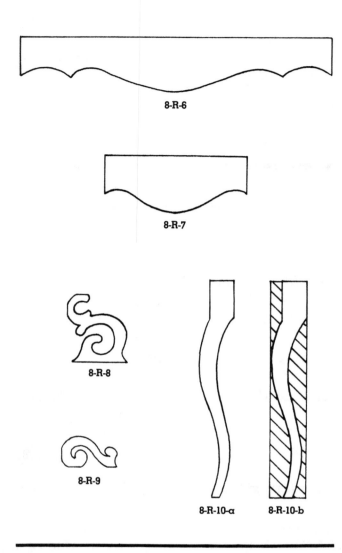

8-R-6

8-R-7

8-R-8

8-R-9

8-R-10-a   8-R-10-b

(P) LOWER SHELF BRACE (Cut 2): 1/16″ × 5/8″ × 3/4″. See Figure **8-R-8** for the shape.

ASSEMBLY: This piece of furniture will be painted and color print will be applied. Refer to Figures **8-R-1** (*front view of writing desk*), **8-R-2** (*left side view of writing desk*), **8-R-3** (*front view of table*) and **8-R-4** (*front view of shelf and drawer assembly*).

1. Glue the top moulding centered atop the table top.

2. Glue the front and back apron pieces between the table legs. See Figure **8-R-3**. Glue the side apron pieces between the above assembly sections, with the top edges flush.

3. Glue the table top atop the top edges of the leg assembly, with equal overhang. See Figure 8-R-3.

4. Glue the drawer chest sides (**G**) against the upright end edges of the back (**F**). Glue the bottom (**H**) between the sides and against the back, with the bottom edges flush.

5. Insert three of the drawers; glue the separator (**H**) between the sides and against the back, resting on the top surface of the drawers. Glue a drawer divider between each of the drawers. See Figure 8-**R**-4.

6. Place the remaining three drawers on the separator. Glue the top (**K**) atop the top edges of the sides and back, with back edges flush and equal side overhang. Glue the remaining two drawer dividers between these drawers.

7. Glue the lower back (**L**) atop the back edge of the drawer cabinet, with back edges flush. Glue the lower shelf brace (**P**) atop the drawer cabinet and against the back. See the location marked by double broken lines in Figure 8-**R**-4.

8. Glue the top shelf (**M**) atop the top edge of the lower back and the shelf braces, with back edges flush. Glue the top shelf back (**N**) atop the top shelf, with back edges flush. Glue the top braces (**O**) atop the top shelf and against the back. See the double broken line location in Figure 8-**R**-4.

9. Glue the upper cabinet assembly atop the table. See Figures 8-**R**-1 and 8-**R**-2.

10. Refer to the color insert sheet. Cut out the section of prints marked 8-**R**. You will note that the background color is a greenish-brown. Paint the writing desk and drawers as close a matching green as possible.

11. Refer to 1-C-2 for application of the color prints. Cut out the various pieces from the section of color prints. Glue these prints against the front, back and side apron pieces, the ends of the drawer cabinet, the fronts of the six drawers, the backs of the two shelves and the sides of the four braces.

12. Finish as instructed in 1-C-2. Apply six drawer pulls. Refer to 1-B-6.

COLONIAL RATCHET CANDLESTAND 9-A

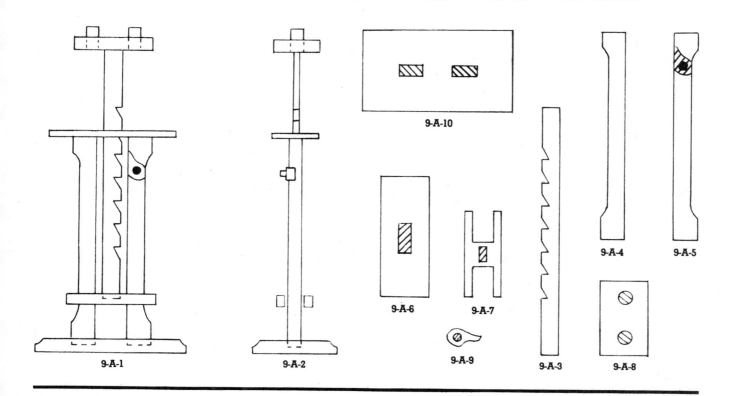

9-A-1 9-A-2 9-A-10 9-A-6 9-A-7 9-A-9 9-A-3 9-A-8 9-A-4 9-A-5

(A) BASE (Cut 1): 1/8″ × 7/8″ × 1 9/16″. Bevel the top edges of all sides. See Figure **9-A-10**. The shaded areas in the diagram represent holes which will be cut 1/16″ deep.

(B) SIDE BRACES (Cut 2): 1/8″ × 1/4″ × 2 1/4″. See Figure **9-A-4** for the shape of these braces. See Figure **9-A-5**; the black dot represents a 1/16″ diameter hole to be drilled through the right brace. The shaded area in this diagram is to be cut 1/16″ deep.

(C) BRACE TOP (Cut 1): 1/16″ × 1/2″ × 1 5/16″. See Figure **9-A-6** (*top view*) for a hole to be cut through the board (*shaded area*).

(D) BRACE BOTTOM (Cut 1): 1/8″ × 3/8″ × 15/16″. See Figure **9-A-7** for a top view of the shape. The shaded area represents a hole to be cut 1/16″ deep.

(E) RATCHET (Cut 1): 1/16″ × 3/16″ × 2 11/16″. See Figure **9-A-3** for the shape.

(F) CANDLE BASE (Cut 1): 1/8″ × 1/2″ × 13/16″. See Figure **9-A-8** for two 1/8″ diameter holes to be drilled through the board.

(G) CANDLE HOLDERS (Cut 2): 1/8″ diameter wood dowel × 1/4″. Drill a 1/16″ diameter hole in the center top of each holder 1/16″ deep.

(H) PEG (Cut 1): 1/8″ × 3/16″ × 3/8″. See Figure

9-A-9 for the shape and a 1/16″ diameter hole to be drilled through the peg.

(I) PIN (Cut 1): 1/16″ diameter wood dowel × 1/4″.

ASSEMBLY: Stain all wood before glueing.

1. Glue the side braces (**B**) into the holes in the base, with the peg depression facing you on the right brace. See Figure **9-A-1**.

2. Glue the ratchet (**E**) into the brace bottom (**D**). Hold this assembly with the ratchet notches to the right, and slip the bottom down over the side braces. See Figure **9-A-1**.

3. Slip the brace top (**C**) down over the ratchet and glue it atop the top edges of the braces. See Figure **9-A-1**.

4. Glue the candle base centered atop the ratchet. Glue the candle holders into the holes in the candle base, with the bottom edges flush.

5. Glue the pin into the hole in the right brace, with the outside edges flush. Slip the peg over the pin so that it swings up and down. The peg will fit into the notches of the ratchet and allow it to stay at various levels.

6. Apply a finish coat to the candlestand. Place a candle in the candle holder.

COLONIAL CANDLESTAND 9-B

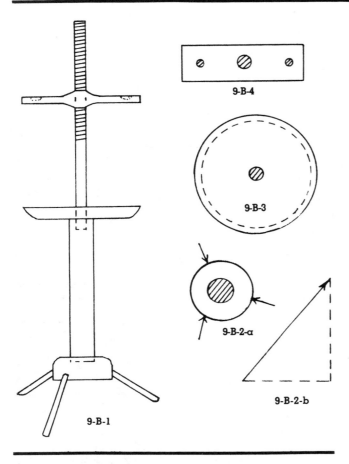

9-B-4

9-B-3

9-B-2-a

9-B-2-b

9-B-1

(A) LOWER POST (Cut 1): 1/4″ diameter wood dowel × 1 9/16″. Drill a 1/8″ diameter hole down in the center top 1/8″ deep.

(B) UPPER POST (Cut 1): 1/8″ diameter wood dowel × 2 1/4″. Secure a nut 3/32″ in diameter and a bolt, the hole of which also measures 3/32″ in diameter. Very slowly turn the nut down around the top end of the upper post, 1 1/4″ from the end. This threads the end of the post. See Figure **9-B-1**.

(C) CANDLE ARM (Cut 1): 3/16″ × 3/8″ × 1 1/4″. See Figure **9-B-4**. Drill a 1/16″ diameter hole 1/32″ deep at each site of the small shaded areas in the diagram. Begin a slightly smaller hole than 3/32″ in diameter. Very slowly turn the bolt in the hole, threading the hole.

(D) TABLE TOP (Cut 1): 1/8″ × 1 1/4″ diameter disc. See Figure **9-B-3** for the shape. Drill a 1/8″ diameter hole through the center of this top (*see shaded area*). The broken line inside the edge indicates the area of 1/16″ deep scoop shaping. Refer to **1-C-3-e**.

(E) BASE (Cut 1): 1/4″ × 5/8″ diameter disc. Drill a 1/4″ diameter hole centered in the top of the disc 1/16″ deep. See the shaded area in Figure **9-B-2-a**. The arrows in the diagram indicate the sites of three holes 1/16″ in diameter in the lower sides of the base. The arrow in **9-B-2-b** shows the angle of the 1/16″ diameter side holes.

(F) LEGS (Cut 3): 1/16″ diameter wood dowel × 1 5/8″.

ASSEMBLY: Stain all wood before glueing.

1. Glue the three legs into the base. Be sure that it sits straight and level.

2. Glue the lower post into the base. Glue the table top atop the lower post, with holes aligned. Glue the top post (*unthreaded end*) down through the table top into the hole in the lower post.

3. Apply a finish coat to all wood, with the exception of the threaded portion of the upper post.

4. Turn the candle arm down on the threaded post. Put a candle in each hole in the candle arm.

HAT RACK c. 1885 9-C

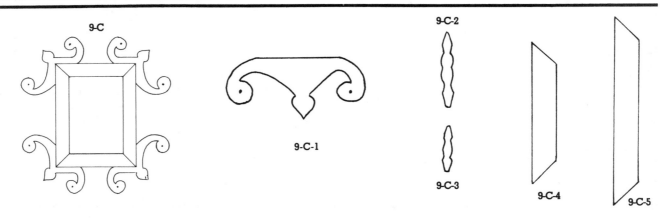

9-C

9-C-1

9-C-2

9-C-3

9-C-4

9-C-5

1.

(A) CORNER DECORATION (Cut 4): 1/8″ × 3/4″ × 1 1/2″. See Figure **9-C-1** for the shape. Drill a 1/16″ diameter hole through each board at the site of the black dot in the diagram.

(B) TOP AND BOTTOM FRAME (Cut 2): 1/16″ × 1/4″ × 1 1/2″. See Figure **9-C-4**. Each end will have a 45° mitre cut.

(C) SIDE FRAME (Cut 2): 1/16″ × 1/4″ × 2″. See Figure **9-C-5**. Each end will have a 45° mitre cut.

(D) LONG SPINDLE (Cut 2): 1/8″ diameter wood dowel × 13/16″. See Figure **9-C-2** for the shape. Refer to **1-C-3-a**.

(E) SHORT SPINDLE (Cut 2): 1/8″ diameter wood dowel × 1/2″. See Figure **9-C-3** for the shape. Refer to **1-C-3-a**.

(F) MIRROR (Cut 1): As thin as possible, but not more than 1/8″ in thickness × 1 1/8″ × 1 5/8″.

(G) PEGS (Cut 8): 1/16″ diameter wood dowel × 3/8″.

ASSEMBLY: Stain all wood before glueing. Refer to **9-C**.

1. Using Figure **9-C** as your guide, glue the frame together. Lay it on the diagram to be sure it is squared. Let the glue dry.

2. *Note:* The two ends of the corner decorations are different. Place them in the correct position on the diagram and glue the assembled frame in place atop them. Let the glue dry.

3. Glue a peg into each drilled hole. The back edges will be flush with the back edge of the decoration.

4. Glue a long spindle (*vertically*) between the corner decorations of the frame at each side. Glue a short spindle (*horizontally*) between the corner decorations of the frame at the top and bottom.

5. Apply a finish coat.

6. Glue the mirror in place behind the frame opening.

ROUND TOP TRUNK 9-D

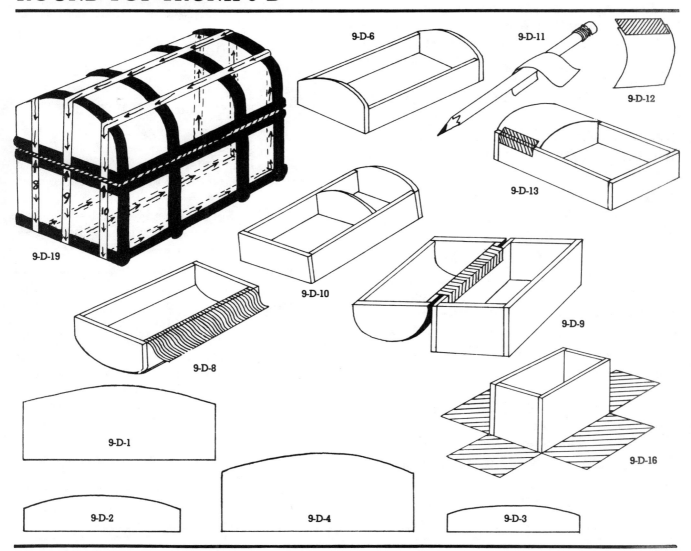

(A) LOWER TRUNK FRONT AND BACK (Cut 2): 1/8" × 1 1/8" × 3 1/4".

(B) LOWER TRUNK SIDES (Cut 2): 1/8" × 1 1/8" × 1 3/4".

(C) TRUNK BOTTOM (Cut 1): 1/8" × 1 3/4" × 3". Refer to 2-E-1 for assembly. See Figure 9-D-5.

(D) TRUNK TOP FRONT AND BACK (Cut 2): 1/8" × 5/8" × 3".

(E) TRUNK TOP ENDS (Cut 2): 1/8" × 13/16" × 2". See Figure 9-D-1 for the shape.

(F) ROUNDED TOP OF TRUNK (Cut 1): Cut from a file card. 2 1/16" × 3 1/4".

ASSEMBLY OF TOP PORTION OF TRUNK: Refer to Figures 9-D-6 and 9-D-7.

1. Glue the front and back boards (**D**) inside of the end boards (**E**), with outside and bottom edges flush. See Figure 9-D-6. Let the glue dry.

2. Glue the file card atop the top edges of the side and end boards. Put rubber bands around this assembly (*see arrows in Figure* 9-D-7) to hold the file card firmly while the glue is drying.

(G) TILL FRONT AND BACK (Cut 2): 1/8" × 3/8" × 2 5/8".

(H) LEFT TILL END (Cut 1): 1/8" × 3/8" × 1 5/8".

(I) RIGHT TILL END (Cut 1): 1/8" × 3/8" × 1 5/8". See Figure 9-D-2 for the shape.

(J) TILL DIVIDER (Cut 1): 1/16" × 1/4" × 1 3/8". See Figure 9-D-3 for the shape.

(K) TILL BOTTOM (Cut 1): 1/8" × 1 1/4" × 2 5/8".

TILL ASSEMBLY: Refer to Figure 9-D-10.

3. Glue the till front and back boards against the side edges of the till bottom board, with bottom edges flush.

4. Glue the left till end board against one end of this assembly, with all edges flush. Glue the right till end board (**I**) against the other end of this assembly, with all edges flush.

5. Refer to Figure 9-D-10. Glue the till divider board inside the assembly, with the right edge 1/2" from the inside surface of the rounded end board (**I**).

(L) ROUNDED TOP OF TILL (Cut 1): Cut from a file card. 3/4" × 1 11/16".

(M) TILL SUPPORTS (Cut 4): 1/8" × 1/8" × 5/8".

(N) HINGE FOR TRUNK TOP (Cut 1): Cut from twill tape. 2 1/2".

(O) HINGE FOR TILL TOP (Cut 1): Cut from twill tape. 5/8".

FINAL ASSEMBLY

6. APPLYING TAPE HINGE TO TRUNK: Figures 9-D-8 and 9-D-9 show this application. Glue to the edge of the trunk top first (*Figure* 9-D-8). Let the glue dry. Place the trunk top (*upside down*) along the top edge of the trunk; glue the tape to the top and inside edge of the trunk back board. Support the trunk top with a scrap of wood, holding the top in this position, until the glue is thoroughly dry.

7. APPLYING AND HINGING TILL TOP: See Figures 9-D-11, 9-D-12 and 9-D-13. Gently "round" piece (**L**) — which has been cut from a file card — using a pencil and pulling the card over the top surface. See Figure 9-D-11. Glue one half of the width of the twill on the rounded top surface of the card. Let the glue dry. See Figure 9-D-12. Place the rounded card over the till compartment edges, glue the tape to the top and back surface of the back board of the till. See Figure 9-D-13.

8. The inside of the trunk and the till can be papered with miniature wallpaper or can be painted.

FINISHING THE OUTSIDE OF THE TRUNK

9. Figure 9-D-14 shows the pattern for material to cover the rounded portion of the trunk lid. Figure 9-D-15 shows the pattern for material to cover the lower portion of the trunk. Figure 9-D-4 shows the pattern for material to cover the trunk lid ends. Choose your material or a paper and trace these patterns onto the material of your choice. Remember that you will need two end pieces.

10. Find a piece of thin leather (*old long gloves, and so forth*) and carefully cut into strips of 1/4" widths. These are glued onto the outside of the trunk. Figure 9-D-17 shows the first step in glueing four strips of leather around the trunk. Begin each strip at the front opening and follow the arrows. Figure 9-D-18 shows the second step in glueing one strip of leather around the lower edge of the trunk top (*begin at the left back and follow arrows*); a second strip at the top edge of the trunk bottom (*begin at the left back and follow arrows*); a third strip around the lower edge of the trunk bottom (*begin at the left back and follow arrows*). Figure 9-D-19 shows the third and final step in glueing three strips over the trunk top (*follow arrows*) and three strips around the trunk bottom (*follow arrows*). Let the glue dry.

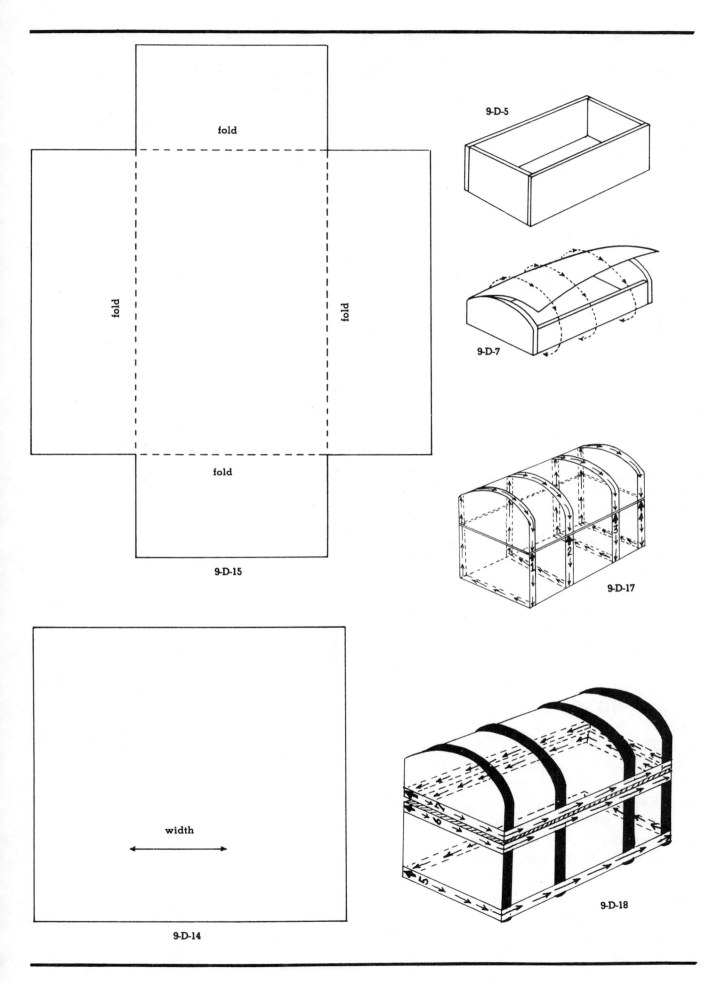

9-D-5

9-D-7

fold

fold

fold

fold

9-D-15

9-D-17

width

9-D-14

9-D-18

VICTORIAN WHATNOT c. 1840 9-E

(A) FIRST SHELF (Cut 1): 1/16″ × 7/8″ × 2 1/2″. See Figure **9-E-1-a** for the shape.

(B) SECOND SHELF (Cut 1): 1/16″ × 3/4″ × 2 1/2″. See Figure **9-E-1-b** for the shape.

(C) THIRD SHELF (Cut 1): 1/16″ × 11/16″ × 2 1/2″. See Figure **9-E-1-c** for the shape.

(D) FOURTH SHELF (Cut 1): 1/16″ × 9/16″ × 2 1/2″. See Figure **9-E-1-d** for the shape.

Note: Drill holes in each shelf as indicated by the shaded area (*denotes size of hole*) in the diagrams.

(E) BACK PILLAR — FIRST TIER (Cut 2): 1/8″ diameter wood dowel × 1 3/8″. See Figure **9-E-2-a** for the shape.

(F) BACK PILLAR — SECOND TIER (Cut 2): 1/8″ diameter wood dowel × 1 1/8″. See Figure **9-E-2-a** for the shape.

(G) BACK PILLAR — THIRD TIER (Cut 2): 1/8″ diameter wood dowel × 1″. See Figure **9-E-2-a** for the shape.

(H) BACK PILLAR — FOURTH TIER (Cut 2): 1/8″ diameter wood dowel × 7/8″. See Figure **9-E-2-a** for the shape.

(I) FRONT PILLAR — FIRST TIER (Cut 2): 1/8″ diameter wood dowel × 1 7/16″. See Figure **9-E-2-b** for the shape.

(J) FRONT PILLAR — SECOND TIER (Cut 2): 1/8″ diameter wood dowel × 1 1/4″. See Figure **9-E-2-b** for the shape.

(K) FRONT PILLAR — THIRD TIER (Cut 2): 1/8″ diameter wood dowel × 1 1/16″. See Figure **9-E-2-b** for the shape.

(L) FRONT PILLAR — FOURTH TIER (Cut 2): 1/8″ diameter wood dowel × 7/8″. See Figure **9-E-2-b** for the shape.

(M) LEGS (Cut 4): 1/8″ diameter wood dowel × 3/8″. See Figure **9-E-3** for the shape.

(N) FINIALS (Cut 12): 1/8″ diameter wood dowel × 1/4″. See Figure **9-E-4** for the shape.

(O) PEDIMENT (Cut 1): 1/16″ × 3/8″ × 2 1/2″. See Figure **9-E-5** for the shape and areas to be cut away.

ASSEMBLY: Stain all wood before glueing. Figure **9-E-6** shows a right side view of the assembly of the whatnot.

1. Glue the four legs in place below the first shelf.

2. Glue the front and back pillars in place, begin-ning with the first shelf. Work shelf by shelf until the whatnot is assembled.

3. Refer to Figure **9-E-6** and glue the 12 finials in place. Glue the pediment atop the back edge of the top shelf, with back edges flush.

4. Apply a finish coat.

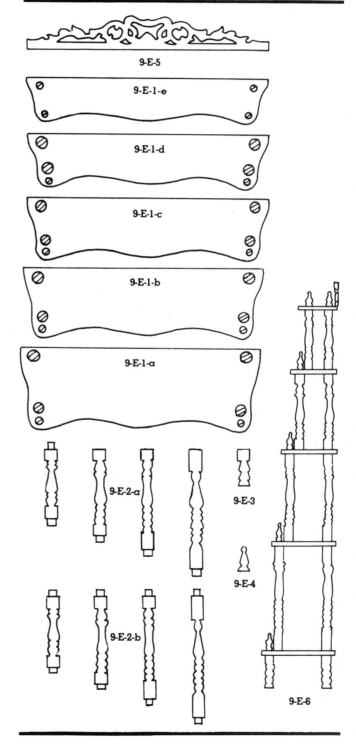

9-E-5

9-E-1-e

9-E-1-d

9-E-1-c

9-E-1-b

9-E-1-a

9-E-2-a

9-E-3

9-E-2-b

9-E-4

9-E-6

CANNISTER BIN 9-F

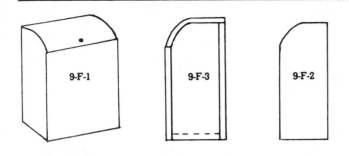

The kitchens and general stores of the Victorian period used tin and papier-mache bins of this design to store such items as coffee, sugar and flour. The bins were usually red, mustard yellow, or black. These are the same colors that were used in tole trays.

(A) BACK (Cut 1): 1/16" × 1" × 1 1/4".

(B) FRONT (Cut 1): 1/16" × 15/16" × 1".

(C) SIDES (Cut 2): 1/16" × 1/2" × 1 1/4". See Figure 9-F-2 for the shape.

(D) HOOD (Cut 1): Cut from 1/16" thick cardboard. 1/16" × 7/8" × 1".

(E) BOTTOM (Cut 1): 1/16" × 3/8" × 7/8".

(F) KNOB (One): Refer to **1-B-6**.

ASSEMBLY: See Figure **9-F-3**.

1. The back, front, sides and bottom are assembled just as the drawer in **2-E-1**.

2. Moisten the cardboard with white glue and glue against the curved edge of each side and atop the top edges of the side boards. Seal the cut edges of the cardboard with glue.

3. Paint the back, bottom surface and all edges red.

4. Refer to **1-C-2**. You will find a section of color prints for the bin marked **9-F** on the color insert page. The top and front prints are joined. Glue these prints and the side prints in place. See Figure **9-F-1**. Attach a knob at the site indicated by a black dot in the diagram.

5. Finish the bin as directed in **1-C-2**.

WALL MIRROR 9-G

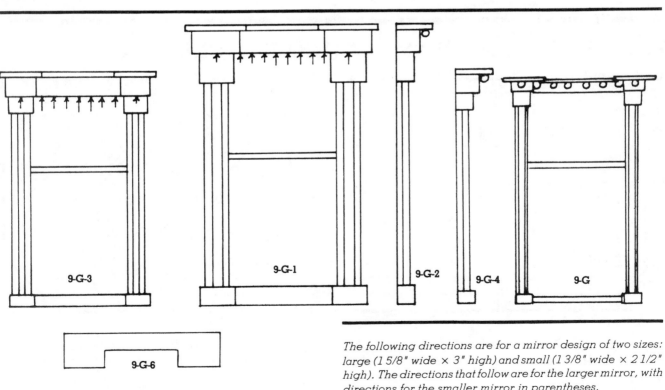

The following directions are for a mirror design of two sizes: large (1 5/8" wide × 3" high) and small (1 3/8" wide × 2 1/2" high). The directions that follow are for the larger mirror, with directions for the smaller mirror in parentheses.

(A) SIDE MOULDING (Cut 2): 1/16" × 1/4" × 2 3/16" (1/16" × 3/16" × 1 15/16").

(B) SIDE PILLARS (Cut 2): 1/8" diameter half-round × 2 3/16" (*1/16" diameter wood dowel × 1 15/16"*).

(C) BOTTOM CENTER MOULDING (Cut 1): 1/16" × 3/16" × 1" (*1/16" × 1/8" × 15/16"*).

(D) PILLAR BASE (Cut 2): 3/16" × 3/16" × 3/8" (*1/8" × 3/16" × 1/4"*).

(E) PILLAR CAPITAL (Cut 2): 3/16" × 5/16" × 3/8" (*3/16" × 3/16" × 1/4"*).

(F) PILLAR TOP MOULDING (Cut 2): 1/4" × 1/4" × 1/2" (*3/16" × 1/4" × 5/16"*).

(G) TOP CENTER MOULDING (Cut 1): 1/8" × 1/4" × 7/8" (*1/16" × 3/16" × 7/8"*).

(H) TOP (Cut 1): 1/16" × 3/8" × 2". See Figure **9-G-5** for the shape. (*1/16" × 3/8" × 1 5/8". See Figure **9-G-6** for the shape.*)

(I) CENTER DIVIDER (Cut 1): 1/16" × 1/16" × 1 1/8" (*1/16" × 1/16" × 1"*).

(J) MIRROR (Cut 1): 1/16" × 1 1/8" × 1 3/8" (*1/16" × 1" × 1 5/16"*).

(K) BEAD TRIM: Ten (*Nine*) 1/16" diameter beads or spheres.

ASSEMBLY: The mirror frame will be painted gold. Refer to Figures **9-G-1** and **9-G-2** (*large mirror*), Figures **9-G-3** and **9-G-4** (*small mirror*) and Figure **9-G** for assembly.

1. Glue the side pillars (**B**) centered atop the side moulding (**A**) with the top and bottom edges flush.

2. Glue the pillar bases (**D**) against the end edges of the bottom center moulding (**C**) with the top, bottom and back edges flush.

3. Glue the pillar top moulding pieces (**F**) against the end edges of the top center moulding (**G**) with the top, bottom and back edges flush. Glue the pillar capitals beneath the pillar top moulding pieces, with the back edges flush and equal side spaces. Glue the top (**H**) atop this assembly, with back edges flush and equal side spaces.

4. Using diagram **9-G-1** or **9-G-3** as your placement guide (*actual size*), locate the position of the center divider (**I**), glue the top assembly, side moulding, bottom assembly and center divider together. All back edges will be flush.

5. Figures **9-G-1** and **9-G-2** contain black arrows denoting the location of the bead trim. Glue the beads in place.

6. Paint the entire mirror frame gold.

7. Glue the glass in the lower opening.

8. Refer to **1-C-2**. Refer to the color insert sheet and cut out the print to fit the mirror which you have made. It will be identified with **9-G**. Glue the print against a piece of file card which measures 1 3/16" × 1 1/4" (*7/8" × 1 1/8"*). Glue the color print behind the upper opening.

PICTURE ALBUM AND MINIATURE PICTURES 9-H

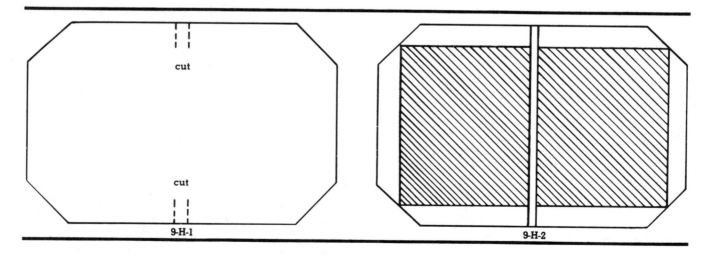

9-H-1

9-H-2

(A) BOOK BACK (Cut 2): 1 5/16" × 1 11/16". Cut from cardboard (*such as the backing of a pad of paper*).

(B) COVER (Cut 1): 2 1/2" × 4". Cut from velvet, cloth, leather (*such as fine glove leather*), and so forth. See Figure **9-H-1** for the shape.

(C) COVER FACING PAGE (Cut 1): 1 1/2" × 2 3/4". Cut from colored writing paper or the tiny pattern paper which is found inside of some envelopes.

(D) BOOK PAGES (Cut 4): 1 1/2" × 2 1/2". Cut from writing paper. *Note:* To increase the number of pages, you must increase the space between pieces

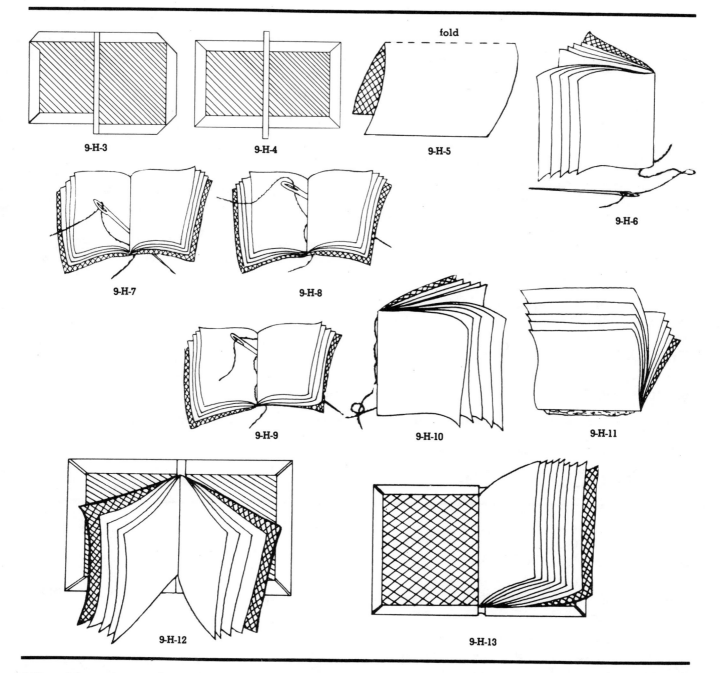

9-H-3

9-H-4

9-H-5 fold

9-H-6

9-H-7

9-H-8

9-H-9

9-H-10

9-H-11

9-H-12

9-H-13

(**A**) and thus increase the length of piece (**B**) from the 4 ".

ASSEMBLY

1. On the reverse side of the book cover material, mark the center with pencil (*2"*). Glue the two pieces of cardboard on either side of this center mark, leaving a space at the center measuring 1/8". See Figure **9-H-2**.

2. Fold the covering over the top edges of the cardboard, with the mitred corners butting together. See Figure **9-H-3**. Glue the top and bottom center flaps of the covering material down in the center 1/8" space. See Figure **9-H-4**.

3. Assemble the book pages, placing the cover facing page (*tiny print*) up and the plain pages stacked (*with edges together*) atop the facing page. Be sure that the center of the book pages is placed atop the center of the facing page before sewing.

4. Sew the pages together in the exact center of the pages, as shown in Figure **9-H-5**, or sew with a sewing machine that can sew a 1/4" stretch basting stitch. Use white thread or clear nylon thread. To sew by hand, begin the stitch from the back (*leave the tag end and do not knot the thread*), sew across and back, using the same needle holes and ending the stitch in back of the pages. Tie the two ends of thread securely together, clip the excess ends, and put a dot of white glue directly on the knot. See Figures **9-H-6** through **9-H-10**.

5. Fold the sewn pages, with the edges together, and crease the back edge.

6. Figure **9-H-11** shows a line of white glue which is applied on the back fold of the pages. Be sure that the glue does not reach the top or bottom edges of the paper. Place the glued edge at the inside center of the book back.

7. Using white glue or bookbinder's paste, glue the cover facing pages down against the inside of the front and back book cover. Press the facing page firmly against the cover, being sure there are no air pockets or wrinkles. Wipe the excess glue away. See Figures **9-H-12** and **9-H-13**.

8. When the glue is thoroughly dry, place the book between two pieces of wood which are larger than the cover and are covered with waxed paper. Clamp all sides (*book press*) for approximately three days to one week. This will aid in firming the pages and cover.

9. Refer to the color insert sheet and cut out the prints marked **9-H**. Glue the album print to the front cover of the album.

PHOTOGRAPHS

10. Cut out the tiny album photographs and glue a picture centered on each of the right-hand pages (*eight*).

ALTERNATE PHOTOGRAPHS

11. You may wish to use family photographs from your own album. It is quite simple to reduce the pictures to the size of this tiny album.

12. Attach your pictures on a firm cardboard. Stand the cardboard (*straight up*) against an outside wall of your house and take color photographs of it. The color photographs will pick up the sepia tones of the old album pictures. You will need to experiment with distance. Take a picture, move back a foot, take another picture, move back another foot, and so on. When the pictures are developed, you will have prints showing your old pictures in various sizes. One set of pictures surely will fit in your album. Cut out the pictures, peel off the backing cardboard, and glue them in your album. This method of reducing your family pictures can be used elsewhere in your miniature work.

VICTORIAN LAMP STAND WITH "MARBLE" TOP AND TRIPOD BASE 9-I

(A) TABLE TOP (Cut 1): 1/16″ thick × 1″ diameter circle. See Figure **9-I-1**. Bevel the edges.

(B) "MARBLE" TOP (Cut 1): 1/16″ thick × 7/8″ diameter circle. See Figure **9-I-2**. Bevel the edges. Refer to **1-C-9** for the "marble" finish on this board.

(C) PEDESTAL (Cut 1): 3/8″ diameter wood dowel × 1 5/8″. Refer to Figure **9-I-4** for the shape and **1-C-3-a** for aid in carving.

(D) PEDESTAL BASE (Cut 1): 1/8″ thick × 13/32″ diameter circle. See Figure **9-I-3**. Round off the top and bottom edges.

(E) LEGS (Cut 3): 1/16″ × 5/8″ × 1 1/4″. See Figure **9-I-5** for the shape.

ASSEMBLY: Stain all wood before glueing. Refer to Figures **9-I** and **9-I-6** for assembly.

1. Glue the "marble" top atop the table top. Glue the top of the pedestal centered against the bottom surface of the table top. Glue the pedestal centered atop the pedestal base.

2. Refer to Figure **9-I-6**. Glue the three legs (*equally spaced*) against the pedestal and its base.

3. Apply a finish coat.

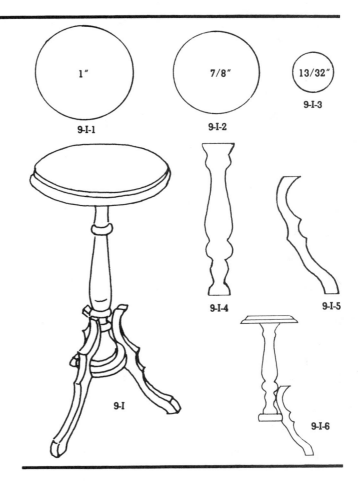

1″   9-I-1

7/8″   9-I-2

13/32″   9-I-3

9-I-4   9-I-5   9-I   9-I-6

VICTORIAN HALL STAND c. 1860-1875 9-J

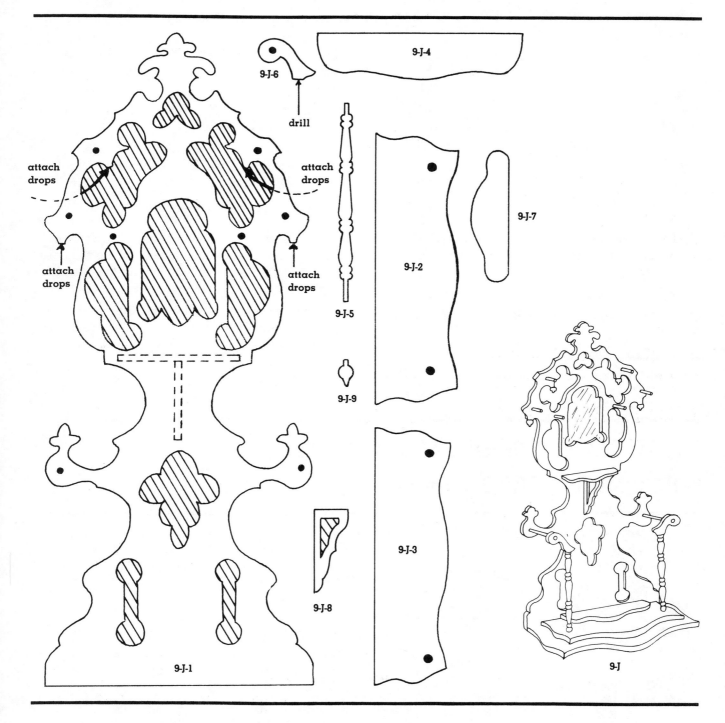

Note: This piece was made of walnut. You can make it of pine or bass wood and stain it to represent walnut.

(A) BACK (Cut 1): 1/8″ × 2 3/4″ × 7″. See Figure 9-J-1 for the shape. The shaded areas are to be cut out, and the black dots represent 1/16″ diameter holes to be drilled.

(B) MIDDLE BASE (Cut 1): 1/8″ × 3/4″ × 2 3/4″. See Figure 9-J-3 for the shape. Drill 1/16″ diameter holes at the sites of the black dots in the diagram.

(C) BOTTOM BASE (Cut 1): 1/16″ × 7/8″ × 3″. See Figure 9-J-2 for the shape. Drill 1/16″ diameter holes at the sites of the black dots in the diagram. Bevel the front and end edges.

(D) TOP BASE (Cut 1): 1/16″ × 1/2″ × 2 1/8″. See Figure 9-J-4 for the shape. Bevel the front and end edges, and paint to represent marble. Refer to **1-C-9** for aid in painting.

(E) "NECK" OF SPINDLE (Cut 2): 1/8″ × 1/2″ × 5/8″.

See Figure 9-J-6 for the shape. Drill a 1/16" diameter hole at the site of the black dot in the diagram, and drill the same diameter hole up into the bottom surface of this piece at the site of the arrow in the diagram.

(F) SPINDLE (Cut 2): 3/16" diameter wood dowel × 2 1/8". See Figure **9-J-5** for the shape. Refer to **1-C-3-a** for aid in carving.

(G) SHELF (Cut 1): 1/16" × 3/8" × 1 3/8". See Figure **9-J-7** for the shape. Bevel the front and end edges and paint to represent marble. Refer to **1-C-9** for aid in painting.

(H) SHELF BRACKET (Cut 1): 1/16" × 3/8" × 7/8". See Figure **9-J-8** for the shape. The shaded area is to be cut away.

(I) DROP (Cut 4): 3/16" × 3/16" × 5/16". Turn four drops, following the shape in Figure **9-J-9**. Refer to **1-C-3-a** for aid in carving.

(J) BAR (Cut 2): 1/16" diameter wood dowel × 3/4".

(K) PEGS (Cut 6): 1/16" diameter wood dowel × 3/8".

ASSEMBLY: Refer to Figure 9-J.

1. Glue the middle base atop the bottom base with back edges flush and both drilled holes aligned.

Glue the top ("marbled") base atop the previous assembly, with equal spaces at either end and the back edges flush.

2. Glue the shelf bracket centered on the underneath surface of the "marbled" shelf, with the back edges flush. Glue this assembly against the back board at the site indicated by a broken line in Figure **9-J-1**.

3. Glue a drop at each of the four sites marked by an arrow in Figure **9-J-1**.

4. Glue a spindle neck onto the top of each spindle (*remember to insert the spindle peg into the bottom of this piece*). Repeat for the second assembly.

5. Glue a bar into each of the lower drilled holes in the back piece. Glue the other end of the bar into the hole in the spindle neck, and glue each spindle down into the holes in the pieces forming the base. *Note:* The spindle necks each face to the outside of this piece of furniture. See Figure **9-J**.

6. Apply the finish coat. When the finish is dry, glue a piece of mirror (*or metal to represent mirror*) behind the large central opening in the back.

7. Apply a finish coat to all pegs and glue into the 1/16" diameter drilled holes in the back board.

VICTORIAN PERIOD WALL-MOUNTED GROOMING MIRROR 9-K

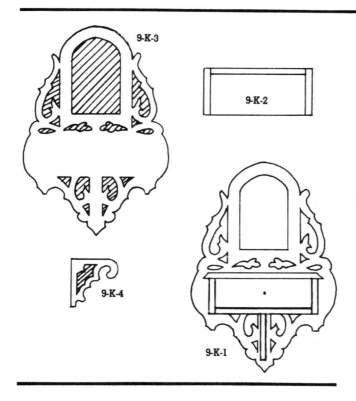

Note: This grooming mirror can be made of 1/16" thick wood or cardboard. If you choose to construct it of wood, stain all wood before glueing. If you choose to construct it of cardboard, apply airplane cement to all cut edges to prevent separation when it is painted, and paint the finished piece a walnut-brown.

(A) BACK (Cut 1): 1/16" × 1 1/2" × 2 1/4". See Figure **9-K-3** for the shape. The shaded areas in this diagram are all cut away. If you are working with wood, bevel all edges of the mirror opening.

(B) CHEST BRACE (Cut 1): 1/16" × 1/2" × 1/2". See Figure **9-K-4** for the shape. The shaded area in this diagram is cut away.

(C) CHEST TOP (Cut 1): 1/16" × 9/16" × 1 1/4". Bevel the top front and side edges of this board.

(D) CHEST SIDES (Cut 2): 1/16" × 3/8" × 1/2".

(E) CHEST BOTTOM (Cut 1): 1/16" × 7/16" × 1".

(F) DRAWER (One)
   (1) **FRONT AND BACK** (Cut 2): 1/16" × 5/16" × 1".

(2) **SIDES** (Cut 2): 1/16″ × 5/16″ × 5/16″.

(3) **BOTTOM** (Cut 1): 1/16″ × 5/16″ × 7/8″.

Refer to **2-E-1** for assembly. Refer to **1-B-6** for a drawer pull.

(G) CHEST BACK (Cut 1): 1/16″ × 3/8″ × 1″.

(H) MIRROR: Choose as thin a piece of mirror as possible and cut it slightly larger than the mirror opening.

ASSEMBLY

1. Refer to Figure **9-K-1** for the overall assembly, and **9-K-2** for a top view of the assembly of the chest back, sides and bottom. Glue together, as shown.

Glue the chest top atop the top edges of this assembly (*beveled side upward*) with the back edges flush and equal overhang on each side.

2. See Figure **9-K-1**. Glue the chest in place against the back (**A**), with the bottom edge at the top edge of the lower pierced area of the back. Glue the chest brace (**B**) against the back and beneath the bottom of the chest, as shown in Figure **9-K-1**.

3. Apply a finish coat to the grooming mirror and its drawer.

4. Glue the mirror in place behind the mirror opening. Attach the drawer pull.

UPRIGHT PIANO 9-L

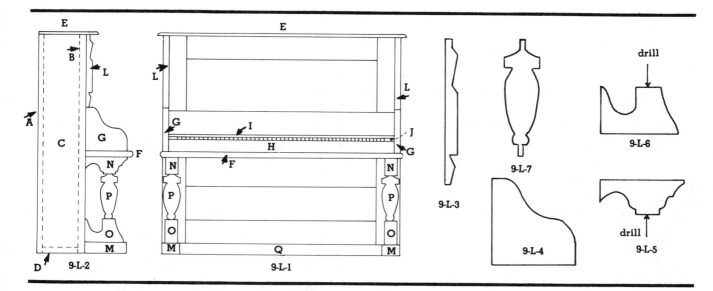

(A) BACK (Cut 1): 1/8″ × 4 3/4″ × 4 3/4″. Cut from 1/8″ thick plywood or 1/8″ thick cardboard.

(B) FRONT: See Figure **9-L-8**.
BOARD 1 (Cut 2): 1/8″ × 1/2″ × 4 3/4″.
BOARD 1-B (Cut 1): 1/8″ × 1/2″ × 4″.
BOARD 2 (Cut 2): 1/8″ × 3/4″ × 4″.
BOARD 2-A (Cut 2): 1/8″ × 3/4″ × 1 3/4″.
BOARD 2-B (Cut 1): 1/8″ × 1/2″ × 3/4″.
BOARD 3 (Cut 1): 1/8″ × 1″ × 4″.

Figure **9-L-8** shows the assembly of these boards. Bevel all edges of the boards which are marked with a letter **B** in this diagram. Stain the wood. When the previous steps have been accomplished, glue butted together as shown in Figure **9-L-8**.

(C) SIDES (Cut 2): 1/8″ × 1″ × 4 3/4″.

(D) BASE (Cut 1): 1/8″ × 3/4″ × 4 3/4″.

(E) TOP (Cut 1): 1/16″ × 1 1/4″ × 5 1/4″. Round off the front and side edges.

(F) BASE — FRONT UNIT (Cut 1): 1/8″ × 1″ × 5 1/8″. Round off the front and side edges.

(G) SIDES — FRONT UNIT (Cut 2): 1/8″ × 1″ × 1″. See Figure **9-L-4** for the shape.

(H) KEYBOARD BASE (Cut 1): 1/8″ × 1/4″ × 4 3/4″.

(I) BOARD BEHIND KEYS (Cut 1): 1/8″ × 1/4″ × 4 3/4″.

(J) KEYS (Cut 1): 1/16″ × 7/16″ × 4 3/4″.

(K) PANEL (Cut 1): 1/16″ × 1/2″ × 4 3/4″.

(L) MOULDING (Cut 2): 1/8″ × 1/8″ × 1 1/2″. See Figure **9-L-3** for the shape.

(M) LEG BASE (Cut 2): 1/4″ × 3/8″ × 7/8″.

keyboard print

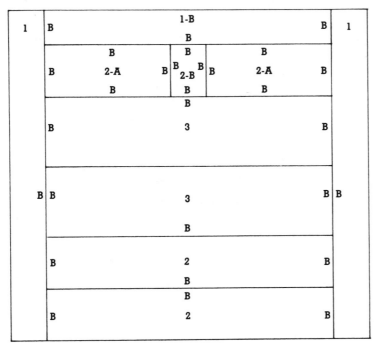

9-L-8

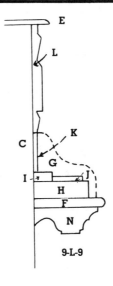

9-L-9

(N) UPPER LEG BRACE (Cut 2): 1/4″ × 3/8″ × 7/8″. See Figure **9-L-5** for the shape.

(O) LOWER LEG BRACE (Cut 2): 1/4″ × 1/2″ × 7/8″. See Figure **9-L-6** for the shape.

(P) LEG (Cut 2): 3/8″ × 3/8″ × 1″. See Figure **9-L-7** for the shape.

(Q) BASE MOULDING (Cut 1): 1/8″ × 1/4″ × 4 1/4″.

ASSEMBLY: Stain all wood before glueing. Refer to Figures **9-L-1** and **9-L-2**.

1. Glue the base (**D**) against the lower front edge of the piano back (**A**) with bottom edges flush. See Figure **9-L-2**.

2. Glue the front (**B**) against the front edge of the base (**D**) with all of the beveled edges of the assembled front boards facing forward. See Figure **9-L-2**.

3. Glue the side boards (**C**) against the end edges of the base and upright edges of the back and front boards. See Figure **9-L-9**.

4. Glue the top (**E**) atop this unit with a 1/4″ overhang in front, 1/8″ overhang at each side, and the back edges flush. See Figure **9-L-9**.

5. Glue a front unit side (**G**) against each end of the board (**H**), with the back edges flush. See Figure **9-L-9**.

6. Glue this unit atop board (**F**), with the back edges flush. See Figure **9-L-9**.

7. Glue this unit against the front of the piano, with the bottom surface of board (**F**) 2 1/8″ above the floor line. See Figure **9-L-2**.

8. Glue the lower leg brace (**O**) centered on top of board (**M**), with the back edges flush. See Figures **9-L-1** and **9-L-2**.

9. Glue the upper leg brace (**N**) against the underneath surface of board (**F**) and against the front of the piano (*left: 1/16″ to the right of the left edge of the piano and right: 1/16″ to the left of the right edge of the piano*). See Figures **9-L-1** and **9-L-2**.

10. Glue a leg (**P**) between the upper and lower braces. See Figures **9-L-1** and **9-L-2**.

11. Glue the base moulding between the two leg units at the lower front edge of the front of the piano. See Figure **9-L-1**.

12. Glue board (**I**) atop the rear edge of board (**H**) and against the front of the piano. See Figure **9-L-2**.

13. Glue board (**K**) atop board (**I**) and against the front of the piano.

14. Glue a piece of moulding at each upper front side edge of the piano. See Figures **9-L-1** and **9-L-2**.

15. Apply a finish coat to the piano.

16. Glue the "keyboard" print, which you will find on these pages with this project, centered on top of board (**J**) and downward covering the front edge of this board. Glue this board on top of board (**H**) and against board (**I**).

17. Find three jewelry findings that will represent the three pedals and attach them to the center of board (**Q**). This completes the piano.

PIANO STOOL 9-M

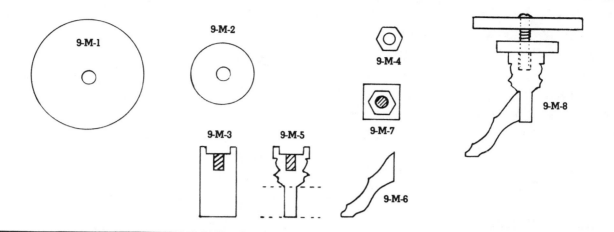

(A) SEAT (Cut 1): 1/8″ thick × 1 1/8″ diameter circle. See Figure **9-M-1** for the shape. Drill a 1/8″ diameter hole in the center.

(B) PEDESTAL DISC (Cut 1): 1/8″ thick × 5/8″ diameter circle. See Figure **9-M-2** for the shape. Drill a 1/8″ diameter hole in the center.

(C) PEDESTAL (Cut 1): 3/8″ × 3/8″ × 3/4″ square. Figure **9-M-5** shows the shaping. *Note:* The top 1/8″ remains square to accommodate the nut. The shaded area in the diagram indicates a 1/8″ diameter hole to be drilled 1/4″ in depth.

(D) LEG (Cut 3): 1/8″ × 1/2″ × 3/4″. See Figure **9-M-6** for the shape.

(E) BOLT (One): 3/32″ diameter × 1/2″ long with a flat head.

(F) NUT (One — to fit bolt): 3/32″ diameter hole × 1/4″ × 1/4″. See Figure **9-M-4**.

(G) THIN CARDBOARD (Cut 1): 1 1/8″ diameter. See Figure **9-M-1**. Cut a 1/8″ diameter hole in the center.

(H) UPHOLSTERY: Velvet or your own choice of material. Place the cardboard disc on the reverse side of the material and cut a circle approximately 1/4″ wider on all edges.

(I) COTTON: For stuffing.

ASSEMBLY: Stain all wood before glueing. Refer to Figure **9-M-8**.

1. Figure **9-M-7** shows the top view of the pedestal. Countersink the nut into the 1/8″ square upper section, so that the top surfaces are flush. Glue in place.

2. Glue the small wooden disc atop the top surfaces of the pedestal and nut, being sure that the holes are aligned.

3. Glue the three legs evenly spaced around the lower portion of the pedestal. See Figure **9-M-8**.

4. Screw the bolt down through the hole in the large wooden disc, until it is resting on the top surface of the wood. Apply glue to the top of the bolt and the wood so that it remains secure. When the glue is dry, screw the bolt into the nut in the pedestal. The seat should now move up and down.

5. Glue a small amount of cotton, evenly spread, atop the cardboard disc. Fit the upholstery over the cotton and the disc, and bring all edges underneath. Snip 1/8″ long cuts all around the edges of the upholstery, and glue the edges securely to the bottom of the disc.

6. Glue the upholstered disc atop the wooden seat, being sure that the top of the bolt fits up into the hole in the cardboard disc.

MANTLE CLOCK 9-N

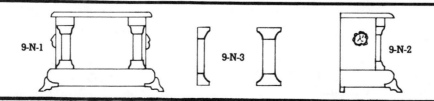

(A) BASE (Cut 1): 1/4″ × 3/4″ × 1 1/2″. Round off the top side and front edges. See Figures 9-N-1 and 9-N-2.

(B) BODY OF CLOCK (Cut 1): 1/2″ × 3/4″ × 1 1/4″.

(C) TOP OF CLOCK (Cut 1): 1/16″ × 3/4″ × 1 3/8″. Round off the top side and front edges.

(D) PILLAR TOP (Cut 2): 1/8″ × 1/8″ × 1/4″.

(E) PILLARS (Cut 2): 1/8″ × 1/4″ × 5/8″. See Figure 9-N-3 for a side view and a front view of the shaping.

(F) CLOCK FACE (One): Refer to **1-C-2**. Find the color print marked **9-N** for this clock face on the color insert sheet. Glue the print onto a piece of a file card and cut out. Apply airplane cement to the edges to seal them.

(G) JEWELRY FINDINGS

(1) **JEWELRY FINDINGS:** You will need two small decorations for the sides of the clock.

(2) **JEWELRY FINDINGS:** You will need two pieces of jewelry findings which you can fashion into the two front feet. Figures **9-N-1** and **9-N-2** will be guides for the type of feet you will need to create. Fit them around the front corners of the clock. When you are satisfied with them, spray the feet and side decorations with an acrylic sealer. Paint the feet and side decorations gold.

(H) BACK FEET (Two): 1/16″ × 1/16″ × 1/16″. Paint gold.

(I) TOP DECORATION (One): Find a tiny figure on a horse or a figure such as the plastic ones made for railroad scenes. Spray the ornament with an acrylic sealer. Paint the ornament gold.

ASSEMBLY

1. Paint the edges of the clock face and the pillars gold.

2. Glue the body of the clock atop the base, with the back edges flush and the sides equal. Paint this assembly black.

3. Refer to **1-C-9**. The top of the clock (**C**) and the pillar tops (**D**) should be painted to represent marble.

4. Glue the top of the clock centered atop the top surface of the body of the clock, with the back edges flush. Glue the top ornament centered atop the top of the clock. Glue the side ornaments in place. Refer to Figures **9-N-1** and **9-N-2**.

5. Glue the pillar tops atop the top surfaces of the pillars, and glue them in place against the front of the clock. See Figure **9-N-1**.

6. Glue the four feet in place. See Figures **9-N-1** and **9-N-2**. Glue the clock face centered against the front of the clock.

VICTORIAN BOX
DECORATED WITH SHELLS
9-O

(A) FRONT, BACK AND TOP (Cut 3): 1/16″ × 3/4″ × 3/4″.

(B) SIDES (Cut 2): 1/16″ × 1/2″ × 5/8″.

(C) BOTTOM (Cut 1): 1/16″ × 5/8″ × 5/8″.

(D) HINGE (Cloth): Cut one piece of cloth 5/8″ wide × 1″ long (*inside hinge*) and one piece of cloth 3/4″ wide × 1 5/16″ long (*outside hinge*). Choose a color that will closely match the color you have chosen for the outside covering.

(E) SHELLS: You can purchase tiny shells from some craft shops or gather them at the seashore, if you are fortunate enough to live near one. Our grandparents gathered exquisite, minute shells by sifting the sands on Florida beaches.

(F) BOX COVERING AND LINING: Choose a fine velvet or satin for the outside covering and a tiny print paper, such as a scrap of miniature wallpaper or the design print from the inside of some envelopes, for the inside lining.

    (1) **OUTSIDE COVERING**
        a. **TOP:** 3/4″ × 3/4″.
        b. **SIDE:** 1/2″ × 3″.
    (2) **INSIDE LINING**
        a. **INSIDE BOTTOM:** 5/8″ × 5/8″.
        b. **INSIDE SIDES:** 3/8″ × 2 1/2″.
        c. **INSIDE LINING OF LID:** 3/4″ × 3/4″.

ASSEMBLY

1. Refer to **2-E-1** for the assembly of the sides, front, back and bottom.

2. Place the top board (*lid*) atop the top edges of the box. Glue the wide piece of cloth hinge covering the top surface of the lid, down against the edge of this board, and down against the outside-side surface of the box. *Let dry.* Open the lid. Glue the narrower piece of cloth hinge against the inside-side surface of

the box, over the top edge of this side, over the same inside edge of the lid, and against the inside surface of the lid. *Let dry.*

3. Paint the top edges of the box, the edges of the lid, and the bottom surface of the box a color that closely matches the color your have chosen to use for the outside covering.

4. Glue the inside bottom lining in place. Glue the inside (*side*) lining around the four interior sides of the box. Glue the inside lining of the lid in place.

5. Glue the outside top covering piece against the top surface of the box lid. Glue the outside covering around the sides of the box.

6. Refer to the color insert sheet, and find a tiny print marked **9-O**. Cut it out and glue it in place atop the box lid. Glue the tiny shells around the edges of the box lid and around the outside-side surfaces of the box. In the Victorian era, this type of box was used for jewelry or trinkets.

GRANDFATHER CLOCK 9-P

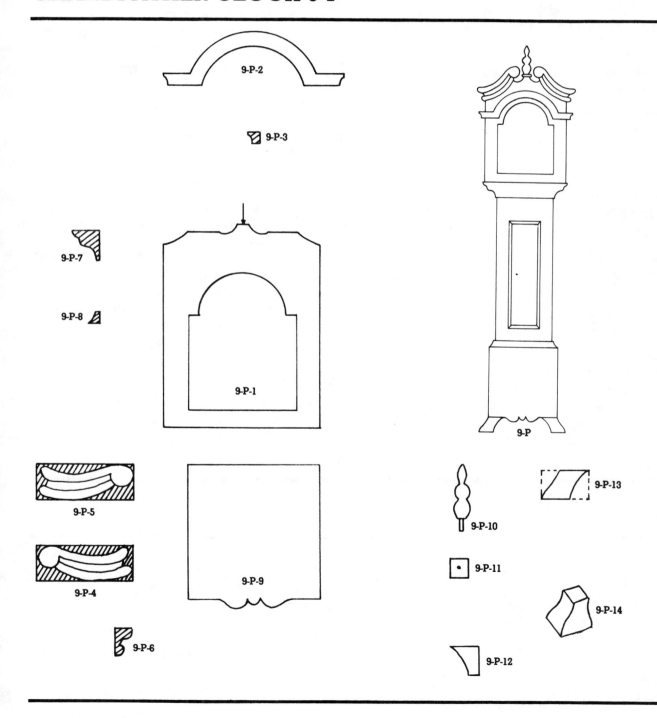

TOP SECTION

(A) **CLOCK FACE BACKING** (Cut 1): 1/16″ × 1 3/8″ × 1 11/16″.

(B) **FRONT** (Cut 1): 1/8″ × 1 5/8″ × 2 3/16″. See Figure **9-P-1** for the area to be cut away. Bevel all inside cut edges.

(C) **SIDES** (Cut 2): 1/8″ × 3/4″ × 1 15/16″.

(D) **BACK** (Cut 1): 1/8″ × 1 3/8″ × 1 15/16″.

(E) **TOP AND BOTTOM** (Cut 2): 1/8″ × 5/8″ × 1 3/8″.

MIDDLE SECTION

(F) **FRONT** (Cut 1): 1/8″ × 1 1/8″ × 3 7/16″.

(G) **BACK** (Cut 1): 1/8″ × 7/8″ × 3 7/16″.

(H) **SIDES** (Cut 2): 1/8″ × 1/2″ × 3 7/16″.

(I) **TOP AND BOTTOM** (Cut 2): 1/8″ × 3/8″ × 7/8″.

(J) **DOOR PANEL** (Cut 1): 1/16″ × 5/8″ × 2 1/4″. Bevel the four edges.

LOWER SECTION

(K) **FRONT** (Cut 1): 1/8″ × 1 3/8″ × 1 9/16″. See Figure **9-P-9** for the shape.

(L) **BACK** (Cut 1): 1/8″ × 1 3/8″ × 1 7/16″.

(M) **SIDES** (Cut 2): 1/8″ × 5/8″ × 1 7/16″.

(N) **TOP AND BOTTOM** (Cut 2): 1/8″ × 1/2″ × 1 1/8″.

LEGS

(O) **FRONT LEGS** (Cut 2): 5/16″ high × 1/2″ × 1/2″. See Figures **9-P-13** and **9-P-14** for the shape. Refer to **1-C-3-d** for aid in shaping.

(P) **BACK LEGS** (Cut 2): 3/16″ × 5/16″ × 5/16″. See Figure **9-P-12** for the shape.

MOULDING

(Q) **TOP FRONT MOULDING** (Cut 2): 1/4″ × 3/8″ × 1″. See Figures **9-P-4** and **9-P-5** for the shapes of the right and left pieces. *Note:* These pieces are carved "rounded" in the top and bottom layers, with the center area recessed. The back surface remains flat

and the ends will be mitred at a 45° angle to fit into the side moulding pieces.

(R) **TOP SIDE MOULDING** (Cut 2): 3/16″ × 5/16″ × 1 1/16″. See Figure **9-P-6** for the end view of the moulding to be carved. *Note:* The front edge will be mitred at a 45° angle to fit into the front moulding and the back end will be flat.

(S) **ARCH MOULDING** (Cut 1): 1/8″ × 9/16″ × 1 7/8″. See Figure **9-P-2** for the shape to be carved. Mitre each end with a 45° angle.

(T) **ARCH SIDE MOULDING** (Cut 2): 1/8″ × 1/8″ × 1″. See Figure **9-P-3** for the end view shape of this moulding. Mitre the front end of each piece with a 45° angle and cut the back end straight.

(U) **MOULDING JOINING THE TOP AND CENTER SECTIONS:** The moulding which is shown in Figure **9-P-7** is approximately the type of moulding to purchase. Keep to the 5/16″ × 5/16″ measurement, if possible.

    (1) **MOULDING** (Cut 1): 5/16″ × 5/16″ × 1 11/16″. Mitre both ends with a 45° angle.

    (2) **MOULDING** (Cut 2): 5/16″ × 5/16″ × 7/8″. Mitre the front end of each piece with a 45° angle and cut the other end straight.

(V) **MOULDING JOINING THE CENTER AND LOWER SECTIONS:** Choose 1/8″ × 1/8″ cove moulding. Figure **9-P-8** shows the shape.

    (1) **MOULDING** (Cut 1): 1/8″ × 1/8″ × 1 3/8″. Mitre each end with a 45° angle.

    (2) **MOULDING** (Cut 2): 1/8″ × 1/8″ × 3/4″. Mitre the front end of each piece with a 45° angle and cut the back ends straight.

(W) **FINIAL** (Cut 1): 3/16″ diameter wood dowel × 3/4″. See Figure **9-P-10** for the shape. Refer to **1-C-3-a** for aid in carving the finial.

(X) **FINIAL BASE** (Cut 1): 1/16″ × 3/16″ × 3/16″. Drill a 1/16″ diameter hole in the center at the site of the black dot in Figure **9-P-11**.

ASSEMBLY: Refer to **2-F**.

SHADOW BOX 9-Q

Note: This is a basic shadow box. It can be constructed of 3/8″ thick plywood or any wood of your choice. The top can be made of wood or can be cut from a piece of 1/8″ thick Plexiglas, which allows the existing light or a table lamp to shine into the box. The outside of the box can be simply painted; add siding to simulate a building, or apply wood veneer to "dress it up."

(A) **TOP** (Cut 1): 3/8″ thick wood or 1/8″ thick Plexiglas × 11 3/8″ × 20 3/4″.

(B) **BASE** (Cut 1): 3/8″ × 11″ × 20″.

(C) **BACK** (Cut 1): 3/8″ × 12 3/8″ × 20″.

(D) **SIDES** (Cut 2): 3/8″ × 11 3/8″ × 12 3/8″.

ASSEMBLY

1. The two sides are glued against the upright edges of the back, with back edges flush.

2. The base is glued between the side boards and

against the lower front edge of the back, with bottom edges flush. See Figure **9-Q-1**.

3. Use 1/2" brads to give the box added strength.

4. The wooden top is nailed and glued in place. If, however, you have chosen to use the Plexiglas you will need to drill holes through the side and back edges to accept 1/2" long screws. See Figure **9-Q-2**.

5. Use a square and level to be sure that the box is "true" as you are constructing it. There is nothing so disappointing as to begin to paper and decorate, only to find that the box is not square. When it is completed, let it dry thoroughly before beginning to decorate it.

6. Leave a 5/8" space around the inside front edge of the box to be used for wood strips and glass or Plexiglas for closure of the box. See Figure **9-Q-3**.

7. Having allowed for the 5/8" closure space, you may now decorate the interior of the box. The size is excellent for a room or an outdoor scene.

BOX CLOSURE

(E) WOOD STRIPS — TOP AND BOTTOM (Cut 4): 1/4" × 1/4" × 20".

(F) WOOD STRIPS — SIDES (Cut 4): 1/4" × 1/4" × 11 1/2".
The above strips of wood should be painted or stained on three sides. Choose a color which is predominant in the shadow box, or the color used on the outside of the box. The 5/8" space should also be painted or stained this same color.

(G) GLASS OR PLEXIGLAS (Cut 1): 1/8" thick × 11 7/8" × 19 7/8". We prefer to use Plexiglas, as it will not break when bumped and is much safer for display when in shows. You will note that these measurements are 1/8" short of the width and height of the opening. This 1/8" will allow for the paint and for space to easily insert and remove the glass.

ASSEMBLY

8. Place one of the 20" long pieces of wood butted against the lower inside line (5/8") as shown in Figure **9-Q-4**. Glue the unpainted side against the box. Repeat for the second 20" piece of wood, which is glued against the inside surface of the top of the box. *Note:* If you have used glass, the top edges of the wood pieces will be painted, and only the ends will be glued. See Figure **9-Q-5**.

9. Glue two of the 11 1/2" long strips of wood (*unpainted side*) butted against the 5/8" line on the inside surfaces of the left and right sides of the box. See Figure **9-Q-6**. You now have a continuous frame of these strips of wood butted against the 5/8" line, leaving a 3/8" space at the front of the box. Let the glue dry.

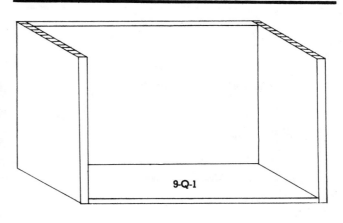

9-Q-1

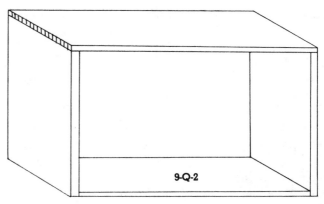

9-Q-2

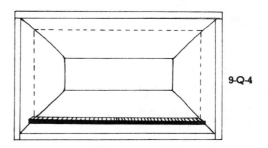

9-Q-4

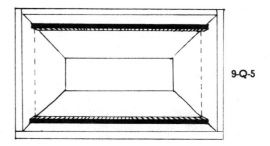

9-Q-5

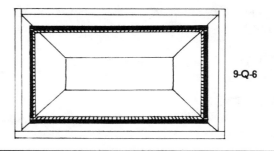

9-Q-6

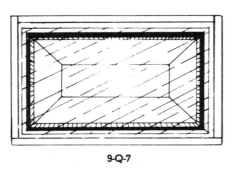

9-Q-7

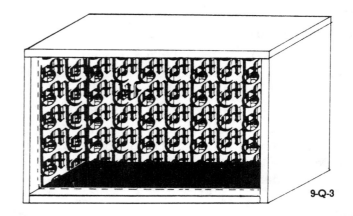

9-Q-3

10. While the glue is drying, thoroughly clean the glass or Plexiglas. Hold it with a towel or rag to prevent unwanted fingerprints. When cleaning Plexiglas for the first time, you will find a residue left after the protective paper covering has been removed. We have found through experimentation that a dampened soft cloth and "Wright's Silver Cleaner" (*paste or cream form*) will satisfactorily remove the residue and yet will not scratch the Plexiglas. Then wash the Plexiglas with mild soap suds, rinse, and then clean it as you would a pane of glass.

11. Insert the glass or Plexiglas in the opening and against the wood strips which were previously glued in place. There is now a 1/4" space still left around the front of the box.

12. Repeat Steps 8 and 9 with this *important exception:* do not glue these last four pieces of wood. Carefully force a brad (*3/8" long*) through each piece of wood and into the box. There will be a brad near each end of each piece of wood. Touch the head of each brad with a dot of the paint which you used to paint the pieces of wood. The shadow box is now closed, as well as being sealed with a double wood stripping against dust. See Figure **9-Q-7**. When you need to open the box, simply pry the outside wood strips loose using a knife or small screwdriver. Reseal it, as you did in Step 12.

BOOK SHADOW BOX 9-R

(A) COVER (Cut 2): 1/4" thick plywood × 9 1/2" × 12".

(B) BACK (Cut 2): 3/4" × 3 1/4" × 12". See Figure **9-R-3** for a side edge view of the shaping of the inside edge. See Figure **9-R-6** for the shaping of the outside edge (*top view*). Cut one of the back pieces into two pieces with one piece measuring 2 1/4" wide and the other piece measuring 1" wide. See Figures **9-R-4** and **9-R-5** (*top views*).

(C) TOP

(1) **COVER** (Cut 1): 1/8" thick Plexiglas × 3/4" × 9 1/8".

(2) **BOX** (Cut 1): 1/8" thick Plexiglas × 5 1/4" × 9 1/8". Mitre the right edge (*3/4" or 5 1/4"*) with a 45° cut.

(D) BOTTOM

(1) **COVER** (Cut 1): 1/4" thick combed plywood × 3/4" × 9 1/8".

(2) **BOX** (Cut 1): 1/4" thick combed plywood ×

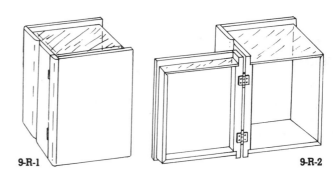

9-R-1

9-R-2

5 1/4" × 9 1/8".

(E) PAGE EDGE

(1) **COVER** (Cut 1): 1/4" thick combed plywood × 3/4" × 11 1/4". Mitre each end edge (*combed surface outside*) with a 45° cut.

(2) **BOX** (Cut 1): 1/4" thick combed plywood × 5 1/4" × 11 1/4". Mitre each end edge (*combed surface outside*) with a 45° cut.

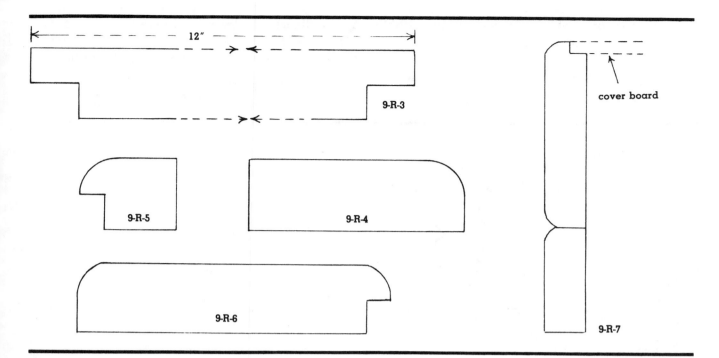

ASSEMBLY

1. Glue the 3 1/4″ back butted against the curved edge of the 2 1/4″ wide back piece, with the inside (*flat*) surfaces flush. See Figure **9-R-7**.

2. Glue a cover board (**A**) butted against the notched edge in the wider back board. See Figure **9-R-7**.

3. See Figure **9-R-2**. Glue the top (*Plexiglas*), bottom and page edge boards together (*with the combed surface of the plywood facing outward*). Glue this assembly against the inside surface of the book cover board (**A**) and glued against the notched edges of the book back.

4. Glue the second book back against the notched edge of the book back board (**9-R-5**). Glue the nar-row top (*Plexiglas*), bottom and page edge boards against this assembly, as you did in Step 3. See Figure **9-R-2**.

5. You will need two small butt hinges. See Figure **9-R-2**. Trace around the hinges and cut out this area, the depth of the hinges. Install the hinges. See **1-B-4**.

6. Select a covering of bookbinder's paper, leather, cloth, velvet and so on. Cut a piece measuring 30″ × 14 1/4″. Refer to **9-H** direction Step 2 and diagrams **9-H-2, 9-H-3** and **9-H-4**. Press the covering into the "valley" between the two curved edges of the back before glueing the edges down.

7. Decorate the interior of the box and glue a piece of bookbinder's paper or wallpaper on the inside of the front cover.

GREETING CARDS 9-S-T-U-V-W-X-Y-Z

The greeting cards will be assembled in a similar manner, which follows:

1. Refer to the color insert sheet and select the color prints for your card. They are marked **9-S, 9-T, 9-U, 9-V, 9-W, 9-X, 9-Y** and **9-Z**. After selecting the prints, refer to **1-C-2**.

2. The diagrams **9-S** through **9-Z** correspond to the color prints of the same number. Select the correct diagram and trace it onto a piece of a white file card. Cut out the color prints.

3. Glue the background print against the face of the top portion of the diagram (*card*). The dotted lines represent a fold. The top section folds downward at the top dotted line, while the bottom section folds upward at the lower dotted line. The card will now stand, with the two sections upright. See Figure **A**.

4. The cards marked **9-S** and **9-U** have a third section, a figure which must be traced onto another piece of a file card. Glue the figure against the face of the upper portion of the diagram (*card*). The lower portion of the cardboard folds down, toward the back, at the dotted line. This figure is glued atop the cardboard between the back and front sections. See Figure **B**.

5. The front color print is glued against the upright front surface of the forward piece of cardboard. See Figures **A** and **C**.

6. Trim any of the white card that may show at the edges of the prints.

7. See diagram **D**. Trace this brace onto a piece of a file card and cut out. Fold at the dotted line, and glue the tab against the back of the card so it will stand.

8. Apply a coat of acrylic sealer to the color prints.

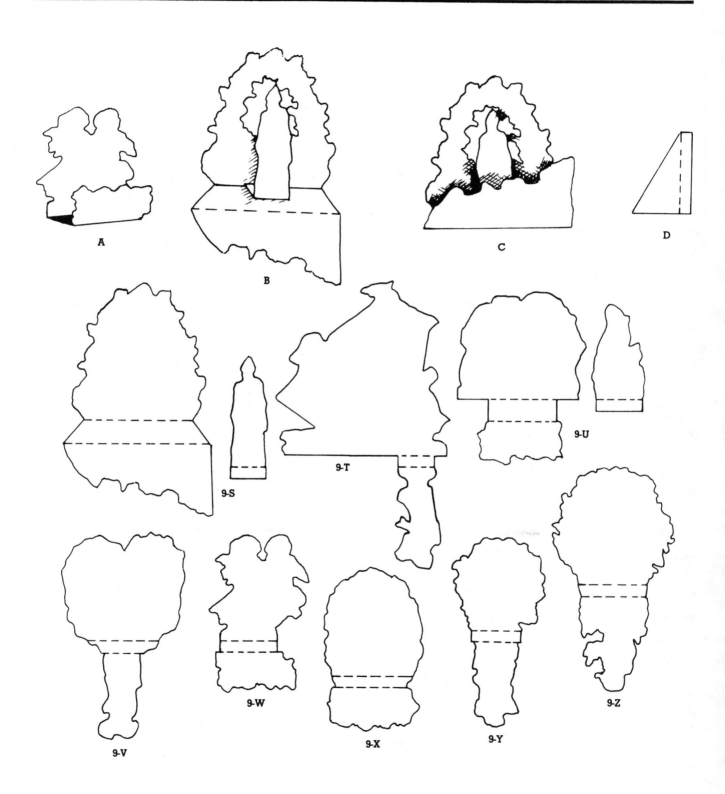

A

B

C

D

9-S

9-T

9-U

9-V

9-W

9-X

9-Y

9-Z

MOTT STABLE 10-A

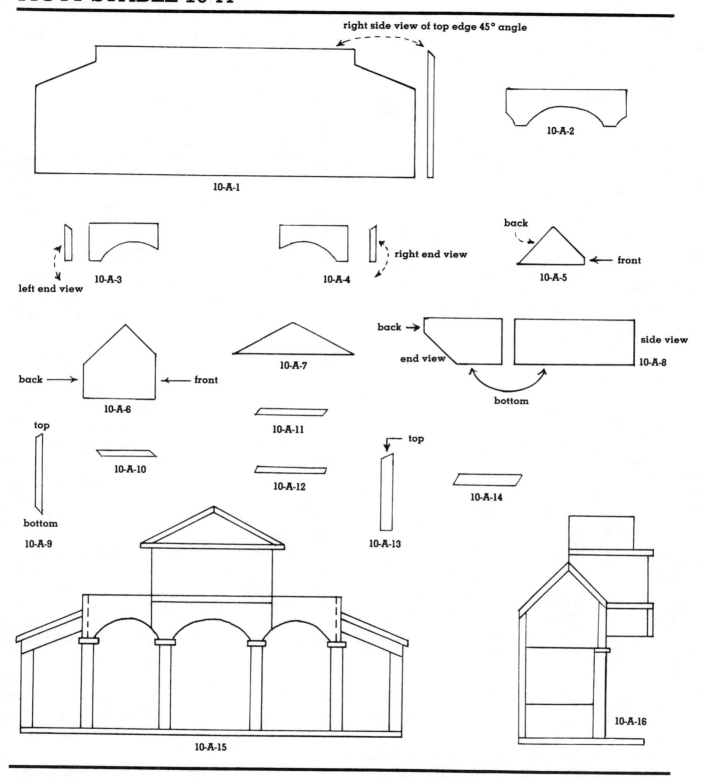

This tiny building is my reproduction of an antique lithographed toy stable which is in our collection. It is of European origin. In the antique toy stable, the floor is lithographed to simulate stone and the stall dividers and other interior walls are stencilled. Use 1/16" thick wood (bass, pine or balsa) or cardboard, unless otherwise noted; oak-brown and blueish-green paint; paper paste; wood glue.

(A) BASE (Cut 1): 1/16" × 1 5/16" × 3 15/16".

(B) BACK (Cut 1): 1/16" × 1 11/32" × 3 15/16". See Figure **10-A-1** for the shape.

(C) CENTER ARCH (Cut 1): 1/16" × 13/32" × 1 1/4". See Figure **10-A-2** for the shape.

(D) CENTER ARCH SIDE (Cut 2): 1/16" × 9/32" × 7/16".

(E) LEFT SIDE ARCH (Cut 1): 1/16" × 13/32" × 23/32". See Figure **10-A-3** for the shape.

(F) RIGHT SIDE ARCH (Cut 1): 1/16" × 13/32" × 23/32". See Figure **10-A-4** for the shape.

(G) END GABLE CORE (Cut 1): Cut from balsa wood. 7/16" × 11/16" × 2 9/16". See Figure **10-A-5** for the shape.

(H) END GABLE FACING (Cut 2): 1/16" thick. See Figure **10-A-6** for the shape.

(I) HAY-MOW GABLE (Cut 1): 11/16" deep. See Figure **10-A-7** for the shape.

(J) HAY-MOW CEILING (Cut 1): 1/16" × 7/8" × 1 1/2".

(K) HAY-MOW (Cut 1): Cut from balsa wood. 1/2" × 13/16" × 1 1/4". See Figure **10-A-8** for the shape.

(L) HAY MOW FLOOR (Cut 1): 1/16" × 1/2" × 1 1/4".

(M) HAY-MOW ROOF (Cut 2): 1/16" × 13/16" × 7/8". See Figure **10-A-9** for the angles at each end of these boards.

(N) FRONT GABLE ROOF (Cut 2): 1/16" × 5/8" × 25/32". See Figure **10-A-10** for the angles at each end.

(O) BACK GABLE ROOF (Cut 1): 1/16" × 3/4" × 2 13/16". See Figure **10-A-11** for the angles at each end.

(P) STALL ROOF (Cut 2): 1/16" × 3/4" × 15/16". See Figure **10-A-12** for the angles at each end.

(Q) STALL (Cut 6): 1/16" × 3/8" × 11/16".

(R) POST CAPS (Cut 4): 1/16" × 3/16" × 3/16".

(S) POSTS (Cut 4): 1/8" × 1/8" × 29/32".

(T) POSTS (Cut 2): 1/8" × 1/8" × 27/32". See Figure **10-A-13** for the angle at the top end.

(U) STALL ROOF FACING (Cut 2): 1/8" × 1/8" × 3/4". See Figure **10-A-14** for the angles at each end.

ASSEMBLY: Refer to **2-G** and **1-C-2**. Figure **10-A-15** is a front view and Figure **10-A-16** is a left side view of the stable.

1. Glue an end gable facing (**H**) against either end of the end gable core (**G**), with the top edges flush. These pieces will extend downward beyond the lower surface of the core.

2. Glue the assembled end gable pieces against the back (**B**) with the back top angle of the end gable assembly matching the back top angle of the back. See Figure **10-A-16**. Note these angles.

3. Glue the back atop the base (**A**) with the back edges flush.

4. Glue the center arch (**C**) butted against the upright ends (*9/32" high*) of the center arch sides (**D**), with the end edges flush. Glue the hay-mow floor (**L**) atop the center arch, with all edges flush. See Figure **10-A-15**.

5. Glue the left side arch (**E**) against the front edge of the left end gable facing (**H**), and with the top edge along the front lower edge of the gable core (**G**) — with angles matching — and the left edges flush. See Figures **10-A-15** and **10-A-16**.

6. Glue the right side arch (**F**) against the front edge of the right end gable facing (**H**) and with the top edge along the front lower edge of the gable core (**G**) — with angles matching — and with the right edges flush. See Figure **10-A-15**.

7. Glue the center arch assembly between the left and right center arches and against the front edge of the gable core. See Figures **10-A-15** and **10-A-16**.

8. Glue a post cap (**R**) centered atop the four posts 29/32" long (**S**). Refer to Figure **10-A-15**. Glue a post beneath each of the four lower points of the arches and atop the front edge of the base.

9. Glue the hay-mow (**K**) atop the hay-mow floor (**L**), with the back angled edge against the front angled edge of the end gable core.

10. Glue the back gable roof (**O**) atop the back angled edge of the back and atop the back edges of the end gable core and the end gable facing. See Figure **10-A-16**.

11. Glue the two front gable roof pieces (**N**) atop the front angled edges of the end gable core and the end gable facing. *Note:* These should have their center edges butted against the side edges of the hay-mow, with their end edges flush with the end edges of the back roof. See Figure **10-A-16**.

12. Glue the hay-mow ceiling (**J**) centered atop the top surface of the hay-mow, with the back edges flush.

13. Glue the hay-mow gable (**I**) centered atop the hay-mow ceiling, with the back edges flush. See Figures **10-A-15** and **10-A-16**.

14. Glue the hay-mow roof (**M**) atop the hay-mow gable (**I**) with the back edges flush and the bottom edges resting on the hay-mow ceiling. See Figure **10-A-15**.

15. Glue the two stalls (**Q**) against the front surface of the back and atop the end edges of the base. Glue the remaining four stalls against the back, atop the

base, at right angles to the back and behind each of the four posts.

16. Paint the gable roof, the top and edges of the hay-mow roof, the two stall roof pieces (**P**) and the post caps green.

17. Paint the back, edges and front surface of the back; the undersurface of the gable core; the bottom surface of the stall roof pieces (**P**); the base; the edges and inside surfaces of the stall boards and all surfaces of the remaining four stall boards brown. Also paint brown the edges of the center and side arches; the edges and back surface of the four posts; the edges and back surface of the remaining two posts (**T**); the stall roof facing — all surfaces — (**U**); the side, front and top edges of the hay-mow floor and the hay-mow roof; the back surface of the hay-mow assembly.

18. Refer to **1-C-2**. Refer to the color insert sheet and cut out the color prints marked **10-A**.

19. Glue the color print to the front and around the end surface of the center arch. Glue the color print to the front surface of the two side arches and around the ends, against the two end gable facing boards. Glue the triangular color print against the front of the hay-mow gable. Glue the four color prints against the fronts of the four posts. Glue the two oblong color prints against the outside surfaces of the two end stall boards.

20. Glue the left and right stall roof pieces (**P**) atop the lower angled end surfaces of the back, with the brown surface downward and butted against the end gable facing. See Figure **10-A-15**.

21. Glue a piece of the stall roof facing (**U**) beneath the front edge of each stall roof and butted against the end gable facing. Glue a post (**T**) beneath the end edge of each facing piece. See Figure **10-A-15**. Glue a color print against each post and facing assembly.

22. Apply a finish coat as instructed in **1-C-2**.

PATRICIA HOUSE 10-B

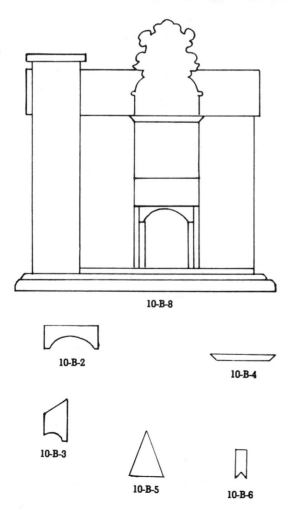

10-B-8

10-B-2

10-B-4

10-B-3

10-B-5

10-B-6

This tiny house is a reproduction of an antique lithographed European doll house which belongs to Patricia Baron. As with all of the antique houses which I have reproduced, I have named each one for the special person who allowed me to reproduce his or her treasure. The Patricia House is named for Patricia Baron. Constructing this house requires 1/16" thick wood (bass, pine or balsa) or cardboard, unless otherwise noted; a file card; white, blue and gilt paint; paper paste; wood glue.

(A) LOWER BASE (Cut 1): 1/8" × 1 5/8" × 2 3/4". Sand the top front and side edges rounded.

(B) TOP BASE (Cut 1): 1/16" × 1 9/16" × 2 9/16". Sand the top front and side edges rounded.

(C) BACK AND FRONT (Cut 2): 1/16" × 1 11/16" × 2 5/16".

(D) SIDES (Cut 2): 1/16" × 13/16" × 2 1/8". See Figure **10-B-1** for the shape.

(E) CENTER FRONT (Cut 1): 3/16" × 11/16" × 1 11/16".

(F) TOWER (Cut 1): 1/2" × 1/2" × 2 5/16".

(G) TOWER MOULDING (Cut 1): 1/16" × 5/8" × 5/8".

(H) CENTER FRONT MOULDING (Cut 1): 1/16" × 1/4" × 3/4". Sand the front and side edges rounded.

(I) CENTER DECORATION SUPPORT (Cut 1): 1/16" × 3/8" × 7/8".

(J) PORCH FLOOR (Cut 1): 1/16" × 1/2" × 13/16".

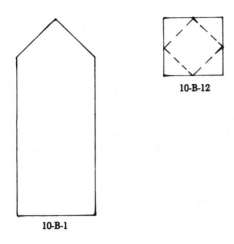

10-B-12

10-B-1

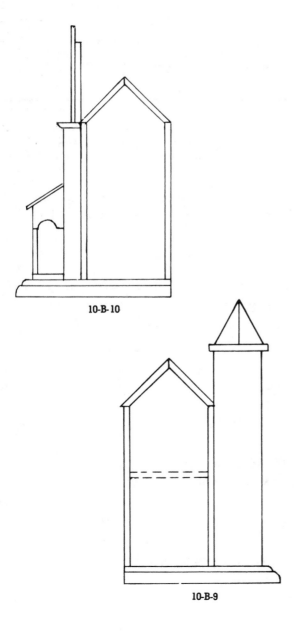

10-B-10

10-B-9

(K) FRONT ARCH (Cut 1): 1/16" × 1/4" × 9/16". See Figure **10-B-2** for the shape.

(L) SIDE ARCH (Cut 2): 1/16" × 1/4" × 15/32". See Figure **10-B-3** for the shape.

(M) PORCH POSTS (Cut 2): 1/16" × 1/16" × 1/2".

(N) SECOND FLOOR (Cut 1): 1/16" × 13/16" × 2 3/16".

(O) HOUSE ROOF (Cut 2): 1/16" × 11/16" × 2 1/2". See Figure **10-B-4** for the end angles.

(P) PORCH ROOF (Cut 1): Cut from a file card. 7/16" × 11/16".

(Q) DECORATION (One): Refer to **1-C-2**. Refer to the color insert page and cut out the color prints marked **10-B-Q**. Glue the color print of the decoration on the file card and cut out.

(R) PYRAMID (Cut 4): Cut from a file card. See Figure **10-B-5** for the shape.

(S) CLOTH HINGE (Cut 2): 1" × 1 5/8".

ASSEMBLY

1. Glue the top base (**B**) centered atop the lower base (**A**) with the back (*not rounded*) edges flush.

2. Glue the back (**C**) centered atop the top base (**B**) with the back edges flush.

3. Glue the two side boards (**D**) in front of the back, with the edges flush and at right angles with the back. See Figure **10-B-11**.

4. Glue the house roof pieces atop the top edges of the back and side boards. Be sure to note placement of the boards so that the angle edges are correct. See Figures **10-B-9** and **10-B-10**.

5. Apply the two cloth hinges. Refer to **2-G**.

6. Paint the front edges of the side boards, the house front board edges and back surface, the front edge of the second floor, all surfaces of the tower moulding (**G**), all surfaces of the porch floor and the porch posts white. Paint the base, roof and back of the house blue.

7. Refer to **1-C-2**. Glue a piece of the color print marked **10-B-E** against the center front board and the two side edges of this board.

8. Glue a piece of color print marked **10-B-C** against the house front with right edges flush.

9. Glue the center front board, with the color print applied, against the front board — to the left of the color print which has just been applied to the house front — with edges flush.

10. Glue the second piece of color print, marked

19-

10-B-13

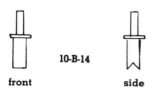

10-B-14

front   side

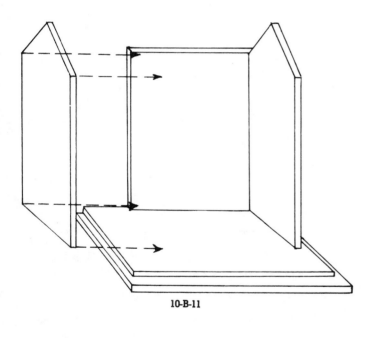

10-B-11

10-B-E, at the left side of the center front board, with edges flush.

11. Glue the color print around the tower. You will note that it covers all four sides of this board at the top. Glue the tower against the front left side of the house front, with the left and bottom edges flush.

12. Paint the center front moulding (**H**) and the center decoration support (**I**) white.

13. Glue the tower moulding (**G**) centered atop the top surface of the tower. See Figures **10-B-8** and **10-B-9**.

14. Glue the center front moulding (**H**) with the shaped surface downward, atop the center front board, with the back edges flush. See Figures **10-B-8** and **10-B-10**.

15. Glue the color print decoration against the center decoration support (**I**) with the bottom edges flush. Glue this assembly atop the center front moulding with the back edges flush. See Figure **10-B-10**. Paint the edges of this decoration with gilt paint.

16. Glue the four pyramid pieces (**R**) together and paint blue. Glue this assembly atop the top surface of the tower moulding, as shown in Figures **10-B-12** and **10-B-9**.

17. See Figure **10-B-13**. Glue the front arch (**K**) against the front edges of the two side arch pieces (**L**). Glue the color print against this assembly. Glue this assembly against the center front board, with the lower front edge 9/16″ above the top surface of the base. See Figure **10-B-10**.

18. Glue the porch floor (**J**) against the center front board (*centered in front of the front door*) with the lower edges of both boards flush. See Figure **10-B-10**.

19. Paint the porch roof (**P**) blue, and glue it centered atop the arch assembly and against the center front of the house. See Figure **10-B-10**.

20. Glue a porch post (**M**) at each front corner, atop the porch floor and beneath the end edges of the front arch.

21. Glue the second floor in place. Refer to **2-G**. See Figure **10-B-9** for placement.

22. Paint and decorate the interior.

23. **OPTIONAL CHIMNEYS**

(**T**) **CHIMNEY STACK** (Cut 2): 1/8″ × 1/8″ × 5/16″. Cut an angle in the base of each stack, as shown in Figure **10-B-6**.

(**U**) **CHIMNEY MOULDING** (Cut 2): Cut from a file card. 1/4″ × 1/4″.

(**V**) **CHIMNEY TOP** (Cut 2): 1/16″ diameter wood dowel × 1/4″.

Assemble these two chimneys as shown in Figure **10-B-14**.

24. Paint the assembled chimneys white. Glue 1/2″ from each end of the house roof.

DOTTIE HOUSE 10-C

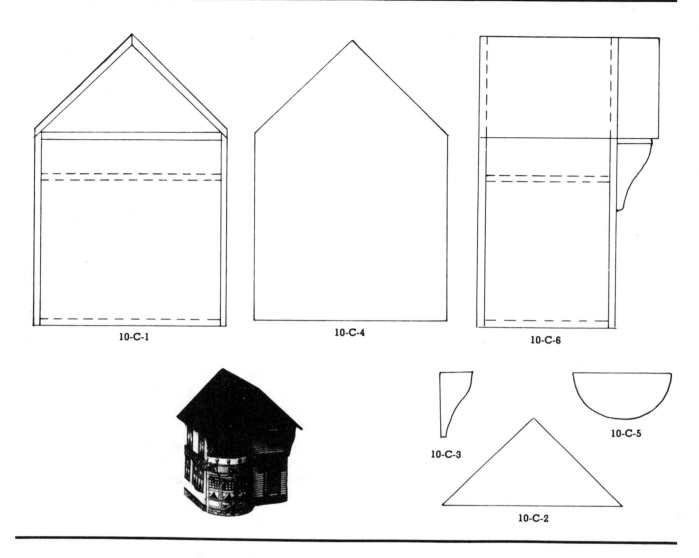

10-C-1

10-C-4

10-C-6

10-C-3

10-C-5

10-C-2

This tiny house is a reproduction of an antique lithographed doll house which we bought from Dottie Von Fliss. I have only reproduced the lithographed design on the outside of the house; however, the interior was also lithographed with charming detail and offered peeks through doorways into views of other rooms. As with all of the antique houses which I have reproduced, I have named each one for the special person who allowed me to reproduce his or her treasure. The Dottie House is named for Dottie Von Fliss. To construct the house will require 1/16" thickness wood (bass, pine or balsa) or cardboard, unless otherwise noted; an oak-brown color paint; paper paste; wood glue; 1" diameter half-round dowel.

(A) FRONT ROOF (Cut 2): 1/16" × 1/2" × 1 1/2".

(B) MAIN HOUSE ROOF (Cut 2): 1/16" × 1 3/8" × 1 1/2". See Figure **10-C-1** for the end angles for all house roof pieces.

(C) DORMER (Cut 1): 3/8" thick. See Figure **10-C-2** for the size and shape.

(D) BRACE TOP (Cut 1): 1/16" × 3/8" × 1 7/8".

(E) SIDE BRACE (Cut 2): 1/16" thick. See Figure **10-C-3** for the shape.

(F) SIDES (Cut 2): 1/16" × 1 5/16" × 2 1/16". See Figure **10-C-1** for the angle at the top edge.

(G) FLOORS (Cut 2): 1/16" × 1 5/16" × 1 7/8".

(H) FRONT AND BACK (Cut 2): 1/16" × 2" × 3". See Figure **10-C-4** for the shape.

(I) BAY CORE (Cut 1): 1" diameter half-round wood dowel × 1 3/16". See Figure **10-C-5**.

(J) CLOTH HINGE (Cut 2): 1" × 2".

ASSEMBLY: Refer to **2-G.**

1. Glue one floor (**G**) centered against the house back (**H**) with the bottom edges flush. See Figure **10-C-6**.

2. Glue a side (**F**) against the front surface of the house back (*with edges flush*) and against the side

edges of the first floor. Repeat for the second side. See Figure **10-C-1**.

3. Glue the main house roof (**B**) atop the top edges of the side boards and the back, with the back edges flush. See Figures **10-C-1** and **10-C-2**.

4. Apply the cloth hinge as instructed in the general directions **2-G**.

5. Glue the dormer (**C**) against the house front board (**H**) with the top edges flush.

6. Paint brown the front edges of the side braces (**E**), the house side edges, the front edge of the second floor and the first floor (**G**), the back of the house, the top of the bay core (**I**), the main house roof, the front roof, the bottom surface and edges of the brace top (**D**), the edges and inside surface of the house front.

7. Refer to **1-C-2**. Cut out the color prints marked

10-C on the color insert sheet. Glue the color print to the house front and sides, around the curved surface of the bay core (**I**), and glue the edges to the flat back surface and to both sides of both side braces (**E**).

8. Glue the unpainted surface of the brace top (**D**) against the bottom surface of the dormer (**C**) and against the house front. Glue a side brace (**E**) beneath each end edge of this board and against the house front. See Figure **10-C-6**.

9. Glue the flat surface of the bay core (**I**) — being sure it is right side up — against the lower left side of the house front, with the bottom edges flush.

10. Glue the second floor in place, being sure that it is straight and level. See Figure **10-C-1** for placement.

11. Decorate the interior of the house.

NOAH'S ARK 10-D

10-D-3

10-D-1

10-D-4

10-D-2

(A) BOAT BOTTOM (Cut 1): 1/4" × 1/2" × 1". See Figure **10-D-4** for the shape.

(B) CABIN (Cut 1): 5/16" × 3/8" × 3/4".

(C) ROOF (Cut 1): 1/8" × 1/2" × 7/8". See Figure **10-D-3** for a front view of the shape.

ASSEMBLY

1. Stain the roof (*all surfaces*) and the boat bottom (*all surfaces*).

2. Glue the cabin centered atop the boat bottom. See Figure **10-D-1**. Glue the roof centered atop the cabin. See Figure **10-D-2** for a front view of this assembly.

3. Refer to **1-C-2**. Refer to the color insert sheet and cut out the section of prints marked **10-D**. Cut out the print for the cabin. *Do not cut out the animal prints.* Glue the cabin print around the cabin.

4. Paint one side of a piece of a file card or file folder an oak-brown color. Glue the animal prints on the reverse side of this piece of card. Using curved-end fingernail scissors or decoupage scissors, cut out the animals. Paint the edges of the animals the brown color. Glue a tiny bead behind each animal to make it stand independently and paint it brown.

5. Finish the ark and animals as instructed in **1-C-2**.

WAGON 10-E

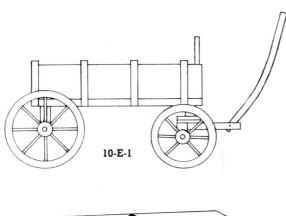

10-E-1

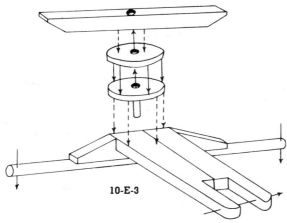

10-E-3

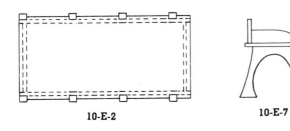

10-E-2

10-E-7

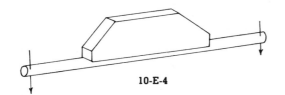

10-E-4

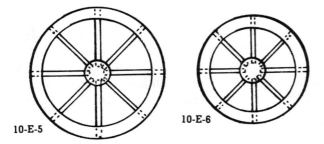

10-E-5   10-E-6

(A) WAGON BED (Cut 1): 1/8″ × 1 1/2″ × 3″. See Figure **10-E-8** for the shape.

(B) SIDES (Cut 2): 1/16″ × 5/8″ × 3″.

(C) RIBS (Cut 8): 1/8″ × 1/8″ × 13/16″.

(D) BACK END (Cut 1): 1/16″ × 5/8″ × 1 1/4″.

(E) FRONT END (Cut 1): 1/16″ × 1 1/4″ × 3″. See Figure **10-E-14** for the shape.

(F) WAGON SEAT (One)

    (1) **LEGS** (Cut 2): 1/16″ × 15/16″ × 1 1/4″. See Figure **10-E-15** for the shape.

    (2) **SEAT** (Cut 1): 1/16″ × 1″ × 1 3/8″.

    (3) **BACK** (Cut 1): 1/16″ × 5/16″ × 1 1/8″. See Figure **10-E-17** for the shape.

    (4) **ARMS** (Cut 2): 1/16″ × 1/4″ × 7/8″. See Figure **10-E-16** for the shape.

(G) TURN-TABLE DISCS (Cut 2): 1/16″ thick × 1/2″diameter disc. See Figure **10-E-12**. Drill a 1/16″ diameter hole through the center. See the shaded area in the diagram.

(H) HANDLE (Cut 1): 1/8″ × 5/8″ × 2 3/8″. See Figure **10-E-20** for the shape. Drill a tiny hole through the side at the site of the black dot in the diagram. This hole will accommodate a piece of fine wire.

(I) HANDLE SUPPORT (Cut 2): 1/8″ × 1/4″ × 1 1/8″. See Figure **10-E-11** for the shape. Drill a tiny hole through the side at the site of the arrow in the diagram. This hole will accommodate a fine wire. Glue these two pieces together along the shorter edge. See Figure **10-E-3**.

(J) FRONT AXLE SUPPORT (Cut 1): 3/16″ × 3/16″ × 1 3/4″. See Figure **10-E-9** for the shape.

(K) FRONT WAGON SUPPORT (Cut 1): 3/16″ × 3/16″ × 1 1/2″. See Figure **10-E-10** for the shape. Drill a 1/16″ diameter hole through the board at the site of the arrow in the diagram.

(L) AXLES (Cut 2): 1/16″ diameter wood dowel × 2 1/2″. Drill a pin-sized hole through the dowel 1/16″ from each end.

(M) REAR WAGON SUPPORT (Cut 1): 3/16″ × 3/8″ × 1 3/4″. See Figure **10-E-13** for the shape.

(N) LARGE WHEEL (Two): 1 3/8″ diameter wheels from a toy, or you can build them as follows.

    (1) **RIMS** (Cut 4): Cut from a file card. See Figure **10-E-18** for the shape. Cut out the inside area.

    (2) **HUB** (Cut 4): 1/4″ diameter wood dowel × 3/16″. See Figure **10-E-21**. The arrows indicate eight holes to be drilled (*centered*) around the outside

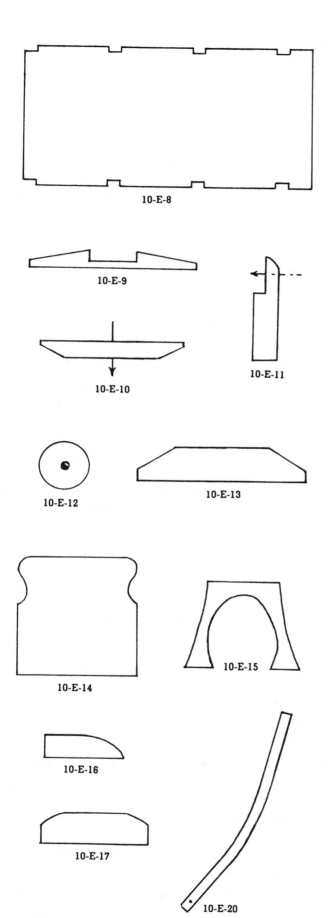

10-E-8

10-E-9

10-E-11

10-E-10

10-E-12

10-E-13

10-E-14

10-E-15

10-E-16

10-E-17

10-E-20

(*1/16" in diameter and 1/16" deep*). Drill a 5/64" diameter hole through the center of the hub to accommodate the axle.

(3) **SPOKES** (Cut 16): 1/16" diameter wood dowel × 5/8".

(O) SMALL WHEELS (Two): 1 1/8" diameter wheels from a toy, or you can build them as follows.

(1) **RIMS** (Cut 4): Cut from a file card. See Figure **10-E-19** for the shape. Cut out the inside area.

(2) **SPOKES** (Cut 16): 1/16" diameter wood dowel × 1/2".

(P) TURN-TABLE PEG (Cut 1): 1/16" diameter wood dowel × 5/16".

(Q) PINS (Four): Sequin pins for axle pegs.

ASSEMBLY OF WHEELS

If you cannot find the correct wheels, the following directions will aid you in the assembly of the two pairs of wheels. Our friend, Elizabeth Watkins, suggested this method. These directions are for one of the large wheels. The other large wheel and the two small wheels are constructed in the same manner.

1. Trace Figure **10-E-5** (**10-E-6** *for the small wheel*) onto a sheet of paper. Place the tracing down on a smooth work surface and place a sheet of waxed paper over it.

2. Place one of the large pre-cut cardboard rims over the area in the diagram.

3. Glue eight of the 5/8" long spokes into the holes in the hub.

4. Glue the spokes onto the cardboard ring at each site indicated in the diagram.

5. Glue a second large cardboard rim atop the spokes and directly over the first cardboard rim.

6. Fill the inside of the wheel rim (*between the spokes*) with wood dough or wood putty, being sure that the areas around and between the spokes are well packed. Keep the putty even with the edges of the rims. *Let dry.* Refill any areas that have shrunk away. *Let dry* again. When the wheel rim is completely filled, gently sand the putty smooth.

ASSEMBLY OF WAGON SEAT: See Figure 10-E-7.

1. Glue the arms butted against the back, with outside and bottom edges flush.

2. Glue this assembly centered atop the seat, and 1/16" in front of the back edge.

3. Glue the above assembly atop the two legs, which will be 1/16" inside the outside edges of the wagon seat, making them 1 1/8" apart (*inside measurement*).

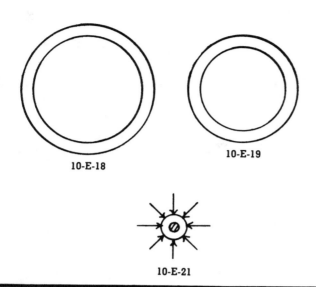

10-E-18

10-E-19

10-E-21

ASSEMBLY OF WAGON BED

1. Glue the ribs (**C**) into the notches in the side edges of the wagon bed (**A**) with the bottom edges flush. See Figures **10-E-1** and **10-E-2**.

2. Glue the sides (**B**) against the inside surfaces of the ribs and atop the wagon bed, with the end edges flush with the ends of the wagon bed. See Figure **10-E-2**.

3. Glue the back end (**D**) between the sides and 1/16" inside of the back edge of the wagon bed. See Figure **10-E-2**.

4. Glue the front end (**E**) inside of the sides and 1/16" inside of the front edge of the wagon bed. See Figure **10-E-2**.

ASSEMBLY OF THE WAGON SUPPORTS AND TURN-TABLE

1. Glue the rear wagon support (**M**) centered atop an axle. See Figure **10-E-4**. Glue this assembly centered beneath the wagon bed 1/8" from the rear edge.

2. Glue the front axle support (**J**) centered atop the second axle. Glue the assembled handle support (**I**) down into the notch at the center of the front axle support, with the top and back edges flush. See Figure **10-E-3**.

3. Glue the turn-table peg (**P**) into the hole in one of the turn-table discs (**G**) with the bottom edges flush.

4. Glue the second turn-table disc (**G**) beneath the front wagon support, with the holes aligned. Glue the top surface of the front wagon support beneath the wagon bed, recessed 3/16" from the front edge. See Figures **10-E-1** and **10-E-3**.

5. Glue the peg and disc centered atop the handle support, with the back edges flush. See Figure **10-E-3**.

6. Slip the handle into the opening of the handle support (**I**). Pass a piece of fine wire through the holes in the handle support and the handle, securing the ends of the wire.

COMPLETION OF WAGON ASSEMBLY

1. Paint the wagon bed, sides, ribs, front and back boards and support assemblies a mustard yellow. Paint the seat, the wheel and spokes red. Paint the bottom surface of the wheel and the handle black.

2. Refer to Figure **10-E-3**. Slip the turn-table peg through the hole in the upper disc and up into the front wagon support. If these holes seem tight, use a file to make them larger. *Do not glue.*

3. Slip the small wheels over the front axle and the large wheels over the rear axle. Push a sequin pin through the hole at the end of each axle. Clip off the excess length of each pin and touch with a drop of glue to secure the pin.

4. Refer to **1-C-2**. Turn to the color insert sheet and cut out the prints marked **10-E**. Glue the prints between the ribs and against the outside surface of the sides, against the front surface of the front board, against the rear surface of the back board, against the front and back and side surfaces of the seat, and atop the seat.

5. Finish as instructed in **1-C-2**.

HORSE SHOO FLY 10-F

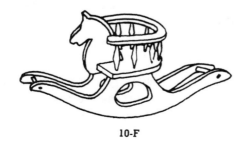

10-F

(**A**) **SPACER RODS** (Cut 2): 1/16" diameter wood dowel × 1 1/4".

(**B**) **FOOT REST** (Cut 1): 1/16" × 1/2" × 1".

(**C**) **ROCKERS** (Cut 2): 1/8" × 7/8" × 3 1/2". See Figure **10-F-1** for the shape.

(**D**) **SEAT** (Cut 1): 1/8" × 13/16" × 1 5/16". See Figure **10-F-2** for the shape. Drill 1/16" diameter holes at the sites of the black dots in the diagram.

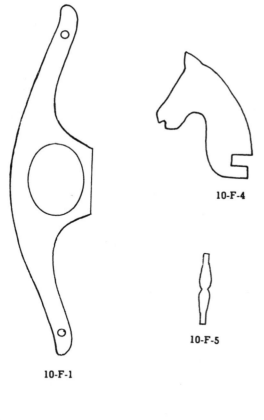

10-F-4

10-F-5

10-F-1

10-F-2   10-F-3

(E) ARM REST (Cut 1): 1/8″ × 7/8″ × 1 1/4″. See Figure **10-F-3** for the shape. Drill 1/16″ diameter holes at the sites of the black dots in the diagram.

(F) SPINDLES (Cut 7): 1/8″ diameter wood dowel × 3/4″. See Figure **10-F-5** for the shape. Refer to **1-C-3-a** for aid in carving.

(G) HORSE HEAD (Cut 1): 1/8″ × 1″ × 1 5/16″. See Figure **10-F-4** for the shape.

(H) REINS (Cut 1): 3″ length of tiny diameter cording.

ASSEMBLY: Refer to Figure **10-F**.

1. Glue the seven spindles into the seat, with the bottom edges flush. Fit and glue the spindles into the arm rest, with the top edges flush.

2. Glue the spacer rods into the holes at the front and back of the two rockers, joining the two sides. Glue the foot rest behind the forward spacer rod, between the two rocker sides.

3. Glue the assembled seat atop the top flat surfaces of the two rocker sides, facing toward the front of the shoo fly.

4. Paint all edges of the horse head white, and paint the assembled shoo fly with your choice of colors.

5. Apply the color print marked **10-F** on the color insert sheet to both sides of the horse head. Refer to **1-C-2**. Glue the horse head in place with the slot fitting centered on the front of the seat. Glue the ends of the cord to either side of the horse's bridle.

ROCKING HORSE SHOO FLY 10-G

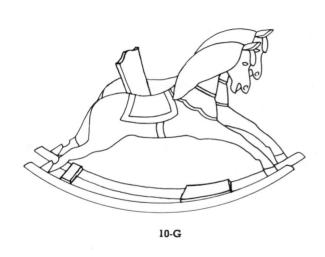

10-G

(A) SIDES (Cut 2): 1/8″ × 2 3/8″ × 4″. See Figure **10-G-1** for the shape. The dotted line above the end of each foot of the horse indicates an area to be cut so that there will be half the thickness of the wood below the line. The two small diagrams by each foot show a side view of the leg with this notch, which will fit against the inside surface of the rockers. When you have notched one side board, notch the reverse side of the other board.

(B) SEAT AND SEAT BACK (Cut 2): 1/8″ × 1 1/8″ × 1 1/2″. See Figure **10-G-2** for the shape.

(C) ROCKERS (Cut 2): 1/8″ × 3/4″ × 4 3/8″. See Figure **10-G-3** for the shape.

(D) ROCKER BOARDS (Cut 1 each): 1/16″ × 1/4″ × 1 3/4″ and 1/16″ × 3/4″ × 1 3/4″.

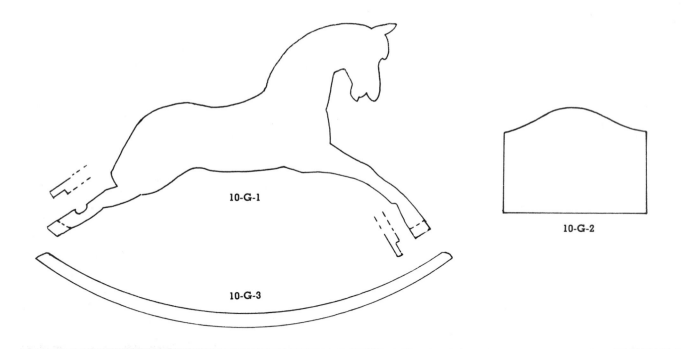

10-G-1

10-G-2

10-G-3

ASSEMBLY: Refer to Figure **10-G.**

1. Paint the edges of both side boards white; the seat back, the seat edges and underneath surface of the seat and the rockers red; the rocker boards blue.

2. Refer to **1-C-2.** Glue the color print marked **10-G-a** on the color insert sheet to both sides of each side board. Glue the color print marked **10-G-c** on the color insert sheet to both sides of the seat back. Glue the color print marked **10-G-b** on the color insert sheet to the unpainted surface of the seat.

3. Glue the seat back atop the top back edge of the seat, with the back edges flush. Glue this assembled seat between the two side boards in the location indicated by dotted lines in Figure **10-G-1.**

4. Glue the top assembly atop the two rockers, with the notched lower edges of the horse's legs glued on the inside of the rockers. Be sure that the feet are glued in exactly the same location on each rocker to assure proper rocking.

5. Glue the narrow rocker board atop the rockers in front of the back feet and the wide rocker board behind the front feet, with the end edges flush with the outside of the rockers. See Figure **10-G.**

SWAN SHOO FLY 10-H

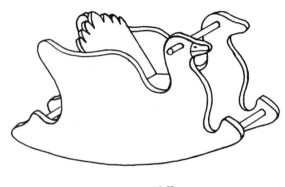

10-H

(A) SIDES (Cut 2): 1/8″ × 1 3/4″ × 3″. See Figure **10-H-1** for the shape. Drill a 1/16″ diameter hole at the site of each black dot in the diagram.

(B) SEAT BACK (Cut 1): 1/16″ × 1 1/4″ × 1 3/8″. See Figure **10-H-2** for the shape. Note the angle at the lower edge of this board.

(C) SEAT (Cut 1): 1/16″ × 1″ × 1 1/4″.

(D) SPACER RODS (Cut 2): 1/16″ diameter wood dowel × 1 1/2″.

(E) HANDLE BAR (Cut 1): 1/16″ diameter wood dowel × 2″.

ASSEMBLY: Refer to Figure **10-H.**

1. Glue the spacer rods into the front and back holes

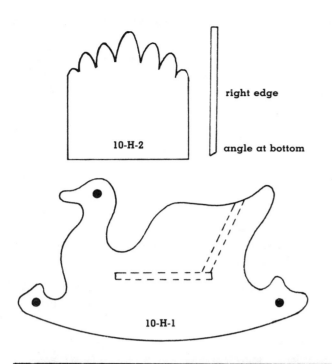

10-H-2

right edge

angle at bottom

10-H-1

of the sides, with the outside surfaces flush, joining the two sides.

2. Paint the edges and inside surfaces of the side boards white, paint the spacer rods and the handle bar a color of your choice. Paint the bottom surface, edges of the seat and edges of the seat back white.

3. Refer to **1-C-2**. Glue the color print marked **10-H-a** on the color insert sheet onto the top of the seat. Glue the color print marked **10-H-c** on the color insert sheet onto the front and back of the seat back. Glue the seat back onto the top back edge of the seat so that it angles back. Glue this assembly inside the two sides in the location marked by dotted lines in Figure **10-H-1**. Glue the color print marked **10-H-b** on the color insert sheet onto the two sides of the shoo fly.

4. Penetrate the side prints at the sites of the eyes and glue the handle bars through the two holes, with the two ends extending 1/4" on each side.

SLED 10-I

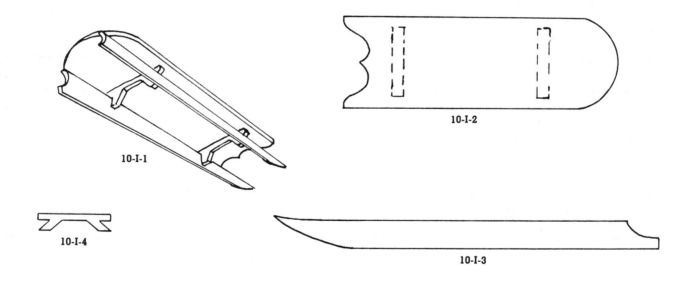

10-I-1

10-I-2

10-I-4

10-I-3

(A) TOP OF SLED (Cut 1): 1/16" × 1" × 2 7/8". See Figure **10-I-1** for the shape.

(B) RUNNERS (Cut 2): 1/8" × 3/8" × 4". See Figure **10-I-3** for the shape.

(C) BRACES (Cut 2): 1/8" × 3/16" × 3/4". See Figure **10-I-4** for the shape.

ASSEMBLY

1. Stain the runners and one side and all edges of the sled top. Paint the braces a flat black.

2. Figure **10-I-2** shows the placement (*broken line areas*) of the brace tops on the underneath surface of the sled top. Glue the two braces in place.

3. Figure **10-I-1** shows an underneath view of the assembly of the sled top, braces, and runners. Glue the two runners against the outside surfaces of the braces.

4. Refer to **1-C-2**. The color print marked **10-I** for the top of the sled will be found on the color insert page. Glue the sled top print in place and finish the sled as instructed in **1-C-2**.

DRUM 10-J

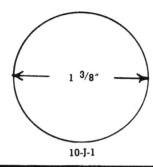

10-J-1

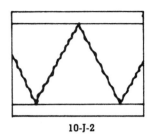

10-J-2

(A) DRUM CORE (Cut 1): 1 3/8″ diameter wood dowel × 1 1/8″.

(B) CORD: A fine gold or white cording × 12″.

(C) UPPER AND LOWER EDGE (Cut 2): 1/8″ × 4 3/8″ from a piece of gold card, such as part of a greeting card.

ASSEMBLY

1. Paint all edges of the two pieces of gold card with gilt paint. Paint the top and bottom surfaces of the drum white.

2. Refer to 1-C-2. Select the color print marked **10-J** on the color insert sheet. Cut out the print and glue it around the drum, glueing the left edge atop the right edge tab.

3. Glue the gold strips around the top and bottom of the drum, with top and bottom edges flush.

4. You will see black dots spaced around the drum print at the top and bottom edges of the print. Glue the gold thread touching a top dot, then a bottom dot, and so on, until the drum is laced with the cord. See Figure **10-J-2**.

STICK HORSE 10-K

10-K-1

10-K-2

(A) HORSE HEAD (Cut 1): 3/8″ × 7/8″ × 1″. See Figure **10-K-1** for the shape. Drill a 1/16″ diameter hole centered up into the flat bottom surface of the horse head. This hole will be drilled 1/4″ deep.

(B) STICK (Cut 1): 1/16″ diameter wood dowel × 3 1/4″. Drill a tiny hole through the stick 1/8″ from one end.

(C) WHEELS (Cut 2): 1/16″ thick × 3/8″ diameter circle. Refer to Figure **10-K-2** for the size. Drill a tiny hole through the center (*marked by a black dot in the diagram*) of each wheel.

(D) REINS (Cut 1): Tiny cording measuring 3 1/2″ in length.

(E) STRAIGHT PIN (One)

ASSEMBLY

1. Paint all edges of the horse head white. Paint the stick and wheels a color of your choice.

2. Refer to 1-C-2. Glue the color print marked **10-K** on the color insert sheet to the side surfaces of the head.

3. Insert a straight pin through one wheel, through the hole in the stick, and through the second wheel. Bend the end with pliers to secure it, and clip off the excess length of the pin.

4. Glue the end of the stick up into the hole in the bottom of the horse head. Glue an end of the cord on either side of the head at the site of the bridle.

DOLL CUPBOARD 10-L

10-L-1

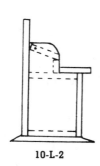
10-L-2

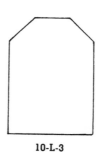
10-L-3

10-L-4

10-L-5

(A) BACK (Cut 1): 1/16" × 7/8" × 1 1/4". See Figure 10-L-3 for the shape.

(B) SIDES (Cut 2): 1/16" × 1/2" × 1". See Figure 10-L-4 for the shape. Note the location of the black dot in the diagram.

(C) TOP AND BOTTOM (Cut 2): 1/16" × 1/2" × 3/4".

(D) BASE (Cut 1): 1/16" × 7/8" × 1 1/8". Bevel the top edge of all four sides.

(E) TOP FRONT (Cut 1): 1/16" × 1/8" × 3/4".

(F) SLANT LID (Cut 1): 1/16" × 5/16" × 11/16". See Figure 10-L-5 for a side view diagram. Note the black dot which indicates the location of a pin hole.

(G) TOP SHELF (Cut 1): 1/32" or 1/16" thick × 5/16" × 1".

(H) DOORS (Cut 2): 1/16" × 3/8" × 11/16".

(I) SEQUIN PINS (Eight)

ASSEMBLY: This piece will be painted and color print will be applied.

1. Glue the sides against the upright front edges of the back board with bottom and outside edges flush. See Figure 10-L-2.

2. Glue the top board (**C**) between the sides, against the back board, and flush with the top edge of the front extension of the sides. See Figures 10-L-1 and 10-L-2. Glue the bottom board (**C**) between the sides, against the back, with bottom edges flush.

3. Glue the top front board (**E**) between the sides and atop the top board with front edges flush. Glue the top shelf (**G**) against the lower front surface of the top front board, atop the top edges of the side front extensions, with side overhang equal.

4. Glue this assembly atop the base with all spaces equal. See Figures 10-L-1 and 10-L-2.

5. Paint the edges, base, back and interior black.

6. Refer to **1-B-4-a** (*pin hinge*). Place the doors against the front. Clip the head end off of four of the sequin pins. Push a pin down through the top shelf into the top edge of each door. Push a pin up through the base into the bottom edge of each door.

7. Refer to **1-B-4-a** (*pin hinge*). Place the slant lid between the upper side boards, against the back and resting on the top edge of the top front board. Push a pin (*clip heads off of two of the sequin pins*) through the side at the site of the black dot and into the left edge of this board. Repeat for the second side.

8. Refer to **1-C-2**. Cut out the prints marked **10-L** on the color insert sheet. Glue the prints against the top front surface of the back, the slant lid, the top front board, the shelf, the doors and the sides.

CHILD'S ROCKING CHAIR c. EARLY 1900's 10-M

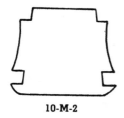
10-M-2

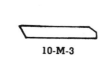
10-M-3

The rocking chair which is pictured is the one which our great-grandfather built for our mother when she was four years old. Of course it is one of our precious possessions, and the miniature replica will fit into any miniature room setting of the early 1900's.

(A) SEAT (Cut 1): 1/16" × 15/16" × 1 1/8". See Figure 10-M-2 for the shape.

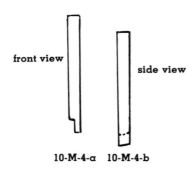

front view   side view

10-M-4-α   10-M-4-b

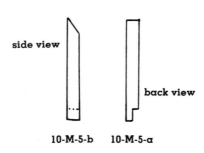

side view   back view

10-M-5-b   10-M-5-α

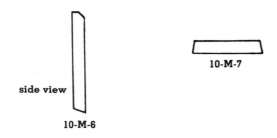

side view

10-M-6

10-M-7

side view

10-M-8   10-M-9

10-M-1

(B) FRONT LEGS (Cut 2): 1/8″ × 1/8″ × 1 1/4″. See Figure **10-M-4-a** for a front view of the leg showing a notch at the lower side edge and Figure **10-M-4-b** for a side view of the leg showing the bottom shaping. Reverse the shaping and the edge with the notch for the right leg.

(C) BACK LEGS (Cut 2): 1/8″ × 1/8″ × 1 1/16″. See Figure **10-M-5-a** for a back view diagram of the left leg showing a notch at the lower edge and Figure **10-M-5-b** for a side view diagram of the leg showing the bottom and top edges. Reverse both shaping and the edge with the notch for the right leg.

(D) SIDE LEG STRETCHERS (Cut 2): 1/8″ × 1/8″ × 3/4″. See Figure **10-M-7** for a side view diagram showing the end angles.

(E) BACK LEG STRETCHER (Cut 1): 1/8″ × 1/8″ × 11/16″.

(F) FRONT LEG STRETCHER (Cut 1): 1/8″ × 1/8″ × 13/16″.

(G) TOP BACK SLAT (Cut 1): 1/16″ × 1/4″ × 11/16″. See Figure **10-M-8** for a left side view of the shape.

(H) LOWER BACK SLAT (Cut 1): 1/16″ × 1/8″ × 11/16″.

(I) BACK POSTS (Cut 2): 1/8″ × 1/8″ × 1 1/8″. See Figure **10-M-6** for a left side view of the top and bottom angles.

(J) ARM REST (Cut 2): 1/8″ × 1/8″ × 13/16″. See Figure **10-M-3** for a left side view of the front and back end shaping.

(K) ROCKERS (Cut 2): 1/8″ × 9/32″ × 1 5/8″. See Figure **10-M-9** for a left side view of the shape.

ASSEMBLY: Stain all wood before glueing. Refer to Figure **10-M-1** (*actual size diagram*) for assembly.

1. Glue the back legs into the back side notches of the seat and glue the back posts atop the side edges of the seat and resting on the top angled edge of the back leg. See the diagram.

2. Glue the top and lower back slats in place between the back posts. See the two broken line areas in the diagram.

3. Glue the back leg atop the rocker. Glue the front leg into the front notch in the seat and atop the rocker. Repeat for the second side.

4. Glue the side, front and back leg stretchers in place.

5. Glue the arm rest against the back post and atop the top edge of the front leg. See the diagram.

6. Apply a finish coat.

DOLL DRESSER 10-N

10-N-1

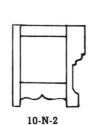

10-N-2

10-N-3

10-N-4

10-N-5

(A) BACK (Cut 1): 1/16" × 1" × 1 1/4". See Figure **10-N-3** for the shape.

(B) SIDES (Cut 2): 1/16" × 1/2" × 1/2".

(C) TOP SIDE MOULDING (Cut 2): 1/8" × 1/8" × 1/2".

(D) BOTTOM SIDE MOULDING (Cut 2): 1/8" × 3/16" × 1/2". See Figure **10-N-4** for the shape.

(E) FRONT SIDE MOULDING (Cut 2): 1/8" × 1/4" × 7/8". See Figure **10-N-5** for the shape.

(F) DRESSER TOP (Cut 1): 1/16" × 3/4" × 1".

(G) DRESSER BOTTOM AND TWO DRAWER SEPARATORS
    (1) **BOTTOM** (Cut 1): 1/16" × 21/32" × 3/4".
    (2) **SEPARATORS** (Cut 2): 1/16" × 1/2" × 3/4".

(H) TWO LOWER DRAWERS
    (1) **FRONT AND BACK** (Cut 4): 1/16" × 3/16" × 3/4".
    (2) **SIDES** (Cut 4): 1/16" × 3/16" × 3/8".
    (3) **BOTTOM** (Cut 2): 1/16" × 3/8" × 5/8".

(I) UPPER DRAWER
    (1) **FRONT AND BACK** (Cut 2): 1/16" × 3/16" × 3/4".
    (2) **SIDES** (Cut 2): 1/16" × 3/16" × 5/8".
    (3) **BOTTOM** (Cut 1): 1/16" × 5/8" × 5/8".

Refer to **2-E-1** for assembly of all drawers.

ASSEMBLY

1. Glue a piece of top side moulding butted against the top edge of the side with the back edges flush. Glue the bottom side moulding butted against the bottom edge of the side, with the edges flush. Refer to Figure **10-N-2**.

2. Glue the front side moulding against the front edge of each side assembly, with the back edges flush. Refer to Figure **10-N-2**.

3. Glue a completed side assembly butted against the front edge of the back (**A**) with the side edges flush. Repeat for the other side. *Note:* The flat surfaces of the side assembly will be toward the inside.

4. Glue the top board (**F**) atop the top edge of the two sides and against the back, with the end edges flush.

5. Insert the top drawer in place between the sides. Glue a drawer separator (**G**) against the sides and back, beneath the drawer. Repeat this process for the remaining two drawers.

6. Remove the drawers and apply a finish coat to all parts of the dresser.

7. Apply two drawer pulls (*a cut off brad or pin*) to each drawer.

TELESCOPING BLOCKS 10-O

A

B

C

The blocks in this project will not nest (fit together) as the antique set does. The blocks will be cubes of wood on which color print will be applied. Refer to Figure 10-O.

(A) BLOCK (Cut 1): 5/8" × 5/8" × 5/8".

(B) BLOCK (Cut 1): 9/16" × 9/16" × 9/16".

(C) BLOCK (Cut 1): 1/2" × 1/2" × 1/2".

(D) BLOCK (Cut 1): 7/16" × 7/16" × 7/16".

(E) BLOCK (Cut 1): 3/8" × 3/8" × 3/8".

D   E   F   G

(F) BLOCK (Cut 1): 5/16″ × 5/16″ × 5/16″.

(G) BLOCK (Cut 1): 1/4″ × 1/4″ × 1/4″.

ASSEMBLY

1. Find the color prints marked **10-O** on the color insert page. Refer to **1-C-2**. Cut out the strips of print and glue around each block. Glue the single square on the top of each block. Finish the blocks as instructed in **1-C-2**.

CHILD'S ALPHABET BLOCKS 10-P

1. Cut twelve pieces of wood 1/4″ × 1/4″ × 1/4″. You will find the color prints for these blocks marked **10-P** on the color insert page.

2. Refer to **1-C-2**. Cut out the prints around the out-side edges. Do not cut apart the joined prints. Glue a series of the joined letters around a wood cube. Glue a single number print on the top and bottom surfaces of this cube. Repeat these instructions until all twelve blocks have been completed.

DOLL BED 10-Q

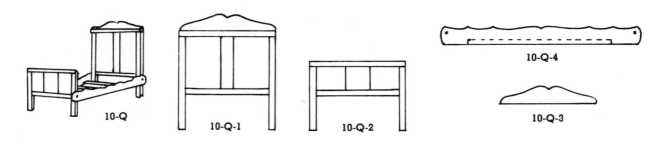

10-Q   10-Q-1   10-Q-2   10-Q-4   10-Q-3

(A) HEADBOARD (Cut 1): 1/16″ × 9/16″ × 7/8″.

(B) TOP MOULDING (Cut 2): 1/16″ × 1/8″ × 1″.

(C) BOTTOM MOULDING (Cut 2): 1/16″ × 1/8″ × 7/8″.

(D) VERTICAL HEADBOARD MOULDING (Cut 1): 1/16″ × 1/8″ × 9/16″.

(E) VERTICAL FOOTBOARD MOULDING (Cut 1): 1/16″ × 1/4″ × 1/4″.

(F) HEAD POSTS (Cut 2): 1/16″ × 1/8″ × 1″.

(G) FOOT POSTS (Cut 2): 1/16″ × 1/8″ × 11/16″.

(H) HEADBOARD DECORATION (Cut 1): 1/8″ × 3/16″ × 1″. See Figure **10-Q-3** for the shape.

(I) SIDE BOARDS (Cut 2): 1/16″ × 3/16″ × 2 1/8″. See Figure **10-Q-4** for the shape.

(J) SIDE BOARD BRACES (Cut 2): 1/16″ × 1/16″ × 1 1/2″.

(K) SLATS (Cut 4): 1/16″ × 1/8″ × 7/8″.

ASSEMBLY

HEADBOARD

1. Glue the head posts against the side edges of the headboard, with the back and top edges flush. The 1/16″ edge will be forward.

2. Glue the top moulding (**B**) and the bottom moulding (**C**) against the top and bottom surfaces of the headboard, with the back edges flush.

3. Glue the vertical headboard moulding (**D**) centered against the headboard, and glue the head-board decoration atop the top edges of the assem-bled headboard. Refer to Figure **10-Q-1**.

4. **FOOTBOARD:** Assemble the footboard as you did the headboard.

5. Glue a side board brace, centered against the in-side surface of the side board, with the bottom edges flush. See Figure **10-Q-4** for positioning.

6. Glue the bed slats evenly spaced atop the side board braces.

7. Apply a finish coat to all pieces of the bed.

8. Insert a tiny brad through each end of the side board at the site of each black dot, and on into the outside surface of the foot post and head post. Do not glue. Repeat this process for the opposite side of the bed. The bed will now fold. Refer to Figure **10-Q**.

DOLL CRADLE 10-R

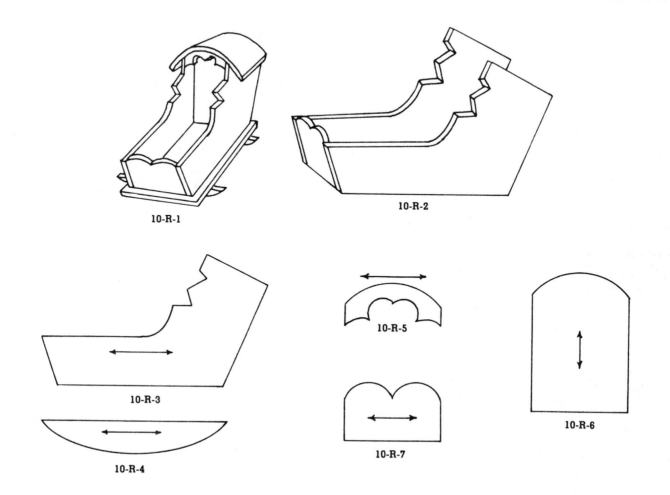

10-R-1

10-R-2

10-R-3

10-R-4

10-R-5

10-R-6

10-R-7

This cradle will be constructed of 1/16" thick wood or cardboard. If you choose to use cardboard, remember to seal all cut edges with airplane glue to prevent separation when painted.

(A) BOTTOM (Cut 1): 1 1/8" wide × 1 7/8" long. The wood grain will run the length of the board.

(B) ROOF (Cut 1): 1" × 1 1/2" long. The wood grain will run the length of the board.

Note: The arrows in the following diagrams indicate the direction of the grain of the wood.

(C) SIDES (Cut 2): 1 1/2" × 2 3/8". See Figure 10-R-3 for the shape.

(D) ROCKERS (Cut 2): 3/8" × 2". See Figure 10-R-4 for the shape.

(E) BONNET APRON (Cut 1): 1/2" × 1". See Figure 10-R-5 for the shape.

(F) HEAD (Cut 1): 1" × 1 1/2". See Figure 10-R-6 for the shape.

(G) FOOT (Cut 1): 5/8" × 1". See Figure 10-R-7 for the shape.

ASSEMBLY: Stain all wood before glueing. Refer to Figures 10-R-1 and 10-R-2 for the assembly.

1. The head (**F**) and foot (**G**) and bonnet apron (**E**) are glued between the two side boards (**C**), with edges flush. See Figure 10-R-1.

2. Glue the above assembly centered on the bottom board (**A**). Glue the rockers (**D**) beneath the cradle, recessed in from both ends. Be sure that they extend equal amounts on both sides, or the cradle will not rock properly. Let the glue dry.

3. Refer to 1-C-6. When the wood bends easily, glue at the top of the two sides, back and apron. See Figure 10-R-1. Place rubber bands around the cradle and the roof to hold this piece securely until the wood and glue are both dry.

4. Use your choice of finishes for the cradle.

SANTA JUMPING JACKS 10-S

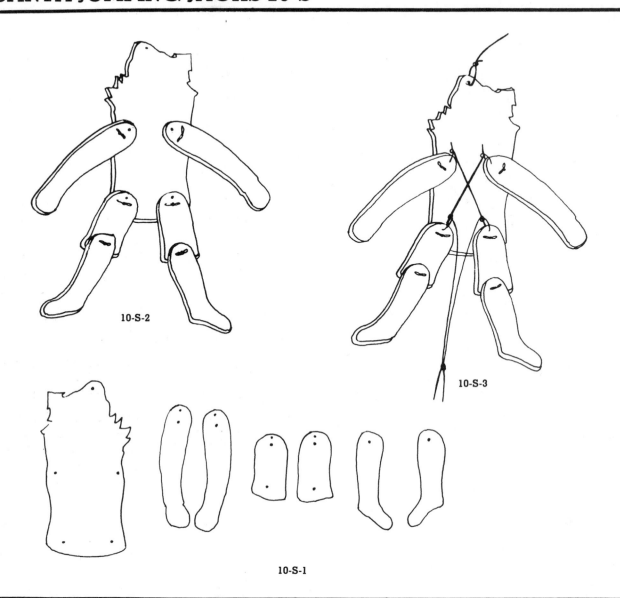

10-S-2

10-S-3

10-S-1

Note: 1" = 1' scale and larger.

1. Refer to the color insert sheet and cut out the section of prints marked **10-S**. Stain a piece of very thin wood veneer 2" × 2 1/2". Glue the entire uncut color print section on the side of the wood which was not stained.

2. Cut out the individual pieces of the jumping jacks. Using a straight pin or a darning needle, punch holes from the front through the back in each piece at the sites indicated by the black dots in Figure **10-S-1**.

3. Attach the various pieces together using pieces of fine wire, as shown in Figure **10-S-2**. Bend each piece of wire in half and twist to make a small loop at the center. Insert both ends through a hole from

the front through to the back, through the second piece which is being attached, and bend the two ends outward against the back surface. Clip short. Continue in this fashion until all of the pieces are wired together.

4. Tie thread in the upper hole in the arm. Cross over to the upper hole of the opposite leg and tie securely, and extend the end to the bottom of the jumping jack. Repeat this procedure for the second arm and leg. Tie a knot in the end of the two strings. Refer to Figure **10-S-3**.

5. Tie a piece of string in the hole in the hat by looping it with a knot at the end.

6. Hold onto the top thread and pull the bottom threads, and the arms and legs will move.

EAGLE RIDING TOY c. 1912 10-T

10-T-1

10-T-2

The Margaret Woodbury Strong Museum of Rochester, New York has kindly given us permission to share with you our miniature replica of the eagle riding toy which is a part of the fabulous collection which will someday be on view in their museum. The original was manufactured by S.A. Smith Manufacturing Company of Brattleboro, Vermont. The full size riding toy is constructed of wood with a stencilled design. The head pivots to change direction. Our replica could be made of wood, but the construction would be quite complicated. The following directions are for 1/16" and 1/8" thick cardboard.

1. Refer to **1-C-2**. Cut the complete section of color prints marked **10-T** from the color insert sheet.

2. Glue the color prints marked **10-T-1**, **10-T-3**, **10-T-4** and **10-T-5** to the 1/16" thick cardboard and let the glue dry. Cut out around the outside line.

3. Glue the color prints marked **10-T-6** and **10-T-8** to the 1/8" thick cardboard. When the glue is dry, cut out around the outside line.

4. Apply airplane cement to all cut edges of the cardboard to prevent the layers of paper from separating when painted.

5. See Figure **10-T-2**. Trace the half wheel once and the whole wheel twice onto the 1/16" thick cardboard and cut out. See Figure **10-T-4**. Trace the seat onto the 1/8" thick cardboard and cut out. Apply glue to the cut edge.

6. Paint all edges and bottom surfaces of the legs and tail, all edges of the head and the body, and all surfaces of the three wheels and the seat an oak-brown color.

7. Glue the color print marked **10-T-7** to the reverse side of the head and **10-T-9** to the reverse side of the body. Glue the color print marked **10-T-2** to the bottom surface of the wings. While the glue is still moist, gently curve the wings. When the glue is dry the wings will retain this shape.

8. Glue the head section (*notched edges*) into the notched front edge of the body. The head can be turned at an angle if you wish. See Figure **10-T-1**.

9. Pierce each leg at the site of the black dot in Figure **10-T-1** and glue the legs in place at either side of the body. Pierce each complete wheel in the center. Push a straight pin through a wheel, through a hole in a leg, through the next leg and then through the second wheel. Snip off the end of the pin and apply a dot of glue to secure each wheel to the pin. See Figure **10-T-1**.

10. Glue the wings (*star side up*) above the top edge of the head. See Figure **10-T-1**. Glue the seat and tail section in place. Glue the partial (*front*) wheel in place at the front base of the neck.

11. Refer to **1-C-2** and apply a finish coat.

KITE 10-U

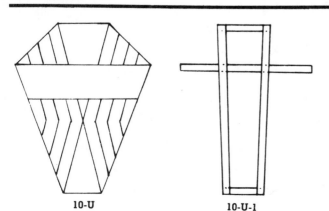

10-U

10-U-1

(A) RIBS (Cut 2): 1/16" × 1/16" × 1 3/4".

(B) RIBS (Cut 1): 1/16" × 1/16" × 1/2".

(C) RIBS (Cut 1): 1/16" × 1/16" × 1 3/8".

(D) RIBS (Cut 1): 1/16" × 1/16" × 7/16".

ASSEMBLY

1. Refer to Figure **10-U**. Glue pieces (**A**) atop the end edges of piece (**B**). Glue the opposite ends of

pieces (**A**) atop the end edges of piece (**D**). Using this diagram for placement, glue the above assembly — with pieces (**B**) and (**D**) downward — over piece (**C**).

2. Refer to **1-C-2**. Turn to the color insert sheet and cut out the color print marked **10-U**. Glue the print atop the top surface of the kite ribs.

PACKING CRATE CAR 10-V

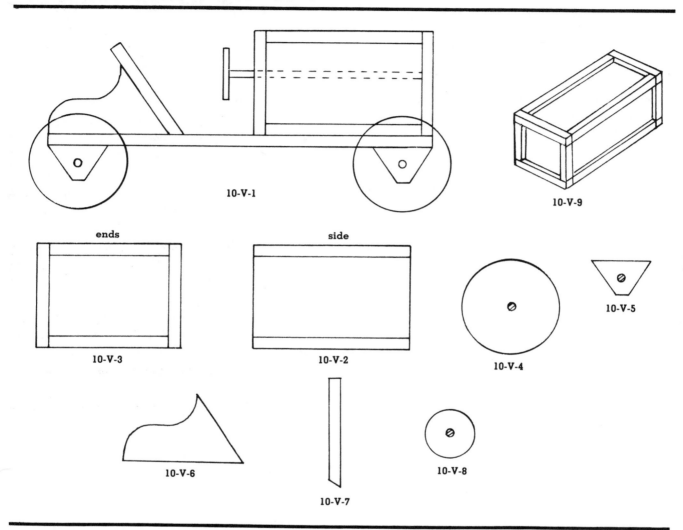

10-V-1

10-V-9

ends

side

10-V-3

10-V-2

10-V-4

10-V-5

10-V-6

10-V-7

10-V-8

(**A**) **FLOOR BOARD** (Cut 1): 1/8″ × 1 1/2″ × 4″.

(**B**) **REAR SIDES** (Cut 2): 1/16″ × 3/4″ × 1 1/4″. See Figure **10-V-6** for the shape.

(**C**) **WHEELS** (Cut 4): 1/8″ thick × 1″ diameter discs. See Figure **10-V-4**. Drill a 1/16″ diameter hole through the center of each wheel. See the shaded area in the diagram.

(**D**) **AXLE SUPPORT** (Cut 2): 1/8″ × 3/8″ × 5/8″. See Figure **10-V-5** for the shape. Drill a 1/16″ diameter hole through each board at the site of the shaded circle in the diagram.

(**E**) **AXLE** (Cut 2): 1/16″ diameter wood dowel × 2″.

(**F**) **SEAT BACK** (Cut 1): 1/8″ × 1 3/16″ × 1 1/2″. See Figure **10-V-7** (*side view*) for the angle at the bottom edge.

(**G**) **STEERING ROD** (Cut 1): 1/16″ diameter wood dowel × 2″.

(**H**) **STEERING WHEEL** (Cut 1): 1/16″ thick × 1/2″ diameter disc. See Figure **10-V-8** for the shape. Drill a 1/16″ diameter hole through the wheel at the site of the shaded circle in the diagram.

(**I**) **PACKING CASE ENDS** (Two)
  (1) **CENTER PANEL** (Cut 2): 1/16″ × 7/8″ × 1 1/4″. Drill a 1/16″ diameter hole through the center of one board.
  (2) **SIDE MOULDING** (Cut 4): 1/8″ × 1/8″ × 1 1/8″.
  (3) **TOP AND BOTTOM MOULDING** (Cut 4): 1/8″ × 1/8″ × 1 1/4″.

(**J**) **PACKING CRATE SIDES** (Two)

(1) **CENTER PANEL** (Cut 2): 1/16" × 7/8" × 1 5/8".

(2) **TOP AND BOTTOM MOULDING** (Cut 4): 1/8" × 1/8" × 1 5/8".

(K) PACKING CRATE TOP AND BOTTOM (Cut 2): 1/16" × 1 1/4" × 1 5/8".

(L) HEAD LIGHT REFLECTOR (Two): Use the backing metal disc of gripper snaps.

ASSEMBLY: Stain all wood before glueing.

1. Assemble the top, bottom and side moulding pieces around the center panels of each end. The back edges will be flush. See Figure **10-V-3** for assembly.

2. Assemble the top and bottom moulding pieces against the side center panels, with back edges flush. See Figure **10-V-2**.

3. Glue the top and bottom panels (**K**) against the back edges of the two side assemblies, with the back edges flush with the bottom edge of each moulding board. See Figure **10-V-9**.

4. Glue the assembled ends against the end edges of this assembly.

5. Glue the assembled packing crate atop the floor board, with side and front edges flush. *Note:* The end of the crate with the hole should be facing toward the rear.

6. Glue the steering wheel onto an end of the steering rod, with the end edges flush. Glue the other end into the hole in the packing crate and against the interior surface of the front panel of the crate. See Figure **10-V-1**.

7. Glue the rear sides (**B**) atop the rear surface of the floor board, with back and side edges flush. Glue the seat (*angled end downward*) against the front upright edges of the side boards. See Figure **10-V-1**.

8. Glue the axle supports (**D**) against the bottom surface of the floor board, with side and end edges flush. See Figure **10-V-1**.

9. Insert an axle through each pair of supports. Place a wheel on each end of each axle, push a pin through the axle which protrudes past each wheel, and bend the pin to secure the wheel.

10. Finish the car in any way you wish. You may wish to use a fine brush and black paint or India ink and fashion signs which may read "To: _____," "Rush," "Fragile," and so forth.

11. Place each head light reflector (**L**) on a piece of scrap wood, drive a brad through the center, remove, and attach to the front of the crate.

MARBLE BAG 10-W

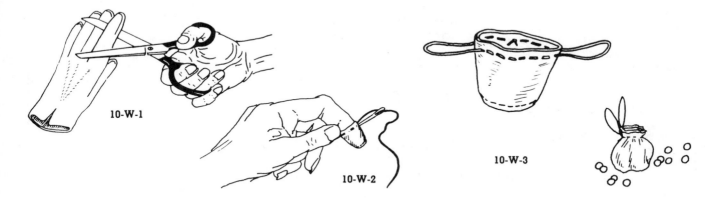

10-W-1

10-W-2

10-W-3

(A) GLOVE: An old, soft thin leather glove.

(B) THREAD: Carpet thread.

(C) NEEDLE: A large-eye needle that will accommodate the thread.

(D) PINS: A card of dressmaker's pins with colored glass ends which can be purchased at the notions counter in a variety store.

ASSEMBLY

1. Cut off the finger of the glove at approximately 5/8", as shown in Figure **10-W-1**.

2. Cut a six inch length of the carpet thread, thread the needle, and begin the first stitch so that the end of the thread is inside of the bag. Sew small stitches around the cut edge of the bag, with the last stitch ending inside. See Figure **10-W-2**.

3. Cut both ends of the thread to 1 1/2". Tie the two ends together with a knot at the extreme end. Pulling the thread from both sides will close the opening. See Figure **10-W-3**.

4. Using cutters, snip off the glass heads from the pins. These will be the marbles.

GLOSSARY OF TERMS USED IN WORKSHOP

APRON: A strip next to or under the top of a chest, table or chair which extends around or between the body, feet, legs, or stand.

ARMOIRE: A large wardrobe or moveable cupboard, with doors and shelves.

BANNISTER: The uprights in a chair back.

BASE: The bottom of an object.

BEVEL: A plane 45° cutting away of the edge in which two plane surfaces meet.

BLANKET CHEST: Any chest used for the storage of blankets.

BONNET TOP: A scrolled top, as on a high chest of drawers or clock, also known as a hood.

BOW TOP or BOW-BACK: A chair top rail with one unbroken curve across the whole width, and receiving the top portion of the spindles.

BREAK-FRONT: The front of a cabinet with a portion advanced by a mitred break.

BUTT: Ends of wood coming together with squared edges.

CABRIOLE: A curved leg with an out-curving top or knee, an in-curving ankle or shaft, and a shaped toe.

CHAIR-TABLE: One with hinged top which can be raised to become a chair back.

COMB BACK: The higher back on a chair resembling a high comb.

CONCAVE: A hollowed surface, such as the seat of a Windsor chair.

CORNER CHAIR: A chair in which the back is set on so that the front leg is in the center front of the chair.

CRESTING: A decoration on a top of a chair rail or the top of a piece of cabinet furniture.

DIAMETER: A straight line passing through the center of a circle or sphere and terminated at each end by the circumference or surface; the length of such a line.

DOWEL: A plain, straight turning.

DOWER CHEST: A hope chest.

FAN BACK: A Windsor chair with a curved top rail and flaring spindles.

FLUSH: Even surfaces which adjoin and make one surface.

FRETWORK: The cutting out of geometrical areas.

GALLERY: A miniature fence or pierced fret, mounted by a rail.

GRANDFATHER CLOCK: Hall clock or tall clock.

HIGHBOY: A high chest of drawers with long legs.

HIGH CHEST OF DRAWERS: A chest with more than five drawers.

HITCHCOCK CHAIR: A chair dating about 1835 with a rush seat and usually stencilled.

JARDINIERE: A box or pedestal which is designed to hold flowers.

LADDER BACK: A chair back with slats or horizontal rails which resemble the rungs of a ladder.

MITRE: The intersection joint at the corner, which changes direction.

MORTISE: A cut-out section to receive a projection.

OVERHANG: To extend, project, or jut over something below.

PEDESTAL: A moulded base supporting a cupboard, table, chest of drawers, and so on.

PIERCED: An open fret, such as in the apron of the harpsichord found in this book.

PILLAR: An upright shaft, relatively slender in proportion to its height, of any shape, used as a support or standing alone.

RAIL: A horizontal piece in the frame of a cabinet, chair, or bed.

ROCKING CHAIR: A chair mounted on curved boards. They became common after 1800.

SAWBUCK TABLE: A table with an X frame, and held together by a truss passing through the center of the intersection.

SCHRANK: A German version of a wardrobe or armoire.

SETTLE: Made all of wood, with solid wood ends and back. It is sometimes hooded.

SIDEBOARD: A side or serving table.

SLATS: Horizontal rails in a chair back; the cross pieces which support a bed spring or mattress.

SLIP SEAT: A framed seat slipped into an open chair frame, which can be removed.

SPINDLE: A small turned pillar used in or applied to furniture.

SPLAT: The central, vertical piece in a chair back.

SPLAY:	A part of furniture that is neither horizontal or vertical.
SQUARED:	That process which results in a piece of furniture being made to have all of its sides at equal right angles.
STENCILLED:	A type of decoration usually found on the Hitchcock chair.
STRETCHER:	The lower connecting or bracing portion of a chair or table to stiffen the legs. When it is turned, it is called a rung.
TRESTLE TABLE or TRESTLE AND BOARD:	The earliest known type of table, which consists of boards placed upon the trestle.
TRUSS:	A beam, bar, tie, or the like so arranged to form a rigid framework.
WARDROBE:	A cabinet with doors and drawers below, for hanging or storing clothing.
WHATNOT:	A tier of shelves which are supported by turned posts.

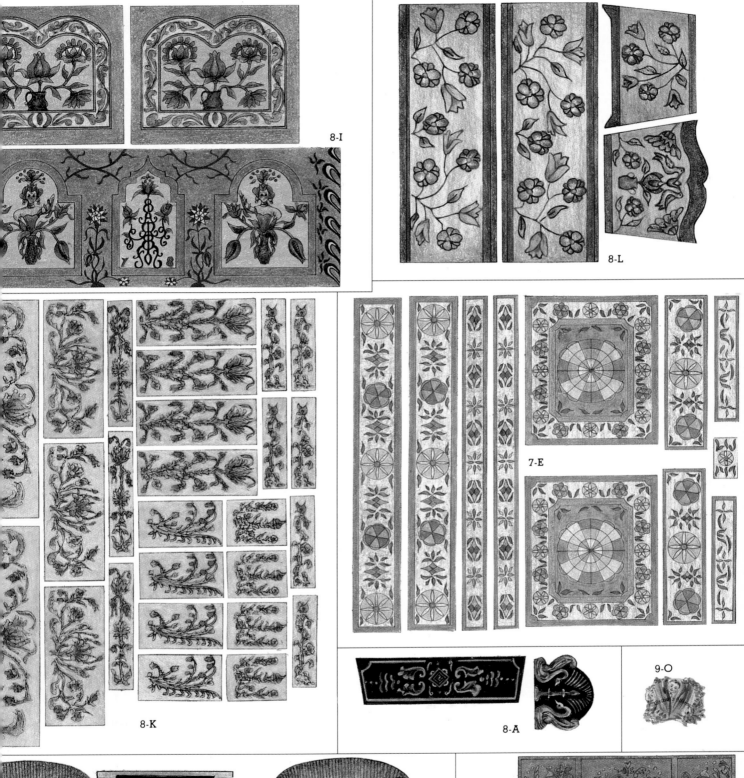

8-I

8-L

8-K

7-E

8-A

9-O

8-F

8-P

10-A

10-P

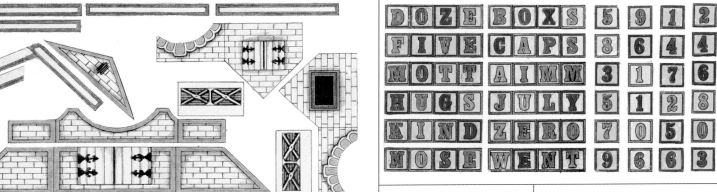

D	O	Z	E		B	O	X	S		5	9		1	2
F	I	V	E		C	A	P	S		8	6		4	4
M	O	T	T		A	I	M	M		3	1		7	6
H	U	G	S		J	U	L	Y		5	1		2	8
K	I	N	D		Z	E	R	O		7	0		5	0
N	O	S	E		W	E	N	T		9	6		6	3

10-B

9-P

10-T

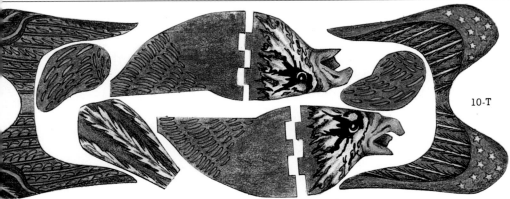

10-S

10-H

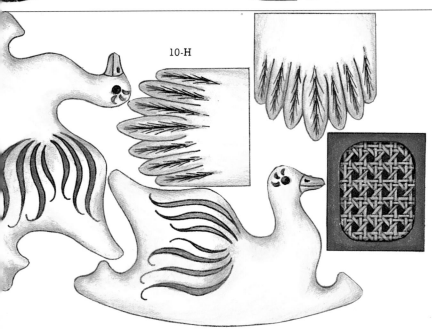

10-D

10-J

8-O

9-N

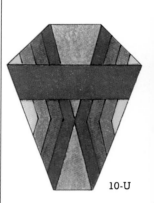

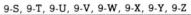

10-U

9-S, 9-T, 9-U, 9-V, 9-W, 9-X, 9-Y, 9-Z

8-R

10-E

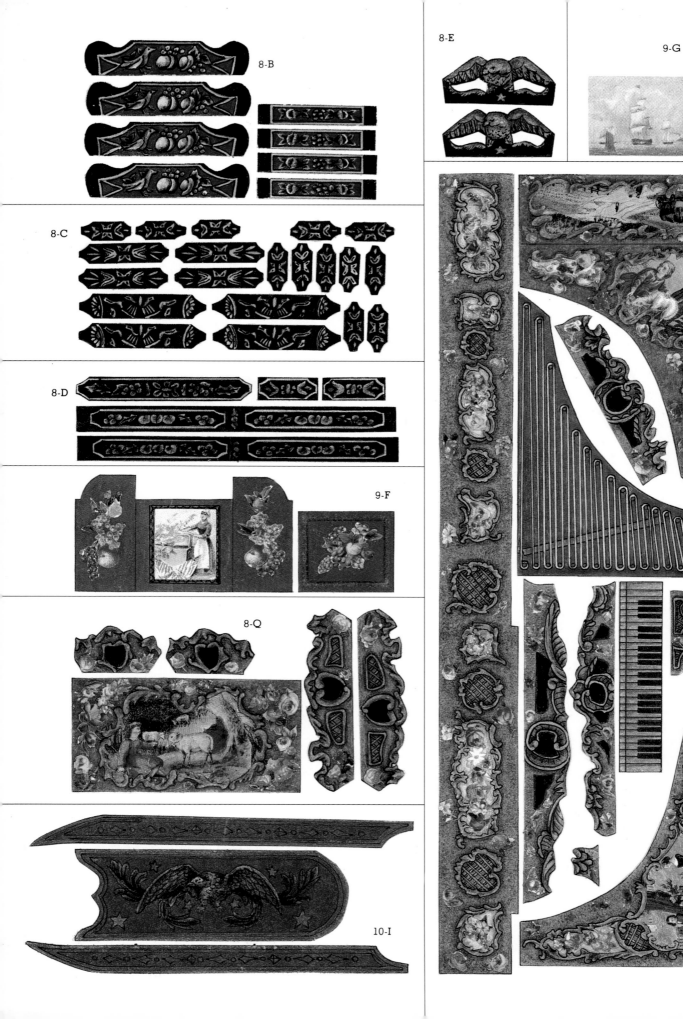

8-B

8-C

8-D

9-F

8-Q

10-I

8-E

9-G

8-N

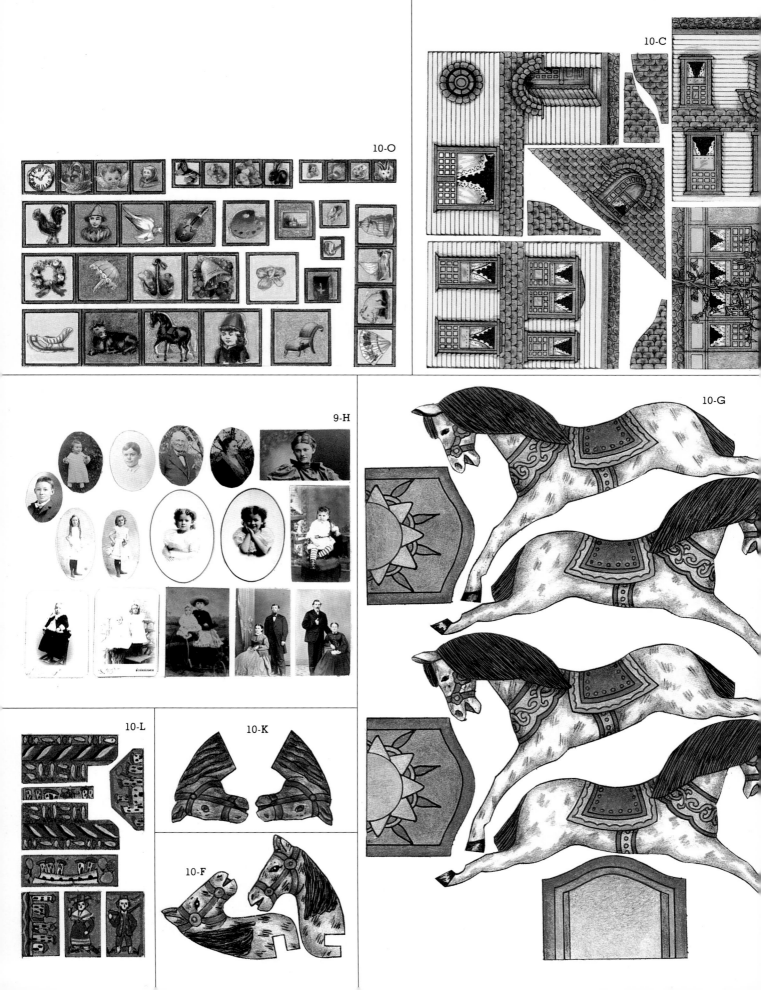

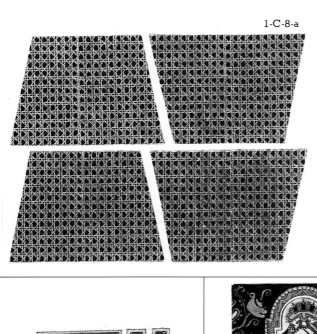

1-C-8-a

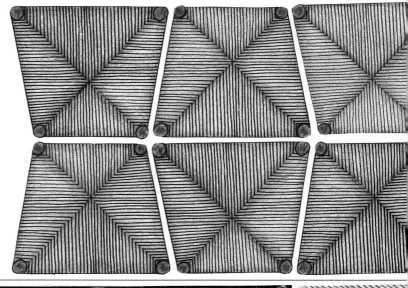

1-C-7-a

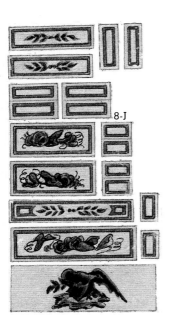

8-J

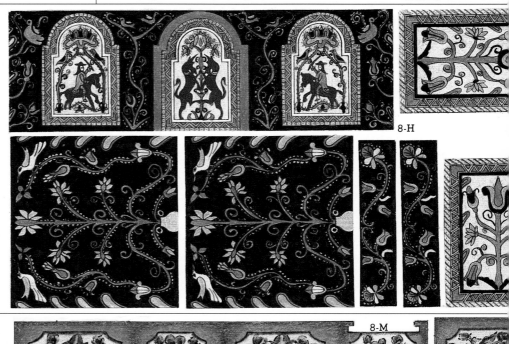

8-H

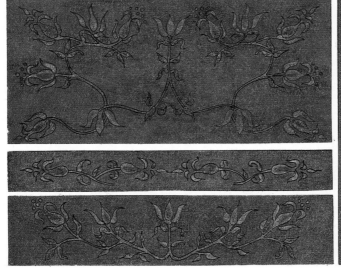

8-M

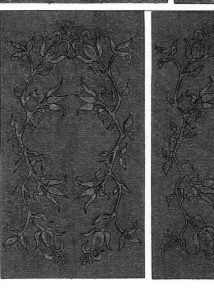

8-G